THE UNEXPLAINED FILES

Enigmas of Mind, Space and Time

INDEX

C O N T E N T S

© Orbis Publishing 1996

This edition first published in Great Britain in 1996 specially for
INDEX
Unit 1,
Garrard Way,
Kettering NN16 8TD

This material has already been published in partwork form as
The Unexplained

Printed in Italy by Cromografica Europea, Milan

WHAT HAPPENED AT HANGING ROCK?

THE BROODING AUSTRALIAN LANDSCAPE, LINKED WITH A WEALTH OF ANCIENT MYSTERIES, PROVIDED A DRAMATIC BACKDROP FOR A STRANGE AND STILL PUZZLING DISAPPEARANCE

St Valentine's Day 1900 dawned sunny and sparkling in the village of Woodend, near Melbourne, Australia. It was the day of the annual school outing at Applegate College on the outskirts of the village. Early in the morning, a party of schoolgirls and teachers drove out with a picnic to a local beauty spot. It all started out as a happy occasion – but, by the end of the day, four of the group had mysteriously disappeared: what is more, three were never to be seen again.

This strange story has become a cause célèbre, as mysterious as the case of the deserted ship, the *Mary Celeste*. It has also become the subject of countless theories, numerous magazine articles, at least two books and a feature film, *Picnic at Hanging Rock* (made in 1975). But, like many historical mysteries, the Hanging Rock affair is perhaps not all it seems.

The story has it that the party of girls and teachers set out in a hired coach to travel to Hanging Rock for their annual picnic treat. A popular place for picnickers at the turn of the century, Hanging Rock is an unusual geological formation. Of volcanic origin and several million years old, it rises

Immense and menacing, the prehistoric volcanic outcrop known as Hanging Rock, above, dominates the surrounding plain like a massive ancient fortress. It is thought to be a focal point for paranormal forces. Were the girls who went missing on St Valentine's Day perhaps caught up by hidden powers and deflected into another dimension?

majestically to 500 feet (150 metres) from an otherwise flat plain and terminates in a jumble of miraculously balancing boulders and monoliths that give it its name. For sightseers, a small picnic area has been laid out a short distance from the base of the rock. It comprises some makeshift stone tables and suitably discreet toilet facilities.

The party from the college included 19 girls, most of them in their teens, and two teachers. These were Mlle Diane de Poitiers, who taught French and dancing; and Greta McCraw, a middle-aged Scottish spinster, who taught maths. The only other adult in the party was Ben Hussey, the coachmaster from the local livery stables. Mrs Appleyard, the headmistress, remained at the college.

The party had set out early that Saturday morning to cover the 41 miles (66 kilometres) to the picnic site, and arrived just before midday. It was warm and sunny; and after their picnic lunch, most of the girls seem to have been content to doze under the shade of the trees and boulders. The only other party at the picnic area was encamped some distance away, on the far side of a small stream that ran down from the face of the Rock. This group consisted of Colonel Fitzhubert (formerly of the Indian Army, but who had subsequently retired to more mellow climes), Mrs Fitzhubert, their nephew – the Hon. Michael Fitzhubert, on a visit from England – and their groom, Albert Crundall.

About 3 p.m., three of the senior girls asked permission from the French teacher to explore the Rock. The three girls – Irma Leopold, Marion Quade and a girl remembered simply as Miranda – were all aged 17 and known to be sensible. After some discussion with the other adults (during which, incidentally, it was noted that the only two watches with the party – belonging to Ben Hussey and Miss McCraw – had both stopped at noon), it was agreed to allow them to go ahead. As an afterthought, Edith Horton, a younger girl aged 14, was given permission to accompany them. All four were warned not to go too far up the Rock, to be careful to avoid its crags, caves and precipices, and to look out for snakes, spiders and other potentially dangerous creepy-crawlies.

The girls walked away from the picnic ground, crossed the stream, and disappeared from sight at about 3.30 p.m. Michael Fitzhubert and Albert Crundall were sitting beside the stream, watching them cross: Irma was first, followed by Marion, Miranda and Edith. Albert let out a wolf-whistle, and Mike got to his feet with the intention of following the girls, but he gave up after only a few yards when they disappeared into a line of trees. At the picnic site, the rest of the school party dozed off.

At about 4.30, Mr Hussey became anxious about gathering his charges together. He and Mlle de Poitiers now discovered that Miss McCraw was missing. No one had seen her go, but it was assumed that she had followed the exploring girls. The Fitzhubert party had by this time packed up and gone home.

Initially with irritation, and eventually with consternation, Hussey and Mlle de Poitiers searched for the absent members of the party. Hussey first checked the toilets, and then organised the girls to search in pairs, calling as they went. A trail of broken bracken and disturbed scrub led them to the

Clyde School for girls, below, *moved from a Melbourne suburb to this building in Woodend in 1919. It was the historical model for Appleyard College, described in Joan Lindsay's novel,* Picnic at Hanging Rock, *as a two-storey Italianate mansion built of solid Castlemaine stone.*

southern face of the Rock from the east; but beyond that, where the stony ground of the Rock itself began, the traces petered out.

HYSTERICAL RETURN

For nearly an hour, the distraught picnickers searched. Then, at about 5.30, Edith Horton suddenly blundered out from the bush on the southwest side of the Rock. She was screaming hysterically and could tell her interrogators nothing of what had happened. Of Miranda, Irma, Marion and Miss McCraw there was no sign.

By now, it was getting late and would soon be dark. Mr Hussey lit fires along the creek and also continued to call out, and to beat upon two billycans with a crowbar. But with night-time coming on, the two adults eventually decided to gather up the remainder of their party and return to the college. On the way back, they stopped at Woodend police station, where Hussey made a statement to Constable Bumpher.

On the following day, Sunday, the search for the missing women began in earnest. It was assumed that the girls and their teacher had got lost in the bush, and the police enlisted the help of local volunteers, including Mike Fitzhubert and Albert Crundall, to search the Rock. This was no easy task, since it is a treacherous place, with many caves and pits (popularly believed at that time to be bottomless), hidden by rough bush. At the end of the first day's search, nothing had been found.

Meanwhile, Woodend's Dr MacKenzie had examined Edith Horton. She appeared to be suffering from mild concussion, and had numerous scrapes, scratches and bruises, acquired during her flight through the bush, but no other injuries. She could remember nothing of her time on the Rock.

But later in the week, on Wednesday, she was interviewed by Constable Bumpher, when she made the almost casual revelation that, on her way back, she had passed Miss McCraw heading towards the Rock. Miss McCraw had been some way off, and had paid no attention to Edith's screams. Even worse, Edith bashfully confessed, the normally prim spinster had been improperly dressed: she had no skirt on, only her drawers.

The search continued for several days, while the police systematically interviewed all the witnesses. Young Michael Fitzhubert seemed a prime suspect, if foul play was involved: he had been the last to see the girls, and admitted to starting out to follow them. But there was no other indication that he might be responsible for the girls' disappearance; and, possibly due to pressure from the influential Fitzhuberts, the police soon abandoned this line of enquiry.

LOST TRAIL

On the Thursday following the picnic, the police brought in an Aboriginal tracker and a bloodhound. Given Miss McCraw's scent from clothes left in her room, the bloodhound followed a trail up on to the Rock and stood bristling and growling for nearly 10 minutes on a circular platform halfway-up. But failing to find any tangible traces and, convinced that no one could have survived that long in the bush, the police called off the search.

The next day, Friday, Mike Fitzhubert and Albert Crundall decided to make a search of their own. At sundown, having found nothing, Mike decided to spend the night on the Rock. Albert returned to Colonel Fitzhubert's residence at Lake View to make Mike's excuses. The next morning, when he returned to the Rock, he followed Mike's trail and

The fateful picnic supposedly took place on St Valentine's Day 1900, and the college cook had, according to Joan Lindsay's account, made a 'handsome iced cake in the shape of a heart', shown above in a still from Picnic at Hanging Rock.

discovered him unconscious, suffering from exposure, and with a badly twisted ankle. Mike was carried home and treated by Dr MacKenzie. That night, Albert found a hastily scribbled note in Mike's pocket which, though largely incoherent, suggested that Mike had indeed found something on the Rock. On Sunday morning, another search party was sent out: to their utter astonishment, they found Irma Leopold.

She was unconscious, had several bruises and minor cuts to the head, and her fingernails were broken and torn: otherwise, she seemed to have suffered little as a result of spending over a week in the bush. Her shoeless feet were clean and unmarked. Most extraordinary of all, her corset was

In a scene from the film Picnic at Hanging Rock, right, *the schoolgirls from Appleyard College drink a toast to St Valentine against the threatening background of the primeval Rock. Within a few hours, three members of the party were to vanish for ever.*

missing – but she had not been sexually assaulted. When she revived, she could remember nothing of her ordeal.

There the story ends. Irma could tell nothing of what had happened; and Miranda, Marion and Miss McCraw were never seen again. As a result of the episode, pupils were removed from Appleyard College, and it was forced to close. Some months later, Mrs Appleyard drove out to Hanging Rock and climbed it alone. Her body was subsequently found at the foot of a precipice.

SPECULATIVE THEORIES

The mystery of Hanging Rock has given rise to endless speculation. For those disinclined to accept a paranormal explanation, there are two possibilities. The girls may simply have got lost and died from exposure on the Rock. Their bodies may have lain hidden in undergrowth at the foot of a cliff or in a cave where they had fallen until disposed of by animals, insects and bacteria (which happens in the Australian bush quite quickly). Edith's amnesia might have been due to hysteria or to a fall; and Irma's might have been caused by the traumatic experience of becoming separated from the others and surviving alone for a week. She may have removed her corset in order to move more freely. This, of course, could also be the reason why Miss McCraw removed her skirt.

The second possibility is that the girls were the victims of some crime. A theory has been put forward that Mike Fitzhubert and Albert Crundall might have kidnapped the girls (after murdering Miss McCraw), holding them hidden on the Colonel's estate to gratify their sexual desires. Marion and Miranda may have died of their injuries, or were perhaps murdered, while Irma may have been saved through some chance. If the motive was sexual, then it has been suggested that Mike may have been a 'remittance man', sent to the colonies to keep him out of the way. It may be tempting to think of him as a pervert; but this theory falls apart since Irma remained a virgin.

One theory to account for the girls' disappearance suggests that Mike Fitzhubert, above left, and Albert Crundall, right, played by Dominic Guard and John Jarratt in the film Picnic at Hanging Rock, *may have kidnapped them for sexual purposes. Others believe that the girls were captured by a UFO, for which the Rock may have acted as an intergalactic beacon, rather like the Devil's Tower, in Wyoming, below, in the film* Close Encounters of the Third Kind.

"" AWESOME... AS IT MIGHT SOUND, THERE'S MUCH CIRCUMSTANTIAL EVIDENCE TO INDICATE ENERGY X MAY DO FAR MORE THAN MOVE OBJECTS IN OUR REALITY, THAT IT MAY EVEN CAUSE PHYSICAL MATTER TO DROP IN AND OUT OF OUR DIMENSIONS OF SPACE AND TIME. ""

MICHAEL H. BROWN, PK, A REPORT ON THE POWER OF PSYCHOKINESIS

Other theories are less earth-bound. It has even been suggested that the girls were spirited away by aliens. Certainly, the Rock itself is distinctive enough – for those inclined to the idea – to serve as some intergalactic beacon, like the Devil's Tower in the film *Close Encounters of the Third Kind*. The presence of a UFO might also explain why the watches stopped. This is a common experience reported by witnesses of alien craft. When recounting how she had seen Miss McCraw, Edith Horton did say she had seen a strange pink cloud around that time – evidence, perhaps, of mysterious goings-on in the sky.

Another theory put forward offers the suggestion that the girls may possibly have slipped into some kind of time-warp, emerging in the past or future. This theory makes much of the strange pink cloud: both Christian Doppler and Albert Einstein suggested that bodies departing from sight at an unnaturally high speed would be seen by those left behind through a 'red shift' – a distortion of the light spectrum. Could this pink cloud perhaps have harboured Miss McCraw, disappearing at high speed as a time-traveller?

The forbidding, jagged crags of Hanging Rock, below, were to claim yet another victim when, according to the novel and the film, Mrs Appleyard, headmistress of the girls' college, drove out alone to the Rock and threw herself from its heights.

Other ideas are that the girls may have crossed into a parallel universe; or that primeval qualities in the Rock itself spirited the victims away, as apparently favoured by the film *Picnic at Hanging Rock*, with its oppressive vision of the Australian landscape, and its view of the Rock as a giant phallic symbol.

So what really did happen on that St Valentine's Day? Sad to relate, there is no concrete evidence that the disappearances ever took place at all.

FACT OR FICTION?

Much of the Hanging Rock story is in fact based on Joan Lindsay's novel *Picnic at Hanging Rock*. Although this is a work of fiction, the author obviously hoped her readers would take it to be based on fact. In the preface, she says: 'Whether . . . fact or fiction, my readers must decide for themselves.' At the end of the book, there is a long quotation, apparently taken from a Melbourne newspaper, describing the outline of the story. All the places mentioned in the story exist, including a Ladies' College at Woodend. The Hussey brothers did run a store near Woodend, and a Dr MacKenzie did practise in the vicinity at the turn of the century. But no contemporary references to the disappearances can be traced.

In fact, St Valentine's Day, 1900, fell on a Wednesday, not a Saturday. The girls' school (named Clyde College) was opened in 1910 in a Melbourne suburb, and did not move to Woodend until 1919. Neither the local newspaper, the *Woodend Star*, nor the two Melbourne papers, the *Age* and the *Argus*, refer to any disappearances on the Rock during February 1900, nor for several years before or after. The newspaper quoted at the end of the novel suggests that Irma gave several interviews to the Society for Psychical Research; but these cannot be traced, nor can the newspaper from which the extract was supposedly taken.

Confronted with this lack of evidence, Joan Lindsay remains mischievously enigmatic. In an interview in 1977, she was asked outright, 'Is *Picnic* fact or fiction?' 'It is an impossible question for me to answer,' she replied. 'Fact and fiction are so closely intertwined.'

Yet it hardly seems to matter whether the story is true or not. It already appears to have passed into modern mythology. People who have read the book or seen the film will assure you that the events described really happened. It seems that the tale has connected powerfully with the Australian collective unconscious, and its characters are already certain of the immortality conferred on many of the world's most familiar legendary figures.

// DO SUCH PLACES MARK THE POSITION OF THOSE DOORS THROUGH WHICH PEOPLE FROM OUR TIME AND SPACE PASS, AND THROUGH WHICH SOMETHING FROM A DIFFERENT TIME AND A DIFFERENT SPACE EMERGES? **//**

MICHAEL HARRISON, VANISHINGS

THE GOOD, THE BAD AND THE UGLY

THE CREATURES DESCRIBED IN CLOSE ENCOUNTER REPORTS COME IN A CONFUSING VARIETY OF SHAPES AND SIZES. WHAT ARE WE TO MAKE OF THEM?

The classic picture of an alien being is of a small, spindly creature with a large head and bulbous eyes, but often no other visible facial features, dressed in a one-piece grey suit that seems to be without buttons or zips. The startling similarity of descriptions of aliens in many close encounter reports has led to speculation that all UFOs probably originate in one place. But for every report of foetus-like aliens, there is one of creatures of a completely different kind, sometimes stiffly moving, like robots, sometimes indistinguishable from human beings, sometimes green and gnome-like.

What can ufology make of this fascinating but bewildering array of descriptions of supposed alien life forms? Are we to suppose that planet Earth is being bombarded with spacecraft from many alien cultures, all conducting reconnaissance missions, and that pilots of the alien craft have some obscure purpose in disguising themselves now in one form, now in another? Or will we be forced to make a more radical hypothesis?

A good starting point is the creating of a tool for analysing the wealth of reports of close encounters of the third kind – those UFO reports that involve aliens. For this, some kind of classification system will be useful, starting with those aliens that take the same basic form as human beings, and that are immediately identified as such by the witnesses. They are generally dressed in one-piece suits, and move and speak normally. Their average height, in all the reports, is between 5 and 7 feet (1.5 – 2.1 metres). Humanoids, meanwhile – perhaps the most commonly reported aliens – resemble humans, but witnesses report clear anatomical differences. They often have disproportionately large heads, pallid skins, underdeveloped facial features, and hairless bodies – giving them an appearance reminiscent of human foetuses. The single feature most often reported is their exceptionally large eyes, sometimes described as unblinking, or with vertical pupils. They are small, with an average height of between 3 and 5½ feet (90 centimetres – 1.7 metres). Unlike human entities, they generally communicate not through normal speech, but telepathically; but like them, humanoid entities are generally dressed in one-piece, close-fitting suits, usually of silver or grey, although space-suits are also sometimes reported.

Somewhat rarer are 'animal entities'. These are characterised by distinctly mammalian, reptilian, fishlike or other features, including fur, claws, a tail, scales or other strange skin texture, pointed ears, a snout, enlarged teeth, and non-human eyes. Their heights range from 6 to 8 feet (1.8 – 2.4 metres). Most are ape-like in appearance, and walk on two legs. Their method of communication ranges from animal cries to telepathy.

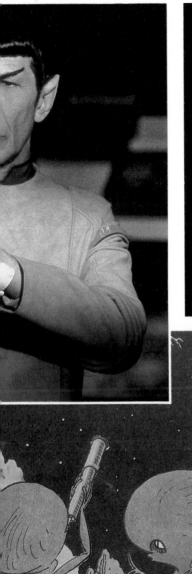

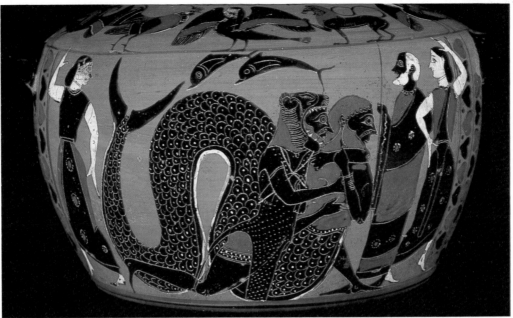

human features, and may combine human characteristics with non-animal ones – humans with robot arms, for instance. Most are bipeds; but some combine the characteristics of two or more of the other categories. They range in height from 1 to 10 feet (30 centimetres – 3 metres). They may move like humans or animals, or like robots, or even float; and they often communicate telepathically, rather than by what for us are more ordinary means.

A final category is also the most puzzling. It consists of 'apparitional entities' – aliens that share many of the characteristics of ghosts. They may materialise or dematerialise, change form, manifest themselves selectively to witnesses, or move matter, including people, at will. Their average height is 5 to 6 feet (1.5 – 1.8 metres); they often float rather than walk; and again, they generally communicate by telepathy. They also most often appear dressed in one-piece suits.

This system of classification can be used to analyse the close encounter cases described in Webb's *1973 – Year of the Humanoids*. Of a total of 66 cases, 16 were humanoids; 12, robots; 10, human; eight, animal; seven, exotic and five, apparitional – while eight were impossible to categorise because the descriptions were so vague.

STRANGER STILL

Some scientists have even gone so far as to speculate about the existence of alien creatures that are so unusual that it would be impossible to classify them under the six-category system already given. In his novel *The Black Cloud*, for example, astronomer Sir Fred Hoyle described a vast, intelligent cloud that 'lives' in interstellar space, complete with molecular heart system, brain and other necessary organs. It feeds on raw energy and its central nervous system functions via radio waves. Ronald Bracewell, in his book *The Galactic Club,* imagines an 'intelligent scum' – colonies of single-celled plants that could, with time, gain technological control of their environment. But, in fact, such creatures are rarely, if ever, encountered in genuine close encounter reports.

Another form of alien is the 'robot entity'. Robots seem to be made of metallic or other artificial body materials, and often move in a jerky, stiff or otherwise unnatural manner. Glowing eyes are often reported, as is the robots' ability to float, or to cause witnesses to float. Their shape varies from bipedal to huge machines; and their height can be anything between 6 inches and 20 feet (15 centimetres – 6 metres). They often wear padded spacesuits with bubble-dome headgear. Their method of communication varies from a flat metallic voice to telepathy.

Other types of alien exhibit a variety of strange characteristics – they are the 'exotic entities'. They may have grotesquely exaggerated animal or

It is also interesting to consider whether any aspects of the above categorisation could be applied to other phenomena. The most well-established single pattern in the groups described has to do with entity clothing – typically a seamless, one-piece outfit that covers the body except for the head. This is distinctly similar to the clothing generally worn by brownies, traditional folklore figures. Another interesting parallel is provided by the many reports of instrument-carrying aliens and similar reports of elves from folk tradition. A close examination of folk tradition also shows that folk creatures fit the six-class categorisation neatly. Giants, for example, are human entities; pookas, gnomes and pixies are humanoid; kelpies are animal; stocks – wooden dolls traditionally substituted by fairies for kidnapped babies – are robotic; the fachan – a bizarre creature with one eye, one hand emerging from his chest, and one leg – is exotic; and fairies – like demons and certain divinities – are 'shape-shifters', or apparitional.

Certain commentators have expressed the opinion that images of traditional Christianity in many ways fall into the same categories. At the centre is the human Christ. The cherubim and seraphim – ageless, sexless beings – are humanoid. The key symbol of the Garden of Eden is the serpent – an animal entity. Adam is the father of all 'robots' – inert matter infused by God with life, consciousness and sensibility. Devils and tempters show horrific bodily distortion, and so fall into the 'exotic class'; and angels, with their capacity for abruptly appearing and disappearing, are apparitional.

Thus, it seems that this system of classification is perhaps more than merely a useful tool for analysis. It may even be that it is actually a set of archetypes, deeply rooted in the subconscious, on which the mind draws when it is subjected to unusual stimuli.

Evidence that this may in fact be correct comes from a series of hypnosis experiments that were conducted by Dr W.C. McCall, John DeHerrerra and Alvin Lawson at Anaheim Memorial Hospital, California, in 1977. In the course of these experiments, a number of subjects were hypnotised and then asked questions about an imaginary UFO 'abduction'. The results were compared with what were reported as 'real' cases; and, startlingly, the descriptions – in particular of the aliens involved – were closely similar. The following is part of such an 'imaginary' description of an abduction:

'They [the aliens] seem to be humanoid in form. They have round heads that are much larger than ... humans. . . . They don't really have fingers. They seem to be kind of webbed.... I can't see any legs, or feet, because they're . . . what looks like possibly a . . . an article of clothing goes right to the floor.... Costume is ... more purplish than blue in color. Seems to be all one . . . all made in one piece. There don't seem to be any seams on the costume.... They stand about four feet, two inches [1.2 metres] tall. Maybe a little taller .... '

This is a typical description of the humanoid type, and seems to provide powerful evidence that the imagery of close encounters of the third kind is stored in the collective unconscious – that it is, in Jungian terms, archetypal.

ILLUSORY EXPERIENCES?

Analysis of hallucinations and the images remembered from near-death experiences frequently shows parallels with reports of close encounters of the third kind. So might such similarities prove that close encounter cases are illusory? This is not necessarily the case – for four reasons. Firstly, many abduction and other close encounter reports involve multiple witnesses, and it seems unlikely that multiple hallucinations, lasting for several hours, occur with significant frequency. Secondly, there are reported physiological, psychological and physical effects associated with abduction experiences that – where authenticated – suggest that something *did*

The detail of a chained devil, below left, is from a stained glass window in the St Lawrence chapel of Strasbourg Cathedral, France. With its goatish beard, cow's horns, ass's ears and bird's talons, he exhibits the characteristics of Lawson's 'exotic' category.

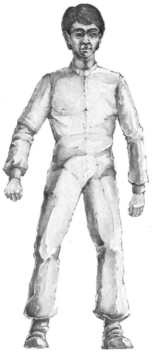

human

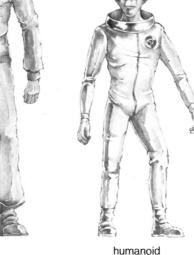

humanoid

animal

happen. Thirdly, hallucinating patients and those who have gone through near-death experiences are generally convinced only by extremely vivid experiences, whereas most close encounter witnesses are convinced very speedily of the 'reality' of the event, however unlikely they know it to be. Fourthly, while the triggering mechanism or stimulus for hallucinations and near-death experiences can apparently be determined with some accuracy, the stimulus for 'real' close encounter experiences continues to be one of the major unknowns of ufology. No one knows what it is that makes a particular person, at a particular place and time, likely to experience a close encounter.

MIXED IMPRESSIONS

Although none of these arguments in itself provides positive proof of the exact nature of witnesses' experiences, taken together, they make it seem likely that close encounter reports are indeed elicited by a real stimulus of some kind. But as the French ufologist Claud Rifat has ventured to speculate: 'UFO reports... do not give us any indication of the true stimulus which elicited the report; they give us only what the subject fancies about the nature of a UFO . . . CE 111s [close encounters of the third kind] are LSD-like experiences, in which a subject perceives a mixture of the real world and of her/his inner unconscious one.'

Accounts given by witnesses may well reflect what their senses have reported – that is, they do actually perceive humanoids, exotics, and so on. But if the six entity-types are indeed already in the collective unconscious, they are, therefore, already in some sense in the mind of the witness before his close encounter. If so, while perceptions of alien entities may well be stimulated in the witnesses by what can only be loosely called the UFO phenomenon, they do indeed indicate that some kind of stimulus is present – but tell us nothing at all about the nature of that stimulus.

It has been said that certain aspects of Christian imagery show striking parallels with reports of alien creatures. The 16th-century window, right, features Adam, the first man, likened by some to a robot infused with life.

> **STORIES OF DWARF FIGURES INCHES TALL AND GIANTS EIGHT FEET IN HEIGHT ARE AMONG WITNESS ACCOUNTS OF UFO OCCUPANTS... CAN THIS INTELLIGENCE VARY SIZE AND SHAPE TO SUIT THE OCCASION?**
> **ARTHUR SHUTTLEWOOD,**
> **THE FLYING SAUCERERS**

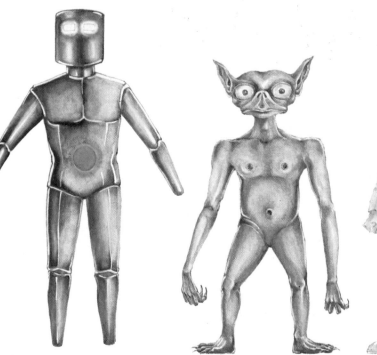

robot   exotic   apparitional

The artist's impressions, left, are of each of Alvin Lawson's six categories of alien. They are, from left to right, human, humanoid, animal, robot, exotic and apparitional. Lawson argues that these categories are archetypal: that they are somehow built into the human psyche, awaiting only the right trigger to bring them to the conscious mind.

DIAGNOSIS BY KIRLIAN AURA

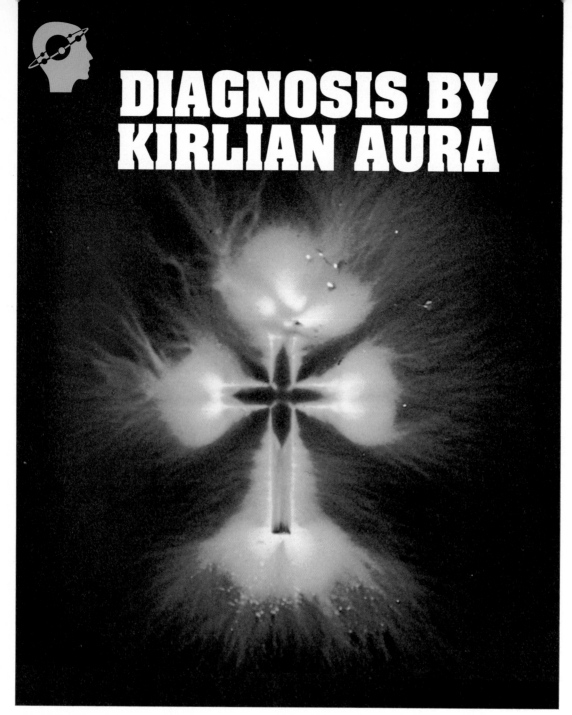

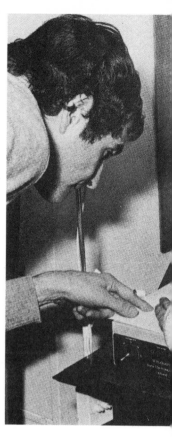

The bright glow surrounding the gold cross, left, is attributed to the influence of the wearer's 'aura'. Gold is said to be able to retain the 'aura' indefinitely.

Brian Snellgrove is seen above, operating a Kirlian machine. The regularity of the corona produced by the subject's hand can provide information about personality and the state of health.

EXPONENTS CLAIM THAT KIRLIAN PHOTOGRAPHS CAN REVEAL THE EARLY STAGES OF CANCER. A DISTURBED 'CORONA' MAY ALSO INDICATE STRESS AND ANXIETY, THEY SAY. WHAT ELSE CAN KIRLIAN IMAGES DETECT?

When Russian scientists first announced the discovery of an 'energy body', composed of so-called 'bioplasma' existing quite separately from the physical body, few scientists in the West were prepared to take them seriously. What evidence was there, they asked, to substantiate such a claim?

This question, despite much scientific investigation, still awaits a conclusive answer. What the Russians believed to be the 'energy body' turned out to be the curious corona shown by Kirlian photography to surround almost all living things. But, as sceptics in the West have asked: what exactly *is* the strange corona effect that Kirlian photography captures on film? Does it really constitute, as some have claimed, positive scientific evidence for the existence of an 'energy body'? Is the corona effect, perhaps, a picture of the 'aura' that has been described by mystics and clairvoyants? Or is there some other perfectly ordinary explanation?

Recent research has concentrated on showing that whatever the nature of Kirlian photographs, they can be used to achieve practical benefits in medical diagnosis, as well as insight into the human mind. A relationship has been found to exist, for example, between the various patterns of Kirlian

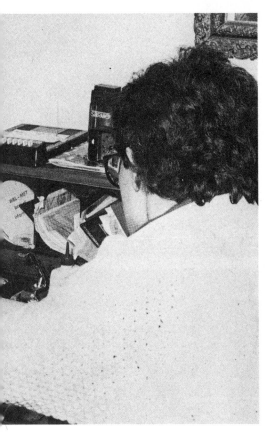

photographs of the human hand and the physical and psychological condition of the subject.

The left hemisphere of the brain corresponds to the right hand, and radiations from it detected by Kirlian photography provide clues, it is said, to the logical ability of the subject. The intuitive potential of the subject, meanwhile, can be discovered by a reading of the corona effect of the left hand, which correlates with the right hemisphere of the brain. A well-balanced Kirlian image of both hands is said to indicate a well-balanced personality.

Characteristics that can be recognised by this method of analysis – characteristics that even the subject himself may not realise he possesses – include healing ability, creative potential and qualities of leadership. Kirlian photographs are also said to show the nature and extent of conflicts arising from professional and emotional life, as well as the existence of physical tension.

Initial investigations into the diagnostic uses of Kirlian photography have revealed a wide range of possibilities. Studies on rats, carried out by Dr Thelma Moss and Dr Margaret Armstrong of the University of Rochester, New York, indicate that marked changes occur in the corona discharge of the tails of cancerous rats, for example. Similar corona patterns have been found in cancerous plants and in the fingertips of cancerous humans. Virtually all areas of the body photographed by the Kirlian method have yielded information about the physical and mental condition of the subject. However, the clearest corona pictures are usually obtained of the hands and feet.

The basic equipment used in Kirlian photography is simple. It consists of a high voltage 'Tesla coil', which is connected to a metal plate and insulated from the subject by a non-conductive layer. A sheet of light-sensitive material – bromide paper or film is generally used – will be placed between subject and machine.

The Kirlian machine radiates a high-voltage, high-frequency field. The 'energy body' of the hand or object to be photographed repels the field and causes a pattern of interference to be established. This 'energy body', or whatever it is that creates the pattern, varies. When the 'energy body' is in a balanced condition, a regular interference pattern is produced when the field of the machine and that of the subject interact. When there is an imbalance in the field of the subject, irregularities appear in the corona that shows up. It is these irregularities, as research has shown, that can often be correlated to some physical or mental ailment.

ENERGY OF THE SOUL?

Despite what seem to be promising uses, Kirlian photography is still beset with many theoretical and practical difficulties. Debate about its reliability continues; and perhaps the most controversial area of Kirlian photography centres on the interpretation of results.

There are at present four broad views taken of Kirlian photography. According to the cynical view, the so-called Kirlian effect is merely the result of normal discharge between the subject, the film and the machine. Any accurate diagnosis produced is purely coincidental and due solely to the intuition of the researcher, sceptics say. And while accepting that Kirlian photography can monitor physical symptoms such as the activity of the sweat glands and temperature, more sympathetic critics maintain that it still needs to be shown that these reflect changes in the physical or psychological state of the subject before proper diagnosis can be made.

Russian experts on nutrition are said to have used the Kirlian process, as in the Kirlian image of a slice of wholewheat bread, above, to improve the quality of grain and other foodstuffs.

The photograph, right, is of a healthy geranium leaf and was taken with a conventional camera. The image, far right, shows the same leaf photographed by the Kirlian method. The Kirlian photograph of the same geranium leaf, below, was taken after the leaf had died. The corona effect has almost completely disappeared, leaving only the outline of the leaf.

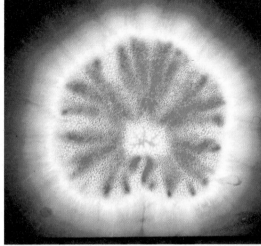

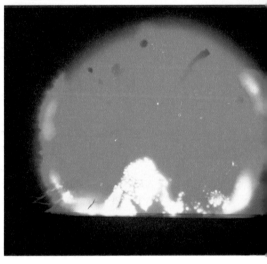

Parapsychologists, however, insist that, although purely physical causes, such as sweat, may play a part in the production of the corona effect, these causes by themselves do not provide a full explanation. According to parapsychologists, Kirlian photography can only be fully understood if the existence of an 'energy body', 'aura', 'bioplasmic body' or some other 'paranormal' phenomenon is accepted.

The most radical interpretation is that of the 'enthusiasts' who claim that Kirlian photography has nothing to do with mundane physical causes, such as sweat. It shows, quite clearly, they say, the energies of the soul. The colours and shapes revealed by Kirlian photography are what mystics and clairvoyants have been talking about for centuries.

Before considering which of these four competing views is most likely to be correct, there are a number of factors that the serious researcher has to take into account. The Kirlian machine used must conform to a certain standard to ensure that skin resistance, sweat, and other physical manifestations do not interfere with the corona. The subject being investigated must also be relaxed. It has been found that, when the subjects try consciously to project their 'aura', the result is a weaker and more irregular radiation. A similar effect is caused

A strong corona surrounding the foot, shown below, suggests good health. But notice the absence of the corona around the big toe. This is said to indicate that the subject is suffering from a headache. Massaging the toe, it is claimed, will relieve this.

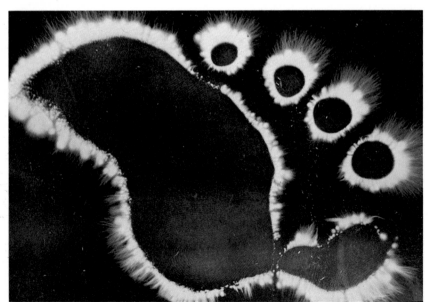

> ❚❚ WE FOUND IN WORKING WITH CANCER PATIENTS AT ST FRANCIS HOSPITAL IN WICHITA, KANSAS, THAT THE KIRLIAN PHOTOGRAPHS CLEARLY REVEALED THOSE PATIENTS WITH CANCER . . . WE ALSO FOUND THAT EMOTIONAL AND MENTAL STATES WERE REFLECTED IN THE ELECTROPHOTOGRAPHS AND POSTULATED THAT THE KIRLIAN PROCESS COULD BE USED AS A PSYCHOLOGICAL TOOL. ❚❚
>
> **BILL SCHUL,**
> **THE PSYCHIC FRONTIERS**
> **OF MEDICINE**

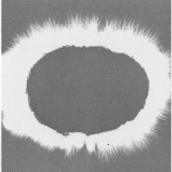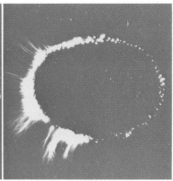

by anxiety or fear on the part of subjects. The researcher must therefore be experienced enough to distinguish between cases where the result is influenced by anxiety, sweat, or some other temporary physical manifestation owing to nervousness, and those effects that indicate some deeper physical or psychological significance.

There are, in addition, several areas in which the exponent needs to exercise caution if he or she is to avoid the more common criticisms levelled against Kirlian photography.

Firstly, the part of the body to be photographed needs to be chosen with care. A fingertip when photographed alone, for instance, presents a different image from that of the finger when photographed as part of the hand.

There is often a temptation to correlate the colours of the corona with an emotional state. The colour cast, however, will often depend on the type of film used. *Ektakrome* 35mm film, for example, produces reds or yellows, while *Polaroid* film produces a red outer corona with a white inner band. Resin-coated paper produces blue and little else. The colours themselves are not always important. What may be rather more relevant is the regularity and extent of any colour effects and what stimuli cause them.

OUTSIDE INFLUENCES

Operator effect also needs to be taken into account. The ability of the mind to cause structural and emotional changes in both living and inanimate objects has been observed on many occasions. An aggressive attitude on the part of observers can sometimes be seen to inhibit the performance of ESP subjects, for instance; and we know that the voltage patterns of wired-up plants will change when disharmonious thoughts are projected. In order to exclude any possible effects of this nature, the operator should stand at least 4 feet (1.5 metres) away from the subject, maintaining a relaxed and open frame of mind.

Excessive voltage, meanwhile, will usually produce an artificially bright corona, so the operator needs to be able to recognise what voltage and waveform characteristics ought to look like. The golden rule is to use the minimum possible voltage to produce a readable pattern.

The 'energy body' takes time – sometimes a matter of days – to settle down after any form of therapy. Results can therefore be misleading when photographing a subject after, for example, a session of meditation. In many cases, the corona will have completely disappeared.

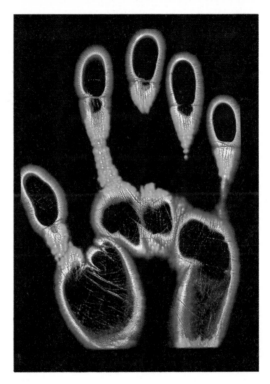

Too long or too short an exposure time can also produce misleading results. There appear to be slow cycles of activity that can be missed if exposure time is too short. For fingertip photographs, one second is sufficient; for a hand, two seconds.

In recent years, Kirlian photography has been used successfully in a number of quite surprising applications. In a study commissioned by a commercial firm in the USA, for example, Dr Thelma Moss was able to predict the incidence of germination of soya bean seeds with almost 100 per cent accuracy. The implications for agriculture are immense. Other areas where Kirlian methods of interpretation might be used include personnel selection and evaluation by employers of prospective employees, compatibility assessment and estimation of the effect on young children of parental conflict. When used in conjunction with acupuncture, counselling or homoeopathy, Kirlian photography, it is claimed, can also produce astonishingly accurate medical diagnoses.

While the practical benefits of Kirlian photography may have been clearly shown, doubt remains, however, as to whether this actually proves the existence of the 'aura'. There does seem to be a 'flow of energy' surrounding almost all living things. But precisely what that energy is remains unknown.

A series of four Kirlian photographs of the same fingertip are shown above, taken at different times of the day. 1: 9.15 a.m. just after breakfast. Note the strong corona. 2: At 12.30 p.m. before lunch. The corona is noticeably weaker. 3: By 3.45 p.m., after only a sandwich for lunch, the subject's corona has faded considerably. 4: At 7 p.m. before dinner, it is now even dimmer.

In general, a tense subject will produce a Kirlian image that is spiky in appearance. The more relaxed subject, however, will generate a softer, more regular corona, as shown left.

witnesses – and only the scarf would be left lying on the ground. 'At last she has forgotten it', a sitter remarked. But, then, the scarf, too, would slowly vanish in the same manner.

Madame d'Esperance was one of the earliest English materialisation mediums and she readily co-operated with investigators who wanted to prove that her manifestations were not produced by fraud – even to the extent of allowing photographs to be taken. But one particular seance experience suggests that materialisation is not in fact entirely straightforward.

SMASH AND GRAB

At a meeting in Newcastle in 1880, one of the sitters became suspicious because another of Madame d'Esperance's materialisations – known as 'the French lady' – looked uncannily like the medium herself. He made a grab for the spirit, which promptly vanished. But the medium suffered a lung haemorrhage and was ill for quite a long time afterwards. On two other occasions, similar incidents occurred; but Madame d'Esperance was never officially found to be producing the strange manifestations fraudulently.

Spiritualists say that touching a materialisation (unless permission has been granted by the 'spirit') or putting a light on during a seance can do untold damage to the medium because it causes the 'ectoplasm' – from which the spirit forms are made – to return to the medium's body at too great a speed. Nevertheless, there have been a number of instances where materialisations have apparently produced in daylight.

It was London medium William Eglinton who was responsible for convincing many sceptics. After

FLESHING OUT THE SPIRIT

CAN UNUSUALLY GIFTED MEDIUMS CAUSE THE DEAD TO MATERIALISE? SUCH CASES ARE NOT UNKNOWN, ACCORDING TO THOSE WHO PURPORT TO HAVE WITNESSED THE PHENOMENON

Yolande was a 15-year-old Arab girl. She was also allegedly a spirit, which meant she could appear and disappear at will in the presence of a famous English materialisation medium, Madame Elizabeth d'Esperance. The way in which Yolande materialised left witnesses in no doubt that she was a genuine paranormal manifestation, even though she appeared to be a normal living person in the course of each seance.

During one particular sitting, Yolande took a liking to a brilliantly coloured scarf that a sitter was wearing. and 'borrowed' it. When she dematerialised, the scarf disappeared with her. She was seen to be wearing it at her next seance appearance, and made it clear that she did not wish to part with the garment.

Sometimes Yolande's spirit form would gradually dissolve into a mist – on occasions, in front of 20

The photograph, above, was taken of the alleged manifestation of Yolande, the 15-year-old spirit-guide of the English medium Madame d'Esperance.

The illustration by Tissot, right, depicts the two materialised spirits he encountered at a seance given by London medium William Eglinton, top right, in the 1880s. It seems logical that a genuine materialised spirit would still be wearing a shroud; but, of course, voluminous clothing would also make an ideal disguise for fake 'spirits'.

attending one of Eglinton's seances, the famous conjurer Harry Kellar declared: 'I must own that I came away utterly unable to explain, by any natural means, the phenomena that I witnessed.' At one point during this seance, both Kellar and Eglinton were levitated.

One of the spirits who regularly appeared at Eglinton's seances was Abd-u-lah. He had only one arm and was adorned with jewels, rings, crosses and clusters of rubies that were apparently worth a fortune. Another materialisation, a bearded man in a long robe, allowed one of the sitters to cut a piece of material from his clothes and a part of his beard. These were later said to match holes in a piece of muslin and a false beard that were found in a truck belonging to Eglinton.

Despite this particular accusation of fraud – which was made by Archdeacon Thomas Colley – Eglinton continued to give seances and impressed many eminent people. He also developed slate-writing powers: spirits were said to write answers to questions on small black slates. The British Prime Minister William Gladstone visited him on 29

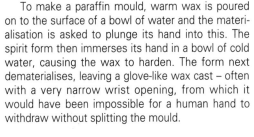

October 1884, and wrote down confidential questions in Spanish, Greek and French. The answers were given in these languages. Gladstone was so impressed that he subsequently became a member of the Society for Psychical Research.

The man who claimed to have exposed Eglinton was, ironically, no sceptic. Archdeacon Colley of Natal and Rector of Stockton, England, was in fact a staunch supporter of another materialisation medium, an English clergyman-turned-medium, the Reverend Francis Ward Monck. Monck was not only accused of being a fraud but was sentenced to three months' imprisonment on the evidence of 'props' found in his room after a seance in Huddersfield in November 1876. Archdeacon Colley was in South Africa at the time, but he was adamant that Monck was genuine.

The problem with materialisations is that they generally leave no tangible evidence. Investigator William Oxley, however, came up with an ingenious method of 'recording' the presence of Monck's materialised spirits – one that has also been used successfully with other mediums. At a seance in Manchester in 1876, Oxley began to make excellent paraffin moulds of the hands and feet of materialisations that appeared.

To make a paraffin mould, warm wax is poured on to the surface of a bowl of water and the materialisation is asked to plunge its hand into this. The spirit form then immerses its hand in a bowl of cold water, causing the wax to harden. The form next dematerialises, leaving a glove-like wax cast – often with a very narrow wrist opening, from which it would have been impossible for a human hand to withdraw without splitting the mould.

WAX IMPRESSIONS

A Polish intellectual, Franek Kluski, was a very powerful physical medium who also produced wax impressions. He was never a professional medium, but offered his services to Dr Gustave Geley and the Institut Métapsychique, Paris, in 1920. This eminent psychical researcher, and other investigators, testified that, in Kluski's presence, phantom limbs materialised, luminous forms glided around the seance room and brilliant lights suddenly appeared. Under strict controls, they were even able to produce photographs of a phantom. Both Dr Geley and Dr Charles Richet, who was a professor of physiology in Paris, obtained excellent moulds of materialised hands and limbs with Kluski. The full-form materialisations that appeared at his seances often arrived suddenly, though at other times they were seen to emerge from a faintly luminous cloud above the medium's head.

The materialisations produced by a Cardiff boot repairer, George Spriggs, seem almost too good to be true; but there is ample testimony from witnesses to the phenomenon who were all aware of precautions against fraud.

Spriggs' powers were first developed in a Welsh Spiritualist circle in the late 1870s. It all began with clairvoyance and automatic writing, and culminated in full-form phantoms. He emigrated to Australia in

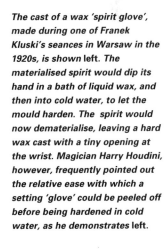

The cast of a wax 'spirit glove', made during one of Franek Kluski's seances in Warsaw in the 1920s, is shown left. The materialised spirit would dip its hand in a bath of liquid wax, and then into cold water, to let the mould harden. The spirit would now dematerialise, leaving a hard wax cast with a tiny opening at the wrist. Magician Harry Houdini, however, frequently pointed out the relative ease with which a setting 'glove' could be peeled off before being hardened in cold water, as he demonstrates left.

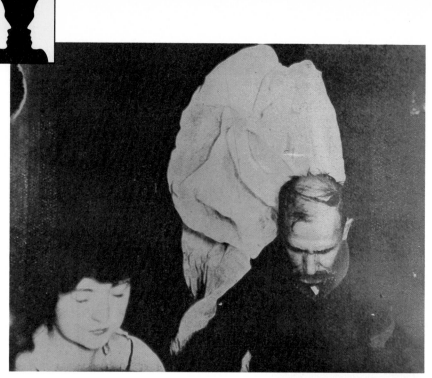

> **"** I FEEL THAT THE AIR IS FILLED WITH SUBSTANCE, AND A KIND OF WHITE AND VAPOROUS MASS, QUASI LUMINOUS . . . IS FORMED IN FRONT OF THE ABDOMEN. AFTER THE MASS HAS BEEN TOSSED AND AGITATED IN EVERY WAY FOR SOME MINUTES, SOMETIMES EVEN FOR HALF-AN-HOUR, IT SUDDENLY STOPS, AND THEN OUT OF IT IS BORN A LIVING BEING CLOSE TO ME. **"**
>
> **MADAME D'ESPERANCE**

In the remarkable photograph, top, a phantom begins to materialise in the gloom of one of Kluski's seances. Spiritualists believe that ectoplasm – the substance from which materialisations are formed – is photosensitive. This is why most seances are held in the dark.

The Australian medium George Spriggs, above right, caused the materialisation of a spirit who wrote a letter and even went to buy a stamp for it, much to the consternation of the shopkeeper who sold it to him.

November 1880, taking his psychic powers with him. A prominent Australian named Donovan, a former member of the legislative Assembly of Victoria, attended Spriggs' seances for 18 months and wrote a book about his experiences.

PHANTOM LETTER

The Evidences of Spiritualism includes a report of an extraordinary incident that occurred at one of the Australian seances. A man materialised and said he wanted to write a letter to a Sydney woman who had visited the seances on a couple of occasions. He was given a pen and paper and wrote a three-page letter, which he placed in an envelope and addressed to the woman. But no one had a stamp. The spirit borrowed sixpence from a sitter and left the seance room to buy one from the shop next door. Word reached the shopkeeper that a phantom was on its way to buy a stamp. Utterly flustered, he forgot to give the dead man his change. The spirit realised the error when he got back to the seance and promptly returned to the shop for the money. The letter was posted and a reply received. This was kept until the spirit materialised at another seance, opened it, and read the contents aloud.

Spriggs' ability to produce materialisations faded after six years, but he developed the ability to diagnose illness psychically. He returned to Britain in 1900 and gave free medical advice in the rooms of the London Spiritualist Alliance.

Medicine also played an important role in the mediumship of English psychic Isa Northage, and the materialisation seances she gave are perhaps the most astonishing ever recorded. She was a popular medium in the 1940s, visiting churches to demonstrate her psychic powers, which included apport mediumship, direct voice and materialisation. But it was the healing work of her spirit guide, Dr Reynolds, that was in particular demand; and eventually a church was built specifically for this work in the grounds of Newstead Abbey, Northumberland. As Isa Northage's powers grew stronger, Dr Reynolds was able to materialise and carry out 'bloodless' surgery. This account, written by Group Captain G.S.M. Insall, is taken from a book about Isa Northage's mediumship, *A Path Prepared.*

'We prepared the room, donned white overalls and masks, as was the rule with Dr Reynolds. This

*In*FOCUS

THE APEMAN COMETH

Not all of Franek Kluski's materialisations would have been welcome at a party – if only because not all of them had a human form. In July 1919, an apeman made the first of several appearances at a Kluski seance. Dr Gustave Geley, present at many of these occasions, reported: 'This being, which we have termed *Pithecanthropus,* has shown itself several times at our seances. One of us. . . felt its large shaggy head press hard on his shoulder and against his cheek.

The head was covered with thick, coarse hair. A smell came from it like that of a deer or wet dog.'

Colonel Norbert Ocholowicz, who published a book about Kluski's extraordinary mediumship in Polish, in 1926, wrote: 'This ape was of such great strength that it could easily move a heavy bookcase filled with books through the room, carry a sofa over the heads of the sitters, or lift the heaviest persons with their chairs into the air to the height of a tall person. Though the ape's behaviour sometimes caused fear, and indicated a low level of intelligence, it was never malignant. Indeed, it often expressed goodwill, gentleness and readiness to obey...'

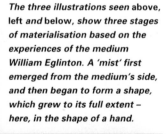

was not new to me as I had been a student in the most up-to-date French hospital before the first World War changed my career to flying... The two patients came in. [Both had hernias.] The first, the one with complications, was partially stripped and placed on the operating table.

'There was a trolley and I checked over the instruments – tweezers, swabs, kidney basins and bowls; no cutting instruments at all except scissors to cut lint. There was also a small white pencil light. I checked the emergency door and saw that it was locked and bolted on the inside, and draught excluded by a mat placed on the threshold. I was just closing the inner door leading into the church when somebody noticed that the medium had not arrived. I opened it again, and she came in. The light was turned low and somebody opened in prayer. I could see the medium sitting in her usual chair, a curtain hanging on either side.

'Immediately the prayer was over, a trumpet rose and Dr Reynolds' familiar voice greeted us all. He then reassured the patients... I was assigned a kidney basin to collect swabs and stepped forward to the operating table.

'The trumpet went down, and almost immediately the doctor appeared in materialised form on the opposite side of the operating table. He is of small stature. The medium was deep in trance .

'He first took the tweezers and swabbed the area with a disinfecting cleaner. The hernia was umbilical. I collected the swab in the kidney basin. Then I saw him place his hands on the patient's flesh, and they just went in deep, nearly out of sight. He stretched out for the tweezers and swabs and I collected eight soiled ones altogether.'

The materialised doctor checked that the patient was comfortable – he had felt no pain – and turned the pencil light on his flesh to inspect the area. There was no sign of a wound or a scar. Dr Reynolds then said he wanted to give the medium a rest before the next operation – and he dematerialised, vanishing in much the same way as others who are 'fleshed out' from the spirit world.

The three illustrations seen above, left and below, show three stages of materialisation based on the experiences of the medium William Eglinton. A 'mist' first emerged from the medium's side, and then began to form a shape, which grew to its full extent – here, in the shape of a hand.

Charles Richet, top left, French scientist and psychical researcher, was president of the Society for Psychical Research in 1905. He was greatly impressed with the mediumship of Franek Kluski, finding no natural or fraudulent explanation for what he witnessed at his seances.

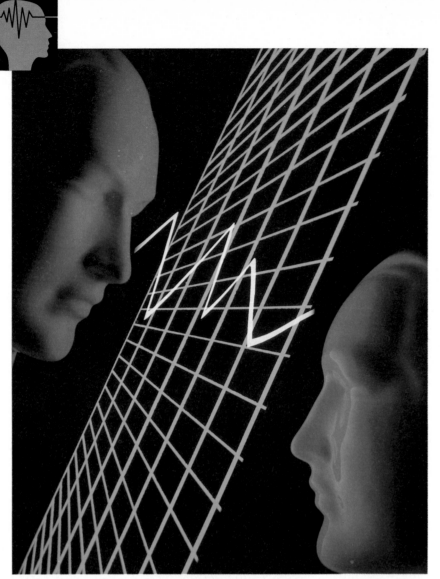

WAKING UP TO PSI

WHEN TWO PEOPLE COMPARE THEIR DREAMS, THEY MAY WELL UNCOVER TELEPATHIC LINKS. HERE, ESP RESEARCHER JOE FRIEDMAN TELLS OF HIS EXPERIMENTS IN THIS AREA

There are few examples of a sustained telepathic link between two people. One is the telepathic link between the American novelist Upton Sinclair and his wife Mary, a link that was tested in a series of ESP drawing experiments, subsequently described in detail in Sinclair's book *Mental Radio.* This book, published in 1930, so impressed Albert Einstein that he wrote an introduction to it.

The illustration, above, depicts the intriguing telepathic link that researchers have found in the dreams of certain subjects with a close relationship.

In the late 1970s, I myself was involved in a sustained and well-documented series of dreams that were telepathically linked to those of a close friend and former student of mine. Most of these dreams took place between May and December 1979. There were more than 20 in all, equally distributed between the two partners.

DREAM AWARENESS

Dave Ashworth first became a student in one of my parapsychology courses, held in London, in April 1978. Aged 23, he had been interested in the occult and psychical research for some time. He was also deeply aware of his dream life, often remembering and recording several dreams a night. After a class that I held on telepathic and precognitive dreams, Dave came up to me and said that, though he had been writing down his dreams for some time, he had never had one that he considered to be precognitive. I told him confidently that he would have such a dream the following week. In saying this, I was partly trying to bring about the desired result – but I also felt a genuine conviction that Dave would indeed have a precognitive dream.

The following week, however, he told me of the failure of his attempt. He had remembered and recorded 13 dreams during the week, but none of them had proved precognitive. I asked him to tell me just one. After looking through his dream diary, he recounted one in which, he said: 'The brat next door comes into my room. I am very hospitable and feed him, but he acts boorishly, as if he owns the place. He opens the wardrobe and, to my amazement, there is another door in the back of the wardrobe, which leads into the attic next door...'

I then told Dave he had just had his first telepathic dream. I had been intending to lead my class in a guided fantasy that evening: they would be urged to have a dream in which they opened their wardrobe door to find that there was another door in the back, a door that opened magically for them.

This experience inaugurated a telepathic dream series that was to last over two years and that was marked by an all-important factor – that of selection. In this case, Dave chose the psychic dream from a total of 13 that he had recorded during the week. He could hardly have picked out the 'right' dream by pure chance; so he must have had some awareness that this dream was precisely the psychic one for which he was looking. Later in the series, this awareness became more explicit, so that each of us became better able to pick out his own psychic dreams.

In March 1979, Dave joined a dream group that I was leading. We met fairly regularly, often once a week, for a period of a little more than a year. It was during this period that most of the psychic dreams occurred. We started the practice of telling each other any dreams in which the other figured. A high percentage contained correspondences with the dreams or waking life of the other person.

Often, Dave and I would dream of similar topics, themes or metaphors on the same night. In one such spontaneous coincidence, I dreamed of visiting a friend who lived in Colliers Wood in south London. In part of Dave's dream of that night, most of which involved eating at my flat, he dreamed of a picnic in a forest. As he recounted: 'All around are

Many psychoanalysts who have studied psychic dreams have encountered this sort of 'tracer' – an indication in the dream itself that it will prove psychic. Indeed, I have found that most people who have regular telepathic dreams have some sort of tracer in them. Psychic dreams also often have a peculiar quality of vividness. On other occasions, they might have a distinctive 'feel' to them. In Dave's psychic dreams, a grey cat often appeared. In other people's dreams, the tracer is to be found in the fact that the dream is set in a certain place of power.

SLEEPING DIALOGUE

Many of the dreams in our telepathic series contained such tracer elements. Their presence indicated that both of us were becoming more aware of the dream dialogue that was gradually developing between us.

people in orange clothes... some single, some in groups. They are either walkers or miners... There are stones and stone circles . . . I stand in one circle and am aware that this is a place of power. I touch my forehead to a tree and then wonder if I am emitting psychic power.'

Could those in the forest, possibly miners, be a reference to *Colliers* Wood? Whether or not this is so, the dream is important for other reasons. In it, Dave seems to have had an awareness that it was connected with me – he dreamt of eating a meal at my flat – and that the dream was psychic – he dreamt that he might be emitting psychic power.

An apparent telepathic dream link was forged between Joe Friedman, seen top, on the right, and his student Dave Ashworth, shown beside him. Friedman once sent a picture postcard, above, to Ashworth from the United States, hoping it would appear in Ashworth's dreams. Before receiving the card, Ashworth did indeed dream of meeting Friedman and discussing SF films – an apparent reference to the picture's fantasy theme.

To test his wife's telepathic powers, American writer Upton Sinclair sent her the sketch of a bird's nest, above left, sealed in an envelope. After concentrating on the 'target', she made her own sketch of it, left. It closely resembles her husband's. Yet she did not see it as a bird's nest. Instead, she wrote on it: 'Inside of a rock well with vines climbing on outside.'

Another sort of psychic dream may involve a reference to an event occurring in the waking life of the other person in the friendship. In one such dream, I had gone to a park with a friend of Dave's and mine called Laura. According to my dream diary, while I was preoccupied with listening to some music that was being played in the park:

'A black youth started to remove my bike. I rushed over to him and started pushing him around, really enjoying myself, saying "What are you doing with my bike?" While I was doing this, the boy's father came and got on my bike and started to ride it off. I realised that I had allowed myself to get carried away...'

Shortly before I dreamed this, in the evening, I later learned that Dave had left his bike outside a friend's house during a visit. While he was inside, his rear light was stolen, for the second time from this location. On the way home, Dave fell to daydreaming of leaving his bike outside this house and hiding, waiting for the thief to come. He then caught the thief and gave him a good beating. His daydream continued with the boy's father coming to his friend's house and asking for the person who owned a bicycle.

I did several forms of informal experiment with Dave. In one, I bought a postcard that I thought would be a good target and sent it to him while I was on holiday in the United States. I wrote on the back: 'Dear Dave, This card was your precog. target for last night – did you dream about it?'

In fact, Dave's dream on the night before he received the card did have a resemblance to the target. It was as follows:

'At Joe's, seeing him for the first time after the break. He tells me of some sci-fi film – did I see it? I didn't, but it seems Roy [Joe's flatmate] did. They talk about it. Joe then mentions a series of sci-fi fantasy films, but I have seen none of them.'

This science fiction or fantasy theme did seem to correspond with the picture on the postcard, which was a fantasy scene. Interestingly, I did not know the date of the postcard's arrival in England,

PERSPECTIVES

DEAR DIARY

If you wish to look for ESP in your dreams, it will be necessary to remember as many as you can, in as much detail as possible. Keep a notebook and pencil at your bedside and write down your dreams immediately you wake up. Often there may be only one fading image: but if you keep going over it in your mind, other parts of the dream will probably be recalled. If you can remember nothing of the dream, go over the thoughts you had at the moment of waking – these are likely to lead back to the dream. It is helpful to carry a notebook during the day to jot down remembered dream scenes that sometimes come to mind without warning.

Write down the dreams – in as much detail as you reasonably can. Selection will be necessary, however, so pay attention to any unusual detail that would provide strong evidence of the paranormal if it were also to occur in someone else's dream (or, indeed, in waking life).

Your partners in the experiment will, of course, need to keep equally detailed dream diaries. Resemblances between your dreams and theirs will undoubtedly occur: your problem will be to decide in an objective way which ones could not be due to coincidence.

The picture of a Chinese film set, below, was used as a target in one of the author's telepathy experiments. He 'sent' it to a group with which he was working. Dave Ashworth, who knew nothing of the experiment, dreamed that night of large, brightly coloured butterflies, and the actors in the background do, indeed, look rather like huge butterflies, because of their extravagant costumes.

and Dave did not even know of the experiment, since I had conceived of it on the spur of the moment. In the dream, there is also a clear tracer element: Dave dreams of seeing me for the first time since the holidays. The dream, seemingly, was a psychic 'meeting'. In the dream, I kept insisting that Dave must have seen one of the films I was telling him about, but he denied it. The dream itself seems to have been alluding to the postcard scene by not actually succeeding in showing it to the dreamer.

On another occasion, Dave picked up a photograph I was 'transmitting' to another group with which I was involved. On the night of this transmission, of which he had no knowledge, Dave dreamed:

'In a street I come unexpectedly upon Jeff [a friend] – he looks absolutely amazing, dressed in a yellow safari suit . . . with a butterfly net in one hand, stalking butterflies... There are many brightly coloured butterflies, large furry ones, yellow ones and somewhere amidst them all is one which is very special.'

The photograph showed a dance troupe which included a number of people wearing wings – they did indeed look like butterflies.

These are a few personal, well authenticated examples of dream telepathy. They suggest that two, or more, people who are open to the possibility of the paranormal can radically increase the amount and quality of ESP occurring in their lives by making a practice of remembering, recording and sharing their dreams.

FROM RUSSIA WITH PSI

RESEARCH AND EXPERIMENT IN PARAPSYCHOLOGY IS KNOWN TO HAVE THRIVED BEHIND THE IRON CURTAIN, ATTRACTING THE INTEREST OF SECURITY AND MILITARY OFFICIALS WORLDWIDE

In 1957, only three articles appeared on the subject of parapsychology in the entire Soviet press, and all were hostile. Yet ten years later, the total had risen to 152, and less than 10 per cent were negative or even critical. Psychic matters had suddenly become respectable; and, as a steady stream of western journalists soon discovered, there was plenty to write about. All over the Soviet Union, it seemed, talented subjects were demonstrating paranormal abilities to scientists who, in turn, were eager to share their new discoveries with western colleagues. The Soviets were, in fact, just as interested as anybody else in telepathy, psychokinesis, UFOs, paranormal healing, and the rest of the *psi* spectrum.

Following the death of the Russian scientist and parapsychologist Leonid Vasiliev in 1966, a new generation of Soviet researchers, many directly inspired by his pioneering research into telepathy, was ready to carry on and expand his work. The young physicist, Viktor Adamenko, for example, had

Until the breakup of the USSR in 1991, Soviet power was usually represented by its missiles, bottom. Some people, however, believed a greater threat lay in its research into telepathy and other forms of mind control.

Dr Genady Sergeyev, a neurophysiologist, is seen above with his invention – a 'bioenergy measuring device'.

started to study the psychokinetic talent of his wife, Alla Vinogradova. Dr G.A. Sergeyev, a mathematician and neurophysiologist, was deeply involved in research into Man's interactions – both normal and paranormal – with his environment. Biochemist Yuri Kamensky had shown himself to be an unusually successful transmitter of images and targets, and his long-distance telepathy experiments with actor Karl Nikolayev fully supported earlier work by Vasiliev. At the Kazakh State University in Alma-Ata, biophysicist Dr V. M. Inyushin was evolving his theory of 'bioplasma' and developing the high-frequency photographic technique popularised by Semyon and Valentina Kirlian.

STAR PERFORMERS

These scientists had many star performers with whom to work. Nina Kulagina, for instance, was willing to demonstrate her psychokinetic abilities to order, whether to scientists in laboratories or to western visitors in hotel rooms. Rosa Kuleshova repeatedly proved her ability to read with her fingertips. Boris Yermolayev satisfied astonished observers, including the eminent psychologist Dr Venyami Pushkin, that he could levitate objects and even people. The young Azerbaijani Tofik Dadashev also set out to carry on the stage tradition set by world-famous 'mentalist' Wolf Messing, and brought publicly demonstrated telepathy into almost every city in the Soviet Union.

Behind all this excitement, scientists led by Dr Ippolit Kogan, head of the newly-formed Bioinformation Section of a Moscow technical institute, were hard at work on theoretical aspects of *psi*. And although parapsychology had never been

Dr Viktor Inyushin, a biophysicist at Kazakh State University, bottom left, undertook research into Kirlian photography, officially approved by the state.

Soviet actor Karl Nikolayev, below right, was the subject of many successful experiments into long-distance telepathy.

Soviet parapsychologist Viktor Adamenko, above, holds a small electric light bulb that lit up when placed beside an object that had been moved psychokinetically by his wife, Alla Vinogradova. In another display of her remarkable abilities, Vinogradova, right, shifts a metal cigar tube by passing her hand over it.

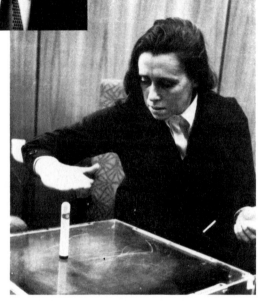

recognised as a scientific discipline in its own right, a young biologist, Eduard Naumov, was devoting himself to it full-time, determined to increase and improve East-West relations by means of his chosen field of research.

Elsewhere in Eastern Europe, the psychic scene looked equally promising, especially in Czechoslovakia, where Dr Milan Ryzl was showing that paranormal skills could be aroused through intensive training and use of hypnosis. Working over a three-year period with a single subject, Pavel Stepanek, he achieved positive results, nine times out of ten, in card-guessing experiments, several of which were witnessed by western visitors. He had, he claimed, published details of the first demonstration of repeatable telepathy under laboratory conditions. 'The subject,' he announced, 'evidently and repeatedly manifested the faculty of extra-sensory perception.'

Also in Czechoslovakia, engineer-inventor Robert Pavlita had begun to arouse considerable interest with his 'psychotronic generators' – small metal objects with which, he claimed, he was able to store 'biological energy'.

Meanwhile, Bulgaria had become the first country in the world to boast a state-supported psychic, a blind woman named Vanga Dimitrova from the small southern town of Petrich, near the Greek border. Any visitor could walk into the Sofia office of Balkantourist, the state travel agency, and book a sitting with her. The subject would then drive to

Petrich, spend the night in the state hotel built especially for Dimitrova's clients and sleep with a sugar lump under his pillow. The next day, he would visit Dimitrova and, when he reached the head of the queue, she would take the sugar lump from him, press it to her forehead, and immediately reel off a flood of information about his past, present and future. Bulgaria also boasted another world first: its official parapsychology institute in the centre of Sofia, headed by Georgi Lozanov, a medical doctor who, like thousands of other Bulgarians, had received accurate personal information from Dimitrova. He was later to become famous for his method of rapid learning through a method termed 'suggestology'.

EAST-WEST DIALOGUE

During the 1960s, Eastern Europe was indeed a centre of parapsychology. But this was not to last. In 1968, Eduard Naumov organised an international conference in Moscow, which was attended by nine westerners, including journalists Lynn Schroeder and Sheila Ostrander from the USA. Hardly had the meeting begun when the Russian newspaper *Pravda* came out with a savage attack on parapsychology in general, and medium Nina Kulagina in particular. Delegates were dismissed from the House of Friendship, and word went round that the East-West dialogue between parapsychologists was over.

Matters were made even worse when Schroeder and Ostrander published *Psychic Discoveries Behind The Iron Curtain* in 1970. This popular book contained an enormous amount of information on developments in Eastern Europe and the USSR, previously unknown to westerners, and

led to a considerable increase of interest in them. It also made it clear that the Soviets were way ahead of the field in most areas of research into the paranormal. But Soviet authorities did not like the book at all. It was, they said, 'overflowing with factual errors and undisguised anti-Soviet thrusts'; and they reacted violently to the suggestion that parapsychology was linked to defence, psychological warfare or espionage.

Reliable observers consider, however, that what really angered the authorities was the indiscretion of Naumov, who had revealed a couple of state secrets: one, that the Soviet military had carried out experiments in animal telepathy between a submarine and the shore; the other, that a method had been devised to intercept telepathy between

humans. Both these reports, if true, could have considerable military significance: conventional communication with a submerged submarine can be extremely difficult; and if telepathy were to become a weapon of war, a means of intercepting it would be of the greatest value.

TRUMPED-UP CHARGE

Although Naumov managed to organise another highly successful international meeting in 1972, he was in serious trouble the following year – allegedly for a financial misdemeanour. He was arrested and sentenced to two years' forced labour in March 1974. Perhaps as a result of vigorous international protest, he was released a year later. However, he was not allowed to resume work and disappeared altogether from the parapsychological scene.

Then, in October 1973, the Soviet press published an article that seemed, at last, to define the official attitude towards parapsychology. It also went some way towards explaining the USSR's apparently erratic international relations. The message was clear. *Psi* phenomena did indeed exist – some of them, anyway – and should be researched, but not by amateurs or 'militant individuals' (a clear reference to Naumov), but by the Soviet Academy of Sciences instead.

Normal international relations were, to all appearances, resumed when, largely on the initiatives of two psychologists – Dr Stanley Krippner (USA) and Dr Zdenek Rejdak (Czechoslovakia) – the first International Conference on Psychotronic Research was held in Prague in 1973: (*Psychotronics* is the Czech term for parapsychology). More than 400 delegates from 21 countries attended, including a group from the Soviet Academy of Sciences, and several Soviet and Eastern European scientists made important contributions. 'There is no doubt that we are experiencing the birth of a unique science,' said Krippner of the study of psychotronics, 'one which requires a combination of the physical and behavioural sciences with a new, holistic viewpoint on the organisation of life systems.'

A solid bridge had at last, it seemed, been built. Several western researchers visited the Eastern bloc countries, and formed close friendships with their counterparts there. Further parapsychological congresses were held at two-yearly intervals; and although there was no Soviet presence in Monaco in 1975 or in Tokyo in 1977, a team of Moscow medical researchers attended the 1979 gathering in Brazil, where Dr Rejdak made a firm plea for placing psychotronic research above politics.

ANALYSING REACTIONS

One might have thought that Schroeder and Ostrander had closed the door for other western writers; but in 1975, two American reporters from the sensationalist weekly *National Enquirer* were given free access to several Soviet research centres, including some that were off limits even to Soviet journalists. Reporters Henry Gris and William Dick were as surprised as anybody else at the privilege they had been granted; but one Soviet scientist speculated that his country's authorities were just as curious about western advances in

Psychokinetic superstar Nina Kulagina is seen, left, moving a matchbox by telekinesis. Before an object moved, she would feel a sharp pain in her spine, her sight became blurred and her blood pressure would rise.

Boris Yermolaev, below, is seen demonstrating the passes he made while paranormally suspending objects in the air.

parapsychology as westerners were about theirs. They wanted to find out how advanced the West really was, he thought, by studying reactions to what Gris and Dick reported.

Yet, even as Gris and Dick were preparing a book on their findings, a bizarre incident took place in 1977 that seemed to put the clock back to the chilliest period of the cold war of the 1950s. On 11 June, the *Los Angeles Times* correspondent in Moscow, Robert C. Toth, was telephoned by a man named Petukhov, who asked to meet him in the street at once. Toth did so, and was handed a document; but before he had time even to glance at it, both men were surrounded by plainclothes police and driven off for lengthy interrogation.

Then, a man claiming to be a senior member of the Academy of Sciences, promptly appeared, read the document, and announced that it contained an account of recent Soviet discoveries on the physical basis of *psi* phenomena – something they had sought in vain for half a century – and that it was a state secret. After 13 hours of interrogation by the KGB, Toth was released, and allowed to leave the country.

This incident baffled western observers as much as it did Toth himself, who had never shown any interest in parapsychology. It was thought at the

authorities in possible uses of it. Practical application had always been a characteristic of all Soviet research; and once it became possible to make practical use of *psi*, Dr Ryzl concluded, 'there is no doubt that the Soviet Union will do so'.

Western researchers have repeatedly been urged by their Eastern counterparts to ensure that psychic forces are used for peace and for the benefit of humanity. 'There is something about the way they say this,' one western parapsychologist has said, 'that makes it clear to me that some people have other ideas.'

▐▐ FROM CIA AGENTS STATIONED BEHIND THE IRON CURTAIN CAME REPORTS THAT THE RUSSIANS WERE ABLE TO INFLUENCE TELEPATHICALLY THE BEHAVIOUR OF PEOPLE, ALTER THEIR EMOTIONS OR HEALTH, AND EVEN KILL AT LONG DISTANCE BY USING ONLY PSYCHIC POWER. ▐▐

GRIS AND DICK, THE NEW SOVIET PSYCHIC DISCOVERIES

A selection of the various types of psychotronic generator, invented by Robert Pavlita, above, are displayed top. They could, he claimed, store biological energy.

In the group portrait, above left, American journalists Lynn Schroeder, left, and Sheila Ostrander, right, are seen with Soviet parapsychologist Eduard Naumov in Moscow in 1968, during the First International Conference on Parapsychology. Ostrander and Schroeder published their findings in Psychic Discoveries Behind The Iron Curtain in 1970, a book swiftly denounced by Soviet authorities.

Vanga Dimitrova, Bulgaria's famous blind prophetess, right, was the world's first known state-financed psychic. Sittings with her could be booked through the Bulgarian state travel agency.

time that he was merely being warned off any involvement with dissidents, but this is unlikely in view of the fact that he had finished his tour and was due to leave anyway. A more probable explanation is that the whole episode was set up by the authorities, and was a clumsy bluff. The Soviets had not solved the *psi* mystery, but they wanted the West to think they had, and hoped that Toth would report something to this effect to his newspaper.

TERRIFYING WARFARE

There was another more alarming theory, too. In 1973, the Soviet leader Leonid Brezhnev had made an enigmatic reference in a speech to a form of warfare 'more terrifying' than even nuclear weaponry, and the need for the USA to agree to a ban on it. He gave the impression that he knew the American leaders would know what he meant. Was this perhaps a veiled reference to biochemical (germ) warfare? Or had the Toth affair been a gentle reminder to the West that the Soviets were now in a position to wage psychic warfare?

After visiting the USSR, shortly before he went to live in the United States, Milan Ryzl reported on a paradoxical state of affairs there. Parapsychology, he said, was poorly funded; yet there were signs of considerable interest from security and military

UFOs SIGHTED OVER WATER

THERE ARE MANY ACCOUNTS OF SUPPOSED UFOS THAT HAVE LANDED ON, EMERGED FROM OR CRASHED INTO WATER. THE THREE THAT FOLLOW ALL TOOK PLACE ON THE BRAZILIAN COAST

The map, above, shows the position of Rio de Janeiro, Curitiba and Santos, Brazil, where the three sightings took place. This artist's impression, meanwhile, shows the mysterious craft spotted by the Machado family in 1970.

A particularly intriguing type of UFO report concerns objects emerging from or disappearing into water – most often, the sea. One such well-documented instance is recorded in an extraordinary series of photographs taken in the Canary Islands in 1979. Some writers have even gone as far as to suggest that there are enormous UFO 'bases' hidden under the world's oceans. In the absence of any concrete evidence, however, we can only regard this as speculation.

All the cases that follow occurred within 200 miles (320 kilometres) of each other along the Brazilian coast, south of Rio de Janeiro, though they were all well-separated in time. All involved several witnesses and what appear to be 'nuts and bolts' craft. Only the Santos case seems amenable to a conventional explanation: but if witnesses were indeed confronted by a stray rocket, aircraft pod, or satellite debris, it seems strange that the authorities were unable to locate wreckage at the site of the crash.

On Sunday, 27 June 1970, Aristeu Machado and his five daughters were playing a game on the verandah of their home at 318 Avenida Niemeyer, Rio de Janeiro, from which they could look out over

It was from the verandah at their house in Avenida Niemeyer, above, which runs north-east along the coast near Rio de Janeiro, that the Machado family, their maid and a neighbour saw the strange craft and its occupants.

Aristeu Machado and his wife are seen, right, at the spot from which they watched the UFO, and subsequent events at sea.

the road below to the South Atlantic Ocean beyond. With them was their friend and neighbour João Aguiar, an official of the Brazilian Federal Police.

Maria Nazaré, their maid, who was preparing lunch in the kitchen, called out to check the time: it was 11.38 a.m. About two minutes after that, João Aguiar happened to look out over the sea, and quickly drew the attention of the others to 'a motor boat striking the water'. As this object descended, it threw up spray on all sides.

The game and lunch were quickly forgotten for, as the family and their guest watched the 'motor boat', they could see two 'bathers' aboard the craft:

they seemed to be signalling with their arms. In a statement to Dr Walter Buhler, who investigated the case, Aguiar said there were definitely two figures on board and that they were wearing 'shining clothing, and something on their heads'. The craft was a greyish metallic colour; it seemed to be between 15 and 20 feet (5 – 6 metres) in length and had a transparent cupola. One strange feature was noted: at no time did the object make the 'bobbing' movement associated with a boat on a swell.

João Aguiar ran down to the nearby Mar Hotel, and telephoned the harbour police. They promised to send help to the occupants of the 'motor boat', who were presumably involved in a mishap offshore. Aguiar then returned to the house and rejoined the Machados on their verandah. He had been away from the house for about 30 minutes.

FLASHING SEQUENCE

Shortly after Aguiar returned, the object – which was now seen to be disc-shaped – took off. It skimmed the water for some 300 yards (280 metres), throwing off a wave from the bows as it went. It now lifted from the sea and made off quickly towards the south-east. It was then that the witnesses realised it was not a motor boat but, rather, an object that looked like a flying saucer. A hexagonal-shaped appendage retracted into the underside of the main body, and a number of lights on the appendage flashed, in sequence – green, yellow, and then red.

Once airborne, the object appeared to be transparent rather than aluminium-coloured, and Maria Nazaré said she clearly saw two entities sitting inside. There was little traffic noise from the road at that time, but the witnesses could hear no sound from the object.

On the sea where the UFO had originally rested, the witnesses saw a white hoop-shaped object 'about the size of a trunk or chest', according to Maria Nazaré. Suddenly the hoop sank, then it reappeared and a yellow oval-shaped section separated from it. This, it was estimated, was some 16 inches (40 centimetres) across with about 8 inches (20 centimetres) projecting above the surface of the water. It remained stationary for about three minutes, then began to move towards the shore, with its longer axis directed at the witnesses. A green flange at the rear of the object separated from the main body and followed it at a distance of about a yard (1 metre). After 15 minutes, the yellow oval was about 130 yards (120 metres) from the shore, when it made a right-angled turn to its left and headed for the beach at Gávea – a movement directly opposed to the maritime current in the area at the time.

The white hoop disappeared several times; but when it came back into view, it was still pursuing its direct course for Gávea Beach, as though it were going to link up once again with the yellow object.

Meanwhile, the police launch from Fort Copacabana had arrived at the spot where the UFO had remained stationary, having come into view about 20 minutes after João Aguiar had gone to make his telephone call. So the crew must surely have seen the UFO take off. At roughly the position where the hoop had been left, the launch was seen to stop and the police hauled on board a strange red

The two-part craft, seen by Captain Rocha and his wife, is illustrated below.

Eight-year-old Rute de Souza and a group of fishermen all saw the silvery object below, as it collided with the top of a palm tree.

cylindrical object, before making off at speed towards their base.

No statement was made by the police regarding what they saw or found. And, although an account of the incident appeared in the newspaper *Diário de Notícias* on 28 June 1970, no other witnesses came forward to confirm the sighting.

On 10 January 1958, Captain Chrysólogo Rocha was sitting with his wife in the porch of a house overlooking the sea near Curitiba, when he was surprised to see an unfamiliar 'island'. He had his binoculars focused on the piece of land and was amazed to see that it was growing in size. He cried out to people inside the house, and very soon eight of them joined the couple on the porch to witness the strange phenomenon.

The 'island' seemed to consist of two parts, one in the sea and the other suspended above it. Then, without warning, both parts sank out of sight. Soon afterwards, a steamer came into sight and passed very near the point where the objects were last seen. Fifteen minutes later, when the ship had gone, the 10 observers saw the objects appear to rise once again from the sea. Now they could see that the upper section was attached to the lower one by means of a number of shafts or tubes, which were quite bright. Up and down the shafts, small objects 'like beads in a necklace' passed in disorderly fashion. This second display lasted for quite a few minutes. Then the sections closed up, and the whole thing started to sink, eventually disappearing beneath the waves.

One of the witnesses, the wife of another army officer, telephoned the Forte dos Andrades barracks at Guarajá, and the air force base was swiftly alerted. An aeroplane was sent as soon as possible to investigate, but it arrived on the scene after the objects had finally disappeared.

MUDDY WATERS

On 31 October 1963, eight-year-old Rute de Souza was playing near her home in Iguape, south-west of Santos, when she heard a roaring noise that was growing rapidly louder. Looking round, she saw a silvery object coming down out of the sky, heading towards a nearby river. After passing over the house, the UFO collided with the top of a palm tree and began to twist and wobble in the air. Then Rute saw it fall into the river, close to the far bank.

The child turned to run home, and met her mother who, alarmed by the noise, had been running towards the river. Then followed Rute's uncle, Raul de Souza, who had been working about 100 yards (90 metres) from the house. The three of them stood transfixed as they watched the surface of the river: at the spot where the object had sunk, the water was now seen to be 'boiling up'. This was followed by an eruption of muddy water, and then one of mud.

Rute was not the only witness. On the far bank, a number of fishermen had watched the spectacle. One of them, a Japanese named Tetsuo Ioshigawa, gave a detailed description of the incident to official investigators and reporters. The object, shaped like a 'wash basin', was estimated by him to have been about 25 feet (7.5 metres) in diameter; it had been no more than 20 feet (6 metres) off the ground when it hit the palm tree. The general assumption was that the object must have been in difficulties after the collision.

Some who had heard about the incident assumed that a wrecked 'flying saucer' was embedded in the muddy bottom of the river, but divers could find nothing in the 15 feet (5 metres) of water. Finally, engineers searched the area with the use of mine detectors; but they, too, failed to locate the object.

Speculating about the incident in the *Bulletin of the Aerial Phenomena Research Organisation* (APRO), Jim and Coral Lorenzon wrote that the reported size of the UFO suggested it could certainly have carried a crew. If so, then repairs may well have been effected that would have enabled the craft to escape.

WITNESSING IMPOSSIBILITY

CAN SOLID OBJECTS DEMATERIALISE, ONLY TO REAPPEAR AT ANOTHER PLACE, OR PASS THROUGH OTHER OBJECTS WITHOUT DISRUPTING THEM? IT HAS BEEN SUGGESTED THAT THIS HAPPENS WHEN 'MISLAID' ITEMS INEXPLICABLY 'JUST TURN UP'

The scientist Johann Zöllner meticulously recorded his teleportation experiments with the medium Henry Slade. In one experiment, right, Zöllner sat with his thumbs pressed down on a loop of string that dangled over the edge of the table. The single knot in the loop was secured with a wax seal. After a few minutes, Slade announced that knots had been created in the string, and those shown in the illustration were found to have appeared. On another occasion, Zöllner requested that wooden rings be linked. The 'spirits' instead transferred them to the leg of a table, as shown below – a feat that should have involved dismantling the table.

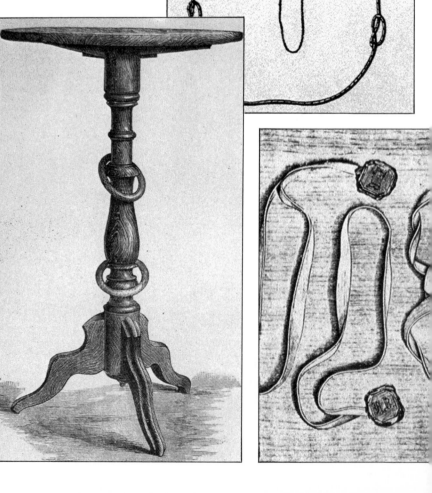

On the morning of 6 May 1878, Johann Zöllner, professor of physics and astronomy at the University of Leipzig, Germany, sat with the American medium Henry Slade in a room that had been set aside for an experiment in parapsychology. No other person was present. Zöllner held both of Slade's hands in his own on top of the card table at which they sat. After about a minute, a small circular beechwood table, standing a few feet away, began to rock to and fro, its top rising above the edge of the card table as it did so. The circular table then slid slowly towards the card table, tipped over backwards and slid beneath it.

Nothing further seemed to happen for another minute. Slade was about to consult his 'spirit controls' about what they should expect next, when Zöllner glanced under the card table to check precisely the position of the circular table – only to find that the latter had disappeared! The two men then searched the room, but found no sign of it.

UP IN THE AIR

Zöllner and Slade then resumed their places at the card table, their hands linked on its top and their legs touching, so that Slade could not make any undetected movements. After five minutes' expectant waiting, Slade saw lights in the air, as he usually did before anything paranormal occurred in his presence. Neither Zöllner nor any of his colleagues ever saw these lights when they participated in sittings with Slade. Nevertheless, Zöllner followed the path of Slade's gaze.

'As I turned my head, following Slade's gaze up to the ceiling of the room behind my back, I suddenly observed, at a height of about 5 feet [1.5 metres], the hitherto invisible table with its legs turned upwards very quickly floating down in the air upon the top of the card table.'

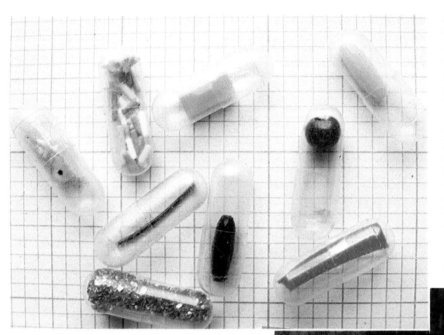

experimental controls). So even parapsychologists who seem willing to accept more 'reasonable' phenomena, such as ESP, join the sceptics in dismissing such tales out of hand, regarding them as tall stories for the gullible. And because these events exceed most people's 'boggle threshold' (to use a term coined by the author Renée Haynes) and cannot be reconciled with conventional physics, they have largely been ignored in parapsychology. Zöllner, certainly, was scoffed at and never taken seriously by the parapsychological establishment – for reasons that seem to have had more to do with the fantastic nature of the events than with any obscurity in his reports or shortcomings in the conditions of observation. Another contributory factor was that Slade – years later when his powers of mediumship were in decline – was declared by an investigating committee to cheat in the production of 'spirit writing' on slates.

The floating table was no mere hallucination – it gave both men a sharp crack on the head as it descended.

This sober and careful account describes what is known as teleportation – the disappearance of matter and its subsequent reappearance at the same or another place, with no known cause being involved. (Such events are also sometimes called 'disappearance-reappearance' phenomena.) A phenomenon that is presumably closely related is the passage of matter through matter – for example, the passing of an object into or out of a sealed container, or the tying and untying of knots without the use of any obvious or 'normal' means.

Such phenomena are reported from seances, experiments with certain psychokinetic (PK) agents, and in some poltergeist cases. However, they are hardly ever witnessed under 'good' conditions (that is, with parapsychologists in attendance and full

The objects inside the capsules, top, were used by researcher Julian Isaacs in experiments. They were intended to be teleported out of the container and were as small and light as possible.

The author, Julian Isaacs, is seen above, second from right, with an experimental group. In the boxes are objects that they attempted to teleport. Two boxes have been sealed with sticking plaster, on which a grid of pencil lines has been drawn. Any tampering inevitably disturbed the grid.

The pair of leather loops, left, are depicted before and after being paranormally linked. The event occurred beneath Zöllner's cupped hands, and he actually felt the loops move.

" IF THE PARALLEL UNIVERSES OF RELATIVITY ARE THE SAME AS THOSE OF QUANTUM THEORY, THE POSSIBILITY EXISTS THAT PARALLEL UNIVERSES MAY BE EXTREMELY CLOSE TO US, PERHAPS ONLY ATOMIC DIMENSIONS AWAY OR PERHAPS IN A HIGHER DIMENSION OF SPACE — AN EXTENSION INTO WHAT PHYSICISTS CALL SUPERSPACE. "

FRED ALAN WOLF,
PARALLEL UNIVERSES

Spontaneous teleportation of a spanner may seem unlikely, but there was a spate of just such events in one family following participation of the parents in Julian Isaacs' metal-bending experiments. The spanner was kept hanging on a hook in a locked garden shed, left. It was seen there in October 1982 – but thereafter went missing and could not be found anywhere, despite a thorough search of the garden and the shed. In March 1983, the spanner was found on a wardrobe, below, in the five-year-old daughter's room. It was now rusty, whereas it was formerly in mint condition. All in the family insisted that they had not put it there.

of the American Society for Psychical Research (ASPR). The report was written by William Button, then president of the ASPR, who was present at the eight sittings reported and who was intimately concerned with the mediumship of 'Margery' – otherwise, Margery Crandon.

In the experiments, the spirit of Margery's dead brother, Walter, ostensibly moved small objects into or out of various kinds of containers – cardboard boxes sealed with sticking plaster, locked wooden and metal boxes, among them. Poor Margery was bound to her chair with sticking plaster at her wrists and ankles; several turns of the plaster were used at each point, and it was marked with pencil lines that were designed to show whether the plaster had been taken off and rewound. When objects were teleported out of a container, the fact could be checked by shaking the container, when there would be no sound of the object bouncing around inside. Then another object might be teleported into the container – all without the container being opened.

A major problem with these experiments was that Margery's husband, Dr Crandon, was allowed to participate in many of the sittings and, in some of them, was even permitted to assist in controlling the medium's movements. The possibility of collusion cannot, therefore, be excluded. And Margery did indeed become embroiled in prolonged and bitter controversy in connection with other aspects of her physical mediumship.

INSTANT JOURNEY

More recently, another highly controversial psychic, Uri Geller, has claimed that a number of spontaneous teleportation events have happened to objects, or even people and animals, connected with him. For example, it is said that Geller suddenly arrived in the glass porch of his friend Andrija Puharich in Ossining, New York, having only a moment previously been walking in Manhattan, an hour's journey away.

The Indian mystic and religious teacher Sai Baba is the subject of a number of tales brought back by westerners who have visited him. His speciality is the materialisation of small objects from thin air; and the most usual gift is *vibhuti*, a powdery, greyish substance sometimes called 'holy ash'. Western parapsychologists who have visited him have never been allowed to impose controls. However, Karlis Osis and Erlendur Haraldsson managed to examine one of Baba's robes and found no pockets or other hiding places. Nor did it bear traces of *vibhuti* down the sleeves, which would be expected if Baba was in the habit of shaking it down into his hand. But the parapsychologists' judgement on him must remain open because he will not perform under controlled conditions.

One of the prime examples of apparent teleportation and the transport of matter through matter is the poltergeist case. In many such instances, stones or other missiles arrive apparently from nowhere, sometimes not becoming visible until they strike an object. A well-known case occurred in 1903. A geologist, W. F. Grottendieck, was conducting a survey in Sumatra. One night, he was sleeping in a hut roofed with a layer of large leaves, when he was awakened by small stones falling on

Other sittings by Slade, witnessed by Zöllner, produced 'impossible' movements of objects: on many such occasions, knots were tied in loops of string, leather or even pig-gut, while Zöllner was holding them or otherwise had them under his control. A sitting that was intended to link two wooden rings did not succeed, however, but ended with the rings 'impossibly' sitting on the central leg of a circular table, the teleportation of which has already been described. This table was well out of Slade's range when the event happened, as he was sitting with Zöllner at the other table at the time. To put the rings on the leg, any human agent would have had to take the table to pieces and reassemble it.

Zöllner's work fills a number of volumes, but only a fraction of this material is available in English translation. Yet if anyone's work deserves an attempt at replication, it is certainly Zöllner's.

Just such an attempt, apparently successful, was reported in the summer of 1932 in the *Journal*

and around him. Several more such showers then occurred, giving him a chance to investigate their origin. The stones seemed to come from the roof, but Grottendieck could find no gap in the overlapping leaves through which they might have arrived. They seemed to fall with unnatural slowness; and when he tried to catch them, they seemed to change direction. 'Intelligent' projectiles of this kind are not uncommon in poltergeist cases. However, they are not usually hot – whereas in this case, they were warm to the touch.

Very many cases, meanwhile, involve the mysterious disappearance of objects. There is even one account of someone who actually saw an object vanish. It happened to a Mrs Kogelnik, in London, in 1922. The Kogelnik household had been experiencing poltergeist disturbances for months, apparently centred on a maidservant. On this occasion, Mrs Kogelnik was working in the loft of the house. Her husband's account records: 'As my wife saw an axe disappearing before her eyes, she quitted the room. All this happened between 10 a.m. and 12 noon, and the light was good for observation.'

Many reasonably well-authenticated 'disappearance-reappearance' events could be cited. Indeed, there is now accumulating evidence that apparently completely ordinary people may experience minor ones fairly frequently. Replies to enquiries made by researcher Julian Isaacs even suggest strongly that teleportation may take place far more often than we would ever assume to be possible. Britain's Society for Psychical Research has woken up to this possibility and has started *Project JOTT* to try to collect a representative selection of such cases. (*JOTT* stands for 'just one of those things'.)

So, what does all this mean? A favourite answer has been that space has a fourth dimension, or possibly even more: that when objects appear and disappear in our world, they are actually moving to another dimension.

This is a perfectly reasonable hypothesis. But there are competing explanations, of course. One is the theory that objects can become invisible temporarily. But while this is consistent with certain kinds of cases, it would not explain the exit of objects from sealed boxes. And hallucination, another frequently proffered explanation, cannot

The subject above, focus of poltergeist events and apparent teleportations, seems to have been bodily teleported on occasions. Once, researcher Julian Isaacs, while at the subject's house, heard a loud thump from upstairs – the usual signal that the subject had 'gone missing'. Isaacs rushed upstairs and pulled open the lower door of the airing cupboard, seen above. There was the subject, seemingly in a dazed condition. Had he hidden himself there? In view of other, better-witnessed events centred on him, Julian Isaacs has expressed the belief that the subject's teleportations are genuine.

account for cases where permanent structural changes take place – such as the knots in Zöllner's loops of string. Where matter passes through matter in ordinary three-dimensional space, others suggest it may be taken apart, transported atom by atom and put together again accurately. Or the atoms involved may somehow be made 'passive' and non-cohesive, so that they do not interact with each other as the objects pass through one another.

QUANTUM TUNNELLING

A process that seems to offer an analogy on the atomic scale to the transport of matter through matter is 'quantum tunnelling', in which an atomic particle 'impossibly' breaks through an energy barrier: the particle is whimsically viewed as tunnelling its way through a barrier that is too high to be jumped. Thus, it could be that the transport of matter through matter is a large-scale quantum tunnelling phenomenon. But two daunting questions then arise. Firstly, how can the tunnelling effect, usually operative only over atomic distances, be multiplied to give the kinds of distances encountered in paranormal reports? Secondly – and this problem is common to all attempts to apply quantum theory to large-scale *psi* events – how are the billions of atoms in normal-sized objects co-ordinated to make each one simultaneously tunnel to the same place?

What is needed is determined research to find people gifted in teleportation, to train them to produce effects under good control, to catalogue the experiences of many ordinary people who also experience similar events, and to use modern electronic technology to explore the phenomenon. If a fourth dimension really exists, this opens up the stunning possibility that there may be an infinite number of other dimensions – perhaps making up an array of parallel universes. The next time you curse an object that has unaccountably disappeared a moment after you have put it down, spare a thought for the possibility that, behind this commonplace event, there may lurk fantastic realities.

The little yellow idol, left, is a stone buddha belonging to a known PK agent who took part in researcher Julian Isaacs' experiments. It disappeared after he had spring-cleaned the shelves on which it normally stood. Several days later, there was a crash as the shell, seen here, fell to the floor and the buddha seemed to tumble out of it. This 'return' may well have been triggered by the psychic's thoughts, for he was watching a television programme on Buddhism at the time.

AGE-OLD MYTHS TELL OF GREAT BIRDS THAT WOULD PREY UPON HUMAN BEINGS. CERTAIN ORNITHOLOGISTS MAY WELL SCOFF AT THE IDEA, BUT SOME PEOPLE CLAIM THEY REALLY HAVE FELT THE CLAWS OF THESE TERRIFYING CREATURES

In Tippah County, Missouri, USA, a teacher had this tragic story to tell in 1878:

'A sad casualty occurred at my school a few days ago. The eagles have been very troublesome in the neighbourhood for some time past, carrying off pigs, lambs, and other animals. No one thought that they would attempt to prey upon

MONSTERS ON THE WING

children; but on Thursday, at recess, the little boys were out some distance from the house, playing marbles, when their sport was interrupted by a large eagle, sweeping down and picking up little Jemmie Kenney, a boy of eight years, and flying away with him. The children cried out; and when I got out of the house, the eagle was so high that I could just hear the child screaming. The alarm was given; and from screaming and shouting in the air, the eagle was induced to drop his victim. But his talons had been buried in him so deeply, and the fall was so great, that the boy was killed.'

This is not the only case of a child being carried away by an eagle. In 1838, in the mountains of Switzerland, a five-year-old girl, Marie Delex, was snatched away from her friends. But she was not carried to the bird's nest – a search party found two eaglets there, with heaps of goat and sheep bones, but no sign of her. It was not until two months later that a shepherd found her mutilated corpse, lying on a rock.

Svanhild Hantvigsen, a Norwegian, claims that, when she was three years old, in 1932, she was seized by an eagle and carried to its nest. She was rescued by a group of people who had noticed the eagle's strange behaviour, and she was lucky

Five-year-old Marie Delex, depicted left, was borne away by a large bird in 1838. Local people assumed it was an eagle.

Svanhild Hantvigsen, below left, displays the torn dress that she was wearing in 1932 when an eagle swooped down and carried her to its nest. The arrival of rescuers saved her from the fate suffered by Marie Delex nearly 100 years previously.

The dog, depicted below, belonged to Peter Swadley, a bear hunter, and attempted to fight off an eagle that attacked his master in West Virginia, USA, in 1895. The dog was carried off, while Swadley was left badly injured.

enough to escape without a scratch, though her dress was badly torn.

Such attacks are frightening, but not mysterious. Sometimes, however, there are reports of a different kind – of monstrous winged creatures that do not seem to fit the description of birds known to ornithology. Sometimes, they seem most like giant flying creatures that became extinct millions of years ago. And sometimes, they seem half-human.

The largest living bird known to science is the wandering albatross, which is seen only in the southern oceans and has the largest known wingspan – 11 feet (3.3 metres). Very close to it in size is the Andean condor, with a 10-foot (3-metre) wingspan. The Californian condor's wings span 9 feet (2.7 metres); but it is thought that today few, if any, of these birds survive.

Even a condor would look tiny, however, alongside the teratorn, a bird that became extinct about 10,000 years ago. It is thought to have been the largest bird that has ever lived on Earth, having a length of 11 feet (3.3 metres), a wingspan of 25 feet (7.5 metres), and a weight of 160 to 170 pounds (72 – 76 kilograms). Fossils have been found in Argentina, Mexico and the southern United States; and some of these are thought to be 5 to 8 million years old.

Huge birds figure widely in mythology. The Illini Indians, for instance, would paint a picture of a monstrous bird, the *piasa* or 'bird that devours men', on a rock face overlooking a river near Alton in Illinois. They used to fire bows or guns at the picture as they passed by in their canoes. The painting was seen by missionary explorers in the 17th century, before the rock face was destroyed; and, in the 1970s, a new *piasa* design, following the traditional one, was repainted at Norman's Landing.

INDIAN MYTHS

According to the Illini, the *piasa* is scaly, with a long tail, horns and red eyes. It can be seen once a year – at dawn on the first day of autumn, as it emerges from the river to pick a cave for the winter. But despite vigils by students on bluffs above the Mississippi River, no one has seen the dreaded *piasa* in recent years.

However, some Indians claim to see another huge creature, the thunderbird, even today. According to James Red Sky, an Ojibwa Indian from the Thunder Bay region of Ontario, Canada: 'We saw a thunderbird a few summers ago. A huge bird it was; a lot bigger than planes you see go by today. It didn't flap its wings. Not even once. It was white on the underside, black on top.'

A carved human face peers out from a mask of a thunderbird, above, made by Haida Indians of the American north-west coast. The Haida believe that a human spirit can take on a thunderbird's form, as symbolised by the closing of the mask's jaws.

The piasa*, a gigantic mythical bird, is shown in the rock paintings, above. Legend tells that the bird terrorised the Illini Indians until the great chief Ouatogo offered himself as bait, while 20 warriors hid nearby. The bird was killed by their arrows, while Ouatogo was unharmed. The paintings commemorate this extraordinary event.*

Modern reports of giant birds in the USA began in the late 19th century. At Dent's Run, Pennsylvania, in 1882, for instance, a certain Fred Murray saw a flock of birds that, he said, looked like giant buzzards, with wingspans of more than 16 feet (5 metres).

In February 1895, the disappearance of 10-year-old Landy Junkins in Webster County, West Virginia, was also ascribed to a giant bird. Landy had been sent by her mother to a neighbour's house, but never arrived. A search party found her tracks in the snow: they left the path and went a few feet into a field. There, a number of tracks were crowded together, as if Landy had turned round and round, perhaps trying to avoid something. No trace of her was ever found.

But an incident a few days later suggested what might have happened to her. A bear hunter, Peter Swadley, was attacked by a massive bird, which swooped down and dug its talons into his back. Swadley was saved from death by his dog, which made for the bird. The winged creature then turned its attention to the dog, ripping open its stomach with one stroke of its claws, before flying off with the unfortunate animal. A deputy sheriff and his son also saw the giant 'eagle', which captured a fawn while they were in the forest, hunting deer. They said the bird had a wingspan of 15 to 18 feet (4.5 – 5.5 metres), and a body as large as a man's.

The same monster was also thought to be responsible for the strange disappearance of a sheep from a locked shed. One morning, Hanse Hardrick found one sheep missing: a hole in the shed roof showed how it had been extracted.

In 1940, in Pennsylvania, author and local historian, Robert Lyman, was in the Black Forest near Coudersport, when he saw a brownish bird standing in the middle of a road. It stood 3 to 4 feet (about 1 metre) tall and had a short neck and short legs. When it flew off, Lyman was astonished to see that its narrow wings, when extended, reached across the road – a span of 20 to 25 feet (6 – 7.5 metres). He wondered how such a large bird could fly so easily through dense trees.

LIVESTOCK ATTACK

In 1947, farmers around Ramore in Ontario, Canada, began to experience problems with a giant black bird that was attacking their livestock. It had a hooked beak, huge talons, and yellow eyes 'the size of silver dollars'. A few months later, an outbreak of sightings of big birds also occurred in Illinois. 'There's a bird outside as big as a B-29!' gasped 12-year-old James Trares of Glendale, Illinois, as he rushed indoors to his mother. That was in January 1948, and James was the first to report seeing the grey-green monster fly overhead.

A former army colonel, Walter Siegmund, saw something similar on 4 April 1948. He estimated that it was 4,000 feet (1,200 metres) up; and from his military experience, he was quite convinced that 'it could only be a bird of some tremendous size.' More sightings followed, including some over St

Fish are the favourite prey of the magnificent bald eagle of North America, above; but it has also been blamed for attacks on small animals and children.

The Californian condor, right, hideous when at rest, is majestic in flight, gliding effortlessly for long distances. One of the world's rarest birds, it can attain 9 feet (2.7 metres) in wingspan. It attacks living animals – though, like other vultures, it feeds mainly on carrion.

The fantasy abduction of an Alpine peasant woman's child by an eagle is depicted right. The artist entitled this picture, published in 1900, The Robber of the Skies.

As shown left, in 1870, a golden eagle attacked a woman rider near the track of the Pacific Railroad. It was beaten off only after severely wounding her.

Louis, Missouri. Several witnesses at first believed they were seeing an aeroplane because of its size – until it began to flap its wings and to perform bird-like manoeuvres. Policemen and flying instructors were among the witnesses. The last sighting seems to have been on 30 April 1948. Charles Dunn could hardly believe his eyes when he saw above him a bird that was 'about the size of a Piper Cub plane', flying at about 3,000 feet (900 metres) and flapping its wings.

Little more was seen of monster birds for nearly two decades – although in 1957, a huge bird with a wingspan of 25 to 30 feet (7.5 – 9 metres) was seen flying at about 500 feet (150 metres) over Renovo, Pennsylvania. In 1966, there were reports from Utah, West Virginia, Ohio and Kentucky, only some of which could be explained as sightings of rare species.

Then, in 1975, during an outbreak of mysterious deaths of animals in Puerto Rico, large birds resembling whitish condors or vultures were seen. On 26 March, Juan Muñiz Feliciano, a workman, was attacked by 'a terrible greyish creature with lots of feathers, and a long thick neck, bigger than a goose'.

At the end of July 1977, a big bird was seen trying to steal a young pig, weighing 50 to 60 pounds (22 – 27 kilograms), near Delava, Illinois. The bird had a companion. Both resembled Californian condors and had 8-foot (2.5-metre) wingspans. But an ecologist at the University of Illinois commented that condors are rare, almost to the point of extinction, and could not lift such a weight – besides which, they feed on dead animals, not live ones.

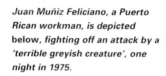

Ten-year-old Marlon Lowe, right, victim of an attack by a large bird in 1977, is seen with his mother whose cry startled the bird into dropping the boy. The incident occurred in Illinois, home of the legend of the piasa.

Juan Muñiz Feliciano, a Puerto Rican workman, is depicted below, fighting off an attack by a 'terrible greyish creature', one night in 1975.

What was it, then, that tried to abduct 10-year-old Marlon Lowe from the garden of his home at Lawndale, Illinois, on 25 July 1977? That bird, too, was accompanied by another; and the near-tragedy took place only a few days before the abortive pig-stealing, and 10 miles (16 kilometres) away. Marlon was playing hide-and-seek when, at 8.10 p.m., one of the birds snatched him off the ground. Fortunately his mother was at hand. She saw Marlon's feet dangling in the air, screamed, and the bird dropped the boy before he had been lifted very high. Mrs Lowe was only 10 feet (3 metres) away from the birds, and afterwards recalled: 'I'll always remember how that huge thing was bending its white-ringed neck. It seemed to be trying to peck at Marlon, as it was flying away.' She described the birds as 'very black', except for the white rings around their necks, which were 18 inches (45 centimetres) long. They had hooked bills, six inches (15 centimetres) long, and a wingspan of at least 8 feet (2.5 metres). She estimated they would have stood 42 feet (1.3 metres) tall if they had landed. Six people watched the birds fly off towards Kickapoo Creek, where there is heavy underbrush and thick tree cover.

But for the fact that the birds were startled by Mrs Lowe's screams, Marlon would probably have suffered the same fate as Marie Delex, Jemmie Kenney and Landy Junkins. As it was, the Lowes suffered in other ways. They were harassed by people leaving dead birds on the front porch, and by unpleasant notes and telephone calls. At school, Marlon – nicknamed 'Bird Boy' – had literally to fight off the taunts of his fellows. His red hair turned grey; and, for a year, the frightened boy refused to go out after night had fallen.

According to a report in Charles Berlitz's *World of Strange Phenomena*, a certain James Thompson also saw a large bird-like object pass over Highway 100 in the Rio Grand Valley in the early hours of 14 September 1982. He later said it had a hide-like covering rather than feathers, and was black or greyish in colour – rather like a pterodactyl, in fact. Could it perhaps be that some of these monsters are surviving winged creatures from prehistoric times?

EVIDENCE FOR T

Britain's Society for Psychical Research (SPR) was fortunate enough in its early days to be able to call upon the services of highly intelligent, well-educated sensitives with open minds – mostly women, incidentally, who according to prevailing custom, used their married names: Mrs Piper, Mrs Thompson, Mrs Leonard, Mrs Garrett, and a number of others.

Some of these women were 'physical' sensitives but most were 'mental' mediums – which may be significant, for physical mediums have become progressively rarer as methods of investigation have become more sophisticated. Cynics may leap to the conclusion that the likelihood of being caught as a fraud is so great these days that few dare to attempt to demonstrate 'physical' mediumship. But an alternative view is that the very act of setting up the elaborate apparatus necessary for investigation may inhibit the delicate, barely understood mechanism that produces the phenomenon. There also seems occasionally to be an 'experimenter effect', whereby sceptical and even merely objective experimenters may have a dampening effect on the activities of the seance room.

Although mediums, such as those listed above, produced very convincing results, members of the SPR were divided over the major question of proof of the afterlife. But they did agree that thought transference – including the communication of feelings, images, sounds, and even scents – had been proved beyond reasonable doubt. And although more than three decades were to pass before J. B. Rhine's work shifted the emphasis from psychical research (the scientific study of the paranormal) to parapsychology (treating psychic phenomena as expressions of little-understood mental activity), extra-sensory perception and psychokinesis were already being taken as alternative explanations for the mediums' purported 'proof' of survival.

It has been suggested that ESP can explain the often uncannily accurate information that a medium gives a sitter. For, through ESP, the human mind may 'pick the brains' of others, without being conscious of doing so, and mistakenly believe the information is coming from a dead relative. *PK* – psychokinesis or 'mind over matter' – meanwhile, is the mysterious force exerted by the mind over inanimate objects. This would explain the so-called 'spirit' table-turnings and rappings of the seance room in terms of a natural, if rare, function of the human mind. Some minds are even thought capable of gleaning information (through a facility known as

A soul being ferried across the river of death – the Styx – is depicted above, in the 16th-century painting by Joachim Patinir. It reveals a blend of Classical and Christian beliefs: the Styx and its ferryman, Charon, were believed by the ancient Greeks to carry the dead to their appointed place for eternity. The dead were buried with coins in their mouths so that they could pay the ferryman. Failure to pay resulted in damnation. The Christian concepts of purgatory, paradise and hell are also shown in this painting on either side of the dreaded river.

AFTERLIFE

Pluto, ruler of Hades, or the realm of the underworld believed by the Greeks to be a real geographical location that dead souls reached through caves, is seen left *on a Greek vase, together with Persephone, whom Pluto made queen. Hades was said to be a shadowy and sinister abode, but not a place of active judgement or punishment. However, at a popular level, there was a widespread suspicion that Hades was much more fearsome territory.*

GESP or general extra-sensory perception) from any written, printed or other kind of record (including presumably, microfilm), arranging and producing it as a coherent account. Such a concept, if true, destroys any chance of proving survival as a fact, for any message from a deceased person – no matter how accurate or how personal the information given – could theoretically be the result of this facility. Such stores of the sum of human knowledge are known by Theosophists as the 'Akashic records'; and certain sensitive people have long been believed to have access to its 'files'. So it could be that, in some unknown way, the 'cross-referencing' necessary for a medium to produce a convincing story of someone's life on Earth has already been done.

There are two other major arguments sometimes presented against evidence for survival as provided by mediums. The first is that a sensitive's so-called 'control' or 'spirit guide' may be no more than an example of dissociated or multiple personality. This condition seems to be formed by the splitting-off of certain mental processes from the mainstream of consciousness. If these 'other selves' come to the surface, they have been known to take over completely, the condition becoming a serious illness. (There have even been cases where over a dozen completely distinct personalities have inhabited the same body, either taking over in turns or fighting among themselves for possession.) Such manifestations have sometimes happened unexpectedly when apparently 'normal' people have been hypnotised. So perhaps a sensitive, by his or her very nature, may be more susceptible to the development of secondary personalities than the more down-to-earth or openly sceptical.

THE VERSATILE FORGER

There is also another extraordinary power of the human mind, known as *mythopoeia*, involving an ability to create myths or detailed stories that are strikingly convincing and that frequently surface during hypnotic regression as 'past lives'. The result may be 'subconscious forgery', enabling some sensitives to imitate the voices, mannerisms, handwriting and even the style of musical composition or drawing of the (sometimes famous) dead. All this may also be at second hand, drawn from the minds of others. *Mythopoeia* may also be responsible for the ability of people in trances to sing or pour out a flood of unintelligible language, known as 'speaking in tongues'. It is a theory that provides an alternative explanation for the many bizarre phenomena that have been taken as 'proof' of survival.

The deaths of the SPR's founder members, notably that of F.W.H. Myers in 1901, were followed by a new phenomenon, that of the 'cross-correspondences'. These were fragmentary messages received at different times and places through two or more sensitives, unconnected with each other. The messages, often apparently non-sensical when taken separately, made perfect sense when fitted together. The compiling of the cross-correspondences took over 30 years. The timing of their beginning, coinciding as it did with the deaths of those whose main preoccupation in life had been to understand the mysteries of death, seems to many investigators to prove beyond doubt who was behind the experiment. Indeed, it seemed

as if the founders of the SPR had arranged a meeting beyond the grave and said: 'Any normal message we send will be ascribed to thought transference. Let us devise a method of communication that will not be open to such an interpretation.'

PAINSTAKING EXPERIMENT

Certainly, no messages easily ascribable to thought transference had ever been communicated in fragments to different mediums before. And the subject matter of the messages – poetry and erudite classical allusions – was highly characteristic of the group of deceased SPR members. Although, to a certain extent, *GESP* could account for much of the material of the cross-correspondences, many researchers believe that they are the best evidence yet of survival. Even so, all they do is attempt to convince us, in as many ingenious ways as possible, of the continued existence of certain individuals. (The dead Myers is alleged to have found the effort of communication trying. To him, 'endlessly presenting my credentials' proved frustrating in the extreme.) But even assuming its authenticity, this massive, painstaking experiment tells us little of what happens when we die, except that we retain something of our earthly habits of thought and some traits of personality.

Some seances have occasionally been interrupted by 'drop-in' spirits, who are unknown to anyone

The ancient Egyptians believed the afterlife to be very similar to that on Earth but more pleasurable, as shown above left, *in a depiction of idealised farming in the world beyond.*

present, and yet provide information about themselves that is later discovered to be substantially correct. Again, this phenomenon could perhaps be explained by *GESP*. But why should a sensitive pick up information about someone in whom no one present has any interest?

Witnesses of the dying often report that dead friends and relatives are apparently seen by them just before death – coming to welcome the newly deceased to the 'other side'. Such experiences may well be hallucinations, a mechanism of nature to ease the passing from life. But this does not, of course, explain those cases where the dying have exclaimed at the 'visit' of a relative whose own death was unknown to them.

" THERE ARE MANY DIFFERENT REGIONS IN THIS AFTERWORLD... THE INDIVIDUAL AFTER DEATH TENDS TO GRAVITATE INTO REGIONS WHERE HE ASSOCIATES WITH PEOPLE WHO ARE LIKE HIMSELF. HERE HIS ENVIRONMENT IS CREATED JOINTLY OUT OF THE COLLECTIVE MEMORIES, ATTITUDES, AND DESIRES OF THOSE WHO ARE SPIRITUALLY IN TUNE WITH HIM. **"**

ALSON J. SMITH, IMMORTALITY:

THE SCIENTIFIC EVIDENCE

Model slaves, such as those above, *were believed to assume real duties in the afterlife in the service of the master in whose tomb they were put.*

An early 15th-century view of heaven as a peaceful garden is shown *right. In days when life was short (and youth and beauty, tragically brief), an eternal period of relaxation in beautiful surroundings had an obvious emotive appeal. Here, the garden of heaven is shown peopled with young, healthy and attractive souls. They relax in each other's company – reading, picking choice fruits, playing musical instruments and holding pleasant conversations. They are also all dressed in the finest and most fashionable clothes. The wall suggests the exclusivity of heaven and a sense of security after the trials of life.*

Since the 1960s, research has been carried out into the experiences of people who have clinically 'died' – often on the operating table – and who have come back to life. They nearly all report similar experiences, whether they had previously believed in survival or not. They report being conscious of leaving their bodies and passing through a dark tunnel with a light at the end. When they emerged from the tunnel, they were met by a radiant figure, often too bright to be seen clearly. This being, however, is identified differently, according to the individual's religious 'vocabulary'; for the westerner, for instance, he is usually taken to be Christ. They may also be aware of the presence of dead friends or relatives, and are filled with tremendous peace and joy. Yet they are told that their 'time' has not yet come and that they have to return. With the greatest unwillingness, they then re-enter their body. Significantly, people who have had this sort of experience are never afraid of death.

Another mass of evidence that we exist apart from our physical forms concerns out-of-the-body experiences, also referred to as *OOBEs*. Many

The medieval concept of hell was a place of brutal torment, believed to be both physical and spiritual. Although sophisticated theologians of the day argued that the real anguish of hell was the knowledge that one was eternally denied the presence of God, most ordinary people believed that hell was the proverbial fiery pit, as illustrated above.

people have had the curious experience of finding themselves hovering over their sleeping – or unconscious – bodies: this most often happens in moments of crisis, during accidents, torture, or while undergoing an operation. Some people later astonish surgeons and nurses by telling them exactly what they had done and said while carrying out the operation. A few even claim to be able to leave their bodies at will: and this, to them, is proof that they exist in a non-physical dimension and that this aspect of them will survive bodily death.

In some instances, tests have been arranged by the living so that, after their deaths, they might prove their continued existence by revealing,

❝ THERE WILL ALWAYS BE PEOPLE WHO REMAIN SEEMINGLY UNTOUCHED BY A DISPLAY OF SPIRIT POWER . . . THE SCEPTIC WHO REFUTES THE FACT OF ANOTHER EXISTENCE BEYOND DEATH AND LEAVES A DEMONSTRATION WITH NOTHING BUT SCORN FOR MEDIUMSHIP MAY BE THE PERSON HOLDING THE GREATEST FEAR OF DYING. ❞

STEPHEN O'BRIEN,

VISIONS OF ANOTHER WORLD

through mediums, the solutions to puzzles. So far, none of these has been notably successful, though the number of tests arranged may be too small to be significant. Lovers or friends have also made pacts that the one dying first should appear to the other, under certain specific circumstances. Allegedly, they have done so. But grief frequently produces hallucinations of the deceased: indeed, they seem to be part of the natural mourning process, acting as a comfort.

Supposed evidence for reincarnation, meanwhile, sets out not only to show that we survive and are reborn (perhaps many times), but also to offer clues as to why we are born at all. Hypnotic regression into 'past lives'; some children's spontaneous memories of being someone else; the 'far memory' of some adults; some *déjà vu* experiences; all these, though subject to other explanations, point to reincarnation as a distinct possibility. Many people even believe that we must submit to a string of different earthly lives until we achieve near perfection of soul: then we become 'gods' or progress on a purely spiritual plane.

Dr Ian Stevenson, of the University of Virginia in the United States, has made a detailed and scholarly investigation into evidence for reincarnation. He has amassed hundreds of cases of alleged 'past lives', reaching the conclusion that 'a rational man . . . can believe in reincarnation on the basis of evidence'. However, for the majority of people, such a belief will remain a matter of faith alone.

The Buddah, above left, *suggests calm and enlightenment. The ancient Chinese painting,* above right, *meanwhile, depicts the Buddhist 'seventh hell', where the souls of the condemned are said to be chased by ferocious dogs and devils into a deadly river.*

Since the 1960s, tape recorders have allegedly been picking up voices of the dead. This phenomenon has since become something of a cult. However, all that can be said of it so far is that, whatever the source of the voices, they do not add to our information about the afterlife.

Despite fast-growing interest in all aspects of the paranormal and psychical research, it is true to say that the majority of believers in survival of the spirit follow some sort of religion; and for them, a belief in the afterlife is entirely a matter of faith. Such faith goes back a very long way; and the oldest known burial customs show that ancient Man believed in survival.

The world's more sophisticated religions, however, differ widely in their concept of Man's ultimate goal. Hindus and Buddhists teach that we finally escape from the miseries of earthly incarnations into a mystical and blissful unity with Brahma, the Supreme Principle, or enter Nirvana, in which the self is lost in the infinite.

In the ancient world, Greeks, Romans and Hebrews believed that the spirit departed to an unsatisfactory existence in a shadowy Hades or *Sheol.* Later, Jews accepted the concept of the resurrection of the righteous to companionship with the Patriarchs; but even today, Judaism does not teach a doctrine of eternal life for everyone.

Believer or atheist, philosopher or materialist, each one of us must die. Only then will we find out the truth for certain.

THE SACRED SERPENTS OF AMERICA

THE ANCIENT LANDSCAPE OF NORTH AMERICA WAS RICH IN EARTHEN MOUNDS, SHAPED LIKE BIRDS, SNAKES AND OTHER ANIMALS. SOME WERE USED FOR BURIALS BUT THE PURPOSE OF OTHERS REMAINS VERY MUCH A MYSTERY

This serpent mound in Adams County, Ohio, is the most famous of the ancient Indian earthworks of North America. Scholars have conjectured that the motif of the serpent swallowing the egg depicts an astronomical event of religious significance.

As European settlers spread westwards through the plains and woodlands and along the river valleys of central North America, they frequently encountered evidence of powerful, populous civilisations that had died out. The most impressive relics were vast earthworks in the form of mounds, embankments and enclosures, often spread over thousands of acres.

They were sited on high ground and among them were huge artificial hills, like that at St Louis, which was once topped by temples. One such hill, discovered by early French colonists at Natchez, on the Mississippi river, was still inhabited by a local tribe of Indians. They were supposedly ruled from the summit temple by a king who was charged with magical power, preserved by his attendants who never permitted him contact with the earth.

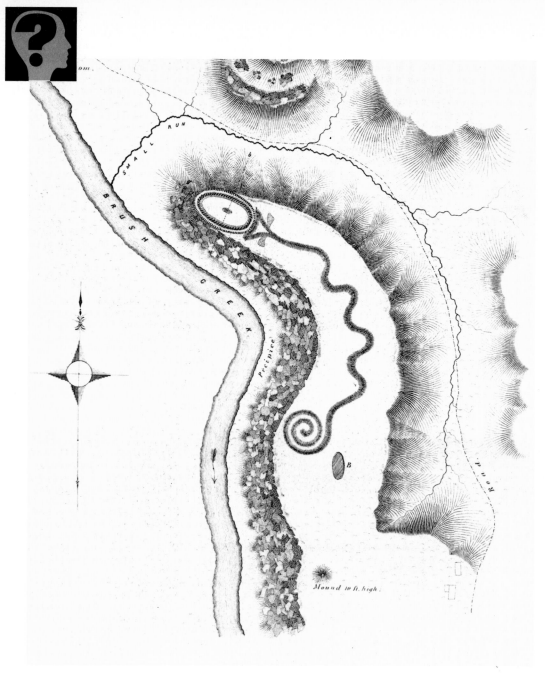

An early survey of the Ohio serpent, made in the mid-19th century by American archaeologists Edwin Hamilton Davis, below, and Ephraim George Squier, bottom, is shown left. But the serpent shape can really only be appreciated from the air.

But strangest of all the ancient monuments in North America were those encountered by settlers in the early 19th century as they began to infiltrate the Indian territories up to the Mississippi and beyond. These monuments consisted of low mounds of earth, often sculpted into the shape of giant birds, men, and real or mythical animals. Also among them were geometrical shapes and other forms of uncertain meaning. Most of these great earth sculptures were found near the rivers of Wisconsin, while others were encountered in Iowa and Illinois, and as far south as Georgia.

Curiously, their shapes cannot easily be made out from ground level, and to view entire groups is impossible except from the air. Even then, many of the mounds can be seen only at certain times of the day or year, when outlined by shadow and sunlight, since they are raised only a few feet (a metre or so) above the ground.

The first printed reference to these ancient American mounds appeared in 1838. Then, in 1848, some examples were described and illustrated in the greatest of all American archaeology books,

Squier and Davis' *Ancient Monuments of the Mississippi Valley*. But they did not become widely known until 1858, when William Pidgeon, who traded with the Indians and was an enthusiastic archaeologist and collector of Indian lore, published his *Traditions of De-coo-dah*. Pidgeon was no writer, and there is much confusion throughout his book, but it caused a sensation at the time.

MYSTERY MOUNDS

After frequent travels among the Indians of both North and South America, Pidgeon had set up a trading post by the walls of Fort Ancient, a vast hilltop earthwork above the Little Miami River in Ohio. Learned visitors would often come to inspect these 'stupendous and wonderful works'. From them, Pidgeon learned that no one had the slightest idea who had built the great American earthworks, or for what purpose. Theories abounded, the most outrageous involving the Lost Tribes of Israel and vanished races of giants, but nothing had been proved, and no one had thought seriously of consulting local Indians on the matter.

" WISCONSIN'S ABORIGINAL MONUMENTS ARE ANOMALOUS AND STRANGE, APPEARING NOT SO MUCH LIKE STRUCTURES FOR ANY SACRED OR CIVIL PURPOSE AS LIKE HIEROGLYPHIC OR SYMBOLIC CHARACTERS... IT MUST BE CONFESSED THAT PICTORIAL WRITING ON SO IMMENSE A SCALE, WITH A SOVEREIGN STATE FOR A TABLET, IS A PHENOMENON UNPARALLELED IN MONUMENTAL HISTORY. "

The Ohio serpent mound is seen from ground level, **below.** *Difficulty in appreciating the design from this position has led some researchers to speculate that the ancient North American Indians may have possessed the gift of levitation.*

A 19th-century artist's impression of the excavation of an Indian burial mound is reproduced **bottom.** *This violation of their sacred sites was one of the factors that led to Indian antagonism towards the white man.*

Pidgeon determined to find out the truth for himself. He built a sailing boat, and in 1840 began a series of great inland voyages through the American continent, travelling up into Wisconsin and the Indian territories of the Winnebago and Sioux, trading and antiquity-hunting as he went on his journey.

Pidgeon sailed into an untouched American landscape that no traveller has seen since, because with European settlement, a great proportion of the ancient monuments and earthworks was destroyed. Many groups of effigy mounds were obliterated, for example, by the building of Madison, Milwaukee (both in Wisconsin) and other cities. Some were also levelled by colonists who wanted no reminder of the native people they had conquered and supplanted.

When Pidgeon saw them, the ancient works were in the care of their Indian guardians and still intact. He saw the long hilltop processions of earthen bears, panthers, lizards, turtles and giant birds; he traced out a series of mounds that formed a great serpent across the landscape; and he found and followed for great distances alignments of earthworks with other effigies at their intersections. He was also fortunate to meet someone who could tell him what they meant.

While surveying ancient earthworks near Prairie la Crosse on the upper Mississippi, Pidgeon attracted the attention of a venerable Indian prophet, De-coo-dah, who introduced himself as a member of the Elk nation, descendants of the original mound-builders. Pleased at Pidgeon's respectful interest in his people's monuments – 'A good white man,' he is said to have cried out in surprise – and disarmed by Pidgeon's gesture of throwing his archaeologist's spade into the river with a vow never more to violate the Indians' sacred places, De-coo-dah offered to inform him about the ancient works. He then proceeded to impart certain traditions to his pupil, while evidently holding back many more, for Pidgeon's account of what he learned is fragmentary and far from clear. But it is neatly summed up in the following words that Pidgeon attributed to De-coo-dah:

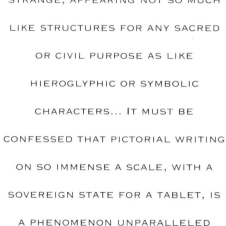

'When this country was inhabited by my early ancestors, game was abundant and easily taken. Consequently they, having leisure in times of peace, used to write their history in figures on the earth. . . The face of the earth is the red man's book, and those mounds and embankments are some of his letters.'

The idea that the effigy mounds and other great earthworks across the face of North America are ancient hieroglyphic records is one to excite the decoders of forgotten languages. It also finds support in the scholarly publication *Archaeology in the United States* by S. F. Haven, who writes:

'Wisconsin's aboriginal monuments are anomalous and strange, appearing not so much like structures for any sacred or civil purpose as like hieroglyphic or symbolic characters. If, instead of being clustered on the surface of the earth, they had been drawn on rocks and stones, efforts would be made to read them as records. They would derive a superior interest from the supposition that they are, as has been suggested, the "totems" of tribes, perhaps memorials of amity or alliance, written upon the ground where adverse nations were accustomed to meet in peace. It must be confessed that pictorial writing on so immense a scale, with a sovereign state for a tablet, is a phenomenon unparalleled in monumental history.'

AERIAL MESSAGE

No one has yet decoded the message of the American mounds, but it is a strange record that can only be read – whether by gods or people – it would seem, from the air. Among the Wisconsin effigies are great human-headed flying creatures, like the thunderbirds of Indian legend or the Garuda bird, which is the agent of magical flight in Hindu mythology. And, along with these magnificent birds, there are the serpents.

The most famous of all America's serpent mounds is the effigy, 1,330 feet (396 metres) in length, measured along its curves, to be found in Adams County, Ohio. An observation tower now gives visitors an overall view of this great earthen reptile; but when Squier and Davis made their fine survey of it and William Pidgeon inspected it on the

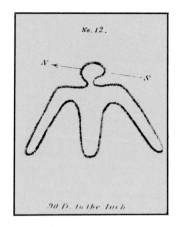

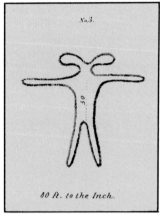

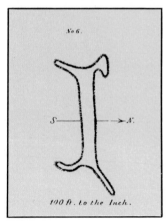

The three drawings, above, come from surveys of ancient Indian animal earthworks in Wisconsin, published by archaeologists E. G. Squier and E. H. Davis in their book Ancient Monuments of the Mississippi Valley *in 1848. The mounds range in height from 18 inches (50 centimetres) to 6 feet (2 metres). Few of the mounds remain today, most having been destroyed by European settlers.*

Mound-builders are shown , left, gathering crops, in the Ohio River Valley. It has been suggested that the mounds may have provided an astronomical calendar for Indian farmers, while some were used for burying the dead.

instructions of De-coo-dah, they could only possibly have appreciated it by walking from the tightly curled tail and along its seven loops to the jaws, which are opened wide in the apparent act of swallowing an egg.

Pidgeon, who had seen other serpent mounds further west, was told by De-coo-dah that: 'When the worshippers of reptiles were reduced by the fortunes of war, and compelled to recognize the sun, moon, and heavenly bodies as the only objects worthy of adoration, they secretly entombed their gods in the earthwork symbols which represented the heavenly bodies.'

He therefore interpreted the Ohio effigy of serpent and egg as an astronomical symbol. Scholars today are inclined to agree with him. In 1975, T. M. Cowan of Kansas University contributed a paper, *Effigy Mounds and Stellar Representation*, to A. F. Aveni's book, *Archaeoastronomy in Pre-Columbian America*, in which he suggested that effigy mounds and other ancient earthworks were based on the pattern of stars and constellations. A traditional image of lunar eclipses in Asia is indeed the moon being swallowed by a serpent, and this may be part of the meaning of the Ohio mound, too. But the seven loops of its body and the tightly winding tail are seen by Cowan as representing the seven stars in Ursa Minor and their annual rotation round the pole star. The connection, as he says, is certainly 'teasingly close'.

The serpent and other such earthworks may well have been used for astronomical observation and for recording astrological lore, but there is something else about their sites that cannot so readily be explained. At first sight, there seems to be no obvious reason why the Ohio serpent mound

should have been placed where it is. Other neighbouring hilltops are higher, with grander views, or with greater areas of flat surface, or would have been more accessible for those carrying up the earth. Yet there is a certain perceptible quality to the place that the serpent seems to have been designed to express. For the serpent is the ancient symbol of a spirit or vital current that identifies the Earth as a living creature, whose magnetic centres are associated all over the world with strange atmospheres, hauntings and apparitions, as well as the sacred sites of early Man.

Local people and visitors alike have told strange stories connected with the great serpent mound. One such report was written by a sociology professor, Robert W. Harner, for the June 1977 issue of *Fate* magazine. As he stood alone on the serpent's head one clear, sunny day in autumn, something happened that threw Harner into abject terror. Something like an evil, elemental force was present; and as Harner felt it move towards him, he saw its shape in the pattern of swirling leaves cast up around it. As the leaves surrounded him, dancing ever closer, he felt himself begin to faint with horror – and then, suddenly, the spell was broken. The energy vortex died down, the leaves became still, and Professor Harner returned to his car, promising himself that he would never venture on to the mound again. 'Perhaps', he concluded, 'they built their mound on that particular hill because very special things happen there.'

> *The graceful curves throughout the whole length of this singular effigy give it a strange, lifelike appearance; as if a huge serpent, slowly uncoiling itself and creeping silently along the crest of the hill, was about to seize the oval within its extended jaws... The effect is heightened when the full moon lights up the scene, and the stillness is broken only by the "whoo-whoo, hoo-hoo" of the unseen bird of night...*
>
> **Frederic W. Putnam,**
> **The Serpent Mound of Ohio**

The mounds, above, part of the Effigy Mounds National Monument, near Marquette, Iowa, were built between 500 BC and AD 1400. Processions of animal figures were common in pre-Columbian North America and may have been tributes to the spirits of forest creatures.

The Campbell mound near Columbus, Ohio, right, is one of many such earthworks in the northern United States.

William Pidgeon, below, was an early researcher who saw and recorded the shapes of many of the North American animal earthworks before they were demolished by early European settlers.

GHOSTS WITHOUT SOULS

IF GHOSTS ARE SPIRITS OF THE DEAD, AS MANY BELIEVE, HOW CAN WE ACCOUNT FOR WHAT SEEM TO BE 'SOULLESS' APPARITIONS – THOSE OF ANIMALS AND INANIMATE OBJECTS?

During the 1930s, a large red London bus on a number 7 route was known to harass motorists in the North Kensington area late at night. The junction of St Mark's Road and Cambridge Gardens had long been considered a dangerous corner: in fact, the bend was 'blind' from both roads and had caused numerous accidents.

The decision of the local authority to straighten out the bend was partially influenced by the testimony of late-night motorists, who said that they had crashed while swerving to avoid a double-decker that was hurtling down St Mark's Road in the small hours, long after regular buses had ceased service.

A typical report to the Kensington police read: 'I was turning the corner and saw a bus tearing towards me. The lights of the top and bottom decks were full on, as were the headlights, but I could see no sign of crew or passengers. I yanked my steering wheel hard over, and mounted the pavement, scraping the roadside wall. The bus just vanished.'

After one fatal accident, during which a driver had swerved and hit the wall, an eyewitness told the coroner's inquest that he, too, had seen the mystery bus hurtling towards the car seconds before the driver spun off the road. When the coroner expressed what was perhaps natural cynicism,

The story of the phantom ship, right, was reported by the American minister and author Dr Cotton Mather in his book Wonders of the Invisible World. *The ship set sail from America but never reached its destination in England and nothing was ever heard of it again. Some months later, however, spectators at the port from which it had sailed witnessed what seemed to be the very same ship, appearing in a cloud. It was seen to keel over and then simply disappeared.*

The junction of St Mark's Road and Cambridge Gardens in Kensington, London, became renowned in the 1930s for the mysterious double-decker bus, like the one shown below, *which travelled at great speed in that area in the middle of the night – when there was no public transport.*

dozens of local residents wrote to his office and also to the local newspapers, offering to testify that they had seen the 'ghost bus' as well. Among the most impressive of these witnesses was a local transport official who claimed that he had seen the vehicle draw up to the bus depot in the early hours of the morning, stand with engine purring for a moment, and then disappear.

The mystery was never solved; but it is perhaps significant that the 'ghost' bus was not seen after the danger of the sharp corner was removed. It was even suggested that the vision had been 'projected' on to the spot to dramatise the inherent danger of the intersection. But if so, by whom? And if, as was also suggested, this all took place in the minds of the motorists themselves – a sort of natural projection of their fears at the corner – how did they manage to superimpose it on the vision of the passers-by, not to mention the bus depot official who saw it all from an entirely different angle?

The phantom bus of Kensington epitomises a problem that, for centuries, has faced those who believe that ghosts are revenant spirits. If a ghost is

In his book **Supernature, Lyall Watson**, *below, suggests that the fact that ghosts appear as people remember them indicates that apparitions are part of a mental process rather than a supernatural one. Certainly, most ghosts do appear fully clothed or are dressed in a shroudlike garment, as was the ghost that terrorised the residents of Hammersmith, London, in the early 1800s,* **bottom.**

'Ghostly' lore is strewn with stories of all sorts of inanimate objects suddenly becoming apparent – everything from the 'phantom' accordion accredited to Daniel Dunglas Home, the 19th-century Spiritualist, to Macbeth's dagger. In the latter case, William Shakespeare, writing in an age steeped in superstition, seems to have been as aware of the anomaly of 'spirit objects' as he was of almost every other field of human experience: '. . . art thou, O fateful dagger, sensible to feeling as to sight, or art thou but a dagger of the mind, a false creation, proceeding from the heat oppressed brain?'

HOVERING SHAPE

One of the most convincing stories of totally 'soulless' apparitions is recorded in the day book of the Tower of London – a place that, according to popular belief, is saturated with ghosts. The man who made the entry was named Edmund Lenthal Swifte. In 1814, he was appointed Keeper of the Crown Jewels, and continued in the office until 1842 – a total of 28 years. The account of what Swifte saw on a Sunday evening in October 1817 is best left to him:

'I was at supper with my wife, our little boy, and my wife's sister in the sitting room of the Jewel House, which is said to have been the "doleful prison" of Anne Boleyn and of the ten bishops whom Oliver Cromwell piously accommodated there. The doors were all closed, heavy and dark curtains were let down over the windows, and the only light in the room was that of two candles on the table. I sat at the foot of the table, my son on my right, my wife fronting the chimney piece, and her sister on the opposite side. I had offered a glass of wine and water to my wife when, on putting it to her lips, she paused, and exclaimed, "Good God! what is that?"

'I looked up, and saw a cylindrical figure, like a glass tube, something about the thickness of my arm, and hovering between the ceiling and table; its contents appeared to be a dense fluid, white and pale azure . . . incessantly rolling and mingling within the cylinder. This lasted about two minutes, when it began to move before my sister-in-law, following the oblong shape of the table, before my son and myself. Passing behind my wife, it paused for a moment over her right shoulder (observe, there was no mirror opposite in which she could then behold it.) Instantly, she crouched down, and with both hands covering her shoulder, shrieked out: "Oh Christ! It has seized me!"

'Even now as I write, I feel the horror of that moment. I caught up my chair, striking at the appearance with a blow that hit the wainscot behind her. It then crossed the upper end of the table and disappeared in the recess of the opposite window.'

There was no recurrence of this curious manifestation; but some years later, it did help Swifte's judgement of a soldier in the Tower who actually died from fright, brought on by what he had seen outside Swifte's front door.

The soldier had been on guard outside the Jewel House when, at around midnight, he had heard a guttural snarl behind him and turned to see a huge black bear, reared up on its hind legs, fangs bared, eyes red with rage, and talons groping towards him.

the 'soul' of a dead person returned to earth, how do we account for phantom buses – and, of course, their lineal ancestors, phantom coaches, which feature so heavily in folklore?

Come to that, why do returning spirits not appear in the nude – for, with very few reliably recorded exceptions, none do?

❚❚ ALL THE GHOSTS OF WHICH I HAVE EVER HEARD WORE CLOTHES. WHILE I AM PREPARED IN PRINCIPLE TO CONCEDE THE POSSIBILITY OF AN ASTRAL BODY, I CANNOT BRING MYSELF TO BELIEVE IN ASTRAL SHOES AND SHIRTS AND HATS. **❚❚**

LYALL WATSON, SUPERNATURE

ACTIVE IMAGINATION

The eminent Swiss psychologist Carl Jung (1875-1961) was deeply interested in many aspects of the paranormal, and keenly recorded his own experiences in this area, as well as following with active enthusiasm discoveries being made by parapsychologists during his lifetime.

One of the most intriguing events to occur to him personally took place during a trip to Ravenna, Italy, with a friend. Here, he was particularly struck by a mosaic that depicted Christ extending his hand to Peter as the disciple appeared to be drowning at sea. Both Jung and his companion apparently looked closely at the mosaic for many minutes and talked in some detail about it. Deeply struck by its imagery and design, Jung had wanted to buy a reproduction of the work but had no luck in finding one.

On his return home, Jung learned that another friend was about to visit Ravenna and so asked whether a photograph could be taken of the favourite mosaic. Strangely, however, it was discovered that no such mosaic had ever existed at Ravenna. The mosaic must therefore have been, Jung was bound to concede, a shared apparition – and one of the most extraordinary experiences of his life.

This bizarre occurrence seems in many ways to relate to what Jung had termed 'active imagination' – a technique that he is known to have taught to some of his patients. In 1935, during a series of lectures given at London's Tavistock Clinic, he described how a young artist he knew was able to project himself into an alpine landscape that was depicted on a poster, even to the extent of walking over the hill that it featured and viewing a fantasy chapel that he was convinced lay beyond.

The soldier rammed his bayonet into the belly of the animal, but the weapon passed clean through and the apparition disappeared.

A patrol found the soldier a few moments later, as he lay senseless. The bayonet, with a heavy 'Tower issue' musket attached, was embedded in the solid wood of the door. The soldier was taken, still insensible, to the guardroom, where a doctor pronounced that he was neither drunk nor asleep. The following morning, Swifte interviewed him; over and over, the soldier repeated his bizarre tale until, three days later, he died.

For about 300 years, until the middle of the 17th century, the Tower of London housed a royal menagerie, and among the animals recorded as having been kept there were a number of bears. Although no account of an autopsy on the soldier survives, the fact that he died three days after his experience could indicate that he was seriously ill without knowing it, and that the apparition was an

Phantom horses, as depicted below, complete with riders, are a common form of haunting and are usually associated with a particular place. According to one theory, they are a kind of recording of a highly emotional or dramatic event which is 'replayed' in certain circumstances.

hallucination caused by his condition. On the other hand, animal ghosts make more sense as 'revenant spirits' than their human counterparts: they at least 'appear' exactly as in life. The fact that Man has lost most of his 'primitive' instincts, while animals retain theirs, may also have an as-yet unexplained bearing on such instances.

PHANTOM BEASTS

Stories of phantom dogs are common to the United States, Europe, and many parts of Africa. Ghostly horses, cattle, and even sheep have their part in folklore, too; and although, like all folk tales, accounts of their appearances have undoubtedly become distorted in the telling over centuries, some are eerily convincing. In 1908, the British Society for Psychical Research (SPR) made exhaustive enquiries into the appearance of what appeared to be a phantom pig in the village of Hoe Benham, near Newbury, Berkshire.

On 2 November 1907, two young men named Oswald Pittman and Reginald Waud were painting in the garden of their house, Laburnum Villa. At around 10 a.m., Pittman got up to speak to the milkman and saw his friend, Clarissa Miles, coming up the lane: she was due to join the men for a painting session. Accompanying her, like a pet dog, was a large white pig with an unusually long snout. When Pittman told Waud about it, Waud asked him to tell Clarissa to keep the animal outside and close the garden gate securely, as Waud was a keen gardener and did not want the pig wandering among his plants.

However, when Clarissa arrived, she was alone, and denied all knowledge of the animal. If it had been following her, she pointed out, she would surely have heard its steps. Nevertheless, she and Pittman went back up the lane and asked several children if they had seen a pig that day, but none of them had.

The following morning, the milkman, pressed by a bewildered Pittman, signed a statement to the effect that he had not seen the pig, and pointed out

that, in any case, the area was under a swine fever curfew, and any stray animal would be destroyed.

Pittman and Waud went to London for few months and, while there, reported the odd incident to a member of the SPR. By the time they returned to Hoe Benham in February, the story of Pittman's apparition had become widespread. Shedding their natural reserve, the villagers inundated them with stories of previous 'phantoms'. Local theory had it that they all stemmed from the suicide of a certain farmer, Tommy King, whose estate, which was demolished in 1892, had bordered the lane. Investigation of the parish records showed there had in fact been two Tommy Kings, one dying in 1741 and the other in 1753, but there was no indication of which one had committed suicide. An old man named John Barrett testified that, when he was a boy in 1850, he had been returning with seven or eight others in a hay cart along the lane when 'a white thing' appeared in the air. All the men had seen it, and the horses obviously had, too, for they suddenly went wild.

'This thing kept a-bobbin' and a-bobbin' and the horses kept a-snortin' and a-snortin' until the wagon reached the neighbourhood of King's Farm, when the shape vanished.' In 1873, at the same spot, Barrett had also seen a creature 'like a sheep' pawing the ground in the lane. He tried to take a blow at it with his stick, but it disappeared before the stick landed.

Another man, Albert Thorne, said that, in the autumn of 1904, he had heard 'a noise like a whizzin'' of leaves, and saw summat like a calf knuckled down' about 2½ feet (75 centimetres) high and 5 feet (1.5 metres) long, with glowing eyes. As he watched, it faded away. Yet another witness, unnamed, said that, in bright moonlight during January 1905, he had seen what he took to be the curate's dog in the lane. It was large and black. Assuming that it had strayed, he went to grab it, whereupon it appeared to turn into a donkey, rising up on its hind legs threateningly before vanishing.

UNEARTHLY SCREAM

Pittman, Waud, and Clarissa Miles reported one more unnerving experience. Once, while walking in the lane, Clarissa was suddenly overcome by an irrational fear, and told her companions that she felt the presence of an evil being, charged with malice towards them. She also felt that she was suffocating. As they reached the spot where Pittman had seen the pig, all three heard an 'unearthly scream', although no one else was about. Waud, who had been sceptical from the start, was finally convinced by this strange and terrible cry that the ghostly animal existed.

The sensitivity of animals, particularly cats and dogs, to paranormal phenomena is almost a truism. Dr Robert Morris, a parapsychologist who has used animals as 'controls' in his experiments, tells of a particular investigation of a haunted house, in one room of which a tragedy had occurred. He used a dog, cat, rat, and rattlesnake.

'The dog, upon being taken about two or three feet [less than a metre] into the room, immediately snarled at its owner and backed out of the door. No amount of cajoling could prevent the dog from

Legend has it that a 17th-century phantom coach, constructed of the bones of the four husbands of the wicked Lady Howard – all of whom she is said to have murdered – travels the road that runs across the moor from Tavistock to near Okehampton Castle, shown below. The sheeted spectre of Lady Howard rides inside the coach and a skeleton-hound runs before it. According to the legend, each night the hound must pick a blade of grass from Okehampton Park to take back to Lady Howard's family home at Tavistock – a penance to be endured until every blade of grass has finally been picked.

struggling to get out and it refused to re-enter. The cat was brought into the room, carried in its owner's arms. When the cat got a similar distance into the room, it immediately leaped upon the owner's shoulders, dug in, then leaped to the ground, orienting itself towards a chair. It spent several minutes hissing and spitting and staring at the unoccupied chair in a corner of the room until it was finally removed,' Morris reports.

The rattlesnake then immediately assumed an attack posture, focusing on the same chair that had been of interest to the cat. After a couple of minutes, it slowly moved its head toward a window, moved back and then receded into its alert posture about five minutes later.

The rat was the only creature not to react at all on that occasion, but all four animals were tested in a separate room some time later, and there behaved perfectly normally.

In the misty world of apparitions, no one – not even the most dedicated psychical researcher – knows quite what is the motivation behind them. What we *do* know is that they are not confined to human beings: the ghosts of both animals and inanimate objects – even the 'soul' of a London bus – have been lucidly recorded by many perplexed witnesses over the years.

UFO

PHOTO FILE

On the evening of 5 March 1979, Antonio Gonzales Llopis, aged 26, was taking photographs of the island of Gran Canaria, in the Canary Islands, when suddenly he noticed a strange, swirling light in the sky over the sea. A moment later, a huge, dark object hurtled straight up into the sky, surmounting a ball of fire, as shown in photographs *1, 2* and *3*. Llopis pointed his camera at the object, checked its setting, and continued to take pictures throughout the sighting, which he estimated as lasting about three minutes – as later verified by several other witnesses.

The brilliant light surrounding the dark object effectively obscured any detail, but it seemed to accelerate rapidly, somehow shooting through the pattern of lights in the sky. After the object had disappeared, a bright trail and a golden cloud illuminated the sky for half-an-hour, as shown in pictures *4* and *5*. Thousands of people on Gran Canaria reported the incident and many of them took photographs. Some of these even found their way into the files of the Spanish government, increasingly sympathetic towards serious UFO investigation.

The bright lights, *right,* were seen near the major airport of Barajas, 6 miles (10 kilometres) from Madrid, Spain, one night in December 1979. An estimated 10 lights appeared suddenly over Madrid, executed a brief aerial ballet, and then sped off in the direction of Barajas, where this photograph was taken. UFOs seem to be attracted to airports and aircraft, naval bases and ships, nuclear power stations and military establishments of all kinds. Indeed, believers in the extra-terrestrial hypothesis claim that UFOs harbour aliens showing an interest in the hardware of our technology in order to compare our progress with theirs. More down-to-earth observers have suggested that UFOs are, in fact, secret weapons accidentally seen while undergoing trials in the vicinity of military bases.

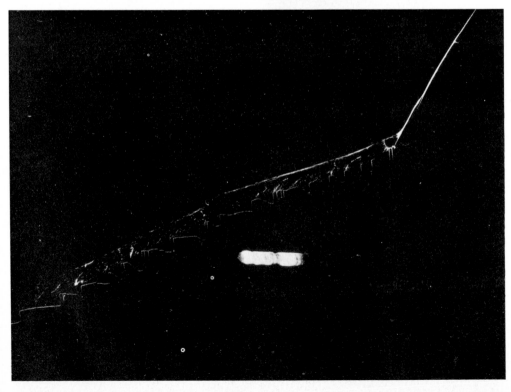

The photograph of a UFO, *left,* was taken near Lakeville, Connecticut, USA, on the night of 23 January 1967, by a 17-year-old pupil from a local boys' boarding school. This was only one of the many sightings of 'bright lights, moving erratically', reported over a four-month period, mainly by boys from the school, although one teacher, and a 12-year-old boy who lived nearby, added their testimony. Condon Report officers Ayer and Wadsworth investigated and went on to study the boy's picture. He described the UFO as 'a bright point of light that blinked or pulsated regularly'. He said it 'pulsated twice', and then disappeared behind Indian Mountain. The investigators left the case open. But could the UFOs have been secret weapons undergoing night trials? Or were they 'nuts and bolts' alien spacecraft?

SCIENCE AND THE

DREAM-MAKERS

PSYCHOLOGISTS STUDYING DREAMS IN THE EXPERIMENTAL LABORATORY HAVE FOUND NOTABLE EXAMPLES OF TELEPATHY AND PRECOGNITION. BUT IS IT POSSIBLE TO PRODUCE DREAM ESP TO ORDER?

The painting of Luis Angel Firpo knocking Jack Dempsey out of the ring, above, was transmitted telepathically to a sleeper, triggering a dream about boxing.

Dr Montague Ullman is seen below, monitoring the brain waves of a sleeper in his dream laboratory.

The artist's dream puzzled him. It had begun with images of a number of posts. Then he had the impression of a prize fight. 'I had to go to Madison Square Gardens to pick up tickets to a boxing fight,' he recalled, 'and there were a lot of tough punks around – people connected with the fight around the place.' Why should he have such a dream? He had no interest in boxing, and had never even been to a fight.

Surprisingly, however, there was a reason for the dream. The artist was a guinea pig in the dream laboratory at the Maimonides Medical Center, at the State University of New York. He had allowed himself to be wired up to a machine that monitors brain activity during sleep. As soon as it registered a reading showing that he had entered a stage of

REM (rapid eye movement) sleep and that he was therefore dreaming, the researchers woke him up and asked him to describe his dream.

In another part of the Maimonides laboratory, meanwhile, a woman was looking at a picture that had been chosen at random from a pool of 12, and was concentrating on trying to communicate it to the sleeping artist. The target picture on this occasion was a painting that showed Jack Dempsey being knocked out of the ring at Madison Square Gardens. When independent judges were shown a verbal description of the sleeper's dream impressions, together with the 12 pictures in the target pool, they had no difficulty in matching it with the painting of Dempsey's fight. The dream was a spectacular telepathic hit.

TRANSMITTED PICTURES

Such experiments at the Maimonides dream laboratory were conducted for over 15 years from the early 1960s, and were designed specifically to look for telepathy between dreaming subjects and agents who set out to 'transmit' pictures to them. They found one particularly good subject, Dr William Erwin, and an equally good agent, Sol Feldstein, who was a doctoral student; and the research team were able to conduct telepathy-in-dream experiments with them that yielded results far better than chance could be expected to produce. (The odds were in fact 1,000 to 1 against chance being responsible.)

But, every so often, the researchers came upon cases where, instead of receiving someone else's thoughts, a dreamer would apparently have a glimpse of the future. This came as no surprise to Dr Montague Ullman, the New York psychiatrist who led the Maimonides team. He had himself experienced a premonition in one of his dreams.

One night, Ullman dreamed that he met fellow dream researcher, Dr Krippner, and was surprised to see that he had a massive, bleeding lesion on his face. The dream startled him so much that he awoke 'with a sinking sense of terror'. Later that day, Ullman visited a part of New York City with which he was unfamiliar. There, he was surprised to see a man whose walk – 'a kind of hunched shuffle' – reminded him of Krippner.

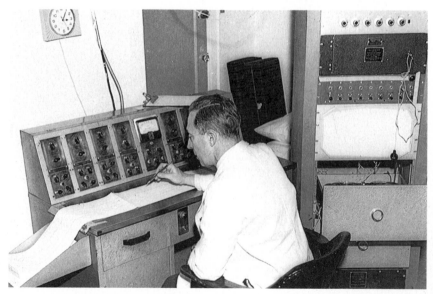

In a major experiment in mass telepathy, a rock band, the Grateful Dead, enlisted their audiences as 'senders'. The 'receiver' was Malcolm Bessent, above, who slept at the dream laboratory. One night, the audience 'sent' the picture of the seven spinal chakras, right. In yoga, these are claimed to be bodily energy centres. Bessent's dream description referred to using natural energy; an 'energy box' to catch sunlight; someone levitating; and a spinal column. Note the figure's halo, which could well have stimulated the idea of sunlight.

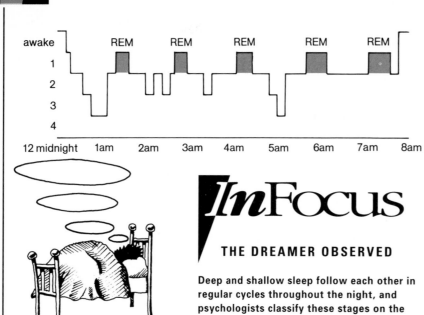

REM   REM   REM   REM   REM

*In*Focus

THE DREAMER OBSERVED

Deep and shallow sleep follow each other in regular cycles throughout the night, and psychologists classify these stages on the basis of the brain's electrical wave patterns. On falling asleep, a person enters stage *1*, the shallowest level, when the brain wave pattern is similar to that of wakefulness. As sleep deepens into stages *2, 3* and *4,* the brain waves become slower, though their voltage increases. Some muscles, such as those of the limbs and the jaw, relax while others, such as those that push food along the digestive tract, continue normally. After about one-and-a-half hours, brain waves suddenly return to the stage *1* pattern, while the body becomes yet more relaxed and completely immobile – except for the eyes, which begin quick, jerky movements behind the closed eyelids. It is difficult to rouse the sleeper from this REM (rapid eye movement) sleep; but when this is done, the sleeper nearly always has a dream to report, which may be vivid and full of action. Typically, REM sleep lasts about 20 minutes; the whole cycle is then repeated. Later cycles are shallower than earlier ones. Volunteers contributing to dream experiments have been deprived of their dreams, however, by being woken when REM begins. Even after months of this, there is usually little effect on waking life, but the volunteers compensate by spending much more of the night dreaming as soon as this is again permitted by the experimenters.

Convinced that it was his colleague, but puzzled that he should also be in that part of the city, Ullman crossed the road to speak to him. As he approached, however, he realised it was not Krippner – but the man had 'the same, horrible, ulcerating lesion around his mouth' that he had seen in his dream the night before.

This was a spontaneous dream experience, but Ullman found the same shift in time occurring in the laboratory, too. In early 1971, a rock band, the Grateful Dead, took an interest in the Maimonides telepathy research and visited the dream laboratory. The research team decided to enlist the musicians' help in an experiment designed to discover whether telepathic communication is stronger if more than one agent is involved. The band was giving six concerts in New York, 45 miles (70 kilometres) from the research unit, and agreed to ask each night's 2,000-strong audience to act as telepathic 'agents'.

On the evening of each concert, an English psychic, Malcolm Bessent, went to sleep at the Maimonides laboratory, under the watchful eye of the research team. At each concert, a picture of Bessent would then be projected briefly on to a screen. Then another picture, selected at random, was shown for 15 minutes, while the Grateful Dead played their music, and the audience tried to transmit the picture.

When Bessent's dreams were analysed, it was found that he had succeeded in scoring four 'hits' out of six. And the story does not end there: indeed, it has an unexpected twist. The researchers wondered if it would be possible for someone to 'intercept' the telepathic communication and describe the pictures. They therefore asked another of their laboratory subjects, Felicia Parise, to try to tune into the concert audience's thoughts, but the audience was not told she was doing so. Taken at face value, her results were disappointing, because there was only one 'hit'. But the team noticed a remarkable displacement effect.

On three nights, Felicia Parise's impressions bore no resemblance at all to the picture that was being shown to the audience at that time: instead, they were impressive descriptions of images that either had been shown to the audience on earlier nights or were still to be randomly chosen and projected. She seems somehow to have seen into both the past and the future.

Psychical researchers have long been aware that dreams provide a wealth of paranormal information. There were apparently many dream warnings of the Aberfan disaster of 1966, when 144 people died in a tiny Welsh village as the result of a coal tip subsiding. When Dr John Barker analysed 31 supposed premonitions of the tragedy, he found that 28 had occurred in dreams.

Until the 1950s, the problem for investigators of dream premonitions was that most people have no recollection of their dreams, or rapidly forget them. But then it was found that, by waking a person after a period of 'rapid eye movement' sleep, an account of a dream was almost always forthcoming. The technique also enabled researchers to time 'transmission' of mental images to a sleeper to coincide with a dreaming phase.

Dreams vary in nature, and studies of one kind in particular – lucid dreams – are currently exciting a great deal of interest. The name might suggest merely a particularly vivid dream, but the term is in fact used to describe experiences in which the sleeper knows he is dreaming and can look at his dream objectively, even critically, and perhaps even control its content.

Lucid dreams have been the subject of study and discussion for many years. As early as 1896, a

Dutch investigator, Dr van Eeden, began recording his dreams; and, after three years, started to distinguish lucid dreams from the others, recording 352 in all. The following had a particular impact:

'In May 1903, I dreamed that I was in a little provincial Dutch town and at once encountered my brother-in-law, who had died some time before. I was absolutely sure that it was he, and I knew that he was dead... He told me that a financial catastrophe was impending for me. Somebody was going to rob me of a sum of 10,000 guilders. I said that I understood him, though after waking up I was utterly puzzled by it and could make nothing of it... I wish to point out that this was the only prediction I ever received in a lucid dream in such an impressive way. It came only too true – with this difference, that the sum I lost was 20 times greater. At

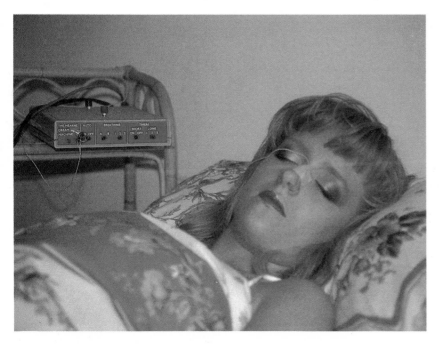

Dr Keith Hearne's dream machine, above, uses a nose-clip to monitor breathing. When the rate and depth of breathing show a lucid dream is possible, weak electrical shocks indicating the fact are delivered to the subject, who can then become the director of his or her own 'dream movie'.

the time of the dream, there seemed not to be the slightest probability of such a catastrophe. I was not even in possession of the money I lost afterwards. Yet it was just the time when the first events took place – the railway strikes of 1903 – that led up to my financial ruin.'

Dr Keith Hearne, author of *Visions of the Future* and *The Dream Machine*, is pioneering a new approach to dream research through lucid dreaming, and coupling his study with experiments in the nature of ESP. When a sleeping person is dreaming, not only does he experience rapid eye movements, but his muscles become virtually paralysed. So, even though the dreamer is having a lucid dream and therefore knows he is dreaming, he cannot signal this fact to the researcher by, for example, switching a button, because his fingers will not move. Hearne therefore decided to see if communication could take place between sleeper and researcher using eye movements as signals.

By pre-arrangement with subjects, it was agreed that eight left-right movements of the eyes would indicate that a lucid dream was happening at that moment. The first such communication was recorded in April 1975 at the dream laboratory at Hull University, where Hearne was working at the time.

AT THE MOMENT THAT THE PERIOD OF DREAM LUCIDITY STARTS, A TRANSFORMATION TAKES PLACE: IT IS AS IF CONSCIOUSNESS HAS BEEN SUDDENLY SWITCHED ON... THE ARTIFICIALITY OF THE DREAM SURROUNDINGS IS REALIZED, BUT THE REALNESS IS SO STRIKING THAT THE WHOLE EXPERIENCE CAN BE ONE OF SHEER WONDERMENT.

DR KEITH HEARNE

Since then, such communication has become more sophisticated. Using pre-arranged codes, subjects can signal that they are flying, or have just landed, or are performing some other deliberate act.

Early work proved laborious, however: after spending 45 nights in the laboratory, Hearne had recorded only eight lucid dreams. So he went on to devise a 'dream machine' that provides 'conscious controllable dreams'. It detects that a sleeper has begun to dream and then signals to the sleeper by applying a small voltage to his wrist. The sleeping mind thereby knows that it is dreaming, and the dream becomes a lucid one.

DREAM TELEPATHY

Hearne also discovered that a lucid dreamer can signal to the waking world by altering his breathing pattern, and has used this fact in a novel way in order to test ESP. When a sleeper realises he is dreaming, he makes rapid breathing movements. A bedside black box responds to this and immediately sets off an automatic dialling machine. When the other participant in the experiment receives a telephone call and there is silence on the line, he or she knows that the subject is having a lucid dream at that moment. A picture card is then selected at random by the recipient of the call and a mental picture is sent to the dreamer, just as in the telepathy experiments at Maimonides Medical Center. Hearne's work on ESP in lucid dreams continues, and further results are eagerly awaited.

Since ancient times, dreams have been regarded as channels of occult or otherwise extraordinary knowledge. It may indeed be that, in the dreaming state, human beings are at their most sensitive to the most subtle of influences impinging on them – from other minds, from the wider Universe, and even from the past and future. Experimental scrutiny of psychic activity during dreaming has begun, and seems to suggest that a great advance in our understanding of this aspect of the paranormal is imminent. As Keith Hearne says: 'Lucid dreams are the ideal state for testing *psi* because the dreamer knows he is dreaming and is taking part in a *psi* experiment. Lucid dreams may well be the royal road to a knowledge of psychic phenomena.'

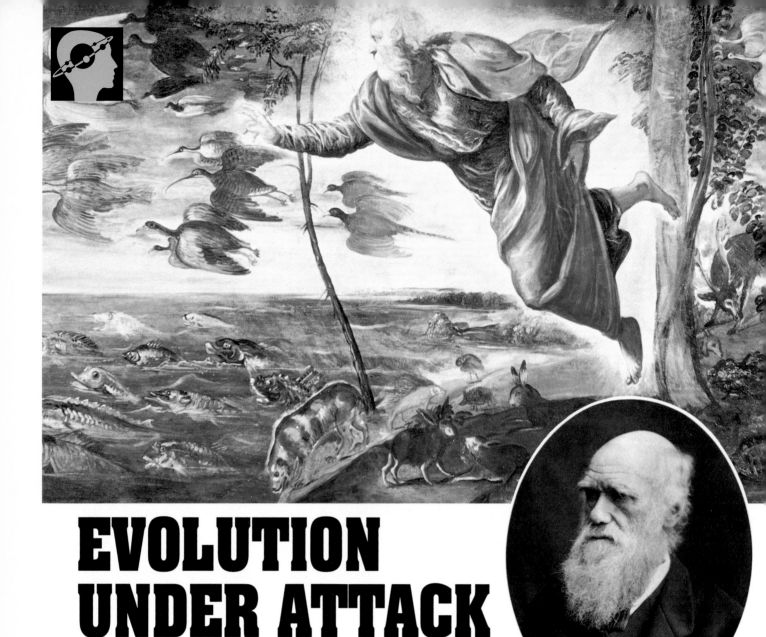

EVOLUTION UNDER ATTACK

MANY WOULD SAY THAT DARWIN'S THEORY OF NATURAL SELECTION – HELD BY MOST MODERN SCIENTISTS TO UNDERPIN EVOLUTION – CONFLICTS WITH THE OLD TESTAMENT STORY OF THE CREATION. BUT CAN DARWIN'S IDEAS ACCOUNT FOR THE ASTONISHING VARIETY OF LIVING THINGS INHABITING THE EARTH?

The 19th century saw a violent clash between two conflicting views on the origin of life on Earth. Christian doctrine stated that the world, and all that lives upon it, was created by God in six days, as depicted in the painting by Tintoretto, above. Charles Darwin, right, introduced a revolutionary new theory in his Origin of Species, *published in 1859, in which he suggested that evolution proceeds by the process of natural selection.*

The theory of evolution, in its most general terms, states that new species of plants and animals evolve from species that existed before them. This is what used to be called the theory of descent, or 'transformism'. It was in fact widely known and discussed for two generations before Charles Darwin published his *Origin of Species* in 1859. Indeed, one version of the theory had been proposed by his grandfather, Erasmus Darwin, as early as 1794; and another had been put forward by the French scientist Jean Baptiste Lamarck in 1809.

Darwin's theory clearly conflicted with the view of the leading philosophers of the ancient world – most notably, Aristotle – that species were eternally fixed and unchangeable. In the light of this classical philosophy, the biblical account of the Creation in the book of *Genesis* was interpreted to mean that God directly created all the different species of plants and animals, and that they remained unchanged thereafter.

The theory of evolution was vehemently opposed throughout the 19th century – and is still opposed by biblical fundamentalists today. However, among scientists, it has been widely accepted for decades, and is generally taken for granted. But to accept that species have evolved from other species naturally raises the questions of why species should change, and of how they do so. This is an area of great controversy.

Natural Selection

In his famous book, the full title of which was *On the Origin of Species by Means of Natural Selection, or the Preservation of Favoured Races in the Struggle for Life*, Charles Darwin put forward a particular theory of the way in which evolution occurs. In doing so, he made the notion of evolution by descent much more credible than it had been before, because he was able to suggest a plausible mechanism – natural selection – for the transformation of species. Thenceforth, the general theory of evolution by descent and Darwin's theory of natural selection became closely associated with each other. However, it is important to realise that it is perfectly possible to accept the idea of evolution without accepting Darwin's explanation of it.

The arguments for evolution are well-known. Firstly, we have fossil records, in which the remains of vast numbers of animals and plants are preserved, often in layers that indicate when they were laid down. These remains clearly seem to indicate that many of the different kinds of animals and plants that once existed on Earth have become extinct. The best-known are the dinosaurs, which died out about 70 million years ago.

Since, in many cases, new types of organism resemble ones that existed before them, it is reasonable to suppose that they were descended from pre-existing species. Birds and mammals, for example, appeared long after reptiles had become established, and share many anatomical features, such as having two pairs of limbs with five digits at the end; and in spite of different modifications in the wings of birds, fingers of men, and flippers of whales, these do show a common underlying pattern.

A second reason for believing that evolution indeed occurs is provided by the many different breeds and varieties of domesticated animals and plants. Think, for example, of the differences

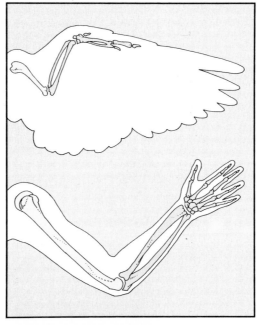

The wing of a bird, top left, and the arm of a human being, below it, although very different in appearance, have similar structures. This fact is strong evidence for evolution, suggesting that birds and men have a common ancestor from which the wing and arm structure evolved. The leading philosophers of the ancient world believed, however, that species were eternally fixed and unchangeable.

When bull-baiting died out in England, around 1835, dog-fighting became popular, and the breed of Staffordshire bull terrier, above, was created by crossing bulldogs and terriers. It is the result of a particularly ruthless form of selection: dogs that were not good fighters were simply drowned.

between dogs such as greyhounds and Pekinese. The fact that these have been produced by selective breeding from similar ancestral stock shows that the form of the species is not rigidly fixed, but is capable of change with time.

Thirdly, the geographical distribution of certain species of plants and animals strongly suggests that they have evolved by descent. An example that greatly impressed Darwin was that of the finches native to the Galapagos Islands, off the coast of South America. Here, distinct finch species, adapted to different methods of feeding, were to be found on the islands within short distances of one another. All these Galapagos species are closely related to finches on the South American mainland. The simplest explanation is that a few finches migrated from the mainland to the islands, and that some of their descendants evolved into new species that adapted to local conditions.

The fact that animals and plants can be grouped together in hierarchical systems of classification also supports the notion of descent. The human species, for instance, is grouped with the primates, together with monkeys and apes; the primates are grouped with other mammals; and the mammals

Dinosaurs, such as the Tyrannosaurus rex, left, died out about 70 million years ago. But fossil remains survive, providing powerful support for the theory of evolution.

Can acquired characteristics be inherited? The neo-Darwinian answer is a categorical 'no' – but there exists experimental evidence that suggests otherwise.

Between 1903 and 1908, a brilliant young Austrian biologist named Paul Kammerer conducted a series of experiments with spotted salamanders, *Salamandra maculosa*. These newt-like creatures have yellow spots on a black ground; and, like the chameleon, they will change colour according to their background.

Kammerer raised two groups of salamanders, one on yellow sand (as shown in the *top* panel, *left*), the other on black sand (*bottom* panel, *left*). Sure enough, the salamanders changed colour.

His next step was to breed from these salamanders, to see whether their adapted colouring was passed on to the next generation. Astoundingly, it was. The colour of the offspring of yellow parents reared on

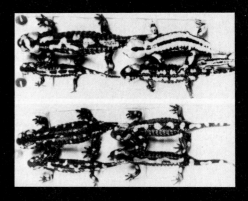

yellow sand (*top* panel, *right*) was almost pure yellow.

These experiments – and others that Kammerer conducted – seemed to prove conclusively that acquired characteristics could be inherited. Such proof would revolutionise genetics, and Kammerer's results deserved – at the very least – careful scrutiny. Instead, his work was greeted by the scientific community with derision and claims of hoaxes that drove him to suicide.

PERSPECTIVES

with other vertebrates. Similarities within each group are most easily explained in terms of descent from common ancestors – the bigger the grouping, the more remote the ancestral links.

The only alternative to an evolutionary interpretation of such evidence is to suppose that species were specially created from non-living matter at frequent intervals over a long period of time, in such a way that new species resembled species that had been created before them, and in the same geographical areas.

This seems extremely implausible, but some people feel bound to adopt this theory in an attempt to harmonise the factual evidence with one particular interpretation of the accounts of the Creation in *Genesis*. But this is completely unnecessary, even for those who accept the authority of *The Bible*. In fact, there is surprisingly little conflict between modern scientific theories of the development of the Universe and the sequence of events described in the first chapter of the *Book of Genesis*.

The Universe is generally supposed by physicists to have originated with an enormous primordial explosion. As the Universe began to cool down after this 'big bang', matter in the form of atoms condensed from incandescent plasma, and vast gas clouds gave rise to galaxies of stars. Relatively small bodies of hot matter were then captured by the gravitational pull of the stars and became planets orbiting around them. One of these was planet Earth. As the Earth cooled, the water vapour condensed and gave rise to the seas. Life originated in the water; and among the earliest living organisms were plants capable of photosynthesis. Animals arose first in the sea, and later colonised the dry land. From these land animals, in the fullness of time, Man eventually evolved.

The first chapter of *Genesis* describes a similar sequence: first, the separation of light from darkness – or in other words, of radiation from matter. Next, the separation of the Earth as a single mass from the heavens, and the subsequent appearance of the seas and dry land. Then, the origin of plants, then of animals in the sea, then of land animals, and finally of Man.

These two descriptions of the origins of things differ in that the scientific one supposes that the time-scale was of thousands of millions of years, whereas *The Bible* speaks of the different stages as taking place on different 'days'. If the term 'day' is interpreted to mean an age, there need be little conflict between the two accounts. The main discrepancy is that, in *Genesis*, the Sun and Moon appear only on the fourth 'day'. But this, in itself, is significant in that it shows that the term 'day' is not to be taken literally, for it could not possibly have a literal meaning if the Sun, by the rising or setting of which days are measured, did not yet exist, according to the very same text. Moreover, other passages to be found in *The Bible* make it perfectly plain that human measurements of time are not the same as divine ones. 'One day is with the Lord as a thousand years, and a thousand years as one day,' (*II Peter, 3:8.*)

In the end, it seems that the protracted controversy between biblical fundamentalists and evolutionists, so often portrayed as a dramatic confrontation of science and religion, comes down to little more than a dispute over the meaning of the word 'day', in a context that provides no basis for assuming that a 'day' must consist of 24 hours. Thus, there seem to be no good grounds, even religious ones, for rejecting the theory of evolution by descent.

Two of the many distinct and specialised finch species that occur on the Galapagos Islands are shown above and below. Darwin cited these birds as evidence for evolution.

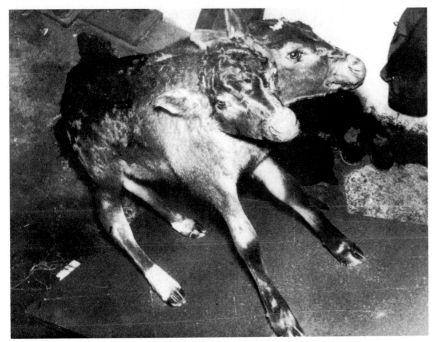

However, a new series of controversies springs up as soon as we accept this theory. Once again, underlying many of them are religious and philosophical questions, although on the surface they may seem to be purely scientific.

The most important of these concerns the origin of new species. Do they come into being gradually, or as a result of sudden jumps? This question has been hotly debated for over a hundred years between two principal schools of thought.

Darwin himself was a gradualist, and so are his modern followers, the neo-Darwinians. Their reasons for adopting this point of view are more philosophical than scientific. Even before the publication of *Origin of Species*, several writers pointed out that the theory of evolution did not contradict the idea of the creation of species by God, because God might just as well have made a new species by transforming an existing one as by forming it directly from non-living matter.

On the other hand, those who espoused the philosophy of materialism had to try to explain the

" THERE IS GRANDEUR IN THIS VIEW

OF LIFE... THAT, WHILST THIS PLANET

HAS GONE CYCLING ON ACCORDING TO

THE FIXED LAW OF GRAVITY, FROM SO

SIMPLE A BEGINNING, ENDLESS

FORMS MOST BEAUTIFUL AND MOST

WONDERFUL HAVE BEEN, AND ARE

BEING, EVOLVED. **"**

CHARLES DARWIN,

ORIGIN OF SPECIES

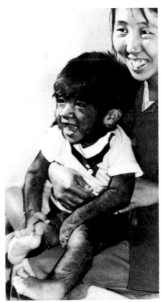

The two-headed calf, top, was the result of a genetic mutation, and lived for only a few days.

The hairy boy, above, was born in north-eastern China in 1977. Strange features such as this can arise through chance combinations of genes, but are unlikely to be favoured by natural selection.

An ancon, or short-legged sheep, is shown right, compared with a normal sheep. Genetic engineering was in fact practised long before the theory was known, the ancon species being bred from a single ram-lamb, born in 1791.

process of evolution in terms of the laws of matter alone, and were at pains to reject anything that smacked of the miraculous. Darwin himself rejected the idea of sudden changes because, as he wrote in *Origin of Species*, it 'seems to me to enter into the realms of miracle, and to leave those of science'.

Although such philosophical views have continued to play a hidden but important role in the debate, there is no real reason for the belief in a Creator to lead to a denial of the gradual evolution of new species – or, on the other hand, for a materialist to deny sudden jumps in evolution. Surprisingly the two concepts can be reconciled. Indeed, there are theologians who argue that God created different forms of life by setting up the Universe and the laws of nature, including the possibility of random genetic change, in such a way that evolution was bound to occur exactly as neo-Darwinians think it does. By contrast, some materialists accept the idea of sudden large changes, but regard them as occurring randomly.

FAVOURABLE SPECIMENS

The main argument used by Darwin in favour of gradualism relied on an analogy with the development of breeds of domesticated animals, such as dogs, pigeons and rabbits, and varieties of cultivated plants, such as cabbages, dahlias and grapes, by the agency of human selection. He reasoned that, just as animal and plant breeders select favourable specimens as parents of the next generation, and thus gradually improve the breed or variety, so – in the wild – natural selection would result in parents well-adapted to the conditions of life leaving more offspring than those less well-adapted. There would thus be a progressive improvement in the adaptation of the race to its environment.

However, the controversial question is not how locally adapted races arise within species, but how species themselves originate. Ironically, this is the very question that Darwin failed to answer satisfactorily in *Origin of Species*. He simply assumed, as his followers also assume, that the same kinds of process, continued over long periods of time, would lead to the gradual divergence of races into new species. No one disputes that this may sometimes

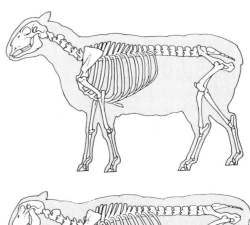

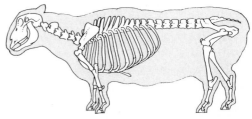

occur; but the opponents of gradualism claim that many, if not most, species arise much more quickly by relatively large and sudden transformations.

This case, like Darwin's own, can be based on an analogy with the breeding of domesticated animals and plants. For while some new varieties or strains have been produced gradually by long-continued selection, others have originated suddenly from occasional freaks or departures from type. In fruit trees, for example, peculiar shoots sometimes appear, differing from all the others, from which new varieties can be propagated. In the history of animal breeding, too, new breeds have been started from spontaneously occurring freaks.

GENETIC MUTATIONS

If, in the course of evolution, freaks occasionally survived and managed to breed successfully, a distinct new type, derived from the original species, could come into existence more or less suddenly. It seems probable, for example, that a fossil rhino genus called *Teleoceras* originated in this way. These dwarf, short-legged rhinos resemble ancon sheep and, like them, may have appeared suddenly as a result of a genetic mutation leading to the improper development of cartilage at the end of bones, a condition known as *achondroplasia*. If this were so, we would not expect to find in the fossil record a whole range of intermediate types between *Teleoceras* and the rhino species from which it evolved. No missing links have indeed been found.

Calculations of the rates of evolutionary change, based on data from fossil horses and other groups of animals, have also shown that they are much too slow to be able to account for the gradual appearance of all the different kinds of organisms in the time available, long though it has been. The neo-Darwinians reply that gradual changes might have been much less slow at some periods than others. But in admitting this, they shift their position so that it comes much closer to the idea of discontinuous or sudden changes.

One of the most convincing reasons for thinking that sudden jumps do occur is that many present-day species differ from more or less closely related species in the number and structure of their chromosomes. Changes in the chromosomes of these types are known to occur occasionally during the process of cell division (meiosis) that produces egg and sperm cells. The chromosomes of the mother cell come together in pairs at the beginning of meiosis, and normally one of each pair then moves into each of the two daughter cells. But, sometimes, pairs fail to separate properly, and one daughter cell gets too many chromosomes; the other, too few. Consequently, offspring derived from such cells have the wrong number of chromosomes. They are often abnormal and sterile as a result; but if they do manage to breed, either through self-fertilisation, as commonly occurs in plants, or by crossing with similarly abnormal organisms (their own brothers or sisters, for instance), they may give rise to a new species straight away. The differences in chromosome numbers thereafter set up barriers to interbreeding and keep the new type separate from the parent species. Other chromosomal changes during meiosis, involving the breaking and rejoining of chromosomes in the wrong places, can have a similar effect.

Those who advocate sudden jumps in evolution do not deny that the great majority of freakish organisms will be weeded out by natural selection. On the long time-scale of evolution, it is sufficient that only very rarely are 'hopeful monsters' able to survive and reproduce. Even neo-Darwinians can hardly deny that this might have happened. The two schools of thought differ mainly in their emphasis: one considers that sudden jumps have played little part in the evolution of new species; while the other claims that many, if not most, new types have arisen in this way. On balance, the available evidence supports the second of these views, although a great deal of work still remains to be done.

This is what the current controversy among evolutionary theorists is all about. At first sight, it is puzzling that these issues should raise such passionate feelings. But as in earlier controversies, some of the contenders are fighting to defend not just scientific theories but their fundamental beliefs.

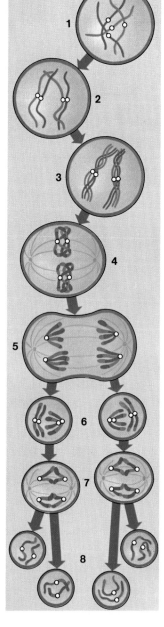

The diagram, above, shows the process of meiosis, which occurs in the production of sex cells. Chromosomes pair (as in 1 and 2), become double-stranded (3) and thicken, exchanging segments of their strands to mix the genetic information (4); the pairs separate (5) and the cell divides (6). The two-stranded chromosomes in each cell divide and the cells split (7). The resultant cells (8) have half the number of chromosomes of the parent cell. This number redoubles in sexual reproduction.

The smooth hawksbeard, left, is a result of faulty meiosis.

▟▟ IF EVOLUTION IS THE PROCESSING OF GREATER STORES OF INFORMATION, AS MANY NOW CONTEND, THEN BIOENGINEERING WILL BE SEEN AS THE INEVITABLE NEXT STEP IN EVOLUTIONARY HISTORY. BIOENGINEERING REORGANIZES EXISTING INFORMATION PROGRAMS AND CREATES NEW ONES. ▟▟

JEREMY RIFKIN, ALGENY: A NEW WORD – A NEW WORLD

GODS FROM THE STARS?

Winged chariots and creatures, part-man and part-animal, are told of in countless legends. Could they perhaps have been visitors to Earth from outer space?

A ccording to *The Bible*, as taught in Sunday schools the world over, we are all descendants of the first human couple, Adam and Eve. But there is a curious textual qualification to this, which is usually glossed over. The *Book of Genesis* states, quite explicitly, that a second strain was added to the human gene-pool – a strain that was not of this world but from a 'heavenly source'.

Perhaps Man did not evolve only from earthly beings like Adam and Eve, above. The Indian god Vishnu, meanwhile, below, is believed by some to have been an early visitor from space.

Immediately before its description of the Flood, chapter 6 of *Genesis* reads (in the *New English Bible* edition):

'When mankind began to increase and to spread all over the earth and daughters were born to them, the sons of the gods saw that the daughters of men were beautiful; so they took for themselves such women as they chose... In those days, when the sons of the gods had intercourse with the daughters of men and got children by them, the Nephilim [or 'fallen ones'] were on earth. They were the heroes of old, men of renown.'

These biblical verses differ strikingly from the rest of the creation narrative and have raised many problems for translators and theologians. Who were the 'gods' involved? *The Bible* denies the very existence of 'other gods'; and the word for 'gods' – *elohim* – can in fact be just as comfortably translated as 'God' (whose name is given a plural spelling throughout most of the creation narrative). But in that case, why do these 'sons of God' interfere in earthly affairs, when God is said to have created Adam in his likeness and as his steward on earth?

The 'sons of God' episode reads like a piece of fossil paganism that escaped the careful editing of later generations of devout Jewish scribes. It could

The abduction of two maidens to the stars finally brought about conflict and disaster for the tribes.

Such unions did not always end in tragedy, however. The Maoris indirectly ascribe their civilisation to an illicit love affair between the daughter of a chief and a prince of 'the country in the sky'. The intruder was caught by the Maori chief, but then accepted as his son-in-law. A Maori deputation was allowed to visit the 'sky-country' where invaluable arts were learned from superior beings there. Similar tales of the days when there were close ties between such beings and mankind can, in fact, be found in widely separated cultures. The Machinguenga Indians of the Peruvian jungle, for instance, tell of 'people of the heavens who came to earth on a shining road in the sky'. Japanese myth, meanwhile, claims that access to the earth from the heavens was once provided by a kind of bridge, enabling the gods to pay frequent visits.

LINGERING QUESTIONS

What, then, are we to make of these curious legends about relationships between people and 'sky beings'? Orthodox anthropology has no standard explanation for such stories, in which the link with what we now term 'paranormal' phenomena is self-evident. Some of the legends even echo the UFO abduction stories of our own time. And it should be noted that a proportion of claimed UFO contacts include some kind of sexual encounter with the aliens – certainly a parallel with the supposed mixed marriages between 'gods' and the 'daughters of men' in tales of old.

Are we perhaps dealing here with some mysterious quality of the human psyche, which compels widely separated peoples to develop similar fantasies around a belief in intelligent beings who are superior to Man? The alternative – that these tales are vestiges of some sort of historical contact between Man and alien beings – is difficult to accept. Nevertheless, it has been argued persuasively by a number of theorists whose reasoning should not be lightly brushed aside.

happily smoulder were it an isolated instance. But the same strange belief in a bygone period, when beings from 'heaven' would descend to take human brides, is found not only in this obscure biblical verse. It is also present, for example, in the well-known Greek myths about the amorous adventures of their gods. Indeed, in classical times, any noble Greek worth his salt would try to trace his ancestry through heroes and princes to one or other of the Olympian deities.

Affairs between mortals and beings from another world feature strongly in the folklore of the North American Indians, too. The Thompson Indians of British Columbia, for example, told how the 'people of the sky' once stole a married woman. Outraged, all the creatures of the earth started a fruitless war against the powerful 'sky people'. To get to the sky, the 'earth people' built a flimsy structure, which collapsed when the 'sky people' retaliated. Massive casualties resulted, and many kinds of animals were extinguished. In the version told by the Quinalt Indians of Washington, the aggressors were said to come from the 'sky country, where the stars are'.

The **Book of Enoch,** *written in the 2nd and 1st centuries BC, tells that rebellious angels were expelled from heaven and made to live on Earth, as shown in the painting* **The Fall of the Rebel Angels** *by Pieter Brueghel, above, where they passed forbidden knowledge on to Man.*

The neo-Assyrian cylinder seal (950-612 BC), below, depicts weird creatures – part-man, part-fish and part-bird, which may well have had alien origins.

" BUT IF A COSMICALLY CAUSED CATASTROPHE IS A POSSIBLE REASON FOR THE DESTRUCTION OF A CIVILISATION ON THE PLANET MARS, THAT WOULD ALSO PROVIDE MATERIAL FOR MY THEORY THAT THE EARTH MAY HAVE RECEIVED VISITS FROM SPACE IN THE VERY REMOTE PAST. "

ERICH VON DÄNIKEN,

CHARIOTS OF THE GODS?

The sketch of an unexcavated figure, 100 feet (30 metres) tall, left, was plotted by T.C. Lethbridge from information he received after using a stainless steel bar as a dowsing-rod at Wandlebury in Cambridgeshire. The number 1 indicates a metal necklace; 2, a shield; 3, could be slingstones; 4, marks the point where an old track has destroyed the legs; and 5, is where a modern pipeline is sited. The drawing is taken from Lethbridge's book, A Step in the Dark.

One serious attempt to penetrate the tangle of myth and belief about the 'sons of God' was made by T. C. Lethbridge, one of the most colourful characters of English archaeology until his death in 1971. Peeved by the lack of imagination of most archaeologists, he found it the last straw when many of his colleagues rejected out of hand his claim that gigantic chalk figures of gods, along with astral symbols, lay beneath the turf of Wandlebury Camp, Cambridgeshire. And so, in 1957, Lethbridge resigned in disgust from his position as the Keeper of Anglo-Saxon Antiquities at the Cambridge Archaeology Museum.

Moving to Devon, Lethbridge now renewed an old interest in dowsing, for which he developed refined techniques, applying them successfully in his archaeological research. His studies and writings soon broadened to take in ESP and other parapsychological problems, and his work culminated in a controversial study, *The Legend of the Sons of God*. 'As it happened,' explained Lethbridge, 'I had been interested in the problem of who were the "sons of God" for many years and had sought enlightenment from archaeologists, anthropologists and theologians at Cambridge and elsewhere, without getting the slightest satisfaction. Nobody knew the answer.'

Lethbridge appreciated the scope of the problem, which touches on fundamental issues. What or who were the gods? And why had the bulk of mankind always, apparently, believed that there were such things? Of course, he had been given plenty of 'explanations' by academic colleagues in terms of their own pet theories, but the 'legend of the sons of God' seemed to defy analysis. 'Now, how does this piece of legend fit in with any known "ism"?' asked Lethbridge. 'It is not totemism, anthropomorphism or anything of that kind. It is a definite statement of fact that a race known as the sons of God intermarried with another, known as the daughters of men.'

REMARKABLE FLYING MACHINES

Lethbridge also drew upon mythological evidence for information about vehicles used by the ancient 'gods'. Elijah was swept up to heaven in a fiery chariot, so *The Bible* tells us. But such transport was not only the product of the Greek and Hebrew imagination, he said, for there were Hindu stories, too, of godlike personages who had remarkable flying machines and destructive weapons. For Lethbridge, the similarity between such craft and the UFOs of modern reports was obvious and led to an inevitable conclusion about the 'sons of God'. Not without a note of embarrassment, he suggested that the myths were memories of extra-terrestrial visitations, and that, perhaps five thousand or more years ago, beings from another world arrived here and thrust mankind a rung or two up the ladder of civilisation by contact and interbreeding.

Such ideas were not new, of course, although Lethbridge arrived at them independently. In 1968, just as he was completing his manuscript, the book *Chariots of the Gods?*, by Swiss hotelier Erich von Däniken, appeared. A string of writers had, in fact, tackled the 'ancient astronauts' theme long before von Däniken's skilful self-publicising made him appear to be its originator. The 19th-century occultist Helena Blavatsky, for instance, had

PERSPECTIVES
ON A GRAND SCALE

Devotees of the ancient astronaut theory seem to be fond of quoting myths and legends of ancient or primitive peoples in an attempt to justify their case. The gods gave fire and the skills of agriculture to mankind, according to the mythology of many peoples. But that does not of course mean that the gods arrived here in space ships – or even that humanity is so simple minded that it could not discover these things for itself. Not only that – ancient astronaut buffs seem not to have noticed a tendency in all mythology to describe the deeds and misdeeds of heroic figures.

Such people are believed to live grander, more expansive, slightly more 'real' lives than do common mortals. The modern mythology of television soap operas likewise exaggerates its characters, simplifying the complexities of life to let us see them (and ourselves) more clearly – and so cope with them.

Myths and legends also deal with deeply shocking events; but because they are inflicted on people slightly removed from the rest of us, we can contemplate such actions with greater calm. And in this, perhaps, lies the secret of the gods and their gifts.

The discovery of fire must have been an astonishing event, full of magic and terror. How else to deal with it but regard it as the property of the gods, which has to be stolen by a Prometheus, who is then cruelly punished? Similarly, one of the most profound changes in human life occurred with the development of agriculture, involving enormous psychological and social upheaval – for which no mere man would want to take responsibility. Safer, then, to say that this was a gift from on high: and, furthermore, if this were the gods' will, what man would venture to resist the change, enormous and shocking though it was?

The Greek goddesses Demeter and Persephone are shown opposite, handing Triptolemus, seated on a winged chariot, the gift of grain for mankind before sending him on his journey to Earth.

Ezekiel's vision of God, depicted below right, must have been a terrifying experience. In the midst of a fiery brightness, the prophet saw winged creatures 'that had the likeness of a man' and who 'sparkled like the colour of burnished brass'. Above them was a throne and a man enveloped in flames. 'This was the appearance of the likeness of the glory of God'.

> THERE ARE THOSE WHO BELIEVE THAT, IN FORMER TIMES, MEN ON EARTH WERE IN CONTACT WITH PEOPLE FROM OUTSIDE OUR GALAXY... THERE IS NOTHING PARTICULARLY ABSURD OR UNLIKELY IN THIS IDEA. SPACE TRAVEL MAY WELL HAVE TAKEN PLACE ... AND IN SOME FORM IT ALMOST CERTAINLY DID.
>
> **JOHN MICHELL,**
> **THE VIEW OVER ATLANTIS**

According to the Aborigines of Australia, beings known as the Wondjina, above, created the world and brought order out of chaos. The Wondjina are believed, by some Aborigines, to visit Earth in UFOs even today.

The earliest Hebrew coin, above, dates from the 4th century BC, and shows Jehovah seated on a winged chariot that resembles that of Triptolemus on the Greek vase opposite. 'Was God an Astronaut?' asked Erich von Däniken in the sub-title to his book Chariots of the Gods?

The Babylonians told of strange beings who taught Man practical and artistic skills. These creatures were often depicted with fish-tails, as is the goddess on the bronze monument, left.

claimed that civilisation, if not mankind itself, had originated on another planet. And the mythological and anthropological evidence that von Däniken used to win fame and fortune had previously been collected by a number of other researchers from the 1940s – most notably, the Frenchmen Louis Pauwels and Jacques Bergier and the English writers Raymond Drake, John Michell and Brinsley le Poer Trench (who, as Lord Clancarty, instigated a debate on UFOs in the House of Lords in 1979).

Together, these writers had accumulated a mass of evidence (of varying quality) from the traditions and beliefs of every corner of the globe, forming an intriguing picture of evidence for extra-terrestrial intervention in Man's history. Most compelling of all are the ubiquitous myths of 'culture heroes' of mysterious origin who allegedly taught Man all the civilised arts. In the words of Lethbridge:

'So many legends affirm that such and such a god taught mankind such and such an art. Hu the Mighty, for instance, so the Welsh Barddas say, taught men agriculture. Man did not evolve it by himself by painfully scratching with a pointed stick in the ground: a god taught him.'

Many of these 'culture hero' legends seem to provide striking confirmation of the 'ancient astronaut' theory. The Babylonians preserved the story of a race of fish-tailed beings who rose every day from the Persian Gulf to teach their ancestors all the arts and sciences; and these are paralleled in Greek myth by the amphibious gods, known as Telchines, who spread metallurgical skills. Similar fish-beings called the Nommo are also said by the Dogon tribe of West Africa to have descended from the skies in a whirling, thunderous craft. Indeed, they attribute their civilisation to these beings, and their traditions about the star Sirius B (home of the Nommo) display an alarming accuracy that has made the 'Sirius mystery' into one of the strongest arguments for extra-terrestrial contact in the past. Australian Aborigines, meanwhile, attribute the creation and ordering of the world to beings known as the Wondjina. They preserve rock paintings of the Wondjina, and believe that these beings reside in the mysterious lights in the sky that white Australians call UFOs.

The culture-bringers featuring in these myths make particularly plausible 'extra-terrestrials' when they are associated with flying craft. Like the ancient Welsh, the Greeks believed that agriculture was introduced rather than invented; and the goddess Demeter is said to have sent her protégé Triptolemus around the world in a flying chariot with winged wheels, drawn by dragons, to distribute grain and teach agriculture and bread-making to all the world. Vase paintings show him perched on a chariot with two wheels, surmounted with wings and serpents.

It is a story reminiscent of the biblical prophet Ezekiel's famous 'vision of God'. Sitting by the river Chebar in Babylonia, Ezekiel saw a 'whirlwind' approach from the distance and turn into a fiery cloud, and then land with a noise like thunder. He was confronted with a dazzling vehicle that

appeared to him to be composed of wheels, wings and living creatures. It carried a throne, on which was seated 'a form in human likeness'. 'And when the living creatures went, the wheels went by them: and when the living creatures were lifted up from the earth, the wheels were lifted up... for the spirit of the living creature was in the wheels' (Ezekiel 1, 19,20). The similarity to the flying chariot of Triptolemus cannot be accidental. Indeed, a Jewish coin, dating from the 4th century BC, shows Jehovah seated on a vehicle similar to that of his Greek counterpart.

But the richest mythology for the believer in extra-terrestrial intervention must be that of India, its picturesque tales incorporating nearly all the essential elements of the 'sons of God' legends. Gods and demi-gods descend from heaven, spreading knowledge and taking mortal women as their wives. They fly on strange beasts or magnificent craft that can leave the wind behind. Indian epics describe aerial battles, involving lightning-like missiles that can turn countryside into wasteland. One such weapon contains the 'Power of the Universe' and unleashes 'smoke brighter than ten thousand suns'. According to writers like Raymond Drake and Erich von Däniken, all one needs to do is read 'extra-terrestrials' for 'gods' and the Indian legends are revealed as a Star Wars-style history of ancient astronautics.

As the ancient writers pile on story after story of sky gods, culture heroes, flying chariots and the like, the idea that extra-terrestrials were somehow behind it all soon begins to seem like an almost natural explanation. The idea is certainly sufficiently intriguing to create a demand for hard proof... or maybe disproof, for we should be careful of trying to explain one unknown, such as the legend of 'the sons of God', by putting forward another unknown – that of extra-terrestrial life. The mythological picture is merely suggestive, and a possible pointer to an uncharted area of human history. The legends of Homer were vindicated many centuries later when archaeologist Heinrich Schliemann uncovered the ruins of Troy and Mycenae; but 'space gods' have not yet found their Schliemann.

SUNK WITHOUT TRACE

WHAT IS THE SECRET OF THE BERMUDA TRIANGLE, WHERE OVER THE YEARS NUMEROUS CRAFT SEEM TO HAVE VANISHED IN STRANGE CIRCUMSTANCES? IS THERE SOME MYSTERIOUS POWER LURKING THERE, OR COULD DISAPPEARANCES BE DUE TO FAR MORE MUNDANE FACTORS?

The Cyclops, below, a US Navy collier, disappeared in March 1918 after leaving Barbados for the Chesapeake Bay area of the eastern USA. The vessel, 540 feet (165 metres) long, carried a crew of about 300 and was laden with manganese ore.

The Bermuda Triangle, an area in the western Atlantic where scores of ships and aircraft have disappeared without trace, has been described as one of the greatest true-life mysteries of all time. This is not simply because ships and aircraft have vanished there, but because – according to numerous writers and researchers – the disappearances are without explanation and therefore seem to be caused by some force or phenomenon as yet unknown to science.

It is a very disturbing, if not highly alarming claim – for precautions can be taken against the known dangers of the highway but not against the unknown forces of the Bermuda Triangle. Every crossing of the region is said to be potentially fatal, in much the same way as every pull of the trigger in Russian roulette is hazardous. For as well as being subject to all the natural dangers of the sea – such as storms, hurricanes and waterspouts – the Triangle is also home to the Gulf Stream, a fast-moving body of water that can carry an unwary or inexperienced sailor miles off course in a matter of hours and quickly disperse wreckage.

Few writers seem to agree about the Triangle's precise size and shape. The American Vincent Gaddis, originator of the phrase 'Bermuda Triangle', placed it within a triangle linking Florida, Bermuda and Puerto Rico. Richard Winer thinks it is a trapezium, however, while John Wallace Spencer sees it as a scalene triangle. Ivan T. Sanderson refers to it as 'a sort of funny blob'.

Strangely, in spite of the Triangle's notoriety, the number of disappearances within it is far from high. About 150,000 boats cross the Bermuda Triangle every year. On average, about 10,000 send a distress call, but only about 100 losses are recorded

Disappearances in the Bermuda Triangle number about 100 annually. The reward poster, left, drew attention to the mysterious fate of the yacht Saba Bank, *which vanished while sailing from Nassau in The Bahamas to Miami in April 1974.*

A British freighter, also called Cyclops, below, went missing in the North Atlantic during the Second World War. It could have been torpedoed, but writer Charles Berlitz maintains that records show no German submarines to have been in the area when the ship disappeared.

The SS Marine Sulphur Queen, *bottom, left Beaumont, Texas, on 2 February 1963, bound for Norfolk, Virginia. She carried a cargo of molten sulphur and was last heard from on 4 February. An official investigation said the ship could have sunk because of an explosion. Alternatively, she may have capsized in heavy seas, or her hull may have broken in two.*

Janeiro to Jamaica. She is known to have been overloaded and is presumed to have capsized. But author Alan Landsberg has wondered why the vessel should have had a safe voyage until she entered the deadly Triangle.

A search in the records at Lloyds reveals a ship of that name built in Liverpool in 1852, but there is no suggestion that it suffered any misfortune. The only ship corresponding with the Triangle's *Bella* is a vessel of that very name, sometimes associated with the famous 19th-century case of the 'Tichborne inheritance'. This concerned the attempt of butcher Arthur Orton to impersonate the heir to the Tichborne estate, Sir Roger Tichborne, who had been lost at sea after leaving Rio de Janeiro aboard the *Bella* of Liverpool. Unlike Tichborne's ship, of which no trace was found, the *Bella* heading for Jamaica did, apparently, leave wreckage, which was found six days after having left Rio.

So assuming perfect sailing conditions and maximum speed, the nearest that this vessel could possibly have been to the Bermuda Triangle when disaster struck was some 2,000 miles (3,200 kilometres) away.

ABANDONED SHIP

A similar case is that of the German ship *Freya*. She is said to have sailed from Manzanillo, Cuba, in 1902 and to have been found in the Triangle, abandoned by her crew and giving every appearance of having been caught in a particularly violent storm. Weather records reveal that only light airs prevailed in the region at the time, however. The *Freya* was, though, in an area where submarine volcanic activity had been reported at about the same time as the ship was abandoned, and it is believed that this probably prompted the crew to abandon ship. Whether or not this explanation is correct does not really matter because records show that the *Freya* did not sail from Manzanillo, Cuba, but from Manzanillo, Mexico, and she was not found abandoned in the Bermuda Triangle, nor even in the Atlantic Ocean, but in the Pacific.

In fact, no hint of mystery was ever attached to either the *Bella* or the *Freya* until writers began searching for Triangle fatalities. And it is questionable whether other ships – such as the *Lotta, Viego,* and *Miramon* or *Miramonde* – also supposedly lost, ever even existed.

annually. And while 100 losses are 100 too many, of course, it is not a significant proportion of 150,000 – 0.07 per cent, in fact.

Charles Berlitz, perhaps the best-known of those who have written about this area, stated that:

'All ship losses are mysterious, inasmuch as relatively few captains set out to lose their ships. When the fate of a ship is established, or even assumed, the mystery ceases. This has not been the case with the many ships which have disappeared in the Sargasso Sea.'

It is there, or near there, that the majority of Bermuda Triangle losses have taken place, Berlitz says.

The British ship *Bella*, for example, is said to have vanished in 1854 on a voyage from Rio de

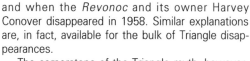

and when the *Revonoc* and its owner Harvey Conover disappeared in 1958. Similar explanations are, in fact, available for the bulk of Triangle disappearances.

The cornerstone of the Triangle myth, however, is the disappearance of five US Navy bombers – Flight 19 – and a sea plane, all on 5 December 1945. Among other aircraft to have vanished in the Bermuda Triangle were the British airliner *Star Tiger* and a Douglas DC-3, both in 1948.

The *Star Tiger*, a Tudor IV aircraft, mysteriously vanished towards the end of a flight from the Azores to Bermuda on 30 January of that year. Contrary to legend, the last message from it was an acknowledgement of a radio bearing requested several minutes earlier, and not 'Weather and performance excellent. Expect to arrive on schedule.' The weather was, in fact, anything but excellent. Cloud cover throughout the flight had prevented accurate navigation; and the aircraft had battled against severe headwinds, forcing the pilot to revise his estimated time of arrival, thereby reducing the safety margin of extra fuel. The airliner disappeared at the most critical stage of her flight. She had

During the 19th and early 20th centuries, ships did not carry radio equipment, so we cannot be certain of where they were when disaster struck or what form any disaster took. The *Atalanta* (not *Atlanta* as many authors call her) disappeared on an intended voyage of 3,000 miles (4,800 kilometres), only 500 miles (800 kilometres) of which were through the Bermuda Triangle. We do not know where she was when she was overwhelmed, but we do know that she had a crew of very inexperienced cadets, and that severe storms swept her route.

CYCLOPS CAPSIZES
The first radio-carrying vessel claimed by the Bermuda Triangle was the 19,000-tonne American collier *Cyclops* in March 1918. As with the *Atalanta*, her route was in the path of a severe storm, winds reaching peak speeds of 84 miles per hour (135 km/h). So it is quite likely that she capsized. Her top-heavy superstructure and the nature of her cargo – which may not have been properly secured – would naturally have ensured that the *Cyclops* sank very quickly.

The Japanese freighter *Raifuku Maru* is said to have vanished in 1925 after sending a strange radio message: 'Danger like dagger now. Come quick!' The message, picked up by the White Star liner *Homeric*, but distorted by electrical interference, was in fact 'Now very danger. Come quick!' The *Homeric* sped to the freighter's assistance but encountered mountainous seas, and only arrived in time to see the *Raifuku Maru* sink with all hands.

Some writers about the Bermuda Triangle state that the 395-foot (106-metre) freighter *Sandra* and her crew of 28 sailed into oblivion in calm seas and under blue skies in June 1950. But the only correct details are the freighter's name and nationality. The *Sandra* was 185 feet (55 metres) long, carried a crew of 11, and vanished in hurricane force winds in April 1950.

Hurricanes and storms also prevailed when the freighter *Anglo-Australian* vanished in 1938, when the yacht *Connemara IV* was abandoned in 1958,

Hurricanes and storms provide likely reasons for some of the losses in the Bermuda Triangle. The **Connemara IV**, *above, for instance, was found drifting and abandoned in September 1955 off Bermuda. The crew were probably lost overboard when the yacht was caught in a hurricane. The racing yawl* **Revonoc**, *right, was to vanish a few years later in 1958, between Key West and Miami, when the Florida coast was being severely battered by near hurricane-force winds.*

The Douglas DC-3, **below**, *is a plane of the type that vanished mysteriously in December 1948.*

*In*Focus

THE ENIGMA OF FLIGHT 19

One of the strangest mysteries of the Bermuda Triangle is the case of Flight 19, the so-called 'Lost Squadron'. On 5 December 1945, 14 US Navy crewmen in five, single-engined Avenger torpedo-bombers, left Fort Lauderdale, Florida, on a training exercise. They were to fly east, make a practice bombing run on a target shipwreck north of the Bahamian island of Bimini, fly north and then head back to base. All went to plan – until, that is, their return flight. An hour after they set out, the squadron leader, Lieutenant Charles Taylor, radioed in to say he and his planes were off-course, and lost. Their compasses, he said, were 'going crazy'.

Two hours later, the Fort Lauderdale control tower could still hear the crewmen trying to work out where they were –

perhaps over the Florida Keys, or later, the Gulf of Mexico. Contact with the squadron eventually grew fainter and the last words the tower heard were: 'Entering white water... we are completely lost.' That was not all. A flying boat, sent up to find them, also failed to return.

For 45 years, the riddle of Flight 19 endured. Then, in May 1991, deep sea divers searching for Spanish treasure claimed to have found the five bombers some 12 miles (20 kilometres) off the Florida coast in 750 feet (230 metres) of water. One of the planes' tail serial numbers, 28, seemed to match that of the Lost Squadron's lead aircraft. In June, however, salvage experts announced the bombers were not the 'Lost Squadron', but older planes, lost in separate accidents. Robots, sent down to the sea-bed, found that the plane serial numbers did not match those of the Lost Avengers either. (As to the number 28, a researcher discovered that the US Navy re-uses serial numbers after a plane is destroyed.) Thus, the Bermuda Triangle – or the waters beyond – still keeps the Flight 19 mystery intact.

---

insufficient fuel to reach any airport other than Bermuda, and was forced to fly at 2,000 feet (600 metres) because of the headwinds. Had anything gone wrong – fuel exhaustion, complete electrical failure or engine breakdown – the *Star Tiger* would have plummeted into the sea within seconds.

DISTORTED EVIDENCE

The case of the Douglas DC-3, lost on 28 December 1948, is an example of how facts have sometimes been omitted and distorted to imply a greater mystery than probably exists. The aircraft, carrying 27 passengers, had left San Juan, Puerto Rico, bound for Miami, Florida. The pilot, Captain Robert Linquist, is said to have radioed that he was 50 miles (80 kilometres) from Miami, could see the city lights, and was standing by for landing instructions. Miami replied within minutes, but the aircraft had vanished. The water over which the aircraft was flying was only 20 feet (6 metres) deep, yet search-craft failed to locate any wreckage.

The DC-3 is actually known to have had a defective radio, so sudden silence does not mean that the aircraft was overcome immediately after sending the message to Miami. It also removes any mystery attached to the lack of a distress call. Furthermore, the pilot did not say he could see the lights of Miami. It seems that some writers have quite literally put these words in the pilot's mouth because he said that he was only 50 miles (80 kilometres) from Miami (from which distance the lights of the city would be visible).

Linquist is known to have been compensating for a north-west wind, but wind direction had changed during the flight and it is not known whether the pilot ever received radio notification of the fact. If not, he might well have missed the Florida peninsula and flown into the Gulf of Mexico. Although the depth of the sea over which the DC-3 was flying at the time of the last message is in places only 20 feet (6 metres) deep; in other areas, it suddenly plunges to depths of up to 5,000 feet (1,520 metres). Nobody is actually certain where the aircraft went down.

As a rule, every air disaster is the subject of an exhaustive enquiry to establish the cause, and such investigations rely largely on minute examination of wreckage. If there is no wreckage, however, it is virtually impossible to hazard a guess at what happened. So, since none of the accepted causes of an air crash can positively be eliminated, how can we be sure that some unknown phenomenon was alone responsible?

A few years ago, it was claimed that the strange forces of the Bermuda Triangle also reached into space when it was learned that a weather satellite malfunctioned over the Bermuda Triangle, and only over the Triangle. But the satellite was not, in fact, malfunctioning. Its job had been to collect visual and infra-red data on cloud cover and transmitted the information to Earth. For convenience, the infra-red signal was transmitted direct, while visual signals were stored on a loop of tape for later transmission. At certain times, the tape became full and therefore had to be rewound, so no visual signal was transmitted. By pure coincidence, the tape was rewinding when the satellite's orbit brought it into position over the Triangle.

A final, hitherto unexplained case – as reported in *The Evidence for The Bermuda Triangle* by David Group – occurred in 1970, in Florida. A National Airlines' Boeing 727 was about to land at Miami Airport when it apparently disappeared from the control radar for 10 minutes. It then reappeared and landed. A subsequent investigation discovered that every clock and watch aboard was 10 minutes slow, suggesting that, for a while, the craft had ceased to exist. However, the flight number, date and time of this event are never given, and there is no record of the incident with either Miami Airport or National Airlines. In short, there is not a scrap of evidence that it ever happened.

Such stories, examined from every angle, do not appear to lend much support to theories about the Bermuda Triangle. Human fallibility, mechanical failure and natural phenomena may account for most of the disappearances: but there may well be other as yet little-understood forces at work in this region.

SYMBOLS, SIGNS AND CEREMONIES

The years from 1480 to 1680 marked the highpoint of interest in the type of ritual magic taught in the so-called *grimoires* – books of spells and magical instruction. Thereafter, there seems to have been a general decline of interest in occult ceremony: indeed, by 1800, practitioners of magical rites were few and far between. Nevertheless, a few isolated individuals had continued to experiment with methods learned from printed and manuscript *grimoires* – sometimes with surprising or unfortunate results. Typical of these experimenters was Thomas Parkes of Bristol, whose occult misadventures were recorded by the Reverend Arthur Bedford, who knew Parkes well.

Necromancy – the art of prediction through communication with the dead – once relied heavily on rituals laid down in the grimoires, medieval textbooks of magic. The magician stood in a circle inscribed with names and symbols, designed to protect him from evil demons. But things could go badly wrong, as in the case of Thomas Parkes, above, whose conjurations produced terrifying supernatural creatures that he could not control.

By trade, Parkes was a gunsmith, but he was also well-versed in mathematics, astronomy and astrology. By the latter art, he would cast horoscopes for friends and acquaintances, his prophecies often proving accurate. Nevertheless, Parkes found astrology an unsatisfactory science, for 'there was nothing in it which tended to mathematical demonstration'.

One day, the Reverend Bedford was approached by Parkes with a theological question. Was it lawful for a Christian, he asked, to raise spirits to visible appearance and converse with them? It was not, answered the clergyman.

Parkes then admitted that, using the processes outlined in a *grimoire*, the Fourth Book of Cornelius Agrippa's *Occult Philosophy*, he had been doing that very thing. He would go, he said, in the dead of night to a causeway where he drew a circle with consecrated chalk. Then, standing within the circle, 'which no spirit had power to enter', he would invoke the spirits – and they would duly appear. According to the Reverend Bedford's manuscript, these manifested themselves as follows: '... in the shape of little girls, about a foot-and-a-half [46 centimetres] high, and played about the circle. At first, he was affrighted, but after some small acquaintance this antipathy in nature wore off, and he became pleased with their company . . . they spoke with a shrill voice, like an ancient woman.'

At first, the Rev. Bedford doubted Parkes' sanity; but, after he had demonstrated the astronomical projection of a sphere, in order to prove himself free 'of the least tincture of madness', the clergyman felt compelled to accept the truth of the story. Nevertheless, he refused Parkes' offer to take him on one of his nocturnal expeditions, and sternly advised the abandonment of ritual magic.

Some three months later, Parkes once again approached the clergyman, saying he wished he had taken his advice, 'for he thought he had done that which would cost him his life'. He had decided, he said, to acquire a familiar spirit – an otherworldly being that would be continually at his service – by following the instructions given in his *grimoire*.

His first step had been to prepare a parchment book; he then went to a crossroads and invoked the spirit that was to be his familiar. The spirit duly appeared, and signed its name in the book. But then other, unwanted and uninvoked, spirits appeared, taking shapes – bears, lions, and serpents – that terrified the unhappy magician. His fears then increased, as he found it beyond his powers to control these supernatural creatures. Eventually, the spirits vanished, leaving Parkes 'in a great sweat'. The rest of the story is best told in the words of the clergyman's manuscript:

'. . . from that time he was never well so long as he lived... he expressed a hearty repentance for, and detestation of, his sins; so that though these matters cost him his life, yet I have room to believe him happy in the other world.'

Shortly after the beginning of the 19th century, there were signs of a small revival of interest in ritual magic. In 1801, for instance, Francis Barrett published a curious magical textbook, entitled *The Magus or Celestial Intelligences*. Although Barrett claimed authorship, it was largely a compilation derived from earlier *grimoires*. Barrett, who lived in what was then the London suburb of St Marylebone, was sufficiently confident of his occult abilities to advertise for pupils, and to announce the setting up of a small 'esoteric academy', the purpose of which was 'to investigate the hidden treasures of Nature'. Barrett assured prospective pupils that they would learn the secrets of natural philosophy, natural magic, the Kabbalah, chemistry, the art of making talismans, astrology and even the art of interpreting human character from facial appearance.

Whether Barrett was really competent to give practical instruction on all these subjects is uncertain; but according to the late Montague Summers, who wrote widely on witchcraft and black magic, some of Barrett's pupils 'advanced far upon the paths of transcendental wisdom'.

Throughout the course of the 19th century, small groups of English occultists studied Barrett's book and experimented with ritual magic in accordance with his instructions. One such group was centred around Frederick Hockley, a tea merchant who experimented with crystal gazing and amassed a large library of occult books and manuscripts, many of them dealing with ritual magic. Then, in the 1870s, students of the paranormal began to take an interest in the writings and ideas of the French occultist Eliphas Lévi (1810-1875). Notable among these was Kenneth Mackenzie, an active freemason who claimed to have been admitted into a secret (allegedly Rosicrucian) society. Mackenzie spent time in France and Germany, and was on friendly terms with several of the earliest members of the Golden Dawn, an organisation that taught a system of ritual magic still employed.

The Order of the Golden Dawn, a secret society whose members received successive initiations that were conferred by ceremonies bearing some resemblance to those of freemasonry, was founded

in 1888 by three masonic occultists. Of these, the most notable was S.L. MacGregor Mathers who, while at first subservient to the other two – Dr William Wynn Westcott and Dr Robert Woodman – came to dominate them in time by the sheer strength of his flamboyant personality.

PATH TO WISDOM

At first, the Golden Dawn was no more than a quasi-masonic society, and the techniques of ritual magic were not taught to its members. Nor, indeed, was any occult teaching imparted to them, save what was to be found in easily accessible books. In spite of this, newly admitted members were assured that 'the Order of the Golden Dawn, of which you have now become a member, can show you the way to much secret knowledge and spiritual progress, it can... lead... to... True Wisdom and Perfect Happiness.'

In actuality, members were far from happy and began to grumble. They wanted to practise the occult arts, particularly ritual magic, rather than just talk about them.

In 1892, Mathers decided to meet their wishes and produced a large body of instructional material that outlined a complex and – so it is claimed by those who have experimented with it – effective system of ritual magic. According to Mathers and his wife Moina, sister of the French philosopher

PHANTASMAGORIA
THIS and every EVENING,
AT THE
LYCEUM, STRAND.

Members of the Golden Dawn are seen, left, at an initiation ceremony. Originally, the society required that, as a novice's knowledge of the occult increased, he should pass through successive initiations based on the progression of the soul through the Tree of Life, illustrated below.

The top of the magic wand belonging to occultist Aleister Crowley, below left, represented the head of Janus – Roman god of beginnings – topped by a triple flame.

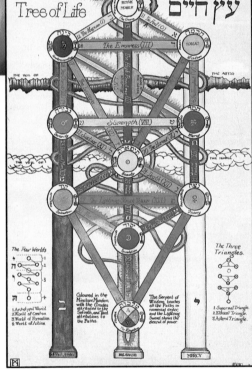

Henri Bergson, it was derived from the 'Secret Chiefs', superhuman beings of the same variety as the Mahatmas (or Masters) whom the Theosophist Madam Blavatsky claimed to represent. Mathers said he had occasionally met these beings in their physical bodies, the appointments with them being made 'astrally'. (Presumably, they either appeared to him in the course of dreams, as disembodied spirits, or perhaps he received messages telepathically from them.)

These meetings apparently exhausted Mathers. After they were over, he felt he had been in contact with a 'terrible force', found such difficulty in breathing that he compared it to being half-strangled by fumes of ether, and even suffered violent bleeding from his nose, mouth and ears.

Whether Mathers' Masters were real or imaginary, there is no doubt that the system of magical practice attributed to their teachings is intellectually coherent and, in its way, impressive. The theories behind the techniques of ritual magic taught are not only more fully developed and better expressed than they are in the writings of Eliphas Lévi, but the practice of the art is taught in a much simpler way than in the *grimoires*. (There is no ritual sacrifices of virgin rams at the dark of the Moon, for example.)

MAGICAL IMPLEMENTS

The Golden Dawn initiate who had reached the stage at which he or she received access to Mathers' instructional material began by making a set of magical implements. These, mostly made from wood, cardboard and coloured paper, included a 'Lotus Wand', signifying the 12 signs of the zodiac and the triumph of spirit over matter, a ceremonial cup – this was usually a wine glass decorated with mystic symbols – a wooden disc, symbolic of matter, and a sword, emblem of the strength and power of Mars. Once made, the implements were ceremonially consecrated.

The magician then began to devise his own ceremonies on the basis of occult knowledge. Sometimes, these were comparatively simple. Thus, for example, when a certain J.W. Brodie-Innes came to believe (on no very good grounds) that a 'vampirising entity' was obsessing himself and his wife, he burned incense on a coal from his fire and drew a pentagram in the air with his right hand, while resonantly chanting the 'name of power', *Adonai ha-Aretz* – Hebrew for 'God of the Earth'. At once, there materialised before him 'a vague blot' that soon formed itself into a terrifying apparition, a foul shape between that of 'a big bellied toad and a malicious ape'. Using the visualisation process outlined in one of Mathers' manuscripts, the magician then imagined something so strongly that it was almost perceptible to his physical sight – a glowing ball of fiery force which he directed against the obsessing entity. There was 'a slight shock, a foul smell, a momentary dimness, and then the thing was gone'.

POWER OF SYMBOLS

Rather more elaborate rituals – those, for example, for raising spirits and the 'making of an astral shroud of darkness' (that is, obtaining invisibility) – were also undertaken. The basic form of these was taken from the *grimoires*, but the ceremonies were enriched by the incorporation into them of additional material derived from the symbol system of correspondences that Mathers claimed to have been given by his teachers. A snake, for example, was said to correspond to both the god and the planet Mercury; so, if a Golden Dawn magician were evoking spirits whose nature was mercurial, he might incorporate snake fat into the candles employed in the ceremony.

The Golden Dawn eventually collapsed into a number of competing schisms. Personality differences in time destroyed even these; but the ritual magic of the Golden Dawn survived. Even today, in both the UK and North America, groups and isolated individuals practising Golden Dawn magic are to be found in almost every large city.

THE ECLIPSE OF VULCAN

OBSERVATIONS MADE DURING A SOLAR ECLIPSE FORCED ASTRONOMERS TO THE CONCLUSION THAT THEY HAD DISCOVERED A 'NEW' PLANET, LYING BETWEEN MERCURY AND THE SUN

The excitement generated by sightings of an unexpected, planet-like object close to the Sun during an eclipse in 1878 was immense. It seemed that this was just the confirmation of the existence of the planet Vulcan that scientists had been looking for. It had apparently first been sighted by an amateur French astronomer, Dr Lescarbault, who claimed to have

During an eclipse of the Sun, above, stars close to the Sun that are normally invisible can be clearly seen.
The French amateur astronomer Dr Lescarbault saw what he believed to be the planet Vulcan, from the observatory below.

seen it by day in 1859, as a silhouette against the Sun. Within 20 years, however, the tide had turned so completely that no reputable astronomer believed in Vulcan's existence. Even in the 1880s, following the supposed 1878 sighting, certain astronomers were openly sceptical. Leading the attack was the brilliant Simon Newcomb, an American theoretical astronomer who had spent his life calculating the orbits of the planets in exacting detail. He had also calculated that flight by heavier-than-air machines was quite impossible: and, although the Wright brothers convincingly proved him wrong on that point in 1903, his astronomical calculations were undoubtedly exceedingly accurate. It was not until electronic computers came along 50 years later that anyone improved on Newcomb's results.

Newcomb suggested that astronomers should be very critical of reports of Vulcan's transits. In the previous century, there had been 19 reports of dark spots moving rapidly across the face of the Sun; and virtually all of these sightings were made by people who were either not astronomers or unknown amateurs with poor telescopes. Yet, during

this time, there had been professional astronomers and skilful amateurs watching the Sun every day.

The German amateur Heinrich Schwabe, for example, started watching the Sun in 1826, and observed it on every clear day for 17 years. Ironically enough, he started in the hope of catching the transit of an unknown planet, but he never saw any such thing. Instead, he noted details of sunspots (dark patches on the Sun's surface) and discovered that the number of sunspots fluctuates over a cycle of 11 years. After that, professional astronomers, too, watched the Sun more carefully. But none of them saw anything that could possibly have been a transit of Vulcan.

Nowadays, special solar observatories photograph the Sun throughout the day, making up movie sequences of gas motions around sunspot regions. If Vulcan existed, it would surely show up in these sequences as it crossed in front of the Sun.

But what of Lescarbault's original supposed sighting? The presence of a new planet had in fact been predicted by the great French astronomer Urbain Le Verrier (1811-77), who seized on Lescarbault's claim as proof of Vulcan's existence. However, the sighting was suspect in several ways. A French professional astronomer in Brazil, E. Liais, had been observing the Sun at precisely the same time, and saw nothing unusual. But, at the time, his negative report carried little weight against the word of the famous Urbain Le Verrier.

Lescarbault, a medical doctor by profession, was only an amateur astronomer. His telescope is also said to have been of very poor quality, giving distorted images. When Le Verrier made his famous incognito visit to Lescarbault, he even openly commented on the 'defects of his instruments and the errors that they led to'. So it is astounding that he should have accepted Lescarbault's evidence for Vulcan at all.

Lescarbault's lack of care and skill also emerged in 1891, when he announced to the French Academy of Sciences that he had discovered a bright new star in the constellation Leo. The 'star' turned out to be the planet Saturn. There is no doubt that Lescarbault was a poor observer, who tricked himself into believing he had seen Vulcan. He may have seen a sunspot, a high-flying bird, or just an image somehow caused by a defect in his telescope – we shall never know.

Two professional astronomers who reported they had seen Vulcan during the total eclipse of 1878 were undoubtedly good observers, but their accounts are nevertheless strangely inconsistent. Lewis Swift saw two stars 'south-west' (towards the south-western horizon) of the Sun: he took one to be the star theta Cancri, and the other to be Vulcan. James Watson reported only one, and its position in fact agrees well with that of theta Cancri itself – a star that Watson does not even mention having observed.

SUSPECT STAR

But there is a much stronger reason for believing that neither Swift nor Watson saw Vulcan. Both agreed that the suspect star was faint: at magnitude 4½ on the astronomer's scale, it would have been only a little brighter than the faintest stars that the naked eye can see. Yet Le Verrier had inferred Vulcan's existence from the peculiar motion of the planet Mercury's orbit, and to perturb Mercury by gravitational pull, Vulcan would have to be three to four times heavier than Mercury itself. If it were larger and closer to the Sun, Vulcan should reflect far more sunlight than Mercury, and so appear far brighter in our sky. In fact, it should have appeared as brilliant as Venus, and ten times brighter than the brightest star in the night sky, Sirius.

If Le Verrier's Vulcan existed, it would not normally be seen in the brilliant blue of the daytime sky (any more than Venus is), but would blaze out during solar eclipses as the brightest object in the sky. Since solar eclipses are seen from some part of the world virtually every year, Vulcan's existence would surely have been known long ago.

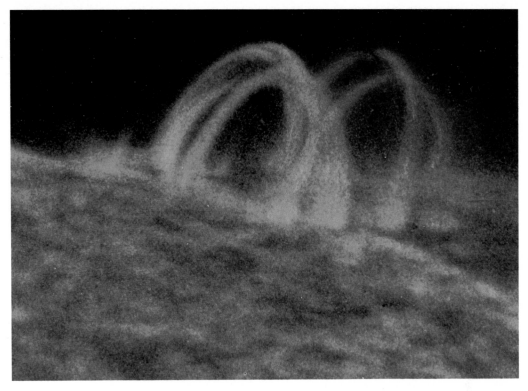

What Swift and Watson saw – if it was real at all – was probably a small comet passing near the Sun. Great comets blaze brilliantly and grow long tails; but small comets look like faint 'woolly' balls of gas. In Watson's telescope, one of these would have appeared more like the tiny disc of a planet.

At the end of the last century, no professional astronomer had yet confirmed Vulcan's existence. Its leading proponent, Le Verrier, had died in 1877, and the general mood was highly sceptical. The name 'Vulcan' therefore dropped out of the indexes of popular astronomy books. But the orbit of Mercury did undoubtedly swing round. Although Simon Newcomb had successfully denounced the supposed observations of Vulcan, his meticulous analysis of Mercury's motion showed that the swinging of its orbit was real, and even a little larger than Le Verrier had calculated. No one could explain it – no one, that is, until Einstein.

For 350 years, scientists had calculated what the planets' orbits should be, and did this using Newton's law of gravitation. Then, in 1915, Albert Einstein proposed a new theory of gravitation, which he called general relativity. Although it looks much more complicated than Newton's law, general relativity does turn out to give the same answer for the gravitational pull of one body on another when that pull is quite weak. When gravity is very strong, though, differences appear between the predictions of the two theories.

The strongest gravitational pull in our Solar System occurs close to the Sun, and Einstein worked out what his theory predicted for a planet in Mercury's orbit. According to general relativity, Mercury should not follow the same oval over and over again, but the oval orbit should gradually swing round. Einstein calculated the rate of swing to be 43 seconds of arc per century. (A second of arc is 1/3600 degree of angle). This is exactly the rate at which Mercury's orbit does swing forward.

America's James Craig Watson, top left, and Lewis Swift, above left, were two experienced astronomers whose independent observations during the solar eclipse of 29 July 1878 seemed to confirm the existence of Vulcan.

Sunspot activity on the solar surface is seen, top. Seen from the Earth, sunspots look like dark patches on the face of the Sun and it is easy for the inexperienced to mistake them for small planets.

So what had appeared to astronomers as a 'perturbation' of Mercury by another planet was not that at all. Mercury's motion disagreed with theory quite simply because astronomers had been using the wrong theory of gravitation.

With publication of the theory of general relativity, any foundation for Vulcan was knocked away. In fact, there can be no massive planet within Mercury's orbit, or its gravitation would upset the agreement between Mercury's motion and Einstein's theory, verified by other tests.

A more recent theory offers other possibilities. Instead of one planet, there may be a million smaller bodies, according to American astronomer Kenneth Brecher. These would be lumps of rock or metal 6 to 30 miles (10 – 50 kilometres) across, like some of the smaller asteroids that orbit the Sun between Mars and Jupiter.

Asteroids within the orbit of Mercury would be so close to the Sun that they would be red-hot. They would emit a lot of infra-red, which is 'heat radiation'. In 1983, a team of Japanese astronomers used an infra-red camera to look near the Sun during a total eclipse. They did not find individual asteroids, but the camera showed a ring of hot dust round the Sun. It was two million miles (three million kilometres) from the Sun, and composed of specks of rock at a temperature of 1,200°C.

Some astronomers thought that this dust probably came from collisions between small asteroids, too tiny for the camera to show directly. But during an eclipse in 1991, astronomers discovered that the ring had disappeared. It was probably just debris from a comet that had disintegrated as it passed too near to the Sun in the early 1980s.

Once again, the trail to the elusive planet Vulcan has led to a dead end. There may well be some very small asteroids close to the Sun, but astronomers are now completely convinced that the innermost planet is Mercury.

SECRETS LOCKED IN STONE

THE SHADOWS CAST BY STANDING STONES PLAY CURIOUS AND EERIE TRICKS, PARTICULARLY AT THE WINTER AND SUMMER SOLSTICES. WHAT DO THESE WEIRD LIGHT-SHOWS TELL US ABOUT WHY SUCH MEGALITHIC MONUMENTS WERE BUILT?

Stone circles and menhirs stand in the landscape like a challenge cast across time by the long-lost people who erected them. The majesty and permanence of these stones alert us to the regard in which they must have been held. But so distant in time are the megalith-builders that it is as if we had landed on another planet and were confronted by the relics of an alien civilisation.

Archaeological investigation of megaliths is thus beset by problems. The megaliths themselves cannot be dated accurately. Radio-carbon dating works only with matter that has once been alive, so that megaliths can be dated only by using such techniques on organic matter that can be assumed to have been associated with the erection of a given stone structure. Carbon dating of burial remains found at the foot of certain British standing stones suggests they were erected around 2000 BC, while similar attempts at dating in north-west Europe indicate a similar or earlier date for the menhirs of

Brittany. Certain menhirs, like the Devil's Arrows and the Rudston monolith, all in Yorkshire, occur in areas where considerable Neolithic earthworks are to be found, and the stones can therefore be dated, with some confidence, to some time in the third millennium BC.

Stone circles, likewise, provide archaeologists with few clues. But the consensus of archaeological opinion seems to be that British circles were in some way associated with the religious life of the late Neolithic and early Bronze Age peoples. Interments have occasionally been found within circles, but it is generally supposed that such human remains were ritually deposited within existing stone circles, rather than that stone circles were built as graves.

ANCIENT RITUAL SITES

Megalithic mounds, like that at West Kennet, close to Avebury in Wiltshire, are probably older than most stone circles. Deposits of bones found within them often show evidence of having been repeatedly disturbed; and in some instances, animal bones, rather than human remains, have been uncovered. All the evidence points to a magical or ritual – perhaps sacrificial – use of such sites. In any event, they cannot have been simply tombs.

The huge megaliths that have been added to some monuments – such as those at Stonehenge, Avebury, or Arbor Low in Derbyshire – are equally enigmatic. They are probably older than ordinary stone circles and, judged simply by the enormous engineering effort that went into their placing, they were certainly of tremendous importance to the societies that erected them.

Archaeology, on its own, can also tell us something about the chronology of the stones, that they were erected with enormous effort, and that they may, in ways not properly understood, have been connected with death rituals. Many archaeologists,

In 1981, it was discovered that the central pillar of the stone circle at Boscawen-un in Cornwall, England, above, leans towards the rising midsummer Sun.

The twin line of standing stones, below, that constitute the West Kennet avenue at Avebury, Wiltshire, are alternately pillar- and diamond-shaped. It has been suggested that these represent male and female attributes.

however, have felt that there has to be something more to the megaliths. A new line of enquiry, during the 20th century, has followed up this intuition, and may well be in the process of contributing important new perspectives to the picture we have so far of the megaliths and their builders. Such research is known as 'archaeoastronomy' or 'astro-archaeology'.

It had been noted by antiquaries, for some centuries, that there seemed to be some sort of astronomical aspect to certain sites – the rising of the midsummer sun over Stonehenge's Heel Stone was a well-known instance. But it was the eminent scientist Sir Norman Lockyer, at the turn of the century, who began to put such observations into a more serious context. As a result of surveying

*In*Focus

In an illustration, taken from William Stukeley's Stonehenge, A Temple Restor'd to the British Druids, *published in 1740, two Druids stand at Stonehenge, as Stukeley imagined it originally to have been built.*

OF GODS AND STONES

Surprisingly, the practice of worship at stone circles persisted well into the Christian era. Then, in AD 452, the Lateran Council forbade the worship of stones; and as late as 1560, the Synod of Argyll found it necessary to destroy a stone circle on the island of Iona.

Until the 15th century, British scholars, such as William Stukeley, believed that Stonehenge and other monuments had been designed as temples by the Druids, the ancient Celtic scholar-priests, something of whose religion was known from the writings of Roman historians.

However, although the Druids most probably used the megaliths of Stonehenge as an observatory for marking the arrival of the seasons, they certainly did not build the complex. Stonehenge is known to predate the arrival of the Druids in Britain by at least 1,000 years.

In modern times, there has been a revival of the Druids who, wearing white robes, have held their midsummer solstice ceremonies at Stonehenge each year. From 1989, however, they have had to hold their rites elsewhere, having been unable to come to an agreement with Stonehenge's official guardians – English Heritage – on the questions of crowd control and access.

ancient sites throughout Britain and in Egypt, he became convinced that the ancients had set up their stones to observe the Sun, Moon and certain stars for calendrical purposes. It was not until the 1960s, however, that the study of ancient sites and their relevance to ancient astronomy began to acquire any general acceptance.

The work of the late C. A. Newham at Stonehenge also showed that there were probably solar and lunar alignments built into the design of stones at this site. In 1965, shortly after the publication of Newham's research, Professor Gerald Hawkins of America's Smithsonian Institution published a controversial book entitled *Stonehenge*

In 1979, excavations at Stonehenge, below, revealed the presence of a stone-hole near the Heel Stone, taken by some to indicate that the surviving stone is one of pair that once framed the rising sun as a gateway to the dawn.

Decoded, which detailed his own investigations at Stonehenge. He, too, found evidence to suggest significant solar and lunar alignments encoded in the relationships of the stones. Furthermore, Hawkins claimed that the ring of pits called the Aubrey Holes, surrounding the stones, could have been used to predict eclipses. Thus, the powerful image of Stonehenge as a sort of prehistoric computer was born.

STATISTICAL SURVEYS

Hawkins made some mistakes, however, and his results were hotly disputed by archaeologists. It therefore took the quieter and more thorough research of Dr Alexander Thom, professor of engineering at Oxford University from 1945 to 1961, to put archaeoastronomy on to a surer footing. Thom spent decades visiting hundreds of British stone circles, making accurate surveys of their ground-plans, elevations and visible horizons. Statistical studies were made from this mass of data, and the results were linked with astronomical information dating back to prehistoric times.

Thom's work led him to three basic discoveries: the ground-plans of the rings were either accurate circles or sophisticated – and exact – geometric constructions; a basic unit of measurement seemed to have been employed – what Thom called the 'megalithic yard' of 2 feet 8 inches (83 centimetres); and statistical data showed, more convincingly than ever before, that stone circles could have been used as observatories for measuring midsummer and midwinter sunrises, as well as the moon's orbit and perhaps other astronomical phenomena, too. Thom's research also showed that such observations could have provided a level of accuracy far exceeding that needed by simple agricultural communities for calendrical purposes.

Although there is still controversy over this approach to standing stones, archaeoastronomical research continues to progress, particularly in Britain and the USA, and interesting details have been revealed. The idea of the Heel Stone at Stonehenge being a solstitial marker, for instance, may be too simple. To begin with, it has been pointed out that the midsummer Sun would have risen slightly to one side of the monolith when viewed from the centre of Stonehenge in prehistoric times, owing to the precession of the equinoxes – the 'wobble' of the Earth on its axis. However, excavations in 1979 revealed a stone-hole near the Heel Stone: this could mean that the stone is the survivor of a pair of megaliths that framed the rising Sun – as a sort of gateway to the dawn. It could be, however, say some archaeologists, that the Heel Stone was never directly connected with solar observations at all: rather, in years when the midwinter full Moon rises over it, a valuable signal of an impending solar eclipse is given.

But the experience of the astronomical alignments of megaliths dwarfs all the facts, figures and arguments. To stand at the Castlerigg circle in Cumbria, north-west England, for example, watching the midwinter rising Sun, is astonishing. It is immediately obvious, as the Sun's rays break over the mountainous horizon, that the two lowest

Shadows certainly seem to play symbolic 'games' at the Castlerigg stone circle in Cumbria, below. At midwinter sunrise, a shadow falls between the two tallest stones of the circle; and at midsummer, the circle's tallest stone casts a shadow for over a mile (1.6 kilometres) across the landscape, as shown bottom.

stones in the circle are diametrically opposite each other, causing a 'cleft' across the circle along this particular astronomical alignment.

Just how subtle the alignments of such places can be was brought home to researcher John Glover in 1976. He was at Castlerigg to photograph the midsummer setting Sun over the stones, and happened to turn round to observe an immensely long, black shadow being cast by the circle's tallest stone – a black line stretching across the landscape for more than a mile (1.6 kilometres). Although this is not, in itself, remarkable, it intrigued Glover, and he has discovered similar 'shadow paths' at other sites. Near the Cumbrian village of Little Salkeld, for instance, a 12-foot (4 metre) tall monolith, known as Long Meg, stands outside a circle of standing stones, called the Daughters. During midwinter sunset, Long Meg throws its shadow to the furthest

perimeter of the circle. It seems that some standing stones may well have been specifically designed with this kind of light-show phenomenon in mind.

SHADOW-PLAY

Martin Brennan, who has carried out archaeoastronomical work in Ireland, became convinced that some of the carvings at Newgrange and other Irish sites were indeed complex forms of sun- and moondials – designed to be used in conjunction with the shadows thrown by sticks of certain lengths. More than that, Brennan's research made him sure that the 70-foot (23-metre) sunbeam that enters Newgrange on midwinter mornings to illuminate the inner chamber with golden light, for example, is clear evidence that the megalith-builders employed shadows and lightbeams for astronomical measurement connected with religious purposes.

Such lightbeams occur at other Irish mounds, too, as Brennan has seen and documented. One of the most beautiful and mysterious of these impressive events occurs at the chambered mound of Knowth near Newgrange. At a particular point in the Moon's approximately 19-year cycle, known as the major standstill, the Sun and Moon both shine down one of the two passages in the mound that is oriented towards them, and the silver, feminine lunar light mingles with the golden, masculine light

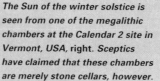

Sunlight illuminates one of the stone passages in the chambered mound of Newgrange in Northern Ireland, left. At the Moon's major standstill, light from the Sun and Moon mingles in the central chamber.

The Sun of the winter solstice is seen from one of the megalithic chambers at the Calendar 2 site in Vermont, USA, right. Sceptics have claimed that these chambers are merely stone cellars, however.

of the Sun – a form of alchemical light-show created as a result of sound astronomical observation.

Other researchers are following different paths. They look, for instance, at legends that might well provide a record of folk-memory for the purposes of prehistoric sites. In Britain, parts of Europe and, to some extent, locations in Africa – such as Senegal and The Gambia – there are motifs in legends specifically linked with the old stones. These claim, variously, that the stones can move at night, to dance or drink; that they are people turned to stone; that they have healing powers; or that they can bring lightning down to afflict a desecrator. Other legends state that certain sites contain buried treasure or are the abodes of fairies and other elementals. A large body of tradition also links fertility and fecundity with certain groups of stones. Indeed, many of those who have investigated such folklore have become convinced that it is a form of race memory that has been handed down from one generation to another, in ever more embellished form, since prehistoric times.

At a site in Cumbria, below, the isolated monolith of Long Meg throws its shadow directly on to one of the so-called Daughters, at midwinter sunset.

The idea has thus come into being that megalithic and certain other prehistoric sites are places of power, where little-understood energies or forces are gathered together and directed. The work of psychics and dowsers, and the findings of some scientists at such sites, tends to support such notions. It has all somehow become inextricably associated with the concept of geomancy – the study of the sacred layout of the landscape – and alignments known as leys, along which standing stones are said to act as markers. We know that geometry was certainly a prime feature of stone circle ground-plans; so perhaps it is not too far-fetched to consider the possibility that the megaliths, together with other types of prehistoric site, were linked together in large-scale relationships across the countryside, and that it was this that gave them their power in the mind of prehistoric Man.

MYSTERIOUS FLYING MACHINES

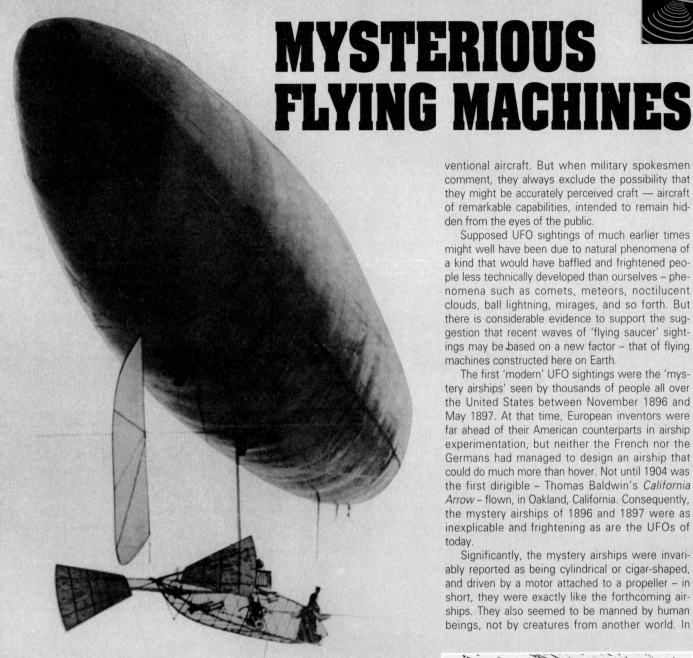

ventional aircraft. But when military spokesmen comment, they always exclude the possibility that they might be accurately perceived craft — aircraft of remarkable capabilities, intended to remain hidden from the eyes of the public.

Supposed UFO sightings of much earlier times might well have been due to natural phenomena of a kind that would have baffled and frightened people less technically developed than ourselves – phenomena such as comets, meteors, noctilucent clouds, ball lightning, mirages, and so forth. But there is considerable evidence to support the suggestion that recent waves of 'flying saucer' sightings may be based on a new factor – that of flying machines constructed here on Earth.

The first 'modern' UFO sightings were the 'mystery airships' seen by thousands of people all over the United States between November 1896 and May 1897. At that time, European inventors were far ahead of their American counterparts in airship experimentation, but neither the French nor the Germans had managed to design an airship that could do much more than hover. Not until 1904 was the first dirigible – Thomas Baldwin's *California Arrow* – flown, in Oakland, California. Consequently, the mystery airships of 1896 and 1897 were as inexplicable and frightening as are the UFOs of today.

Significantly, the mystery airships were invariably reported as being cylindrical or cigar-shaped, and driven by a motor attached to a propeller – in short, they were exactly like the forthcoming airships. They also seemed to be manned by human beings, not by creatures from another world. In

WERE THE STRANGE AIRSHIPS, SIGHTED IN HUGE NUMBERS IN THE 1890S, ALIEN CRAFT? OR WERE THEY PERHAPS CREATED BY HUMAN ENGINEERS, ADVANCED IN AERONAUTICS?

Explanations offered for unidentified flying objects have been numerous and varied. In past ages, they were at times regarded as supernatural visitants or omens, divine or demonic in origin. In our own technological age, they are sometimes thought to be visitors from distant civilisations in space, time-travellers, or even emissaries of dwellers inside the Earth. Those who despair of ever finding evidence for such conjectures speculate that UFOs might be 'thoughtforms', created by those who believe they perceive them, or that they could be the results of governmental mind manipulation. Scientific debunkers, meanwhile, insist that they are misinterpreted natural phenomena or con-

The non-rigid airship, above, was built by Santos-Dumont of France at the turn of the century. Nothing as advanced as this was publicly known in the USA.

An aerial object, seen over California in 1896, was portrayed in a local newspaper, as shown right. Witnesses saw a dark body above a brilliant light, apparently descending.

fact, their occupants were often reported to have talked to witnesses, usually asking them for water for their machines.

IN GREEN PASTURES

Perhaps the most intriguing of all such cases were those involving a man who called himself Wilson. The *Houston Post* of 21 April 1897 carried an account of an event that took place in Beaumont, Texas, two days previously, when J. B. Ligon, the local agent for Magnolia Brewery, and his son noticed lights in a neighbour's pasture a few hundred yards away. They went to investigate and came upon four men standing beside a 'large, dark object', which neither of the witnesses could see clearly. One of the men asked Ligon for a bucket of water. Ligon gave it to him and the man gave his name as Wilson. He then told Ligon that he and his friends were travelling in a flying machine, that they had taken a trip 'out of the Gulf' and that they were returning to the 'quiet Iowa town' where the airship, and four others like it, had been constructed. When asked, Wilson explained that the wings of the airship were powered by electricity. Then he and his friends got back into the passenger car at the bottom of the airship, and Ligon and his son watched it ascend and fly away.

The next day, 20 April, Sheriff H. W. Baylor of Uvalde, also in Texas, went to investigate a strange light, as well as voices behind his house. Here, he encountered an airship and three men. Again, one of the men gave his name as Wilson, and said he came from Goshen, New York State. Wilson then enquired about a certain C.C. Akers, former Sheriff of Zavalia County, saying that he had met him in Fort Worth in 1877 and now wanted to see him again. Sheriff Baylor, surprised, replied that Akers was now at Eagle Pass, 60 miles (96 kilometres) to the south-west. Wilson, apparently disappointed, asked to be remembered to him the next time

In 1900, the world's conception of air travel was still dominated by the image of the airship. In the illustration, top, an artist imagines an aerial ironclad of the year 2000, suspended from a somewhat vulnerable gasbag and battling with aeroplanes and ships.

One of Samuel Pierpont Langley's designs for a pilotless aeroplane, powered by a light petrol engine, is shown above. Some of his small aircraft were successful; but in 1903, two of his full-scale planes crashed.

Sheriff Baylor visited him. The men from the airship then asked for water and requested that their visit be kept a secret from the townsfolk. They now climbed into the passenger car of the airship, before its great wings and fans were set in motion. They then sped away northward in the direction of San Angelo. The county clerk also claimed to have seen the airship as it left the area.

Two days later, in Josserand, Texas, a whirring sound awakened a farmer, Frank Nichols, who looked out of his window and saw 'brilliant lights streaming from a ponderous vessel of strange proportions' in his cornfield. Nichols went outside to investigate; but before he reached the object, two men walked up to him and asked if they could have water from his well. Nichols agreed, and the men then invited him to view the airship. He said there must have been six or eight crew members. One of these told him that the ship's motive power was highly condensed electricity and that it was one of five that had recently been constructed in a small town in Iowa with the backing of a large company in New York.

The next day, 23 April, witnesses, described by the *Post* as 'two responsible men', reported that an airship had descended where they lived in Kountze, Texas, and that two of the occupants had given their names as Jackson and . . . Wilson.

On 27 April, the *Galveston Daily News* printed a letter from C.C. Akers, who claimed that he had indeed known a man in Fort Worth named Wilson, that Wilson was from New York, and that he was 'of a mechanical turn of mind and was then working on aerial navigation and something that would astonish the world.'

SIGHTING AT DEADWOOD

Subsequently, the *Houston Post* reported that, in Deadwood, Texas, a farmer called H. C. Lagrone had suddenly heard his horse bucking, as if about to run amok. Going outside, he then saw a bright white light circling around the fields nearby and illuminating the entire area before descending and landing in one of the fields. Walking to the landing spot, Lagrone found a crew of five men, three of whom talked to him, while the others collected water in rubber bags. The men informed Lagrone that their airship was one of five that had been flying around the country recently, that theirs was the same vessel that had landed in Beaumont, and that all the ships had been constructed in an interior town in Illinois (which borders Iowa). They were reluctant to say anything more because they had not yet taken out any patents on their machine.

By May 1897, the mysterious airship sightings had stopped. But what lay behind them? Could such airships indeed have been financed by a powerful company in New York and constructed secretly in the wilds of Iowa or Illinois?

This is certainly a possibility. During the late 1890s, numerous inventors in the United States obtained patents for planned airships. But since most of them worried constantly about the possible theft or plagiarism of their designs, they also kept

The German engineer Otto Lilienthal is seen flying one of his biplane gliders, above. Lilienthal was the first inventor to build and fly successful controllable aircraft. He steered by shifting his dangling body and legs from side to side. Although he was killed in a flying accident in 1896, soon after this flight, his successes inspired several other pioneers, including the Wright brothers.

many of their ideas completely secret. Knowing this, many Americans came to believe that Wilson and his friends could well have invented successful airships.

Experimentation in aerodynamics was highly advanced by the 1890s, particularly in Massachusetts (an area having numerous mystery airship sightings) and New York, reportedly Wilson's home city. At the Massachusetts Institute of Technology (MIT), there were plenty of informal courses on propulsion and the behaviour of fluids, relevant to aerodynamics. What is more, by 1896, instructors and students at MIT had built a wind tunnel and were experimenting with it to get practical knowledge of aerodynamics. A man such as Wilson could have attended those courses and then

A WAVE OF SIGHTINGS

CASEBOOK

The American mystery airship wave began in November 1896, as citizens of Sacramento, California, watched a light moving through the night sky. Further sightings were reported from all parts of California throughout the month, with a few from farther north, in Washington State and Canada. A dark shape supporting the light could sometimes be glimpsed, and was variously said to be shaped like a cigar, a barrel or an egg. The airship's motion was slow and undulating, suggesting a wind-blown craft. Some newspapers named inventors who, they speculated, could be responsible. Others floated the idea that the airships were visitors from Mars. Occasionally, airships were seen on the ground: in one such case, two Methodist ministers saw a fiery object taking off as they approached. Three strange beings, very tall and with bald heads, allegedly attempted to kidnap two men on a country road, and then fled in a cigar-shaped craft.

After a two-month lull, the sightings again came thick and fast – this time, from all over the United States and Canada. At one point, each day saw a score of reports coming in – some of them quite startling. A citizen of Michigan, for example, reported that a voice from above the clouds asked him for four dozen egg sandwiches and a pot of coffee – which were duly hauled up to the unseen craft in a scoop. One witness even claimed to have seen a landing ship manned by Oriental-looking crew.

The main 'flap' was over by mid-1897. But later in the year, there were isolated sightings reported from other parts of the world, including Sweden, Norway and Russia.

In September 1897, for instance, some sort of balloon that seemed to have a bright sheen to it was seen by an engineer in the Russian town of Ustyug. Its exact nature was never discovered; but we do know that motor-controlled balloons had indeed been built in England and France by this apparently early date.

gone on to Cornell University in Ithica, New York. Here, by the mid 1890s, it was possible to obtain a bachelor's degree in aeronautics.

PIONEERS IN THE PUBLIC EYE

One of those who gave a series of lectures at Cornell University – noted nationally for its courses in aerodynamics – in 1897 and 1898 was Octave Chanute, the world-famous engineer. In 1896, he had emulated the successful manned hang-glider experiments of the German engineer Otto Lilienthal. The courses at the University included experimental engineering, mechanical and electrical engineering, as well as machine design and construction. Aeronautical texts would have included the Smithsonian Institute's *Experiments in Aerodynamics*, Sir Hiram Maxim's reports on his experiments with engines, propellers and aircraft designs, and the *Aeronautical Annual*, which contained highly innovative contributions from most of the leading aeronautical scientists of the time.

By 1896, the first successful flights of S.P. Langley's flying machines had taken place in Washington, DC; and by the following year, numerous patents for other types of flying machine had been registered. The scientific advances of the last decade of the 19th century were of staggering magnitude, laying the all-important ground work for advanced aeronautical experimentation. So if a particularly dedicated team of scientists did indeed happen to be working on an airship project, it certainly becomes possible that the sightings all over the country that took place during that period were indeed of man-made flying machines.

No more was heard of the mysterious Wilson, however. But the following years saw remarkable further advances in the field of aeronautics. By 1901, the Brazilian Alberto Santos-Dumont had succeeded in flying an airship from St-Cloud, on the western edge of Paris, to the Eiffel Tower and back in less than 30 minutes; two years later at Kitty Hawk, North Carolina, the Wright brothers made the first known heavier-than-air manned flight; and by 1906, the American Robert Goddard had begun his exciting experiment in rocketry. On the last day

The Flyer, above, **built by the Wright brothers, takes off on its first brief journey and inaugurates a new age. Four flights were made on that day, 17 December 1903 – the first sustained powered and controlled flights known to history. But could other inventors working in secret have anticipated the Wrights and been responsible for earlier airship sightings?**

Louis Bleriot's Number XI *flying machine,* **right,** *soars above the* **cliffs of Dover at the end of the** *prize-winning cross-Channel flight* **on 25 July 1909.**

of December 1908, Wilbur Smith flew 77 miles (123 kilometres) in just two hours and thirty minutes. Seven months later, the French aviator Louis Bleriot became the first to fly across the English Channel, from Calais to Dover.

Since these were all highly publicised achievements, is it possible that even greater advances were being made away from the public gaze? The numerous UFO sightings of the early 20th century and the rapid pace of technological development suggest that this may have been so. In 1904, US Navy Lieutenant Frank H. Schofield – later to be Commander-in-Chief of the US Pacific Fleet – officially reported seeing, from the deck of his ship, three bright lights that were travelling in echelon. They remained above the clouds, and ascended before disappearing. In 1909, numerous unidentified aircraft were reported over Massachusetts. On 30 August 1919, at about 9 p.m., a long black object flew low over Madison Square, New York City, and was witnessed by hundreds of people. The nature and origin of this object were never determined.

In 1933 and 1934, a wave of sightings occurred over Scandinavia. 'Ghost planes' were reported on scores of occasions, frequently appearing or heard overhead in 'impossible' conditions for aircraft of that time. They were described as monoplanes, usually grey in colour. Sometimes their crews could be glimpsed. Often their engines would cut out, and the aircraft would glide for long periods before their power was turned on again – an unlikely feat for conventional aircraft. Sometimes brilliant search-lights would be directed from them on to the ground below.

INVADED TERRITORY

In 1934, the Swedish Air Force began a thorough search of those remote areas from which the 'ghost plane' reports were emanating. Twenty-four aircraft took part in the search, and two of them actually crashed during it. No traces were found of the bases that would be required to support the activities of the intruders, however. In April 1934, a high-ranking Swedish military officer stated in an announcement to the press:

'Comparison of these reports shows that there can be no doubt about illegal air traffic over our secret military areas. . . . In every case, the same remark has been noted: no insignias or identifying marks were visible on the machine. . . . It is impossible to explain away the whole thing as imagination. The question is: Who are they? And why have they been invading our air territory?'

The same questions were by now being asked in Norway and Finland, too, where similar sightings were said to be occurring. But they were never satisfactorily answered either – so that the origin and purpose of these 'ghost planes' still remained utterly elusive.

Aeronautics now advanced from initial crude experiments with wind tunnels in Massachusetts to highly complex rocket research at Peenemünde on Germany's Baltic coast that led to the *V-2*. On the principle that all scientific research resembles an iceberg – in other words, nine-tenths is hidden from public view – the possibility arises that secret research in America, Europe, or both, had led to the construction of machines much more powerful and unorthodox in design than those that were officially put into use. Certainly, it is a fact that, from the First World War onward, more and more technological research was being financed and controlled by governments who were interested mainly in the military applications of craft built as a result of such research.

So the question inevitably remains: is it possible that citizens of the United States and certain European countries had witnessed the clandestine aeronautical experiments being carried out by their very own leaders?

The pace of aviation development accelerated still further during the years of the Second World War. Jet aircraft, radar navigation and detection, ballistic missiles and bombers of unprecedented size all appeared in response to the desperate necessities of the principal combatants. And sightings of equally mysterious craft – such as the balls of light, which became known as 'foo fighters' – then began to enter a new phase, in the skies over embattled Germany.

Only 40 years after the Wright brothers' first flight, air warfare had advanced to the point where rocket propelled, long range ballistic missiles were being prepared for use against cities. In the photograph below, three experimental V-2 rockets stand on their trailers at the Nazis' Peenemünde research centre.

❚❚ IT CONSISTED OF A GREAT CIGAR-SHAPED PORTION, POSSIBLY THREE HUNDRED FEET LONG, WITH A CARRIAGE UNDERNEATH... IT WAS BRILLIANTLY LIT WITHIN AND EVERYTHING WAS PLAINLY VISIBLE... THEY WERE JABBERING TOGETHER, BUT WE COULD NOT UNDERSTAND A WORD THEY SAID. ❚❚

YATES CENTER (KANSAS) FARMER'S ADVOCATE, 23 APRIL 1897

IN SEARCH OF LOST SOULS

example – are seen as the results of supernatural happenings in which the hunter is perhaps the subject of an attack by malicious spirits, or has failed to show due respect to the gods and thus incurs their displeasure. Perhaps – and this is the worst possibility of all – a part of his spirit has wandered from his body without the hunter realising it, to become lost or imprisoned by evil demons.

In many shamanistic tribes, bodily sickness, particularly illnesses associated with high temperature and delirium, such as typhus and smallpox, are attributed to the latter cause. Thus, among the Altaic tribes of Siberia, the belief was – and still is, for, in spite of many decades of communism, primitive communities still survive in this area – that really severe fevers were often caused by the imprisonment of the sick man's soul in the realms of Erlik Khan, one of the supreme rulers of the Underworld. It is clear that, in this context, the word translated into English as 'soul' means something more closely

THE TRIBAL SHAMAN OFTEN USES HALLUCINOGENIC DRUGS TO ENABLE HIM TO LEAVE HIS BODY AT WILL AND ENTER THE SPIRIT WORLD. HOW DOES THIS HELP HIM TEND THE SICK?

During the 1960s, the village of Huautla de Jimenez, Mexico, attracted American hippies because of the local shamans' practice of eating sacred mushrooms, as shown above right, *known for their capacity to produce visual and auditory hallucinations. Mushrooms are often eaten by the entire community in rituals to honour the dead. The woman,* above, *is on her way to a funeral, where she will partake of these sacred plants.*

akin to 'vitality' or 'life force' than to the 'soul' of Christian belief; for the Altaic tribesman believes it is perfectly possible to remain conscious, and even to conduct a rational conversation, when his 'soul' is absent from his body.

Just as it is believed that the shaman can travel upwards to the heavens while his body lies in trance, so it is thought possible for him to descend into the seven *pudaks* (literally, 'obstacles' – but the word 'hells' indicates the meaning of the word more precisely) of the infernal regions. This downwards journey is considered far more difficult and dangerous than the upwards transformation of consciousness into the nine heavens, so only the most powerful of shamans can undertake it. Even these supposedly risk death or madness when visiting the hells, and only the 'blue shamans' – men who are specialists in dealing with evil spirits – can make the journey in complete safety. And before a shaman will travel to Erlik Khan's black palace in search of the soul of a sick person, he will first set about searching more readily accessible locations.

The shaman, occupying an important position within many of the world's tribal societies, tends to see the physical world as inferior to, and conditioned by, the spirit world with which he communicates and to which he believes he travels when in trance.

Even the most ordinary physical events – a hunter's broken leg, or his failure to find game, for

The shaman therefore begins by entering a trance state, 'leaving his body', and looking for a strayed soul in the immediate vicinity of the sick person's yurt, or tent. If he finds the soul, he can usually coax it back into the body to which it properly belongs, so it is believed.

If, however, the soul is not nearby, the shaman searches further afield. He sends his spirit to examine the beds of lakes and rivers (both unlikely locations appear to be popular with truant Siberian souls), the depths of the forest, and the vast plains of the steppes. From all these places, the shaman's spirit can usually persuade the lost soul to return home, although the task is not quite as easy as when the soul has remained near its yurt. If the shaman's urgings are still in vain, and the soul will not return to its bodily home, the illness continues and the patient dies.

If the soul cannot be found, it is concluded that it is held hostage in the palace of Erlik Khan. The only way to get it back is to conduct a kind of infernal exchange of prisoners: Erlik will release a soul only if he is given another in exchange for it.

The shaman then negotiates a fee for the ransoming of the lost soul, either with the sick man's family or, if the patient is capable of conversation, the man himself. At the same time, it is decided whose soul shall be stolen and delivered to Erlik – most likely, some individual who has displeased both shaman and patient. While the chosen victim is asleep, the shaman enters a trance and leaves his body. He then transforms his spirit, usually into the form of an eagle or another bird of prey: shape-shifting is one of the arts in which shamans excel. The shaman-eagle now flies to the victim's yurt, dives upon his body, and seizes the struggling soul.

The palace of Erlik Khan – in Siberian mythology, one of the supreme rulers of the Underworld – is shown right. In order to cure the illness of a patient, the shaman, in the form of an eagle, captures the soul of an innocent victim and carries it struggling to the palace of Erlik Khan. There, he exchanges it for the soul of the sick person which which thereafter will be imprisoned within the walls of the palace.

Then begins the journey downwards to Erlik Khan's palace. When this sinister dwelling, built of black boulders cemented together with black clay, is reached, the shaman politely asks the infernal ruler to make the exchange of souls, and the latter usually agrees. The shaman then returns the released soul to the body of the patient, who now begins an immediate recovery. But the man whose soul has been stolen and delivered to Erlik Khan falls ill, soon becomes sicker, and eventually dies.

Sometimes, a shamanistic procedure involving trance is undertaken, not so much for the sake of curing an illness but in order to determine its eventual outcome – to find out whether the gods have decreed life or death for the patient. A team led by R. Gordon Wasson has actually tape-recorded a Mexican ceremony of this type in its entirety.

This rite was performed on the night of 12 July 1958, in the Mazatic village of Huautla, by three shamans, two of them women, for the purpose of finding out whether a 17-year-old boy, Perfeto, would eventually recover from the chest illness –

probably tuberculosis – with which he was afflicted. On the basis of divine messages they received at the height of the ritual, the shamans prophesied death, a gloomy prognosis that was to be fulfilled a few weeks later. These messages were directly heard by the shamans: any visions they saw were transitory and regarded by them as being comparatively unimportant.

DIVINE CONTACT

The emphasis on what is heard, rather than what is seen, in Mexican shamanistic trance, is in marked contrast to its Siberian counterpart, and probably originates in a purely physical cause. Mexican shamans generally induce trance states by eating a particular type of semi-poisonous mushroom that is noted for its ability to produce auditory hallucinations. This 'divine mushroom' is unique only in that the hallucinations it produces are primarily aural rather than visual; for in every part of the world shamans use hallucinogenic plants as a way of 'loosening the girders of the soul', entering into trance and, so it is believed, coming into contact with gods, demons and lost souls. In Siberia, for example, shamans drink an infusion of the dried heads of *amanita muscaria*, the fly agaric mushroom or red, white-spotted 'toadstool' that often features in illustrated books of fairy tales as a quick method of achieving trance and vision.

The use of fly agaric has been, and remains, very widespread in Siberia. In the 18th century, Count von Strahlenberg, a Swedish officer who had been a prisoner in Siberia for some years, described how the local population reached a state of 'drunkenness'. They did not, he reported, know the use of fermented liquors, but instead relied on an infusion of fly agaric, a sort of 'mushroom tea'. This drink, he added, was so highly valued by the tribesmen that the dried heads of the mushroom had become an article of commerce, a luxury that only the rich could afford. 'Those', added the observant Swede, 'who cannot afford to buy in a store of these mushrooms, post themselves... around the huts of the rich, and watch the opportunity of the guests coming out to make water; and they hold a wooden bowl to receive the urine, which they drink off greedily, as having still some virtue of the mushroom in it, and by this way they also get drunk.'

BAD TRIPS

The 'drunkenness' observed by von Strahlenberg was very different from alcoholic intoxication. Steven Krassenikov, another 18th-century observer of Siberian tribal culture, remarked that those who underwent it were subject to various visions, terrifying or happy, depending upon differences in temperament. Some would jump, some dance, others cry and apparently suffer great terrors, while some might deem a small crack to be as wide as a door, and a tub of water as deep as the ocean.

In other words, the drinking of fly agaric was often productive of something closely resembling both the 'bad trip' of the LSD-user and a shamanistic trance, in which the shaman loses control over the flood of images that suddenly fills his consciousness during a trance state.

Many anthropologists and students of ancient religion assert that the use of fungi and other plant substances to induce changes of consciousness is of great antiquity, probably almost as old as humanity itself. Thus, for example, in classical Greece, ergot – a fungus that grows on rye and other grasses – was administered to initiates of the mystery cult of Eleusis in order that they might be able to 'see the goddess'.

The object below is a 'soul-catcher' of the mid 10th century, found on the north-west coast of America. Like the Siberians, many of the North American Indian tribes believed that the souls of sick people went wandering in the underworld, and that shamans could cure a patient by retrieving his soul and then returning it to the body.

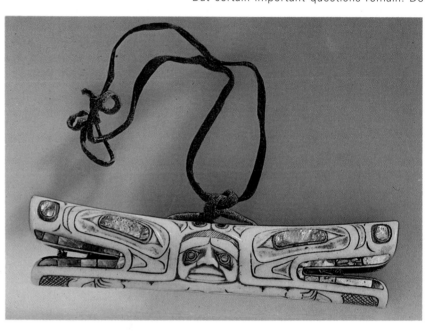

The puppet, left, was found by the Nass river in British Columbia, USA, in 1910. It was used by shamans of the Tsimshian tribe in both dramatic performances and healing ceremonies.

Similarly, in ancient India, a substance called *soma* was reputed to be both 'the food of the gods' and the chosen food of those wishing to come into contact with those gods. While the nature of soma has been the subject of much scholarly dispute – one eccentric academic of the last century believed it to have been rhubarb, a substance with laxative properties that seemed to him to be almost supernatural – it is now thought that it was some hallucinogenic substance taken by shamans in order to experience something supposed to resemble the life of the immortals.

But certain important questions remain. Do shamans have genuine supernormal powers? Can they transcend normal consciousness? Or are they simply inducing vivid hallucinations?

Roman Catholic priests, who accompanied Spanish soldiers and administrators to the Americas in the 16th and 17th centuries, had no doubt of the answer to these questions. Some shamans, they averred, were able to obtain knowledge of the future and of things happening in distant places. But these supernormal abilities owed nothing, they said, to the personality of the individual shaman: rather, they were the gift of Satan, master of all shamans and wizards.

More than one Spanish chronicler asserted that the information given by shamans was 'perfectly

❚❚ ONE OF THE MOST EFFECTIVE HALLUCINATION-PRODUCING DRUGS IS THAT USED BY THE INDIANS OF COLUMBIA... YAGÉ... THE NATIVES BELIEVE IN ITS CLAIRVOYANT EFFICACY... ❚❚

D.H. RAWCLIFFE, OCCULT AND SUPERNATURAL PHENOMENA

" THE MEDICINE MAN IS NOT ALWAYS

A PARAGON OF VIRTUE AND SEX

MORALITY... ON HIS RECOVERY FROM

THE THEOPNEUSTIC TRANCE, HIS

REPRESSED EMOTIONS SOMETIMES

EXPLODE WITH ABNORMAL

VIOLENCE... IT NOT INFREQUENTLY

HAPPENS THAT AFTER THEIR RETURN

TO NORMAL CONSCIOUSNESS, THE

REPRESENTATIVES OF THE GODS ARE

GUILTY OF UNSPEAKABLE

DISSOLUTENESS. **"**

J.L. MADDOX, THE MEDICINE MAN

exact'. Thus, Gonzalo d'Oviedo y Valdez stated that American-Indian shamans had secret means of putting themselves into communication with spirits 'whenever they wish to predict the future'. He had personally witnessed shamanistic rites and claimed to have observed the accuracy of the predictions made. The shaman, he wrote, 'appeared to be in ecstasy and to be suffering strange pains . . . while he lay senseless on the ground, the chief, or some other, asked what they desired to know, and the spirit replied through the mouth of the inspired man in a manner perfectly exact.'

Spanish-speaking theologians, particularly Jesuits, regarded shamanism as a dangerous and diabolical parody of the genuine physical and psychical phenomena associated with Roman Catholic mysticism. Priests were instructed to question Indian converts to Christianity closely as to whether they had drunk peyote – the favourite hallucinogen of Mexican shamans, made from cactus tops 'in order to find out secrets or discover the where-abouts of lost or stolen articles'.

The very nature of shamanistic activity dictates that there can be no hard scientific proof of the validity or otherwise of many of the claims made by its practitioners. On a purely anecdotal level, there is a good deal of evidence that some shamans do experience what seems to be genuine clairvoyance and clairaudience. And in the absence of hard scientific evidence, there is no proof that they do not leave their bodies to enter the spirit world.

SQUATTERS IN THE MIND

CERTAIN INDIVIDUALS SEEM TO POSSESS A HOST OF DIFFERENT SELVES THAT COME AND GO CONTINUALLY. WHAT LIES BEHIND SUCH CASES OF FLUID AND UNCERTAIN IDENTITY?

The history of Man's advance since the medieval period has been the story of his gradual realisation of how little he seems to matter in the scheme of things. From the pre-Copernican view that he lived at the centre of the Universe – a Universe that was not very much larger than the Earth – he has been forced by modern astronomical discoveries to accept that the Earth is but an insignificant dot in the Galaxy, while the Galaxy, in relation to the visible Universe, is the size of a speck of dust in a cathedral. His fond conceit that he was 'Lord of Creation' over the beasts of the field has been swept away by Darwin and his

Are such creatures as those in **The Sleep of Reason Brings Forth Monsters,** *by Goya,* above, *the products of our own unconscious minds – or are they sometimes intruders from outside? Evidence suggests that our minds may not in fact enjoy undisputed possession of our bodies.*
In **The Three Faces of Eve,** *Joanne Woodward,* right, *played a multiple personality victim, with one self who behaved uninhibitedly.*

successors: indeed, to many, he seems simply to be an animal species that grew a large brain and is now in serious danger of following both the dinosaur and the dodo to extinction. In the 19th century, his assumption that he was at least in charge of his mind, overseeing its workings and guiding it according to rational purposes, was also undermined by Freud's theories of the subconscious. Freud discovered that large tracts of Man's thinking processes lay behind a barrier. Often, decisions were taken there and then surfaced: thus, in implementing them, Man was cast more in the role of public relations officer than of managing director.

Notwithstanding such withdrawals to more modest estimates of his position, Man could still console himself with the belief that, at any rate, his mental processes, conscious and unconscious, originated within his skull, woven on the marvellous electrochemical loom of his brain. The raw materials feeding the brain came both through his five senses and the nerves monitoring his body.

THE SPIRITUAL FACTOR

This view is even held by a large proportion of those who still pay lip service to the religious teachings that there is a non-material factor – the spiritual – capable of influencing and being contacted by human beings. Some believe that their thoughts are their own, and that their dreams, by night or by day, are the products of their mind and brain: their fantasies, their wishful thinking, belong solely to them. If they are surprised or terrified by the events in their dreams, they attribute this to the fact that the dream-producer, the 'master of ceremonies', is their unconscious, that they have had too much to eat for supper, or that they are worried about something. In their dreams, they are like a person at the cinema who views a film he has had no hand in producing. 'What an imagination I have!' they say in self-admiration.

Unfortunately, not all people can believe this to be the case – among them, multiple personality cases, in which a number of distinct characters dispute the possession of one body. In some such individuals, it seems that the original personality has been shattered by one or more traumatic experiences and has given rise to 'secondary' personalities. But others, carefully studied by psychiatrists, demonstrate such bizarre features that the possibility of actual invasion by independent personalities, or parts of personalities, has to be seriously considered. If such a theory seems to the man in the street to be a woeful return to the superstitions of the Dark Ages, its proponents would reply that he is simply ignorant of the facts.

During the last 100 years or so, scores of multiple personality cases have been treated and carefully studied by authorities such as Freud, Jung, William James, Morton Prince, Walter F. Prince and others. Many have common features; but it is rash to assume that the same explanation will suffice to cover all of them.

Let us suppose that the personality is a girl. Often she is quiet, reserved, joyless, hyperconscientious. Often she has had a very unhappy upbringing, and is the product of a violent home. She may find herself puzzling over lost stretches of time, the events of which she cannot remember. Strange clothes appear in her wardrobe, and she gradually comes to fear for her sanity. If she consults a psychiatrist, she may be fortunate enough to find one who recognises her condition and encounters one or more secondary personalities that from time to time surface to take control of the body and obliterate the dowdy, everyday personality.

In a number of cases, the major secondary personality turns out to be bright and fun-loving, openly contemptuous of the quiet girl with whom she shares a body. Dislike and contempt of the secondary personality may find an outlet in playing

Dr Walter Franklin Prince, a minister of religion and also a psychologist, above, investigated many cases of multiple personality and of apparent possession by spirits. One of his most celebrated cases was that of Doris Fischer, who had five personalities – one of whom claimed to be a form of guardian spirit.

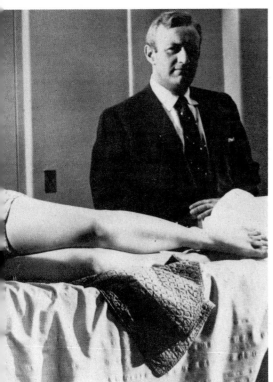

tricks upon the bewildered rival, who has no knowledge of the fun-lover's existence, nor memories of the experiences of the other. On the other hand, the fun-lover is often fully aware of everything the dowdy one experiences when the latter is in control. So different are the two characters that the psychiatrist treating the case knows which personality is in control immediately the girl enters the room – a knowledge due not only to different tastes in fashion but also to an almost physical transformation of the patient's face. Truly, Robert Louis Stevenson displayed remarkable insight into the complexities of the human mind when he wrote *Dr Jekyll and Mr Hyde* in the late 19th century.

ONE BODY, FIVE OCCUPANTS

As many as five or six separate personalities in one body, quite distinct in their beliefs, ethics and mental ages, have been displayed in a number of cases. In that of an American woman, Doris Fischer – studied by Dr Walter F. Prince of Pittsburgh – for instance, there were five personalities: Doris, Margaret, Ariel, Sick Doris and Sleeping Real Doris. Doris was the 'normal' quiet, bewildered personality, while Margaret was the mischievous one who got Doris into trouble. Ariel appeared when Doris was asleep and always claimed to be a spirit who had come to protect her. Sick Doris gave the impression of being a dull, nervous, timid, almost simple-minded person. Sleeping Real Doris seems to have had predominantly the role of guardian of memories: she had no marked separate personality, but could reel off memories of past events, like a living tape-recorder. Dr Prince described her as 'sleeping' because this ability lay dormant most of the time.

Dr Prince and his wife took the sorely troubled girl to stay with them, almost as a daughter; and thanks to the Princes' care and psychiatric treatment, the girl's mental and physical health improved over the next few years. During that time, the complex relationship among the five personalities inhabiting the body of Doris Fischer altered. At first, Margaret had access to the contents of Doris' and Sick Doris' minds, while Ariel was acquainted with the minds of all three. Sometimes, quarrels would occur for control of the body. As time went on, Doris extended her control, as Sick Doris and then Sleeping Real Doris gradually deteriorated and finally disappeared. It was then the turn of Margaret, the sharp, fun-loving one who was slowly to recede until she, too, vanished.

There is a touching and thought-provoking account of the last days of Sick Doris. As she began to disintegrate, she seemed to realise that she was going to disappear. She accompanied Dr Prince on a last walk and left a letter for Margaret. (One of the ways by which each entity communicated with the others was by writing letters when in control. These would be read when the appropriate personality took over the body.) In her letter, Sick Doris instructed Margaret as to what to do with her possessions after her demise and tried to leave her sister-personality some helpful advice.

To the end, Ariel maintained her claim that she was a spirit, sent to look after Doris. In his account, Dr Prince admits that, to him, she was the most

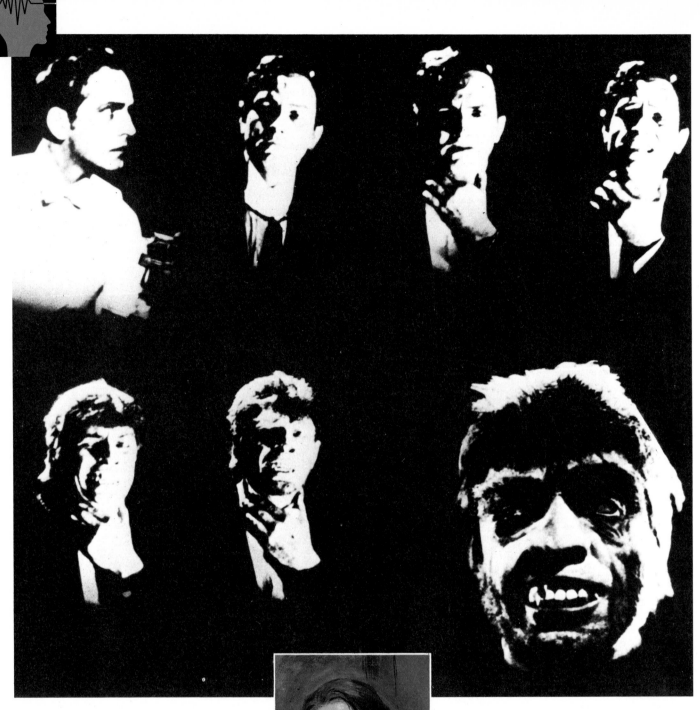

mature and wise of all the personalities and that he had to consider seriously the hypothesis that her claim was in some way true.

The Christine Beauchamp case displayed many similarities to the Doris Fischer case and is quite often confused with the latter, especially since it was treated by another Dr Prince – this time, Dr Morton Prince, a professor at the Tufts Medical School in Boston, USA. Christine Beauchamp was a student, and was approaching a nervous breakdown when she first consulted him. He tried hypnosis, finding that she was a good subject. But to his surprise, a distinct personality emerged – a relaxed, very much calmer version, whom Prince called *B-2* to distinguish her from the first Christine, *B-1*. But more was to follow. *B-2*, under hypnosis, was always rubbing her closed eyes. Prince discovered that it was a third personality, at first called *B-3*, who did the rubbing in an effort to get them open.

B-3 insisted that she had a right to see; and on a subsequent occasion, she at last managed to open Christine's eyes. From then on, she insisted on being known as Sally. She was a bright, mischievous person, not nearly so well-educated as Christine, but exhibiting perfect health in contrast to Christine's debilitated and nervous state. She seemed to hate Christine and claimed that she never slept, but stayed awake while the other personality was asleep. She also continually tormented Christine with practical jokes. According to Dr Prince, Sally went out into the country where she collected in a box some snakes and spiders. She packed them up and addressed the package to Christine, who opened the box in due time and went into screaming hysterics – not surprisingly, since she had a horror of snakes and spiders.

Sally would also force the strait-laced Christine into embarrassing situations in which she would

The transformation of the decent Dr Jekyll into the bestial Mr Hyde, is shown, **left,** *in stills from a film version of the classic tale by Robert Louis Stevenson,* **inset.** *Hyde was in fact a fragment of a personality – the repressed evil side of Jekyll's nature. In many ways, Stevenson, writing in 1886, anticipated Freud in his view of a potentially destructive, dark side of the mind that threatens the world of reason and light.*

have to tell lies. In spite of Dr Prince's efforts, this feud continued until, quite suddenly, a fourth personality, *B-4*, surfaced. *B-4* was a mature, responsible, firm personality who defended the luckless Christine from Sally's torments by giving Sally as good – or as bad – as she gave Christine.

Dr Prince decided that, if he could merge *B-1* and *B-4* and suppress Sally, he might get in tune with the true Christine. Using his hypnotic skills, he attempted to achieve this goal. It is not surprising to learn that Sally resisted to the end, claiming that she had every right to live and enjoy life. But Dr Prince succeeded in producing a more complete personality for Christine, though not quite eliminating Sally. As the years went by, Sally appeared from time to time, as if revisiting old haunts, to indulge herself by playing tricks on Christine.

If a personality under shock can shatter into fragments, so that each fragment is made up of a fraction of all those moods, emotions, beliefs, prejudices, and desires that contribute to the 'normal' person, then – even though, in the Doris Fischer case, Ariel claimed to be a spirit – we can still cling to the belief that no outside influences are at work. But there are a number of cases that, to certain investigators, stretch this hypothesis almost to breaking point.

*In*Focus

OF MORE THAN ONE MIND

It has been suggested that population figures for the United States should be increased – so many of its citizens seem to be afflicted, or favoured, by extra personalities.

William Milligan, **left,** *was finally diagnosed as having ten different personalities – one of them, a teenage lesbian.*

William Milligan, for instance, was found guilty of raping four young women in Columbus, Ohio, in 1976. He was diagnosed as having ten personalities – of whom the guilty one was an 18-year-old lesbian. One of the psychiatrists who hastened to interview Milligan was Dr Cornelia Wilbur. She had previously treated 'Sybil', the subject of a book and a film, who is said to have had as many as 16 personalities.

But these cases are surely excelled by that of 'Charles' – the pseudonym given by a psychiatrist to what he hoped was the core personality of one of his patients, Eric, who had been found wandering in a daze in Daytona Beach, Florida, in February 1982. Eric immediately 'split' into two selves – 'young Eric' and 'older Eric'.

'Young Eric' told a (fictitious) tale of how he had been brought up by drug dealers, of having been raped, and of having witnessed murders committed by his stepfather.

Further personalities emerged over a period of weeks. These included violent 'Mark', arrogant 'Michael', and blind and mute 'Jeffrey'. Finally, the psychiatrist identified no fewer than 27. The youngest of them was a foetus.

Many of the selves were in conflict and created problems for each other. 'Michael', for example, was athletic and once went on a long jog that left 'Eric' – and all the other occupants of his body – physically aching for days. 'Charles', supposedly the true personality, said afterwards of his existence: 'I've lived through hell. I'm surprised I didn't go crazy.'

As more and more cases of poltergeist activity are subjected to rigorous investigation by parapsychologists, a clearer picture is emerging not only of the possible causes of such phenomena, but also of those who are generally the victims. There are, of course, cases that evade classification, but research into recurrent spontaneous psychokinesis (RSPK) appears to support certain broad conclusions.

The sexual drive, or libido, seems to be at the root of many paranormal experiences. In the 1840s, for instance, when the case of the Fox sisters stirred up a great deal of interest in the United States and elsewhere, it was widely assumed that the girls' experiences were associated with the fact that they had just reached puberty. Other cases that were examined at that time appeared to confirm the assumption that girls on the threshold of sexual maturity were to be blamed for all such

SEX AND THE MISCHIEVOUS SPIRIT

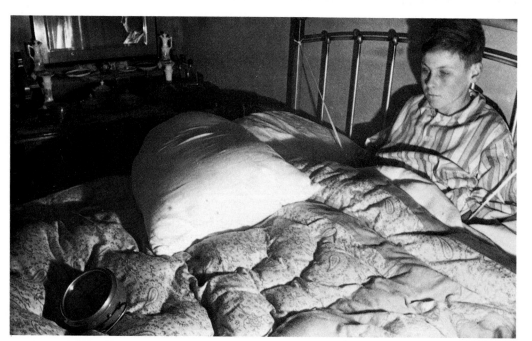

The 10-year-old boy, above, was being filmed when the walking-stick hanging from his bed head jerked and jumped about of its own accord.

12-year-old Alan Rhodes, left, had his hands taped to the bedclothes to guard against trickery when his poltergeist was investigated by researcher Harry Price in 1945. Even so, the alarm clock managed to jump on to his bed, and was later joined by a trinket case from the dressing table.

mysterious incidents: only young women, it was thought, could summon up reserves of energy capable of moving tables, producing strange sounds and causing objects to appear and disappear – the familiar signs of poltergeist activity.

Certainly, many cases today also involve girls at about the age of puberty. In the classic case of the family living in the London suburb of Enfield, who experienced intense and protracted disturbances between 1977 and 1978, for example, Janet – the 12-year-old daughter – was clearly the epicentre. Shirley Hitchings of Battersea, another famous victim of poltergeist activity, was 14 years old at the time. One middle-aged mother with a 12-year-old daughter, meanwhile, told a parapsychologist that her family had experienced a number of incidents of RSPK during the course of a few weeks, both in the kitchen and in her daughter's bedroom.

'Bumps, crashes and saucepans flying about – you know, the usual type of thing. But when Sheila started her menses, it all stopped, of course. It was all a bit of a nuisance at the time, but we are all right now.'

Eleanora Zugun, above, would develop mysterious marks on her face whenever she felt insulted.

> **❝ At five minutes past midnight on Monday, 16 December 1968, I was walking behind twelve-year-old Roger Cullihan as he entered the kitchen of his house. When he came to the sink, he turned toward me and at that moment the kitchen table... jumped into the air, rotated about 45 degrees and came to rest on the backs of the chairs that stood around it... ❞**
>
> **Dr W.G. Roll, The Poltergeist**

Fox case, for instance, two sisters out of three were involved; and at Enfield, both Janet and her sister were at the centre of many of the incidents. (Interestingly, another family member, Janet's brother, was at the time attending a school for the mentally subnormal; subnormality is often – though by no means always – associated with outbreaks of poltergeist activity.)

In some cases, girls are not involved at all, though a hundred years ago, male victims of RSPK were often ignored or discounted, so entrenched was the view that pubescent girls were always the source of poltergeist activity. The experiences of one sensitive, D.D. Home, did provoke more serious examination of paranormal incidents associated with men, however; but investigators were content to conclude that Home was a homosexual and left the matter there.

Apart from the onset of puberty, another common feature has been observed in young victims of RSPK. Janet and her sister in Enfield were obsessed with Starsky and Hutch, the heroes of a television series; Shirley Hitchings adored James Dean, the film star; and another poltergeist victim was infatuated with Dr Who, the character in a major science fiction serial. It has been suggested that this sort of passion, involving fictional characters, serves to ensure that the powerful force deployed by such girls is unconstrained by the influences of normal day-to-day life.

Such isolation from the norm was even more apparent in the case of a young Romanian peasant girl, Eleanora Zugun, who was able, between the ages of 12 and 15, to produce marks on her body whenever she felt that her personal 'devil' was being insulted. At the slightest word or gesture that she interpreted as offensive, scratches and bites would appear on her face and arms.

Although young girls are often the focus of RSPK, however, it has been observed that they are rarely the sole agents of the disturbances. In the

Rappings regularly disturbed the Fox family, above, in a case that helped to establish the assumption that poltergeist activity was particularly associated with young girls.

The scratches on the arm of a 19-year-old girl from Rotherhithe, England, right, erupted spontaneously, apparently as a result of emotional disturbances.

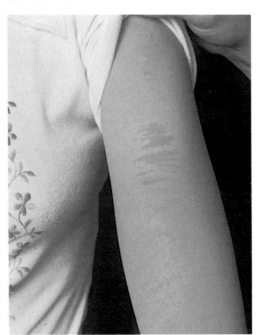

The Harper family from Enfield, left, *were affected by some of the most elaborate and remarkable poltergeist activity on record.*

In recent years, male sensitives, young boys and men alike, have received a more sympathetic hearing. One 10-year-old boy was filmed as he lay in bed, awake, while a walking-stick moved of its own accord, in erratic jerks, behind the head of his bed. Like many young epicentres, he was of an extremely nervous disposition and, again in common with other victims, was anaemic.

Another fascinating case involved two boys in Glasgow, between August 1974 and May 1975. The boys were 15 and 11 years old, and lived with their parents in a tenement flat. A series of 'peculiar sounds' was heard, followed by communicative raps. It turned out that the boys, without knowing it, were linked telepathically with an old man who lived in a flat on the ground floor and who was afflicted by a malignant tumour. As the old man's condition deteriorated, the raps became more frequent. They ceased, suddenly, when the old man died. But perhaps the most celebrated case of all is that of Matthew Manning – the well-known healer – who, at the age of 11, was able to produce a variety of genuine phenomena at will. Disturbances occurred both at his Cambridge home and at school: beds moved; stones appeared inexplicably; and sudden cold spots were discovered. His brother and sister, meanwhile, seemed to be unaffected by the experiences.

But it would be inaccurate to assume that RSPK is linked exclusively with puberty. Indeed, a survey carried out in the 1950s indicated that seven was the age at which most children were particularly sensitive and receptive, and this finding has been confirmed by subsequent studies – although children as young as four or five have also been identified as epicentres. Most are quite unaware that they are responsible for the disturbances. Their powers vary: some, like Shirley Hitchings, have to 'screw up their eyes as if concentrating' in order to produce intelligent raps; and many of the children who are able to bend metal (in the manner of Uri Geller) have only to gaze at the object for a moment or two, and then glance away, for the metal to move or twist.

Anne-Marie Schneider, below, *sent her employer's telephone bill soaring when her poltergeist constantly dialled the speaking clock. Once she married, however, the activity ceased.*

At the other end of the age range, adults long past the age of puberty also experience poltergeist activity, although in many cases there does appear to be an unequivocal link between sexuality and RSPK. Interestingly, the majority of mediums who provoke – or claim to provoke – physical phenomena are women in their middle years, who have reached the menopause, when their metabolism is disturbed, much as it is at puberty. In this connection, it is worth mentioning that Janet's mother, at Enfield, was just at that age – a fact that may well have contributed to the intensity of the poltergeist activity in the household. Among mediums of both sexes, there are also those who admit to sexual frustration and who acknowledge that seances provide a form of sexual release.

PENT-UP EMOTION

Sexual maladjustment may indeed contribute to, or heighten, sensitivity; and certainly, a number of recent cases suggest that RSPK may be related to frustration and distress. One involved a man of 48, who was living with his elderly uncle in a large house in York, England. Whenever the younger man entered his study, the room appeared to react to his presence: his desk moved; chairs shuffled across the floor; the curtains blew into the room even on airless days; and the windows would open and shut rapidly. Such incidents persisted for nearly three years, increasing in frequency and intensity all the time, until mental exhaustion eventually forced the man to seek medical assistance. He was found to be sexually impotent and given treatment. Within a week, the phenomena ceased.

Another case was that of a family of four who lived in Somerset, south-west England. For some months, the household had been disrupted by paranormal incidents of all kinds, and the two teenage children were assumed to be the cause. But when the case was investigated, it appeared to be the father, and not the children, who was the source of the disturbance. He was a professional man of 49, who had become increasingly concerned about his promotion prospects at work, had developed insomnia and had become sexually impotent. Anxiety finally pushed him towards the brink of breakdown. But once he had been given the help and encouragement that he needed, the family experienced no further disruption.

A similarly strange case of this kind was documented in Bavaria, in Germany, in 1967. A number of inexplicable incidents were observed by employees at the office of a lawyer, accompanied by an alarming increase in the size of the telephone bill. The electricity and telephone companies were alerted and requested to check all equipment in the building, and Professor Hans Bender undertook an investigation of the case. A survey of the numbers dialled from the office revealed that one particular number was constantly being activated, though no one was dialling it: the number was that of the speaking clock, O119. Eventually, Professor Bender traced the incidents to the source – a 19-year-old girl called Anne-Marie. He concluded that she was dissatisfied with her working conditions and was generally unhappy, for she seemed to have a remarkable effect on the machines in the office, which she admitted she disliked, and on other electrical

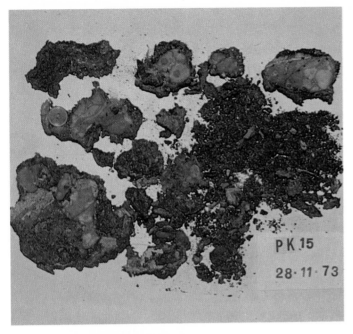

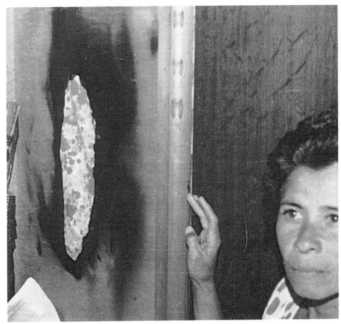

Two worrying cases of spontaneous combustion – a feature of poltergeist activity – both involved girls in Brazil. One, which affected a family in Sao Paulo for six years, caused clothes to be set on fire inside a closed wardrobe and reduced them to ashes, as shown above left; *while the other, occurring in Suzano in 1970, burned the wardrobe,* above right. *When the police were called, they too became the victims of mysterious fires.*

Council house tenants Mary Sharman and her two sons, left, *were victims of poltergeist disturbances for 12 years. The trouble stopped when the family moved house.*

equipment. Overhead lamps would swing to and fro whenever she passed underneath them, and the fluid in photo-copying machines would spill on to the floor. The only plausible explanation for the steep rise in the telephone bill was that Anne-Marie was bored with her job and was mentally clock-watching, stimulating a response from the speaking clock. On the day that Anne-Marie was married, all such incidents seemed to cease.

Sexual maladjustment is not the only source of tension or distress, however: indeed, researchers believe that RSPK may be related to many other conditions. Migraine and temporal lobe epilepsy are common among middle-aged epicentres and sensitives, for example; and there is evidence to suggest that there could be some link between these disorders and 'psychic' faculties. It has even been observed that the parents of many young epicentres hold conflicting religious views, which appear to trigger distress in their children that in turn leads to outbreaks of RSPK.

But perhaps the most significant finding of recent research is that 86 per cent of all poltergeist activity is experienced by families that have recently moved into council houses. It is not hard to find an explanation for this. Any move is bound to be disturbing; and in these circumstances, it is hardly surprising that tension generated by the members of the family, both individually and as a group, should provoke incidents and noises that cannot be readily explained away, or that ultimately many families – frightened and distraught – should demand to be rehoused.

Any attempt to provide a definitive categorisation of actual and potential poltergeist epicentres needs to be based on thorough psychological and medical examination of all victims who can be identified, but such examinations are hardly ever conducted. Investigators have, on the whole, been too anxious to record incidents, or to eliminate the possibility of fraud, to concern themselves with study of the mental and physical state of victims and their families.

// THE POLTERGEIST WAS PLAYING UP EVERY TIME HE WENT TO SEE HIS GIRLFRIEND AND TORMENTED HER IN HIS ABSENCE. IT TORMENTED HIM, TOO, AT NIGHT. IT WOULD GET HOLD OF HIM IN BED, AND HOLD HIM FAST WHILE IT TICKLED HIS FACE AND TUGGED HIS HAIR. //

MARY WILLIAMS, THE POLTERGEIST MAN, JOURNAL OF ANALYTICAL PSYCHOLOGY, VOL. 8

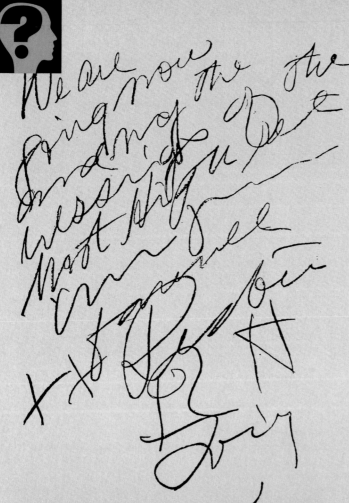

MESSAGES FROM BEYOND

A GROUP OF DEDICATED PSYCHICAL
RESEARCHERS PLANNED – AFTER THEIR DEATHS
– TO SEND EVIDENCE OF THEIR SURVIVAL TO
CERTAIN CHOSEN MEDIUMS

An ardent and vociferous believer in the after-life, Frederic Myers – classical scholar and founder member of the Society for Psychical Research (SPR) – wished passionately to communicate his belief to others. But to judge from an impressive body of evidence, he never desired it more than after his death in 1901. For the following 30 years, the SPR collected and collated over 2,000 automatic scripts, said to be transmitted from Myers and other deceased members of the Society, through the mediumship of several ladies. These messages seem to have been specifically designed to prove to the living the reality of the afterlife.

What have become known as the 'cross-corre-spondences' do indeed seem to point to some kind

Frederic Myers, above, respected
founder member of Britain's
Society for Psychical Research, is
said to have tried to prove his
survival after death to his living
friends and colleagues. He
supposedly sent messages
through various mediums, in
widely separated parts of the
world, by means of automatic
writing, which he had studied
intensively in life. The fragment,
above left, is in a hand markedly
different from the normal script of
the medium who produced it.

of intelligent communication between the living and the dead – arranged in such a way as to confound critics. Whoever thought up the system, on this or the other side of the veil, was very ingenious.

Apart from Myers, the purported spirit communi-cators were Edmund Grundy (died 1888) and Professor Henry Sidgwick (died 1900). The medi-ums included 'Mrs Holland' (pseudonym of Mrs Alice Flemming), who lived in India and was the sis-ter of Rudyard Kipling; 'Mrs Willett' (pseudonym of Mrs Combe-Tennant), who lived in London; Mrs A. W. Verrall, a teacher of Classics at Cambridge University, England; her daughter, Helen (later, Mrs W.H. Slater); and the famous American trance medium, Leonora Piper of Boston, Massachusetts.

A COMPLEX PLAN

The purpose and design of the cross-correspon-dences is bold yet at the same time complex. But it is this very complexity that gives them their unique air of authenticity. The plan, as far as it can be understood, was as follows.

After Myers' death, he and his deceased col-leagues from the SPR worked out a system by which fragments of automatic script, meaningless in themselves, would be transmitted through differ-ent mediums in widely separated parts of the world. When brought together, however, they would prove to make sense. To make understand-ing them all the more difficult, the fragments were to be in Greek or Latin, or contain allusions – some-times fragmentary in themselves – to classical works. In Myers' words, as dictated to Mrs Verrall: 'Record the bits and, when fitted, they will make the whole . . . I will give the words between you neither alone can read, but together they will give the clue he wants.'

The classical references were way beyond the scope of most of the mediums, except for the Verralls, showing that the scripts were not the products of their own minds. The fact that the fragments were unintelligible to the mediums themselves also ruled out the possibility of joint telepathic composition by them.

It seems that Myers thought of this plan once he had the ultimate personal proof of the afterlife. None of the thoughts he recorded during his earthly life even hints at this scheme. But at least he knew how to set about proving his point since, as an ex-president of the SPR, he knew which mediums were genuine and competent automatic 'scribes'.

The various automatists – in England, India and the United States – were instructed to send their apparently meaningless scripts to certain investigators, whose addresses were supplied. Each piece of automatic script was to be carefully dated and, if possible, witnessed.

An example of what H. F. Saltmarsh, in *Evidence of Personal Survival,* calls a 'simple' cross-correspondence is as follows. Mrs Piper, in America, heard – in a trance state – a word she first took to be *sanatos.* She then corrected herself (she was speaking her impressions out loud to be written down) to *tanatos.* That was on 17 April 1907. Later in the month, the word came through as *thanatos,* and on another occasion was repeated three times. On 7 May, the whole phrase 'I want to

Leonora Piper, below, was one of the most celebrated mediums of modern times. Several of the distinguished researchers who studied her, including Myers, allegedly communicated through her after their deaths.

say *thanatos'* came through. Mrs Piper did not recognise the word as being the Greek for 'death', however.

Meanwhile, on 16 April 1907, Mrs Holland in India received a curious opening phrase in her automatic script: 'Maurice Morris Mors. And with that the shadow of death fell on his limbs.' The two names seemed to be an attempt to get to the word *mors* – Latin for 'death'.

SYMBOL OF DEATH

On 29 April 1907, Mrs Verrall – in Cambridge – received this cryptic communication: 'Warmed both hands before the fire of life. It fades and I am ready to depart.' Then her hand drew what she took to be the Greek capital letter *delta* (a triangle). Next came these disjointed phrases: 'Give lilies with full hands [in Latin] . . . Come away, Come away, *Pallida mors* [Latin, meaning 'pale death'].

There are several allusions to death here: apparently, Mrs Verrall had always seen *delta* as a symbol for death; the 'lilies' quotation is a distortion of a passage in the *Aeneid,* where the early death of Marcellus is foretold; and 'Come away... ' is from the song in Shakespeare's *Twelfth Night* that begins: 'Come away, come away, death.' (The first passage, 'Warmed both hands... ', is a slightly altered quotation from a poem by W. S. Landor.)

So it was that three automatists, in three countries and in three languages, received both straightforward and allusive references to the subject of

PERSPECTIVES

LITERARY PROOF

Myers tried to send quotations from the poem The Pied Piper of Hamelin, *illustrated below, by Robert Browning, above.*

One of the most famous of the cross-correspondences has been labelled the 'Hope, star and Browning' case. In January 1907, one of the communicators (unidentified) proposed – through the medium Mrs Verrall – an experiment. The cryptic message read as follows: 'An anagram would be better. Tell him that that – rats, star, tars and so on...'

A few days later, Mrs Verrall received a script, beginning:

'*Aster* [Latin for 'star'] *Teras* [Greek for 'wonder' or 'sign'] . . . The very wings of her. A WINGED DESIRE . . . the hope that leaves the earth for the sky – *Abt Vogler* . . . '

Mrs Verrall recognised these as fragments from poems of Robert Browning: *Abt Vogler* and *The Ring and the Book.* Within a week, Mrs Verrall's daughter Helen also produced an automatic script that included drawings of a bird, star and crescent moon, and verbal references to songbirds.

On 11 February, Mrs Piper had a sitting with J. Piddington, a member of the Society for Psychical Research. Myers 'came through' and said he had previously communicated something of interest to Mrs Verrall. 'I referred to Hope and Browning . . . I also said Star.'

The investigators noted that 'hope' had been emphasized by the very fact that, in the

quotation, it had been substituted for another word: the quotation should have read 'the passion that left the ground . . . ' and not 'the hope that leaves . . . ' Mrs Verrall, who knew her Browning, had remarked after reading through her script: 'I wondered why the silly thing said "hope".'

There was now a clear correspondence between the 'hope, star and Browning' reference of Mrs Piper and the texts of the elder and younger Verrall ladies. Mrs Verrall told her daughter that there had been such a correspondence; but, in order not to influence her script, she referred not to 'hope, star and Browning' but to 'virtue, Mars (the planet) and Keats'. Two days later, Miss Verrall produced another script that included the phrase: 'a star above it all rats everywhere in Hamelin town'. This was a clear reference to the poem *The Pied Piper of Hamelin* – written by Browning.

Now, Frederick Myers had an extensive knowledge of the works of Browning, and had always expressed a sympathy with many of the poet's aspirations and ideals. So perhaps it was natural that his disembodied mind should turn to his old literary favourites when trying to prove his continued existence to those left on earth.

A letter, left, from the still-living Myers to the physicist Sir Oliver Lodge reveals a hand that differs considerably from the scripts he allegedly 'sent' through mediums after his death.

Mrs A. W. Verrall, below, was the key medium in Myers' elaborate post-mortem plan.

death. H.F. Saltmarsh explains in his book how more complex cross-correspondences might work.

'Suppose that the topic chosen was "Time". Automatist *A* might start the ball rolling by a quotation from the hymn "Like an ever-rolling stream". Automatist *B* might follow on with a quotation from *Alice in Wonderland*, dealing with the discussion concerning "Time" at the Mad Hatter's tea-table, such as "He won't stand beating" or "We quarrelled last March – just before he went mad, you know". Then, Automatist *C* gives the clue with "Time and Tide wait for no man". Most of the actual cases are far more subtle – and it was not until after much research that connections were discovered. It is probable that, even now, a good many have been overlooked.'

" I CONFESS THAT AT TIMES I HAVE BEEN TEMPTED TO BELIEVE THAT THE CREATOR HAS ETERNALLY INTENDED THIS DEPARTMENT OF NATURE TO REMAIN BAFFLING, TO PROMPT OUR CURIOSITIES AND HOPES AND SUSPICIONS ALL IN EQUAL MEASURE... **"**

WILLIAM JAMES (1842-1910), FOUNDER OF THE AMERICAN SOCIETY FOR PSYCHICAL RESEARCH

Alice Fleming (alias 'Mrs Holland'), above, was part of the group of women who apparently received cryptic messages from SPR members in the afterlife. The sister of Rudyard Kipling, she was living in India when the supposed cross-correspondences were being produced.

This scholarly jigsaw puzzle may seem, at first glance, to be no more than some sort of post-mortem game of intellectual snobbery. In fact, more than one critic has pointed out that the hereafter, if we are to judge from the communications made in cross-correspondences, seems to be peopled solely with upper-class Edwardians who had a solid classical education and a background of SPR membership. But if the next world were to be more or less a continuation of this one – without the hindrance of physical bodies, that is – then what could be more natural than choosing one's ex-friends and colleagues for an enormous, epoch-making venture? To take an analogy, one would not bother to take someone who has no head at all for heights on an Everest expedition.

To suspend disbelief for one moment, it seems that Myers was passionately trying to 'get through', and was also intent on using some means that could actually constitute proof. On 12 January 1904, Myers wrote (through Mrs Holland in India): 'If it were possible for the soul to die back into earth life again, I should die from sheer yearning to reach you to tell you that all that we imagined is not half wonderful enough for the truth... '. Through Mrs Piper in the United States, he wrote: 'I am trying with all the forces... together to prove that I am Myers.' And again, through the Indian connection, he wrote: 'Oh, I am feeble with eagerness – how can I best be identified?'

SCEPTICAL CHALLENGES

The whole subject of the cross-correspondences has been subject to analysis and is still the focus of much research. On the evidence of the examples given above, there are bound to be be many sceptics who will suggest that the whole business must have been no more than a kind of genteel collusion, perhaps arranged in secrecy by Myers and his SPR colleagues some time before their deaths. Or, if conscious fraud seems unlikely, perhaps the series of bizarre word-games was the result of telepathy among the mediums concerned. The relationship between Verrall and her daughter was surely too close for them to keep secrets from each other. What is more, detailed study has shown that the classical words and allusions actually came mainly through the mediumship of those women who had the benefit of a classical education – they were almost totally absent in the case of Mrs Willett and Mrs Piper, who did not have this educational background.

The fact that the 'Myers' of, say, the Piper scripts, sounds entirely different from the 'Myers' of, say, the Willett scripts must also be taken into consideration. And although the handwriting that came through differed from the women's own hands, it was not actually that of Myers himself, nor was there a resemblance.

However, it seems that Myers and his friends were determined to nip in the bud any such sceptical 'explanations'. In life, they had both known and challenged both frauds and cynics, and so knew what to expect. So, marshalling their spirit forces, they began a barrage of fragmentary and intellectual cross-corresponding communications, spanning continents and decades, so those who give credence to such phenomena believe.

TANTRIC SEXUAL RITES

SOME BELIEVE THAT CERTAIN SECRET CULTS HAVE FOUND THE KEY TO ETERNAL YOUTH. WHAT TRUTH IS THERE BEHIND THIS AMAZING CLAIM THAT LIFE CAN BE PROLONGED?

Although most Western writings on the subject of Tantra are somewhat vague about its inner mysteries, certain works by Kenneth Grant – known as *The Typhonian Trilogy* – go some way towards revealing and analysing the system. In these books, Grant unfolds some of the arcana underlying the symbolism of so-called Left-Handed Tantrism, as practised in the West.

According to Grant, the lotus – sacred flower of the Orient – is a symbol of the female genitalia and of psychic energy, and is composed of all the mystical essences. Its secretions are therefore said to be collected for use in various magical rites and for the consecration of talismans. As Grant explains, quoting from an initiate:

'What is not (generally) known is that these secretions are not mere excretions but are valuable fluids which contain in themselves the secretions of the endocrine glands in a much purer form, and more fit for human use than the gland extracts and desiccated gland products of the present-day

The lotus, above, is the mystical sacred flower of the Orient, and the Tantrics use it to symbolise the unfolding of the self and the expanding of consciousness. It is also the Tantric symbol of the chakras, or psychic energy centres, of the human body. Used in this way, each petal signifies the blossoming of a special quality or mental attribute.

organotherapy... The secretions of women are made in the laboratory of the Deity, the Temple of the Mother, and they supply just what is needed by the human...

'Of the three kinds of fluids, the urine is the least and the weakest; *rajas*, or menstrual secretion, is next; and *bindhu*, the last, is a secretion not at present known to the West, and obtainable only by means of the Shakta-Tantra and their analogies in Mongolia, Tibet, China, Peru, Mexico and elsewhere; a fluid that bisexualises . . . and rejuvenates to an extraordinary extent.'

The commentator goes on to say that at least 16 different types of bodily fluid from women are used in the Eastern Tantric system – the sixteenth, *sadhakya kala* (also known as the ray of the Moon) being the most secret. To lend some support to these assertions, Grant cites Havelock Ellis, the pioneer sexologist. In his book *Studies in the Psychology of Sex*, Ellis says that only 14 of the bodily secretions known in Tantrism are recognised by Western science.

Exactly how the various essences are obtained and applied, however, is not revealed. Nor are the precise results of their supposed effects. But there are indications that, in some way, they are able to retard or even halt the ageing process.

One highly secret group that would appear to have been successful in this technique is known as

reported that he did not think the cult had any powers greater than those claimed by other occult groups he had encountered.

COUNTING THE YEARS

Weech did confirm, however, that the group appeared to have the power to arrest the ageing process. In his opinion, a further 20 to 40 years could be added to normal life expectancy, together with the retention of a youthful appearance. When he first encountered what he accepted ultimately as evidence of age-retarding, Weech found it difficult to believe. He met a young girl who looked about 18 years of age and reported: 'Only after I had met her daughter and granddaughter (who did not possess this power) did I even begin to believe that such a power existed.'

Later, however, Weech met another member of the cult, a man who appeared to be in his mid-thirties. 'And by sheer chance I was able to check and completely confirm his claim that he was born before the turn of the century.' The man mentioned that he had served on *HMS Iron Duke* during World

the Cult of Priapus and Ayana, thought still to function in Britain, Europe and the United States. The cult was named after two ancient gods. Priapus was the fertility god, venerated by the ancient Romans, Etruscans, Greeks and Pompeians and symbolised by his large phallus. His consort Ayana had three breasts, and she was regarded as submissive to him.

According to the Roman author, merchant and traveller Lucius Marcellus, the cult's followers would present their daughters to the Temple of Ayana to be trained as priestesses. In return, they would be admitted to the inner sanctum where they were taught magical powers, including the secret of eternal youth.

The onset of Christianity and its persecution of pagan religions caused the cult to go into hiding, however, and it has remained underground ever since. Like the Tantrics, the Ayana cultists practised indiscriminate sex, incest and other forms of sexual rites considered to be morally degenerate. But despite the persecution of its adherents, the cult apparently survived and later spread.

One of the ways in which the cult stays secret is by dispensing with regular mass gatherings. Its aspirant priestesses are usually trained individually, or in small groups of two or three, by a priestess with whom they reside. The inner sanctum of the cult's various branches meets only twice a year, and always at different venues.

The survival of the cult into contemporary times was discovered in the late 1950s by an American occultist, James McNally. But McNally's discovery was quite by chance and, being a devout Christian, he was horrified at what he found. Consequently, he uncovered little more about the cult and its activities. Another investigator, Justin C. Tanner, gleaned additional information. He found that there were three temples of the cult in the United States, one in Denmark, one in Britain, and possibly others.

Another researcher, meanwhile, Arnold Weech, gained the confidence of the inner circle of the British temple and, in 1978, published a pamphlet about his assessment of the Cult of Ayana. He

Kenneth Grant, top, writer and occultist, has revealed some of the inner mysteries of the Ordo Templi Orientis (OTO) in a trilogy of books. The sexual rites of the order link it to those of Tantrism, symbolically depicted above.

War I. Weech happened to know a man in his home village who had been an officer on the same ship at the same time and arranged a meeting between the two – on the proviso that the officer would promise not to mention the encounter to anyone else afterwards.

'The meeting duly took place, and within the first few minutes it became obvious that there could no longer be any doubt. They spent nearly five hours discussing old times and past events. The clincher came when our host produced a collection of photographs. One was of a gun crew standing in front of a gun turret; and there, smiling at the camera, with the same tell-tale scar on the point of the chin, and looking only a little younger, was the Cult member.'

As a result of his investigations, Weech came to the conclusion that initiates of the cult did have the power to arrest the ageing process, along with 'the ability to alter or change certain physical characteristics and develop mental powers to a very high degree, and one other power, which I have promised not to disclose'.

SECRET SUBMISSION

This secret power appears to comprise some manner of ensuring that each member will remain absolutely submissive to the Cult and will not disclose its existence nor its secrets to anyone. According to Weech, the Cult of Ayana does not charge at all for membership, nor does it even accept voluntary donations. Moreover, it does not actively seek new members for its ranks and certainly does not pander to the curious.

Would-be members have their life thoroughly checked before being admitted to the Cult and, if any of the details they have given turn out to be false or misleading, they are immediately rejected. Those who are admitted are then put in touch with a mentor, who remains their only contact with the Cult until the preparatory period is over. At this point, the candidate is then given the choice of joining – for life – or of withdrawing.

The Elders have complete control, and any member who offends an Elder is subjected to severe penalties, including corporal punishment. Weech states in his monograph that none of the members with whom he came in contact had any regrets. A young married man told him:

'We have literally to grovel sometimes. Our particular Elder has total power over us and can use us

Priapus Disarmed, below, *is a painting by Austin O. Spare. Priapus was the ancient god of fertility, usually depicted with an enormous and erect phallus. Ayana – the three-breasted goddess – was his consort. Members of the secret cult of Priapus and Ayana, which emphasises sexual rites, are said to be able to halt the ageing process by their magical practices.*

as he wishes, we can only obey. If he desires my wife, then he takes her and I have no say in the matter. Some of the ceremonies strip away all human dignity and yet we have no regrets. The diminishing of one's ego is a small price to pay for the priceless powers we now command.'

In an attempt to investigate the cult further, Magdalene Graham, editor of the quarterly *Occult World*, which originally published Weech's pamphlet, was contacted. She gave her opinion: 'Unfortunately, the Cult of Priapus and Ayana has now gone deep underground and severed all links with other organisations.' Asked if she believed the cult used Tantric methods to attain their age-retarding process, she replied: 'I should think it extremely unlikely that the Cult used Eastern methods as they . . . were extremely scathing of Eastern mysticism. They did state that they used sexual magic but, from the deliberately vague hints, it is obvious that this took somewhat unusual forms and probably consisted of acts which even in these enlightened times remain illegal.'

At one period, it is known that an occult group known as the Society of the Third Eye began to prepare a correspondence course, including a lesson on the Cult of Ayana, but the sect subsequently asked that it be withdrawn. Magdalene Graham, who was involved in this project, reported: 'My personal contact with the real thing was of course via the Society of the Third Eye when we were preparing the lesson on P & A [Priapus and Ayana] for the Course, and I am sorry that I cannot give any details of this, except to say that we required proof before attesting to their powers... '

It is clear that there are cults in Britain, Europe and the USA today that practise sex magic. It will, they claim, endow their initiates with occult powers. Even if they deny the Tantric source, it is almost certain that the ancient cult of Tantra, based upon the symbolic union of the god Shiva and his consort Shakti, provided the initial impulse for such practices and beliefs.

PSYCHIC
PHOTO FILE

Stella Lansing, *right,* a housewife from Massachusetts, found she had the ability to capture phantom forms, flashes of light or UFO-like objects on film after a close encounter in the 1960s. Following that episode, she produced well over 500 colour ciné films as well as still photographs showing strange artefacts that were not visible when the pictures were taken. Particularly interesting is the compulsion she felt to aim her camera at, say, a street scene by a sudden sensation of cold or simply a strong intuition. Psychiatrist Dr Berthold Schwarz spent several years investigating Mrs Lansing and became convinced of the genuineness of her images.

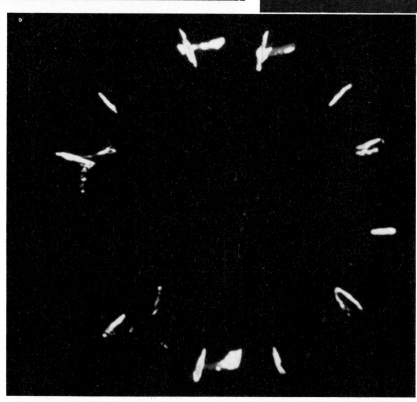

Can the camera 'see' what the human eye cannot? Spiritualists and psychics have often offered photographic 'proof' of their beliefs; but all too frequently what seemed to be paranormal effects have turned out to be the result of faulty equipment – or downright fraud. Yet, as we show, some psychic photographs, although controversial, remain essentially unexplained

London medium Gladys Hayter began to specialise in psychic photography in 1970, when she bought an Instamatic and noticed bizarre effects in her photographs – shadowy figures, swirls of light and the apparent disappearance of objects or people actually present when the photograph was taken. The fuzzy ball of light in her lap, *above,* was interpreted by her as the spirit form of a dead poodle. Sceptics have explained away her pictures as the result of a leaking camera, but a few other people also obtained odd results when they took photographs of the medium using their own equipment.

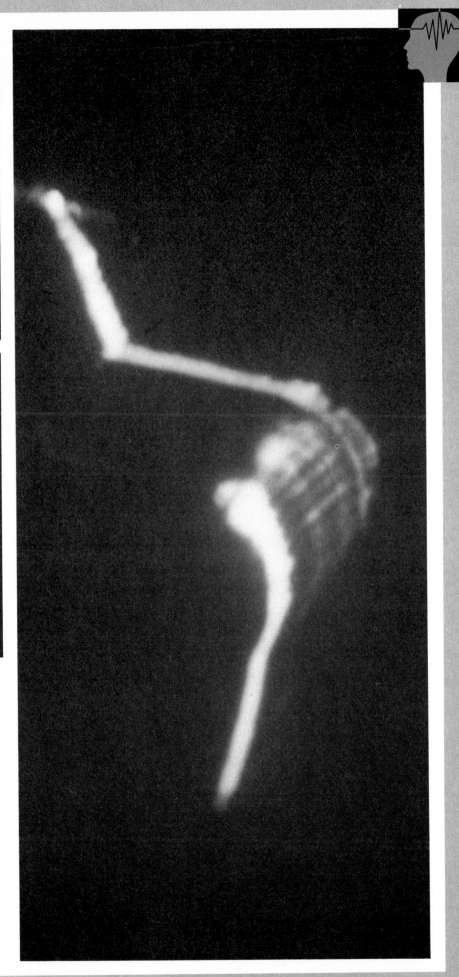

The detail, *above,* from Stella Lansing's 'clocklike' formations *left,* seems to be a classic UFO disc shape when 'frozen'. She actually saw this object as a single light moving in 'fast, erratic patterns', which appeared as this circular formation only when the *Super 8 Kodachrome* ciné film was scrutinised frame by frame. What she considered to be a 'madonna-like' figure can be seen at the top of the picture, as if moving in a fast spin from a 12 o'clock to a 1 o'clock position.

The frame from a ciné film, *right,* was taken by Stella Lansing in February 1967, and is said to show a UFO that 'took off from the knoll of a hill within a high tension line area . . . in a sudden burst of white light which, as it ascended, changed colours and then became a mere star-like flashing light... ' She considered that the leg-like protrusion that can be seen at the top of the luminescent UFO was landing-gear of some sort.

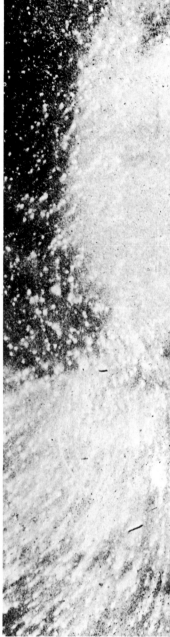

The picture, *left,* shows two UFOs, including one described by Stella Lansing as a 'Saturn-type', and was taken with a *Super 8* movie camera from Route 32A near Petersham, Massachusetts, in October 1974. She described the object on the left as 'travelling on edge' and as 'coming through into our dimension'. Many such sightings apparently occurred both at night and during the day. According to Stella Lansing, the attraction is the reservoir dam and the power lines, which implies that she assumed these UFOs to be 'nuts and bolts' objects, not subjective psychic phenomena that can be seen by others only on film.

Although the mechanism behind thoughtography – the impressing of mental images on to film – remains a mystery, the phenomenon seems to exhibit marked characteristics. Typical feathery, swirling effects seen in the work of Ted Serios have also been noted in that of Charles Lancelin, as *left,* and in that of Professor Tomokichi Fukurai, as reproduced *bottom,* of the Imperial University, Tokyo, during the period between 1910 and 1913.

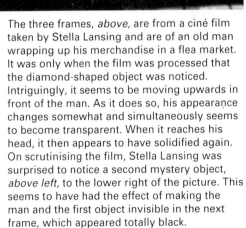

The three frames, *above,* are from a ciné film taken by Stella Lansing and are of an old man wrapping up his merchandise in a flea market. It was only when the film was processed that the diamond-shaped object was noticed. Intriguingly, it seems to be moving upwards in front of the man. As it does so, his appearance changes somewhat and simultaneously seems to become transparent. When it reaches his head, it then appears to have solidified again. On scrutinising the film, Stella Lansing was surprised to notice a second mystery object, *above left,* to the lower right of the picture. This seems to have had the effect of making the man and the first object invisible in the next frame, which appeared totally black.

The second object also then seems to have risen above the man's head and, instantly, both the first object and the man were visible once more. Stella Lansing said: 'However fantastic this may sound, I feel that there is a human image inside of the... object... ' One of the frames appears to be suffused with an amber tint, a phenomenon frequently noted by her. She could offer no straightforward explanation for her psychic films, but said: 'It's like a psychic connection with something, or someone, which causes me to grab my camera and film... Not that I hear a voice but I sense something, as though I am being controlled.'

ALIEN SPACECRAFT – HALLUCINATIONS OR FRAUD? HERE, WE LOOK AT VARIOUS POSSIBLE EXPLANATIONS, AND CONSIDER WHETHER THE PHENOMENON POSSIBLY LIES OUTSIDE OUR USUAL CATEGORIES OF THOUGHT

road ahead. He instantly thought of a works bus that regularly travelled the route and idly wondered why it was a little early. Then, as he approached the glow, it became obvious that he had been wrong.

The object that confronted PC Godfrey was like a spinning top with windows. It was hovering just above the road surface, spanning the gap between two lamp posts, and was rotating. He could see his headlights reflected in its metallic surface, and that leaves on the roadside bushes were moving in the vortex created by its rotation. The road surface, soaking wet in other places, was dry in blotchy patches directly beneath the object. There was no doubt in his mind that the object was real.

Keeping calm, the officer propped his clipboard on the windscreen and carefully sketched the object. But then something inexplicable happened. He suddenly found himself further down the road, driving the car away from the scene. He turned the car round and drove back past the spot, now deserted, where the object had been. He then carried on the short distance into town and collected a colleague. Only at this point did he notice the time. Somehow, since the moment he first saw the UFO, all of 10 minutes had disappeared.

UFOs - ASSESSING THE EVIDENCE

Alien beings must exist somewhere in the Universe, in some form or other. Of this, there is little doubt. The problem confronting us is therefore whether the evidence we possess proves that some of them are visiting the Earth right now. If this is so, then proving the fact would be of the utmost significance, and would certainly constitute the most momentous occasion in the history of the world.

Unfortunately, we do not possess reliable photographs, movie films or tape recordings of aliens, or artefacts manufactured in another world... or anything that goes beyond mere testimony. In view of this paucity of hard evidence, we can hardly say, with any definiteness, whether aliens are or are not visiting us. Instead, we can only make a reasoned assessment of the facts.

The dilemmas posed by close encounters of the fourth kind are starkly illustrated by a case that occurred in the north of England on 28 November 1980. Police Constable Alan Godfrey had been called out to pursue some cows that were allegedly roaming a housing estate. By 5.15 a.m., still not having found them, he was ready to give up the search. Then, while making one last trip in his patrol car before coming off duty, he saw a glow on the

This was not all. Constable Godfrey reported having a dim memory of a strange voice saying: 'This is not for your eyes. You will forget it.' Additional fragmentary recollections gradually filtered back to him until, nine months after the incident, and with the help of ufologists, he underwent regression hypnosis. This was conducted by an eminently qualified and rather sceptical psychiatrist, but what appeared to be a coherent memory of the incident emerged.

The story was of the usual type: the officer had been taken on board the UFO and given a medical examination by two distinct types of humanoid creature – one tall, the other small and somewhat ugly. Remarkably, this is almost exactly what the Day family claimed happened to them during their abduction at Aveley in Essex. In fact, contact cases reported from Britain share many such similar features. Cases reported from other countries show similarities among themselves, too.

What happened to the police constable? Did he lie? If not, did he have an hallucination or did he undergo the events he described? Or was it something between an hallucination and a straightforward experience – a distortion or misinterpretation of some extraordinary event?

There happens to be unusual and powerful support for the 'face-value' interpretation of the story. Four police officers on patrol 8 miles (13 kilometres) away had to duck as an object streaked low over their heads, moving directly towards the town near which the encounter took place. And a caretaker lighting a school's boilers saw, in the direction of the town, an object that fitted PC Godfrey's description, climbing into the sky. These stories were reported.

There are many questions posed by reports of alien sightings. Why should aliens look like us? Why do they behave like us? Why do they never tell us anything valuable to which we do not already have access? Taken together, these facts seem to suggest a mental origin for these strange experiences.

In the north of England, a craft resembling a spinning top, left, hovers above a road. The witness was a police constable, Alan Godfrey, seen below left. Later, he recalled the experience of being taken aboard the craft, where he was examined by terrifying creatures.

Research into lucid dreams has also proved revealing as far as supposed sightings are concerned. These are dreams in which the dreamer knows he is dreaming. Often, the course of the dream can be controlled by conscious effort.

Although they seem so real at the time, lucid dreams give away their 'unreal' nature by means of various subtle hints. For example, the subject does not react with normal responses. He may feel no fear, despite the weirdness of the experience. He will not wake up a sleeping partner to witness the events. In one case, a lucid dream was of an atomic bomb exploding in a garden. The subject's response was to yawn and fall asleep. The behaviour of contact case witnesses is often just like this.

SENSORY DEPRIVATION

Interestingly, such symptoms also occur in hallucinations that follow long periods of sensory deprivation. When a person is kept in darkness and silence, and even his sense of touch is deprived of normal stimulation because his hands are enveloped in special gloves, the mind starts to manufacture its own 'perceptions' – hallucinations of sound, sight and touch. When we consider the usual setting of certain contacts – night-time, a tired driver, a lonely country road, and the sudden appearance of a slightly unusual sight, such as a bright light in the sky – it does not stretch credulity very far to suggest that these could be hallucinations brought about by lack of sensory stimulation.

In the USA, Dr Alvin Lawson, a professor of English at the University of California, conducted experiments that are relevant to the hallucination theory. He advertised for people of a 'creative' turn of mind to take part in an unspecified experiment. He screened out all those who seemed to have a knowledge of, or interest in, UFOs. The rest were asked to imagine, under hypnosis, that they were being abducted by aliens. They were led on with certain key questions, and the results, he claimed, were so closely akin to the stories told of allegedly

---

*In*FOCUS

WORDS OF WISDOM?

In 1976, an American contactee group published a letter which they said had been channelled by telepathy from outer space. Addressed to Terrestrial Brother Carter (U.S. President at the time), it warned him: 'Remember, do not do as others have done! We remind you that this authority has been granted from above... your action could render it constructive and effective, prosperous, salvaging light for all mankind. Remember, Jimmy Carter, Remember! From the Heavens to Earth.'

Such a message is something of an exception. Surveying 16 years of editing

Flying Saucer Review, Charles Bowen commented on the general absurdities featured in alien messages. In 1968, in Argentina, two 'men' with transparent legs gave a farmer's son a message, rendered as: 'You shall know the world. F. Saucer.'

In 1965, in Venezuela, two beings, said to be 7 to 8 feet (2.1 – 2.4 metres) tall, with long, yellow hair and protruding eyes, were asked whether there were 'any human beings like you living among us?' The answer was: 'Yes. 2,417,805.'

During the 1954 'flap', a French witness encountered a small being standing before a glowing disc-shaped craft. The alien repeated several times in a mechanical voice: 'La veritée est refusée aux constipés,' and 'Ce que vous appelez cancer vient des dents.' Translated, these messages from another civilisation read: 'Truth is denied to the constipated' (or 'to the ill at ease'), and 'That which is known as cancer comes from the teeth' (or 'through what you eat').

In 1977, Professor Alvin Lawson began to investigate the validity of UFO abduction reports obtained under hypnosis. He hypnotised a total of 16 volunteers who knew very little about UFOs. Once in trance, they were asked to imagine a series of events – seeing a UFO, being taken on board, given an examination, and so on. Lawson hoped to find differences between their imaginary accounts and those given by alleged UFO contactees. Such differences would enhance the credibility of the 'real' reports.

To his surprise, it was the similarities that were most striking. For example, among his test subjects' narratives were descriptions of tubes of light, which extended from UFOs or retracted into them, perhaps levitating the subject aboard.

Sometimes, the subject described the UFO imagined during the hypnotic trance as 'getting bigger and smaller'. Patterns of pulsating colours, rotating spirals and geometric patterns were also often reported. All these features are common in 'real' UFO reports, but they are rare in science fiction stories and films, a likely source of UFO imagery.

The experiments showed that authentic-sounding reports could be produced in abundance during trance states by subjects asked to imagine close encounters, but who have never claimed to have been abducted by a UFO. Dr Lawson concluded that contact case witnesses were not lying – but he could offer no hypothesis as to the nature of the stimulus causing their experiences.

PERSPECTIVES

'real' abductions that it was likely that these also were, wholly or in part, subconscious fantasies.

Such different types of evidence constitute impressive support for the contention that alien contacts are hallucinatory. But there is a fair amount of negative evidence too. Some contact experiences are shared. But while collective hallucinations can occur, they are not well-understood, and some encounters stretch this hypothesis to breaking-point. One Italian case involved as many as seven witnesses; one British case involved four. In some cases, meanwhile, such as those in Puerto Rico and that involving the English police officer, there is at least some degree of independent corroboration.

Alvin Lawson's work, as he himself recognised, showed major differences between allegedly 'real' abductions and imagined ones, as well as similarities. When, in a UFO contact case, memories emerge by way of hypnosis, they are almost invariably associated with very strong emotions, more consistent with the memory of a real event than a fantasy. The 'abductions' imagined in the laboratory did not display this effect; and in general those who took part in the experiment knew afterwards that

Alpha Centauri, right, a well-dressed science fiction monster from the television series Dr Who, is more outlandish than most descriptions of aliens provided by UFO contactees. 'Real' ufonauts are far more similar to human beings – or to gnomes, giants, dwarves and other traditional mythical creatures.

Two high officials of the Draconian race, left, are another instance of the television designer's imagination outstripping the diversity of reported aliens. Animal forms, or hybrid animal-human forms like these, might be expected among ufonauts – whether they were genuinely extra-terrestrial or the products of the human imagination. In fact, both 'real' accounts and 'imaginary' ones, produced under laboratory conditions, are seldom of this type.

" THE GREATER THE EDUCATION, THE HIGHER THE PROPORTION THAT INDICATED THEY HAVE HEARD OF FLYING SAUCERS, WHO THINK THEY ARE REAL RATHER THAN THE PRODUCT OF IMAGINATION AND WHO BELIEVE THAT THERE ARE PEOPLE SOMEWHAT LIKE OURSELVES LIVING ON OTHER PLANETS... "

ALDORA LEE,

COLORADO UNIVERSITY REPORT

they had been fantasising. Contact witnesses, however, are never in any doubt that their regression memory is of a 'real' event.

We must also consider the frequent reports of physical effects on the body of a witness, such as burns on the skin. Marks on the ground sometimes accompany these cases. But, on the other hand, there is almost no photographic support for contact witnesses' stories, and it is known that physical effects can be produced psychosomatically.

Looking at more subtle features of such accounts, considerable consistency and a kind of lucid cohesiveness appear in all but certain 'bedroom visitor' cases. This tends to make the UFO investigator doubt that he is dealing with experiences more akin to dreams than reality.

Perhaps the fairest judgement we can make at present is to say that some such experiences seem more like vivid hallucinations than reality. Some cases have elements suggesting hallucinations but may offer data that casts doubt on this assumption. Some also seem to be of a unique type, almost a hybrid between dreams and reality.

So what of the other extreme? Are these contacts extra-terrestrial in nature? This, the 'face-value' hypothesis, implies that hundreds of different races (most of them not very imaginative variants on ourselves), from many different worlds, are taking a great deal of interest in the Earth. They perform medical examinations interminably, and gather up endless cargoes of soil and rock samples.

Sceptics invariably ask why the aliens fail to contact anyone important. Why do they not land on the White House lawn and thus dispel all doubts? Contactee Gaynor Sunderland asked Arna, one of the aliens she claimed to have met, this very question. In reply, she was told that people in authority had so much credibility to lose that there was no point in contacting them, although this had been tried on a few occasions. Fear of the consequences always kept such people silent. Instead, the aliens prefer to pursue a policy of contacting children or simple folk, knowing that some of these will brave ridicule and speak out.

This argument makes an intriguing amount of sense. A slow, covert process of conditioning world opinion to the idea of extra-terrestrial visitors fits well with the provocative, but not probative, evidence that we possess. Solid proof would be detrimental to such a policy: it might be impounded, or hidden, or denied outright. Suggestive indications, on the other hand, avoid the unwelcome attention of authority, while providing a stimulus to continued interest and the long, slow build-up of belief. Even the confusing and ridiculous behaviour of aliens would fit this theory.

A great deal of fascinating work remains to be done before we can even hope to know the truth. There is no hard evidence that a superior intelligence has made contact with the Earth – but we do have suggestive hints that this might be true. And, since most of us would probably wish UFOs to come from space, our judgement is clouded by an enormous emotional bias.

> **"** IF SUCH THINGS AS UFOS... DID NOT EXIST AS A POSSIBILITY, THEN THE WORLD WOULD BE A DULL PLACE TO LIVE IN... DOES IT REALLY MATTER THAT 90 PER CENT ARE NOT TRUE UFOS? **"**
>
> **JENNY RANDLES AND PETER WARRINGTON, UFOS: A BRITISH VIEWPOINT**

Of the six drawings below, three were made by witnesses in UFO contact cases, and were offered as bona fide representations of alien beings. The others were made by participants in Alvin Lawson's 'simulated abduction' experiments. These subjects, though they produced their accounts under hypnosis, were never in doubt about the imaginary nature of their experiences. Is there a different 'feel' about the two types of drawing? Can you pick out the three 'real' contact witness drawings? The answer is printed at the lower right.

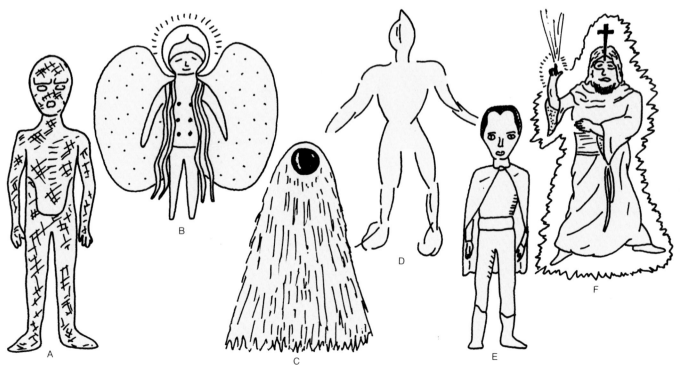

CASEBOOK
UFOs CAN KILL

OVERWHELMING TERROR,

BLINDNESS AND EVEN

DEATH FEATURE IN THREE

REMARKABLE BRAZILIAN

CLOSE ENCOUNTERS

Ever since the wave of UFO sightings that followed World War II, debate has raged among ufologists as to whether or not the objects seen in the sky are hostile.

Some researchers cling to the belief that a surveillance of this planet is being carried out by extra-terrestrial explorers. A number take this a step further and proclaim that 'space beings' come to the Earth to warn Man of the evil of his ways.

The artist's impression, below, shows the eerie orange light that surrounded a UFO sighted at São Vicente in November 1957.

Others believe that the extra-terrestrials (or meta-terrestrials, to those who consider them denizens of parallel universes) are engaged in a struggle for possession of the human race, and that they have no interest in human welfare.

Still other investigators claim that UFOs are psychically caused phenomena, while others counter by suggesting that UFOs may themselves cause manifestations of psychic phenomena. Then, there are those who have come to the conclusion that UFOs are mere products of the imagination.

On the whole, however, UFO researchers assume that they are dealing with a benign phenomenon. If human beings occasionally suffer harm from UFOs, they say, it is either an unintended

consequence of UFO activity that had no malicious purpose, or it was a purely defensive response. In the cases discussed here, human witnesses of UFOs suffered substantial injuries – in one case, death. The injured could perhaps be held guilty of provoking the trouble. Nonetheless, these incidents invoke the spectre first raised by H. G. Wells in *War of the Worlds* – of attack on mankind by alien beings.

The Brazilian coastal fort of Itaipu is situated at São Vicente, close to the port of Santos in the state of São Paulo. To the two sentries patrolling the gun emplacements during the small hours of 4 November 1957, everything seemed quiet. Nothing warned them that within a few minutes they were to be put through a nightmare ordeal that still lacks explanation.

At 2 a.m., the sentries spotted what looked like a bright star that suddenly appeared above the horizon over the Atlantic. It was growing larger and the soldiers soon realised that it was approaching them at high speed. At first, however, they thought it was an aeroplane, and so gave no thought to sounding the alarm.

Within a few seconds, the UFO, travelling silently, had reached a point high above the fort and halted. Then it floated down until it stopped motionless some 150 feet (50 metres) above the highest gun turret, bathing the ground between the turrets with an eerie orange light. The object appeared to be circular and was, in the soldiers' words, about the size of a 'big Douglas' (meaning, presumably, a Douglas DC-6). The sentries could now hear a gentle humming noise that seemed to be associated with it.

Without warning, a wave of searing heat suddenly engulfed the men. Fire now seemed to be burning all over their uniforms, while the humming sound intensified.

One sentry staggered, dazed, and then fell unconscious to the ground, while a comrade managed to stumble into a relatively sheltered spot beneath one of the guns. But, once there, his mind seemed to give way. He was seized by horror and rent the air with bloodcurdling screams.

These terrible cries awakened the rest of the garrison, and within seconds the power supply cut off, lights went out and equipment failed. An officer tried to start the emergency generator, but that, too, failed. Meanwhile, the horrifying screams continued and confusion turned to panic in the dark subterranean corridors.

Suddenly, the lights returned. Those officers and men who were first to get into the open were in time to see a great orange light climbing away vertically, before shooting off at high speed. The last of the soldiers to arrive found those who had preceded them examining the unconscious sentry, while his colleague was still crouched in hiding and crying hysterically.

When they reached the sick bay, both men were found to have 'first- and deep second-degree burns mostly on areas that had been protected by clothes'. The sentry who had retained consciousness was in deep nervous shock and many hours were to pass before he could talk.

Subsequently, it was noticed that the fort's electric clocks had stopped at 2.03 a.m., which suggested that the whole nightmare experience had lasted no more than about four minutes.

Later that morning, the colonel in command of Fort Itaipu issued orders forbidding the communication of the incident to anyone outside the unit. Intelligence officers were quickly at work conducting an investigation, and a report was sent to army headquarters. Some days later, officers from the US military mission arrived, together with Brazilian Air Force officers. Meanwhile, the sentries were flown to Rio de Janeiro and admitted to the Army Central Hospital, where a security net was promptly drawn around them.

Three weeks later, an officer from the fort who was interested in UFO reports sought out Dr Olavo Fontes, who had been involved in other such investigations. The officer had been present at the fort during the incident and, once he was satisfied that his name would never be divulged, he gave Fontes full details of the case. Dr Fontes then approached medical colleagues at the Rio de Janeiro hospital, who confirmed that two soldiers were being treated for severe burns, but would tell him nothing more about their case.

Without further corroboration, Dr Fontes could not publish an account. So the case lingered in the files until mid-1959, when, by chance, the doctor met three other officers who, in the course of conversation, confirmed what had happened. Thanks to the unauthorised disclosures of these officers, the world now has some knowledge, tantalisingly incomplete though it is, of a UFO's unwelcome visit to Fort Itaipu on that terrifying night.

Illiterate, simple, honest, trustworthy and reserved – this was how Inácio de Souza, a 41-year-old Brazilian ranch worker, was described by his employer. But he was to meet a tragic end, apparently as a result of an encounter with a UFO during which, gripped by fear, he resorted to violence, and was repaid in kind.

On 13 August 1967, at about 4 p.m., de Souza and his wife Luiza, the parents of five children,

Following a close encounter of the third kind, with three beings, illustrated below, Inácio de Souza became seriously ill with mystery symptoms and subsequently died.

were returning to the ranch after a shopping trip on foot to the nearest village. The ranch was near Pilar de Goias, some 150 miles (240 kilometres) from Brasilia, the country's capital. The couple had almost reached the first building on the ranch when they saw three 'people', apparently playing on the landing strip. (The ranch owner, a well-known and extremely wealthy man, possessed several aircraft.) De Souza thought the trespassers were naked, but his wife said they were wearing skin-tight, yellow clothes. At the same time, the intruders seemed to see the couple, and started to approach them.

It was then that de Souza spotted a strange aircraft at the end of the runway. It was either on or just above the ground, and looked like an upturned wash-basin. The ranch-hand suddenly became very frightened, unslung his .44 carbine, took aim and fired a shot at the nearest figure.

Almost immediately, a beam of green light was emitted by the strange craft. He said it hit de Souza on the head and shoulder, and he fell to the ground. As his wife ran to his assistance, she saw the three 'persons' enter the craft, which thereupon took off vertically at high speed, and with a noise like the humming of bees.

During the following few days, de Souza complained of numbness and tingling of the body, of headaches, and of severe nausea. On the third day, he developed continuous tremors of the hands and head. The rancher was informed of the incident on that day, and flew his sick employee to Goiania, more than 180 miles (300 kilometres) away, where he was examined by a doctor.

Marks were discovered on his head and trunk, in the shape of perfect circles, 6 inches (15 centimetres) across. The doctor thought they could be a rash produced by a poisonous plant. When he offered this theory, the rancher told him de Souza's story of the encounter with the UFO and its occupants. The surprised doctor proposed some tests of de Souza's faeces, urine and blood, prescribed an ointment and expressed his opinion that de Souza had suffered an hallucination and that he had contracted some disease. He made no secret of the fact that he had no time for flying saucer stories, that he did not believe de Souza, and that the whole affair should be hushed up.

The sick man and his employer stayed on in Goiania for five days while investigation and treatment continued. When de Souza was discharged, the illness was diagnosed as leukaemia. The prognosis was poor: he was expected to live no more than 60 days. And he did indeed waste away quickly, his skin covered with white and yellowish-white blotches. He died on 11 October 1967.

The doctor in Goiania might well have wished to suppress de Souza's story because he feared the panic that such a disturbing tale could cause among the public at large. So this may have been the motive behind his 'hallucination' theory. But if de Souza did have an hallucination, then his wife shared it – unless she dutifully lied about her experience out of loyalty to him. And if there was some form of joint hallucination, then there must have been some agency responsible for causing it – an agency whose nature is as mysterious as the strange 'aircraft' and 'people' that the couple thought they saw that August afternoon.

ONE OF THE BEST-DOCUMENTED CASES OF A MEDIUM PRODUCING ECTOPLASMIC FORMS IS THAT OF EVA C, MANY OF WHOSE MATERIALISATIONS WERE PHOTOGRAPHED

During the first decade of this century, a young French girl living in Algiers began to exhibit remarkable psychic powers. Marthe Béraud, the daughter of a French army officer, was apparently able to produce full-form materialisations of an ectoplasmic substance during seances. As her abilities as a medium became known, she came under the scrutiny of some of Europe's leading psychical researchers, many of whom were convinced that the phenomena produced by 'Eva C' – the pseudonym of Marthe Béraud – were genuine ectoplasmic 'teleplasms'.

But suspicion of fraud arose very early in Eva's career. In 1904, a lawyer name Marsault attended seances held at the Villa Carmen, home of the Noel family who ran a Spiritualist circle, and claimed that the young medium had confessed that she faked the phenomena for fun. Yet less than a year later, one of the most respected investigators of the day, Professor Charles Richet, published a favourable report of Eva's mediumship.

Richet elaborated upon his experience with Eva in his book *Thirty Years of Psychical Research*, and said he had been able to:

'See the first lineaments of materialisations as they were formed. A kind of liquid or pasty jelly emerges from the mouth or the breast of Marthe, which organises itself by degrees, acquiring the shape of a face or a limb... I have seen this paste spread on my knee, and slowly take form so as to show the rudiment of the radius, the cubitus, or metacarpal bone... '

Richet (who was professor of physiology at the Faculty of Medicine in Paris) admitted that these formations were often very imperfect. Sometimes

Eva C was born in around 1890 and grew up in Algiers, below, where she became engaged to the son of General Noel, at whose house seances were held, and where her powers as a medium were discovered. Unhappily, Eva's fiancé died before they could be married, but her career as a medium flourished. At seances in Paris, like the one held on 7 June 1911, left, Eva was able to produce ectoplasmic materialisations, even though her hands and feet were held by two witnesses throughout the proceedings.

SHAPES FROM THE SHADOWS

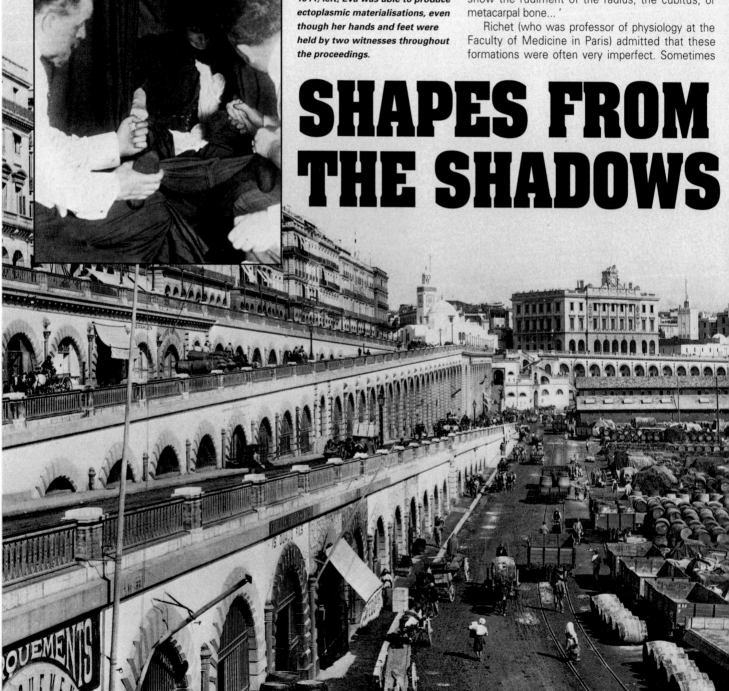

they looked like flat images 'so that in spite of oneself, one is inclined to imagine some fraud, since what appears seems to be the materialisation of a semblance, and not of a being.'

But at other times, Eva did produce recognisable spirit forms. Richet witnessed one such materialisation at the Villa Carmen:

'At first, it was only a white, opaque spot, like a handkerchief, lying on the ground before the curtain, then this handkerchief quickly assumed the form of a human head level with the floor, and a few moments later it rose up in a straight line and became a small man enveloped in a kind of white burnous, who took two or three halting steps in front of the curtain and then sank to the floor and disappeared as if through a trap-door. But there was no trap-door.'

BEARDED SPIRIT

A spirit who regularly appeared at Eva's seances was Bien Boa, said to have died 300 years previously. One remarkable picture shows him with a thick beard, wearing a helmet, and draped with ectoplasm. Richet maintained that, on five or six occasions, he saw both Bien Boa and Eva at the same time. The phantom's eyes moved, and so did his lips as he tried to speak. The witnesses could also hear him breathing, and the professor used a flask containing a chemical solution to test if Bien Boa's breath contained carbon dioxide: it did.

At another seance, a beautiful Egyptian princess was seen. This spirit, said Richet, was well-defined and wore a gilt ribbon or diadem in her fair hair. She was laughing, and he could see her pearly teeth. Richet was told to bring scissors the following day so that he could cut a lock of the spirit's hair. When the woman materialised again, he saw that she had very abundant hair, though he had trouble distinguishing her face. Richet reported:

At a seance held in Paris on 13 March 1911 with Schrenck-Nötzing, Richet and Mme Bisson in attendance, Eva produced ectoplasm that assumed the shape of hands, left.

Eva's manifestations were carefully investigated by such eminent psychical researchers as Baron von Schrenck-Nötzing and Professor Charles Richet, top, and Mme Juliette Bisson, shown above in her seance room.

> **WITH SOME MEDIUMS, A KIND OF LIQUID OR PASTY JELLY EMERGES FROM THE MOUTH, FOREHEAD OR BREAST; WITH OTHERS, THIN, NARROW STALKS WHICH THICKEN... INTO MUSLIN-LIKE CURTAINS OR EVEN SOLID-SEEMING LIMBS AND BODIES ARE EXTRUDED.**
>
> **CYRIL PERMUTT, PHOTOGRAPHING THE SPIRIT WORLD**

'As I was about to cut a lock high up, a firm hand behind the curtain lowered mine, so that I cut only about six inches [15 centimetres] from the end... I have kept this lock: it is very fine, silky and undyed. Microscopical examination shows it to be real hair... Marthe's hair is very dark and she wears her hair very short.'

Was it perhaps possible that Eva was producing these phenomena by smuggling props into the seance room? Many other mediums have been caught doing so before and since, but Richet and other investigators went to great lengths to satisfy themselves that the medium was not using trickery.

At seances conducted by the German physician Baron von Schrenck-Nötzing over a four-year period, the most stringent precautions were taken. The seance cabinet, which was usually a curtained section of the room, was searched; and Eva was stripped naked in front of witnesses and then clothed in a close-fitting garment from neck to feet. Often her head was completely covered by a veil of tulle, which was then sewn to the other garment.

Despite all these measures, sceptics still suggested that Eva was somehow able to secrete props about her person. The investigators carried out mouth, vaginal and anal examinations, but the medium was never found to be hiding anything. Another theory was that she was able to swallow

the props and regurgitate them during a seance. She was therefore given syrup of bilberries to drink, so that it would colour anything she had swallowed. But the ectoplasm that subsequently appeared was as white as before. On one occasion, Eva was even given an emetic before a seance, to make sure she had not swallowed muslin or paper. Within 10 minutes, she had vomited, and another theory was disproved. Even if she had managed to smuggle props into the seance room, the controls were so strict that it would seem to have been impossible for her to use them.

Throughout Schrenck-Nötzing's investigations, not a single seance was held in total darkness. A red light was used: at first this was a single lamp; but later on, the phenomena were witnessed beneath a six-lamp chandelier of more than 100 watts. The medium sat behind a curtain, or curtains, to provide her with the darkness necessary to produce ectoplasm. But she usually sat with her hands visible, drawing the curtains apart when phenomena occurred. At other times, witnesses held her hands all the time.

DAMAGING EVIDENCE

One of the investigators who conducted the seances with Schrenck-Nötzing was Juliette Bisson, in whose house Eva C lived for several years. To record their visual observations, the two researchers used a number of cameras (sometimes as many as nine), including stereoscopic equipment. These were arranged to take pictures simultaneously in order to record phenomena from a number of vantage points (including above and behind the curtain), not usually accessible to investigators. It was this arrangement that produced one of the most damaging pieces of evidence against Eva C. At a seance held in Paris on 27 November 1912, at which Schrenck-Nötzing and Mme Bisson

Eva is seen, above, producing ectoplasm in the form of a human face at a session in Paris on 22 November 1911. Although sceptics said that Eva's materialisations were unconvincing, others – such as Dr Gustave Geley – were sure that they were genuine. Geley described in detail how her ectoplasms were produced. Eva was first seated in a dark cabinet, and then entered a hypnotic state. When the phenomena started to appear, they produced painful sensations in her. She would sigh and moan, her groaning only ceasing when the forms were complete.

were the only observers, photographs were taken that showed the side view of a flat, creased disc, on which the words 'Le' in small type and 'Miro' in large type were visible. Schrenck-Nötzing commented: 'That is evidently meant to be "Le Miroir". We can just recognise the top of an "I" following the "O", but the next "R" is covered. I cannot form any opinion on this curious result.'

Others could, however, and were quick to suggest that the medium had used an image cut from the magazine *Le Miroir*. Yet Eva C's hands were in full view during the production of this ectoplasmic shape, according to Schrenck-Nötzing.

Schrenck-Nötzing published the picture, together with some candid criticisms, in 1914 in his book on the *Phenomena of Materialisation*, in which the pseudonym 'Eva C' was used for the first time. Perhaps Schrenck-Nötzing concealed the identity of the medium because he was afraid that an earlier allegation of fraud against her (in Algiers, when she was supposed to have confessed to cheating) would discredit his work.

This allegation had been made by an Arab coachman who had been dismissed by General Noel (in whose home the earlier seances took place) for theft. The coachman, who was called Areski, said he had 'played ghost' at the seances; he was even put on show dressed in white by a doctor in Algiers who wanted to expose the medium. But Areski's allegation is barely credible. He claimed that he entered the seance room with everyone else; and that, while the other sitters were examining the furniture, he would slip behind the curtain in readiness to play the part of a phantom. Richet, who attended these seances, dismissed the claim indignantly: 'Now, I declare formally and solemnly that during the seances – 20 in number – Areski was not once permitted to enter the seance room.'

KEEPING WATCH

Another allegation of fraud came from an observer who believed that Mme Bisson was collaborating with the medium, in order to dupe Schrenck-Nötzing. This doubting Thomas employed a Paris detective agency to keep watch on the two women, gather information and even acquire copies of Schrenck-Nötzing's seance photographs. But in the course of an eight-month enquiry, the agency failed to find any evidence of fraud, nor did it discover what material was being used to produce the materialisations.

The photographs themselves, many of which were published in Schrenck-Nötzing's book, would not convince anyone of the reality of materialisation. They appear to be crude fakes. Many show crumpled and creased two-dimensional images that seem to be attached to the medium's hair. They are a far cry from the fully-formed spirits that are said to walk and talk at the materialisation seances of the most powerful mediums.

Nevertheless, much of what occurred in the presence of Eva C is difficult to explain in normal terms, considering the strict controls imposed on her. At those seances that produced results (on average half the sittings were negative), it was a white substance that often appeared. This would change shape, move around slowly and throw out antennae-like spikes. Sometimes it would form

" THE SOLID SUBSTANCE IS MADE UP OF AN AMORPHOUS PROTOPLASMIC MASS, USUALLY WHITE, OCCASIONALLY GREY, BLACK OR EVEN FLESH COLOUR. IT EMANATES FROM THE WHOLE SURFACE OF THE MEDIUM'S BODY, BUT ESPECIALLY FROM THE SIDES, THE FINGERS, OR THE NATURAL ORIFICES... WHETHER THE SUBSTANCE IS VAPOROUS OR SOLID, IT IS AS A RULE VERY RAPIDLY ORGANISED AND THEN GIVES PERFECT OR IMPERFECT MATERIALISATIONS. "

DR GUSTAVE GELEY

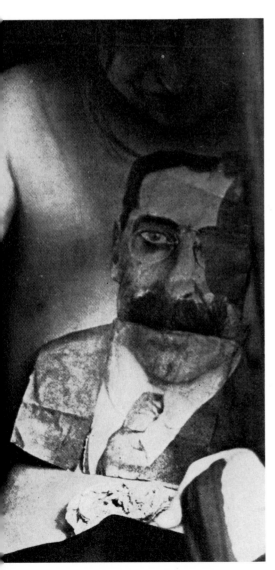

The photograph above was taken by a camera over Eva's head on 27 November 1912. It did considerable damage to her reputation.

At a session on 19 January 1913, left, Eva was alone with Mme Bisson and completely nude, as she sometimes was when the two were working together. Eva nevertheless managed to produce a materialisation. However, many people found the two-dimensional image unconvincing.

itself into a perfect hand, in which nails and bones could be detected. It would then return to a blob of white and disappear.

Further testimony comes from Dr Gustave Geley's book *From the Unconscious to the Conscious:*

'From the mouth of Eva there descends to her knees a cord of white substance of the thickness of two fingers... the cord... detaches itself from the medium and moves towards me. I then see the extremity thicken like a swelling, and this terminal swelling expands into a perfectly modelled hand. I touch it... I feel the bones, and the fingers with their nails. Then the hand contracts, diminishes, and disappears in the end of the cord.'

Geley held a number of experimental sessions with Eva in 1917 and 1918 at his own laboratories. Before these seances, she was stripped, searched and dressed in a garment that was then sewn at the back and wrists. Her hands were also held in full sight outside the curtains throughout the seances.

Whatever others many have thought of Eva's strange mediumistic powers, Geley was in no doubt. 'I do not merely say: There was no trickery; I say there was no possibility of trickery... The materialisations took place under my own eyes.'

After her run of successful seances with Geley, Eva's powers seem to have declined. She visited London in 1920 and held 40 seances for the Society for Psychical Research over a two-month period. But half of these were blank and the others resulted only in weak phenomena. Although no fraud was detected, the SPR committee suggested that regurgitation could have produced the materialisations they witnessed. In 1922, Eva gave a series of 15 seances at the Sorbonne in Paris, but these were equally inconclusive. Both Eva and her materialisations then faded into obscurity.

VINDICATING VELIKOVSKY

VELIKOVSKY'S WORK WAS ONCE DERIDED BY OPPONENTS; AND HIS THEORY OF 'CATACLYSMIC EVOLUTION' WAS DISMISSED AS PROOF OF INTELLECTUAL IRRESPONSIBILITY. BUT RESEARCH NOW SUPPORTS MANY OF HIS BELIEFS

The story of the publication of Immanuel Velikovsky's *Worlds in Collision* in 1950 – and subsequent attempts to suppress it – is one of the sorriest chapters in the history of ideas. In his book *Scientists Confront Velikovsky*, the sociologist Norman Storer does his best to excuse the attitude of scientists, pointing out that 1950 was in many ways a bad year, with the Cold War at its chilliest, and reactionary forces – exemplified by Senator Joe McCarthy's 'un-American activities' campaign – steadily gathering strength. Storer pleads disarmingly for the scientists:

'If we add to this the fact that Velikovsky could be only marginally distinguished from the myriad of eccentrics who have always assailed science, perhaps the initial response to his work can be understood.'

Plausible as this is, however, it fails to explain the gibbering rage with which respected scientists greeted the book, nor their determined efforts to suppress it.

To be fair, it is true that Velikovsky's basic thesis sounds lunatic at first. He asks us to believe that, sometime before 1500 BC, a comet erupted out of Jupiter. But, as far as we know, comets do not erupt out of planets. He also asks us to believe that this comet came close to the Earth at the time when Moses was trying to persuade Pharaoh to let the Israelites out of Egypt and that, as the Earth passed through the comet's tail, Egypt was smitten with the plagues described in *The Bible* – among them, water turning to blood, locusts, and the death of all the firstborn. He asks us to believe, too, that, as the centre of the comet came closer to the Earth, so the waters of the Red Sea rose until the two bodies met, when an almighty electrical discharge caused the waters to fall again so that the Israelites were able to cross the Red Sea when the waters were sucked back, while the pursuing Egyptians were drowned when the waters were once more released. Life on Earth might have become extinct were it not for the fact that the comet also dropped a kind of food in the form of carbohydrates – manna – that kept the survivors alive. Then, fifty years later, Velikovsky tells us, the comet returned just as Joshua was leading the Israelites into the Promised Land, and the walls of Jericho collapsed in the resultant earthquake

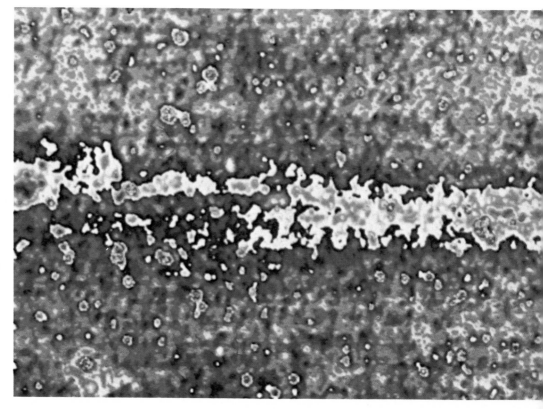

The computer-enhanced photograph of the 3-million-mile (5-million-kilometre) tail of Comet Kohoutek, right, was taken by Skylab in 1973. Velikovsky believed that the catastrophes described in The Bible – such as the plagues that afflicted Egypt, illustrated above right – occurred when the Earth passed through the tail of a comet that later became the planet Venus.

Most reasonable people feel that Velikovsky's hypotheses go too far. In a sense, he is a true Freudian in that he cannot resist seeing all the facts he comes across in terms of his theory – just as Freud, for example, saw just about every genius in history as an illustration of the Oedipus complex. But the fact remains that Velikovsky has presented a case to be answered.

While the controversy over *Worlds in Collision* was still raging, Velikovsky moved from New York to Princeton, New Jersey, and began to spend his days in the library of the Department of Geology at the University. Here, he gave time to studying material on the tremendous convulsions that are believed to have distorted the surface of our Earth at remote epochs in the past. In doing so, he was aware that he was reviving a theory that had actually been discredited in the 19th century – that of catastrophism. This was an attempt to explain such mysteries as fossil dinosaurs. How had these species come to vanish? The answer, according to eminent scientists like Georges Cuvier (1769-1832), was that a series of violent catastrophes had wiped out these species, forcing nature to start again from scratch. But Lyell's *Principles of Geology* and Darwin's *Origin of Species* destroyed the catastrophe theory by showing that our Earth is in fact thousands of millions of years old – not just a few thousand, as had been assumed – and that dinosaurs became extinct over a long period by the gradual process of natural selection. Or did they?

One of the unexplained facts of prehistory is that dinosaurs may have vanished quite suddenly. They had lasted a hundred million years, compared

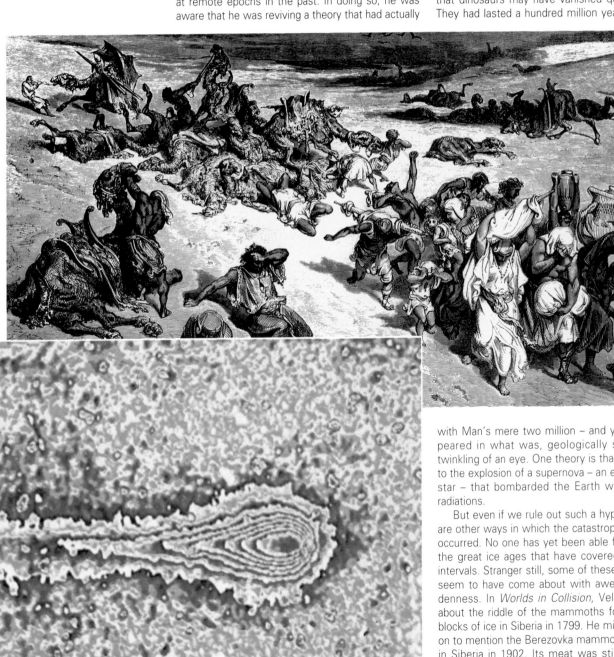

with Man's mere two million – and yet they disappeared in what was, geologically speaking, the twinkling of an eye. One theory is that this was due to the explosion of a supernova – an exploding giant star – that bombarded the Earth with poisonous radiations.

But even if we rule out such a hypothesis, there are other ways in which the catastrophe could have occurred. No one has yet been able fully to explain the great ice ages that have covered the Earth at intervals. Stranger still, some of these ice ages also seem to have come about with awe-inspiring suddenness. In *Worlds in Collision*, Velikovsky wrote about the riddle of the mammoths found frozen in blocks of ice in Siberia in 1799. He might have gone on to mention the Berezovka mammoth, discovered in Siberia in 1902. Its meat was still as edible as quick-frozen steak, and there were grasses and fresh buttercups in its stomach. Experts consulted a quick-freezing firm, who admitted that it had no idea of how to go about freezing a whole mammoth so that the flesh remained edible after thousands of

intervention. Meanwhile, Velikovsky's heterodox theory in many ways begins to look more like a genuine scientific inspiration.

It was unfortunate for Velikovsky that, by the time *Earth in Upheaval* appeared, the general public had largely lost interest in the controversy. By this time, he had published the first volume of his 'revised chronology of ancient history', *Ages in Chaos*, and most ordinary readers found this work confusing and boring. It is a lengthy comparison of various dates in Egyptian and Jewish history, together with an attempt to show that historians have got it all wrong. Even for the intelligent layman, the question of whether Queen Hatshepsut of Egypt was the same person as the Queen of Sheba is scarcely a vital issue.

There was also the fact that *Worlds in Collision* had been over-exposed. The mass onslaught on

The wall paintings at Deir el-Bahri, above left, show the Egyptian Queen Hatshepsut on a journey to the mysterious land of Punt. But Velikovsky suggested that the paintings show the Queen on her way to Jerusalem to visit King Solomon, and that Hatshepsut was actually the Queen of Sheba, shown left, in an illustration from a 15th-century manuscript. Hatshepsut is believed to have lived some centuries before Solomon – but Velikovsky boldly argues that she actually lived some 600 years later than is generally assumed.

years. Now, it takes 30 minutes to quick-freeze a mere side of beef. But a creature the size of a mammoth – covered with hair – could not be penetrated by cold in less than several days, and by then the stomach would have begun to decompose. Yet this had not happened in the case of the Berezovka mammoth. According to Velikovsky, probably 'the mammoths... were killed by a tempest of gases accompanied by a spontaneous lack of oxygen caused by fires raging high in the atmosphere.' Once asphyxiated, their bodies were almost immediately frozen when the land mass of Siberia moved into the polar region. But another explanation suggests a sudden lowering of the temperature.

One way in which this could have happened was for volcanoes to have shot out vast quantities of gas and dust into the atmosphere. Howling gales could have built up cold fronts, causing huge clouds of icy snow; and such a freezing cloud, encountering a patch of still, warm air – in a protected valley – would descend like a ton of bricks. Any mammoths in the valley would have been quick-frozen to death.

CATACLYSMIC EVOLUTION

The result of Velikovsky's study at Princeton was his most readable and fascinating work *Earth in Upheaval*. In this book, published in 1955, we can glimpse something of the daring intuition that makes his thought so exciting to follow. After discussing Darwin's theory of evolution, he raises serious doubts about its adequacy, and suggests instead a theory of 'cataclysmic evolution', according to which new species might appear by mutation of genes. At that time, every good biologist in the world was a Darwinian, and Velikovsky's 'cataclysmic evolution' was cited as evidence of his intellectual irresponsibility. Yet now biologists have come to recognise that Darwin's theory of evolution is probably highly questionable. Immense biological changes do occur in sudden leaps. Geneticists are still trying to understand the mechanism by which these occur, and may well find satisfactory explanations that do not require the hypothesis of outside

The head and leg of a young mammoth, below, were found in the Alaskan permafrost. Velikovsky suggested that the sudden disappearance of the mammoths was due to asphyxiation or electrocution, caused by fires in the atmosphere.

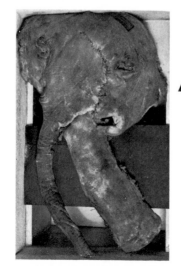

Velikovsky gave readers the impression that his theories had been totally discredited, while the titles of his books – *Worlds in Collision, Ages in Chaos, Earth in Upheaval* – gave rise to the suspicion that he was no more than a sensationalist. What happened might be compared with the events that followed publication of *The Third Eye* by T. Lobsang Rampa, when its author was revealed to be an Englishman using a Tibetan pseudonym. Despite his assurances that he was actually the reincarnation of a Tibetan monk, only the faithful stayed around to listen to the sequel. Fortunately, in Velikovsky's case, the 'faithful' finally succeeded in having the whole affair reopened.

" WE ARE MOST LIKELY TO GET ANGRY AND EXCITED IN OUR OPPOSITION TO SOME IDEA WHEN WE OURSELVES ARE NOT QUITE CERTAIN OF OUR OWN POSITION, AND ARE INWARDLY TEMPTED TO TAKE THE OTHER SIDE. **"**

THOMAS MANN

MOST CHRISTIANS BELIEVE THAT CHRIST DIED ON THE CROSS. BUT A LEGEND FROM THE REMOTE HILLS OF NORTHERN INDIA SUGGESTS THAT HE SURVIVED THE CRUCIFIXION AND LIVED OUT HIS OLD AGE THERE

At Lake Nagin, near Srinagar, the capital city of Kashmir, below, many local inhabitants believe that Jesus Christ got married, raised children, and lived out his last days in the area.

The Kashmiri city of Srinagar, in the hills of northernmost India, houses – so it is claimed – one of the world's most precious and controversial archaeological relics. In front of a Muslim cemetery, towards the centre of the city, stands a solitary rectangular building, described on a notice in the street outside as a *rauza bal* – a 'prophet's tomb'. Inside, a carved wooden plaque bearing the inscription 'the tomb of Yuz Asaf' indicates a chamber containing a simple stone tomb, confirmed as a holy monument by a state document of Srinagar from 1766. The text gives brief details of the tomb's enigmatic occupant:

'In the reign of rajah Gopadatta . . . a man named Yuz Asaf came. He was a royal prince and renounced all worldly claims, becoming a legislator. He used to spend his nights and days in prayer to God, and passed long periods in solitary meditation... He preached the oneness of God until death overcame him... '

And so the matter would rest with this epitaph to an obscure holy man, who lived, taught and died in Kashmir – except that this particular holy man is held by local tradition to have been none other than Jesus Christ.

The apparently incredible claim that Jesus died in Kashmir is upheld not only by the hereditary keepers of the tomb in Srinagar but by adherents of the world-wide Ahmadiyya Muslim sect, who number several hundred thousand. The Ahmadiyya, as well as various writers sympathetic to their cause, have assembled a fascinating collection of legends and scraps of historical information from records held in Iran, Afghanistan, Pakistan and India. From

DID CHRIST DIE IN KASHMIR?

PARADISE ON EARTH

In his fascinating book, *Jesus Lived in India*, German-born author, traveller and teacher Holger Kersten recounts how, in the middle of the 19th century, the Identification Society of London was formed. Its purpose was specifically to investigate what happened to the ten lost tribes of Israel.

One of their prime findings was that the population of Kashmir is very likely to be of Jewish descent. Several factors led them to this conclusion. There are, for instance, many place and family names that are similar to those cited in the Old Testament. It is also apparent that Kashmiris are rather different from the other peoples of India – not only in their facial characteristics but also in their mode of dress and certain customs. The men, for instance, wear small caps, rather like those worn by Jewish males during prayer and by the more orthodox at all times.

There are a number of notable similarities between the language of Kashmir and Hebrew, too. Kersten tells how the women practise certain rituals when it comes to bathing after childbirth that echo age-old Jewish custom; and even preferences for the mode of preparation for certain foods are reputed as showing a striking likeness.

To the south of Srinagar, the capital of Kashmir, meanwhile, can be found the Temple of Martand, featuring numerous Hindu carvings but otherwise with an architectural style that is essentially Jewish in character.

It seems that there is much to indicate early Jewish settlement in various regions of the Indian sub-continent. Abraham, patriarch of the Jewish people, lived at one point – according to the *Book of Genesis* – in Haran but was commanded by God to leave. It could, of course, be a matter of coincidence, but there is actually a small town by this very name just a few miles north of Srinagar.

Some have even ventured to suggest that Kashmir may well be the biblical Promised Land. In the language of Kashmir, the country's name does in fact signify 'Paradise on Earth'. Indeed, the land is known worldwide for its predominance of beautiful lakes, wooded mountains and fertile valleys. What is more, it has always been a region of great spiritual influence, too.

It would seem, therefore, that there is much to indicate early Jewish settlement in various regions of the Indian sub-continent. Dr George Moore is even known to have discovered a stone with an inscription in Aramaic – the language in which Jesus, born in Palestine, some 2,000 years ago, would have been raised.

P E R S P E C T I V E S

The plain building, below, which stands outside a Muslim cemetery in the centre of Srinagar, allegedly houses the tomb of Yuz Asaf – a holy man whom the local inhabitants believe to have been Jesus Christ himself. Inside, ornate trelliswork, below right, conceals the simplest of tombs, right, in an east-west alignment. Muslims bury their dead facing north-south, and Hindus do not bury their dead at all. Jewish graves, on the other hand, are often aligned east-west. So Yuz Asaf may well have been a saint of the Jewish tradition.

these, they believe, there can be written a final chapter in Christ's life – a chapter unknown to Western historians.

After the last deeds told of him in the *New Testament* – the resurrection, appearance to various disciples and ascension to heaven – according to the Ahmadiyya's reconstruction, Jesus left Palestine to escape the jurisdiction of the Romans and the possibility of being crucified again. He took the road north through Damascus, bringing about the conversion of St Paul on the way, to seek refuge with scattered Jewish communities further east. Accompanied by his mother Mary, he walked on through what are now Iraq, Iran and Afghanistan (then parts of Rome's rival empire, Parthia) to India, where he wandered, teaching prayer, monotheism and godliness. In the East, he acquired the name Yuz Asaf – meaning, in Persian, 'leader of those cured of sores [leprosy]'.

Some say that Yuz Asaf came to Kashmir via Pakistan, and that when his aged mother died he buried her in the city of Murree, some 30 miles (50 kilometres) north-east of present-day Rawalpindi. Others say he travelled and taught in Ceylon (now Sri Lanka) before arriving in Kashmir, where he lived out the rest of his natural days. He was buried by his disciple Ba'bad in Srinagar, where his tomb has remained a venerated holy spot until this day. And if these tales of a 'second life of Christ' are not enough, there are further stories to shock believers

story does show that identification of Jesus with Yuz Asaf goes back some thousand years.

As one reads the legends of Yuz Asaf – gathered by the Ahmadiyya from sources as far apart as Iran and Sri Lanka – conviction grows that we are dealing with a facsimile of Christ, albeit in most unfamiliar surroundings. Local traditions describe him as 'an auspicious man, fair in colour and clad in white garments', who performed miracles, communicated with angels and announced himself to be the son of a virgin. In fact, every detail of his character and behaviour is 'Christ-like', making it most unlikely that the story represents Christian mythology foisted on to a genuine Hindu saint called Yuz Asaf. Indeed, the traditions seem indisputably to be talking about Jesus Christ, whatever their origin. It is an integral part of all the tales that he was a foreigner, a prophet from much further west. One Persian manuscript even specifies his point of origin as the Holy Land, the term used by Muslims, as well as others, for Palestine (now Israel).

As for the tomb itself, while the stone cover is of Muslim date, underneath is a more ancient burial chamber, aligned east-west. Since Muslims bury their dead aligned north-south, and Hindus do not bury their dead at all, the likelihood is that the occupant was a Jew. (Jewish graves, including many in Kashmir, are often aligned east-west.) Islam recognises no prophet after Mohammed, so the strong local tradition that the tomb houses a prophet suggests, in predominantly Muslim Kashmir, that it

in Christ's death upon the cross. According to one Persian tradition, Yuz Asaf was persuaded by an Indian king to take on a local woman as housekeeper. Her duties evidently extended beyond cooking and cleaning, however, as she is said to have borne him children. There is even a man in Srinagar (a local politician and newspaper editor, as well as official keeper of the tomb of Yuz Asaf) who claims to trace his ancestry directly back to Jesus.

The initial temptation to reject the whole story as a delusion or ludicrous and elaborate hoax is strong. But legends about Yuz Asaf are both prolific and ancient, and the fact that they tell of a figure with an extraordinary resemblance to the founder of the Christian religion surely merits their consideration. The 10th-century Islamic scholar Al-Said-us-Sadiq, for example, recounts a Hindu story of the arrival of the holy Yuz Asaf in Kashmir. His extensive travels, death and burial are described in detail, as are his teachings of the desirability of shunning worldly desires, the value of humility and the impending arrival of the kingdom of heaven. The inclusion of a parable about truth falling like scattered seeds – similar in many ways to Jesus's own parable of the sower (*Mark* 4:3-20) – also suggests that we may be dealing here with the life of Jesus Christ himself. Sadiq wrote, of course, at a time when the teachings of the *New Testament* were widely available to Islamic scholars and he could easily have added such details himself. But his

We can assess the Ahmadiyya theory by looking again at evidence from the other end of Yuz Asaf's long journey – Palestine, and the biblical account. There are two main questions. Could Jesus really have survived the rigours of the crucifixion? And if he did, is India historically plausible as the last resting place of a first-century guru from Palestine?

Christian theology, of course, has much to say about the first question. It insists both that Christ died on the cross and that he continued to live, after the resurrection, in more than spirit form. Indeed, the *New Testament* is most insistent that Christ's resurrection is also to be understood in the physical sense. When Mary Magdalene and her friends came to the tomb they found the body had gone and that the stone sealing it had rolled away. (If Christ had appeared only as a wraith, rolling away the stone would have been unnecessary.) Shortly afterwards, he appeared to Mary; then, meeting two travellers on the way to Emmaus, he joined them at supper in most unghost-like fashion (*Luke* 24: 13-32). He then arrived at a meeting of the remaining 11 disciples, who 'were terrified and affrighted, and supposed they had seen a spirit', until Christ persuaded them to feel him and see that he was real flesh and blood (*Luke* 24:36-40; *John* 20:27-8). As a further demonstration, he then sat down and had a meal, while he talked to the baffled disciples.

As well as these appearances recorded in the Gospels, St Paul adds that Christ was seen by

dates from before the life of Mohammed (c. 570-632). These pointers strongly suggest that the tomb contains the remains of a prophet of Jewish race, buried at some time before the rise of Islam.

Investigation of the tomb was carried out by Professor Fida Hassnain, director of the archives and antiquities of Kashmir. Study of documents concerning the tomb convinced him of its authenticity, though solid archaeological evidence of its date and character is still conspicuously lacking. A plan for a full-scale excavation in the 1950s, backed by Ahmadiyya funds, eventually foundered, but Hassnain's surface probings turned up one intriguing find. In the north-east corner of the chamber is a stone block once used as a table for lighting candles by pilgrims to the tomb. Scraping away thick layers of wax, Hassnain found a rosary and a crucifix that had been left by Christian visitors, and then uncovered the surface of the stone itself. It shows, curiously enough, what appears to be the impression of two human feet, deeply gouged on the insides. The 'impressions' are obviously carved and are perhaps intended – it has been conjectured – to represent the feet of a crucified man.

In the absence of firm archaeological corroboration, the case for Christ's burial in Kashmir stands on the evidence of legends. The approach of the Ahmadiyya sect to these is straightforward. The obvious explanation, they say, is that Christ retreated to the East after his ordeals in Palestine. To tie up the story, the Ahmadiyya also point out that the dates of the kings, such as the rajah Gopadatta, in whose reigns Yuz Asaf was said to have been active, all fall around the middle of the first century AD, in the decades following Christ's crucifixion in around the year 33.

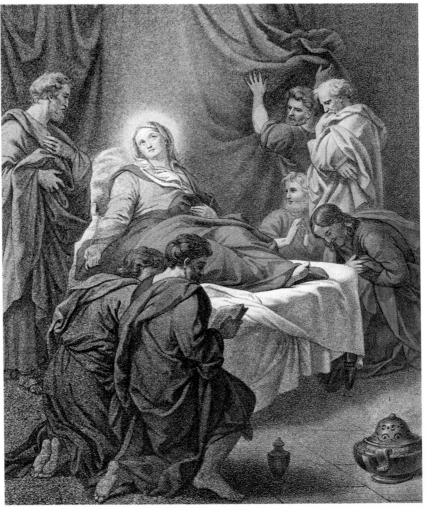

The conversion of St Paul on the road to Damascus, is shown left, in a detail from a 19th-century stained glass window in Lincoln Cathedral. If the account of Christ's survival of the crucifixion is true, such stories, in which Christ allegedly made physical appearances, take on entirely new significance.

The Srinagar poet Sahibzada Basharat Saleem, below, believes he can trace his ancestry back to Jesus Christ. According to legend, Christ married a Kashmiri girl.

A stone block found in the north-east corner of the Yuz Asaf shrine, above left, shows what appears to be the impression of two human feet bearing the marks of Christ's wounds.

A 19th-century engraving after a painting by Carle Maratte of the death of the Virgin Mary is reproduced left. Kashmiri legend has it that, after survival of the crucifixion, Christ and his mother travelled through what are now Iraq, Iran, Afghanistan and Pakistan where, at Murree, Mary died. Jesus is said to have then travelled on to India alone.

and scholar Robert Graves, who added as a footnote to his own study of the crucifixion that he was himself logged 'died of wounds' by an experienced medical officer after the battle of the Somme in 1916, and was left in a corner, unattended, for a whole day before showing signs of recovery:

'I managed to conserve my vital heat for little less than the thirty hours which Jesus spent in the tomb, with only a stretcher between myself and the bare earth; and the physical resistance of Oriental saints is notoriously greater than that of European sinners.'

It does not seem beyond the bounds of reason to entertain the idea that someone with the extraordinary strength of mind exhibited by Jesus could revive after remaining in a death-like state of suspended animation for up to two days. This feat is, after all, a commonplace 'trick' performed by Indian yogis, who survive after days of burial underground. Such a solution would seem to satisfy the evidence of the *New Testament*. But it would, of course, be unacceptable to those Christians who insist on a real resurrection from the dead as a sign of Christ's true divinity.

However, neither the extreme Christian nor the outright sceptical view is acceptable to the historian. It is not reasonable to treat an article of faith as historical evidence; on the other hand, the sceptics' light dismissal of the post-crucifixion appearances of Christ flies in the face of what is, after all, the most natural explanation for the explosive growth of the early Christian Church. For, although we have only the word of the *New Testament* writers for the reappearance of Christ (unlike the crucifixion, for which we have evidence from Roman and Jewish writings of the period), we do know that Christianity spread like wildfire in the middle of the first century AD. What can account for this? The *New Testament* presents the highly plausible scene of a small group of followers, made doubtful and utterly disillusioned by the arrest and crucifixion of their leader, subsequently inspired and revitalised by the return of the Messiah. The resurrection of Christ, testified by numerous witnesses, is the lynchpin of the faith of the early Christian apostles; 'And if Christ be not raised, your faith is in vain,' says St Paul (*1 Corinthians* 15:17). But what if Christ really did continue to live after the crucifixion – not because he was resurrected, but because he did not die in the first place?

'about five hundred brethren at once', and on other occasions by himself and St James. What are we to make of these claims about Christ's resurrection? According to a rational, materialistic approach, no resurrection of a completely dead man could have happened; and if the stories of Christ's appearance after the crucifixion are authentic, then Christ must have been buried in a comatose state from which he later awoke. Today, doctors are still arguing about the precise definition of 'death', and the annals of 20th-century medicine are full of cases of apparently 'dead' people coming back to life. One interesting example comes from the English poet

❚❚ ALMOST EVERYTHING THAT HAS EVER BEEN SAID ABOUT JESUS HAS PARALLELS IN ANCIENT INDIAN LEGENDS... NOT UNTIL RECENTLY HAVE TRANSLATIONS BEGUN TO AROUSE INTEREST IN THE WESTERN WORLD. **❚❚**

HOLGER KERSTEN,

JESUS LIVED IN INDIA

THE LEY LINE PUZZLE

ARE THE STRAIGHT LINES THAT JOIN THE SACRED MEGALITHICS OF EUROPE MERELY A RELIC OF ANCIENT PATHWAYS? OR DO THEY SHOW THAT EARLY MAN WAS FAR MORE ADVANCED THAN WE GENERALLY SUPPOSE?

Looking out over the countryside near Bredwardine, one June day in 1921, Alfred Watkins, a respectable Herefordshire brewer, had a startling vision – one he later described as 'a flood of ancestral memory'. What he saw was a totally new pattern in the familiar countryside that lay before him – a complex network of straight lines, linking burial mounds, hilltops,

ancient churches and crossroads to make 'a fairy chain, stretched from mountain peak to mountain peak, as far as the eye could reach, and paid out until it touched the high places of the earth at a number of ridges, banks and knowls.'

Watkins, who had his reputation in a small town to consider, did not at first tell anyone about his discovery. Instead, he sat down with maps and rulers,

Herefordshire brewer Alfred Watkins, above, discovered that many of the megalithic sites of ancient Britain are aligned. It was he who coined the word 'ley' for these alignments because many of the places located on them have names ending in 'ley', 'lay', 'lee', 'lea' or 'leigh'.

At 25 feet 6 inches (7.7 metres), the monolith in the churchyard at Rudstone, Humberside, shown left, is the tallest standing stone in Britain. A ley runs through the stone itself – but not through the adjacent Norman church.

Circular moats count as ley points, too, for they have often developed from ditches around tumuli. But square moats are frequently much later developments and cannot really be counted as 'safe' primary ley markers. Ponds sometimes fall on leys, as the light reflected from the surface of the water provides a clear landmark. Yet while ponds and fords are not generally considered to be primary markers, they can act as points of confirmation of leys. Holy wells, such as St Ambrew's Well at Crantock, in Cornwall, and St Hilda's Well at Hinderwell in North Yorkshire, are also important markers, often indicating the starting point of a ley.

Castles and early churches appear on leys, it seems, because many of them are built on the sites of more ancient buildings or earthworks: castles, for instance, were generally built on hills because this gave their protectors a good view of the countryside and a strong defensive position. The hill itself was also often a prehistoric earthwork. Indeed, excavations at Worcester, Penworham and Warrington have brought to light pre-Norman artefacts in the mounds of each of these castles.

There is in fact a great deal of evidence to show how churches replaced and supplanted pagan shrines on the same sites. Pope Gregory, writing at the end of the sixth century AD, complained: 'The English nation, placed in an obscure corner of the

and began checking carefully for evidence that would back up his inspired vision. Time and again, he found that the lines on his maps passed through the same kinds of places – all ancient, and all of some significance to Man.

PRIMARY MARKERS

It was Watkins, in fact, who coined the term 'ley' to describe these lines. Others call them scemb lines, geomantic corridors, or simply alignments – but all who believe in their existence agree on the features that can be taken as their primary markers. Stone circles – of which there are about 900 in Britain alone – are important markers, as are stone rows, such as the one on Stall Moor that continues for 2 miles (3 kilometres) across Dartmoor, linking a stone circle with a prehistoric cairn on Green Hill. Other standing stones are also possible ley markers, but not all of them are shown on Ordnance Survey maps. It is difficult to miss a stone like the Rudston monolith, which towers 25 feet (7.5 metres) high in a churchyard near Bridlington, Humberside, or the Devil's Arrows near Boroughbridge, North Yorkshire; but other stones are much smaller and more difficult to find, sometimes lying hidden in hedges or converted into churchyard crosses.

Cairns, tumuli, prehistoric camps and mounds are said to form another group of ley markers. The oldest of these are the Neolithic long barrows – mounds of earth or chalk that can be several hundred feet long and 100 feet (30 metres) wide. One feature making them easily recognisable is that one end is generally higher than the other. Round barrows are the most common sort of mound. There are about 20,000 of them in Britain, and sometimes they are clustered together – like the collection close to the A35 road at Winterbourne Abbas in Dorset; sometimes they are solitary.

were obtained from formulae that were, if anything, loaded against the ley concept, for many alignments feature six or more points in a length of perhaps only 10 or 12 miles (12 or 15 kilometres).

RIFLE-BARREL ACCURACY

A completely separate and detailed computer analysis was also prepared to test certain work that John Michell published in *The Old Stones of Land's End*. Michell had surveyed 53 sites in Cornwall, using only those that were known to be prehistoric. He found 22 leys between them, 'of rifle-barrel accuracy', with the sites visible from one to the next and forming precise alignments up to 6 miles (10 kilometres) long. The computer analysis verified all but two of Michell's alignments – and added 29 more leys he had not identified!

Professional archaeologists form another group that looks on the idea of a ley system linking Britain's ancient sites in some meaningful grid as totally absurd. They have shown not only a complete lack of interest in, but a positive hostility to, the notion. Professor Glyn Daniels, former editor of *Antiquity*, a mouthpiece of the profession, is said even to have refused to accept advertisements for the monthly journal *The Ley Hunter*. The question of leys, when brought up in interviews with archaeologists, also frequently elicits the sort of response that the flat-earthers must have given to the first brave person who began to think of the world as a sphere.

Yet it was an exceedingly reputable scholar, Sir Norman Lockyer, Astronomer Royal, who – at the beginning of the century – first rediscovered an important alignment that centres on Stonehenge. Lockyer found that the principal axis on which Stonehenge is aligned – the angle of the midsummer sunrise – joins with the Neolithic settlement at Grovely Castle. The distance between the two is 6 miles (10 kilometres). He then found that Old Sarum, another prehistoric hilltop site where Salisbury's first cathedral had been built, also lay exactly 6 miles (10 kilometres) from Stonehenge,

world, has hitherto been wholly taken up with the adoration of wood and stones,' but concluded that: 'It is not well to make people of an obstinate turn grow better by leaps, but rather by slow steps.' The missionary Augustine was also advised not to destroy the old shrines and temples, but to modify them, sprinkle them with holy water, incorporating the healing qualities of the pagan wells, and to convert the local people slowly. This is why many churches stand on top of ancient man-made hills, such as Brent Tor on Dartmoor, or inside henge monuments, like the ruins of the strange church at Knowlton in Dorset, a 12th-century building that stands centrally in a huge prehistoric religious enclosure, a quarter of a mile (350 metres) from the village, surrounded on all sides by other enclosures and burial mounds.

Despite such evidence, there are many people who do not believe in the existence of these strange patterns and alignments. Statisticians discount the existence of leys by saying that, in an island as small, as varied and as densely populated as Britain, straight lines drawn in any direction on Ordnance Survey maps are bound to run through ancient sites, holy wells, tumuli and other features that ley hunters consider to be significant. Mathematicians have even prepared formulae and tested them on a computer in an attempt to prove that ley lines occur simply by chance. Unfortunately for the statisticians, however, their formulae turned out to be enemies rather than allies. Analysis showed that the chance factor was only one in 200 for a six-point ley – that is, for six significant and generally accepted ley markers to fall exactly in a straight line not more than 30 miles (50 kilometres) long. For a seven-point ley, the random element soars to one in 1,000. What is more, these results

The holy well of St Ambrew at Crantock, Cornwall, is shown above. Holy wells often mark the ends of leys.

The ruined church at Knowlton, Dorset, below, stands at the centre of a huge earthen circle. Churches were often built on sacred megalithic sites, and frequently act as ley markers.

The Iron-Age hill fort of Old Sarum is in alignment with Salisbury Cathedral and another hill fort, Clearbury Ring, as shown above. These sites form part of the important Old Sarum ley, which also passes through Stonehenge.

and that the same distance separated Old Sarum from Grovely Castle. The three points make a perfect equilateral triangle, too perfect to have occurred by chance. It was a first hint of early Man's obsession with patterns and numbers.

Another bombshell for the archaeologists came in 1967 from the research of Alexander Thom, Professor Emeritus of Engineering Science at Oxford. Thom surveyed more than 600 megalithic sites in Britain and France, and concluded that prehistoric Man had laid them out, with astonishingly precise engineering skill, in an astronomical alignment. Thom also discovered a basic unit of measurement, the 'megalithic yard' that corresponds to 2 feet 8 inches (81 centimetres).

These discoveries forced many people to revise their ideas. As the eminent archaeologist Professor Richard Atkinson wrote in the journal *Antiquity*:

'It is important that non-archaeologists should understand how disturbing to archaeologists are the implications of Thom's work, because they do not fit the conceptual model of the prehistory of Europe which has been current during the whole of the present century and even now is beginning to crumble at the edges... In terms of this model, it is almost inconceivable that mere barbarians on the remote north-west fringes of the continent should display a knowledge of mathematics and its applications hardly inferior, if at all, to that of Egypt at about the same date, or that of Mesopotamia, considerably later.'

Professor Thom's meticulous research established beyond doubt that early Man had constructed his monuments with precision and forethought. One question, however, remains. What was it that inspired him to do so?

> **"** FAINT TRACES OF ANCIENT TRACK OR EARTHWORK ARE MOST EASILY SEEN WHEN THE SUN IS LOW ON ONE SIDE – IN LATE EVENING... THE METHOD IN THE FUTURE IS AN AEROPLANE FLIGHT ALNG THE LEY. FAINT TRACKS ARE TO BE SEEN FROM THE AIR... WHICH ARE INVISIBLE ON THE GROUND. **"**
>
> **ALFRED WATKINS,**
> **THE OLD STRAIGHT TRACK**

*In*Focus

A 'LEYMAN'S' VIEW

Alfred Watkins, the discoverer of ley lines – ancient straight tracks that criss-cross the British Isles and other parts of Europe – was born in the town of Hereford, England, in 1855. After leaving school, he became a representative of his father's brewery, travelling widely in the area, and gaining intimate knowledge of the county's topography and legends. In 1921, the 65-year-old Watkins – by then, a prominent merchant, landscape photographer (he invented the pinhole camera) and local magistrate – was struck by the realisation that many ancient sites seemed to be aligned by a network of tracks, some visible, some not. They also appeared to be aligned either with the sun or the path of a star. For the next 14 years, until his death in 1935, Watkins explored this idea further. Finally, he came to the conclusion that these tracks – or leys – were man-made paths laid down between 4,000 and 2,000 years BC, but later abandoned and forgotten. Much of his work on leys was set out in his two books, *Early British Trackways* and *The Old Straight Track*.

THE MIRACLE SURGEONS

CERTAIN NATIVES OF THE PHILIPPINES AND BRAZIL ARE ALLEGEDLY ABLE TO OPERATE USING ONLY THEIR BARE HANDS. THEIR SKILL IS ENTHUSIASTICALLY PRAISED BY PATIENTS – BUT HOW DOES IT FARE UNDER SCRUTINY BY WESTERN SCIENTISTS?

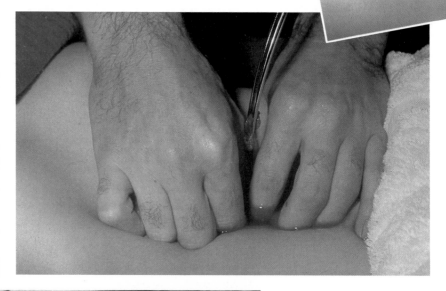

Of all paranormal phenomena, that which has become known as psychic surgery is undoubtedly one of the most extraordinary. Since the 1950s, there have been many reports of such bare-handed surgery, allegedly witnessed by scores of observers and undergone by thousands of willing patients. There is, remarkably, nothing at all furtive about the practice, and it can be seen taking place in broad daylight.

Despite extravagant claims, however, psychic surgery is now regarded by many people as no more than a shabby deception – or, more kindly, if patronisingly, as the product of primitive and super-stitious cultures. Its history seems to have followed a now familiar pattern: it looked good at first, but its credibility was soon whittled away by criticism levelled at it.

Investigators at first assured Western scientists that uneducated, medically ignorant men and

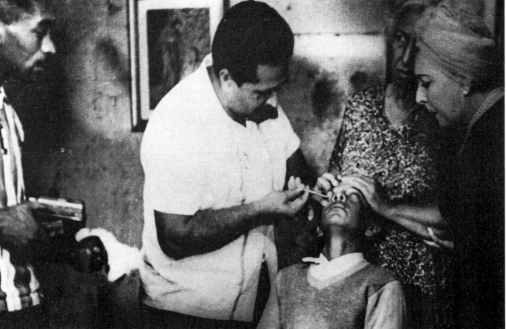

The Brazilian psychic surgeon José Pedro de Freitas, left, nicknamed Arigó, or 'yokel', is seen performing an eye operation. Arigó's surgery, often practised with such crude instruments as rusty scissors and kitchen knives, attracted a great deal of attention in the West. His operations appeared to effect genuine cures – although the work of other psychic surgeons has been laid open to doubt.

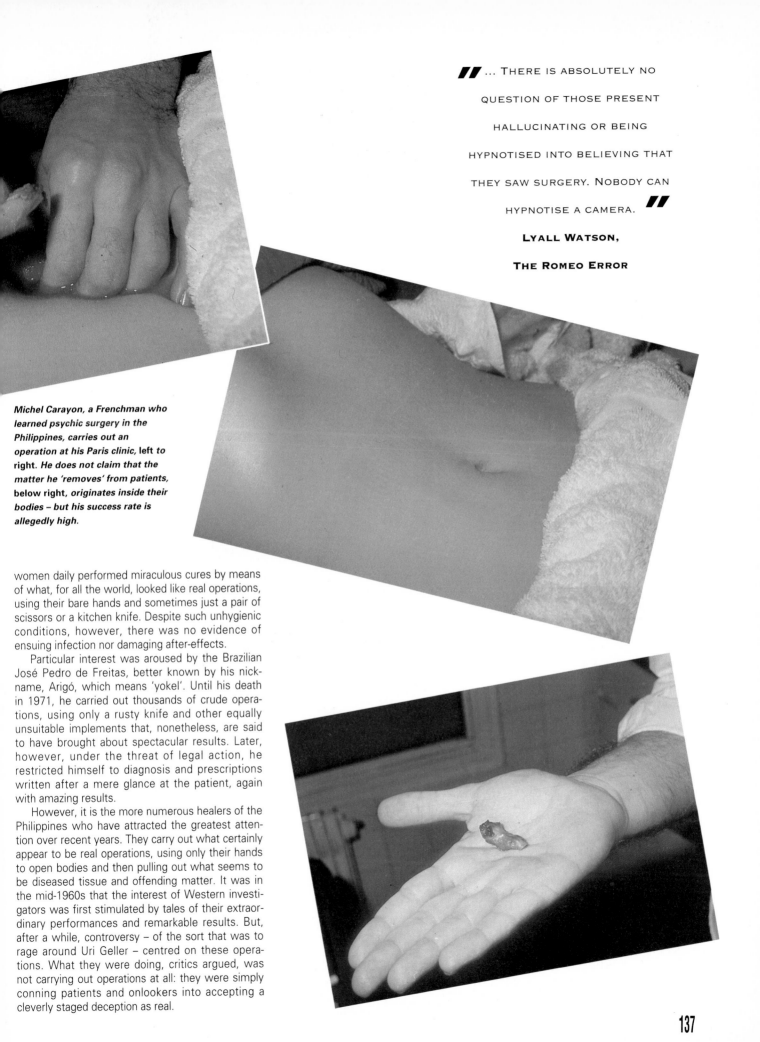

Michel Carayon, a Frenchman who learned psychic surgery in the Philippines, carries out an operation at his Paris clinic, left to right. He does not claim that the matter he 'removes' from patients, below right, originates inside their bodies – but his success rate is allegedly high.

women daily performed miraculous cures by means of what, for all the world, looked like real operations, using their bare hands and sometimes just a pair of scissors or a kitchen knife. Despite such unhygienic conditions, however, there was no evidence of ensuing infection nor damaging after-effects.

Particular interest was aroused by the Brazilian José Pedro de Freitas, better known by his nickname, Arigó, which means 'yokel'. Until his death in 1971, he carried out thousands of crude operations, using only a rusty knife and other equally unsuitable implements that, nonetheless, are said to have brought about spectacular results. Later, however, under the threat of legal action, he restricted himself to diagnosis and prescriptions written after a mere glance at the patient, again with amazing results.

However, it is the more numerous healers of the Philippines who have attracted the greatest attention over recent years. They carry out what certainly appear to be real operations, using only their hands to open bodies and then pulling out what seems to be diseased tissue and offending matter. It was in the mid-1960s that the interest of Western investigators was first stimulated by tales of their extraordinary performances and remarkable results. But, after a while, controversy – of the sort that was to rage around Uri Geller – centred on these operations. What they were doing, critics argued, was not carrying out operations at all: they were simply conning patients and onlookers into accepting a cleverly staged deception as real.

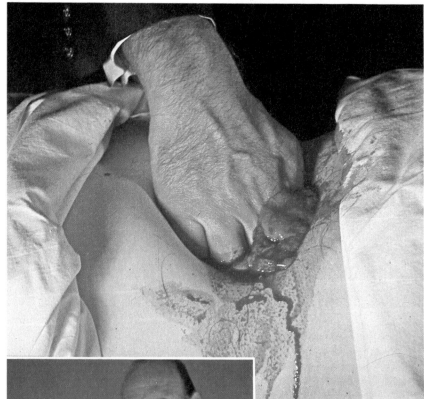

Evidence against the psychic surgeons then started to stack up heavily, and cries of fraud grew louder as teams of investigators began to return, not with the glowing accounts of miraculous recoveries of earlier days, but with evidence of shabby deceit and exploitation.

DAMNING EVIDENCE

In the early 1970s, debunking articles appeared first in the German press and on television. Then, in Britain, in 1975, Granada Television screened its own damning investigative programmes on psychic surgery, and these were followed in 1979 by the BBC's *Nationwide* exposé of the Elizaldes, a husband-and-wife team who visited the UK to treat patients. Yet again, what had looked like a promising, repeatable demonstration of paranormal powers in action was subjected to the same kind of public demolition.

But can the case really be said to be closed? Some are convinced that there is nothing more to be said about psychic surgery. It is simply a case of gullible observers being taken in by impressive but, in the end, identifiable sleight of hand. Is this really all that can be said? To answer these questions, first of all we need to trace the story of psychic surgery back to its roots and take a look at the evidence more closely.

The Filipino psychic surgeons were discovered among their own people, on their own territory, and within the context of their own culture and traditions. They did not ever advertise their talents, nor did they go out of their way to prove their abilities, but were tracked down by investigators from the other side of the globe.

The Philippines have a long tradition of belief in the reality of the spiritual and psychic worlds. This provided fertile ground for the Spiritist movement that took root there in the 19th century. Indeed, there are still flourishing chapters of the Spiritist society to be found throughout the Philippines. But the focal point of Spiritist activity is found on Luzon, the largest island in the archipelago, where biologist, writer and researcher Lyall Watson located the densest concentration of healers in an agricultural community 60 miles (100 kilometres) north of the capital, Manila. The majority of the healers living and working on Luzon belong to the Union Espiritista Cristiana de Filipinas, a network of rural Spiritist churches.

Lyall Watson was one of the first Westerners who went to discover for themselves what psychic surgery was all about. During three separate visits to the Philippines, occupying eight months in all, he witnessed over one thousand operations performed by 22 different healers. He was duly impressed, and what is more, he remained so despite the controversy that had already begun to detract from the credibility of earlier fulsome accounts of the Filipinos' powers.

Watson went as a scientist to carry out an unbiased investigation of the healers, and his book *The Romeo Error* tells of what he found. Also featured is a blow-by-blow account of a typical operation lasting about five minutes that, as far as Watson is concerned, was a genuine demonstration of psychic surgery.

" WHAT FIRST STRIKES EVERYBODY WHO IS ABLE TO WITNESS PSYCHIC SURGERY IS THE AMAZING SPEED AT WHICH SOME, BUT NOT ALL, SURGEONS WORK, AND THE COMPLETE SELF-CONFIDENCE THEY ALL SHOW IN THE PROCESS. "

GUY PLAYFAIR, THE FLYING COW

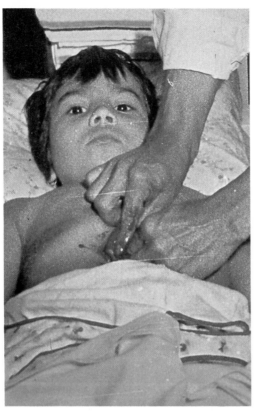

The subject of the operation was a middle-aged woman who complained of a nagging pain in the stomach. She was asked to lie down on a wooden table, fully dressed; her abdomen was bared and her skirt covered with a towel. Like a true sceptic, Watson examined the towel for anything that might be concealed within it: 'I find it innocent, if none too clean,' he said. The healer, dressed in cotton trousers and a short-sleeved shirt, entered and showed Watson he was concealing nothing in the folds of his clothes.

The healer said a prayer. Watson handed him some cotton wool and a bowl that Watson had himself filled with water from an ordinary tap. The healer used them to cleanse the woman's abdomen.

'He is now working just to the right of her navel, and suddenly there is red colour. It could be blood. At first it is watery, mixing with the moisture on her skin, but now it darkens and gurgles quite strongly up between his fingers... I can see what looks like connective tissue, thin, almost transparent, obviously elastic, red and bloody.'

The healer next appeared to push his hands deep into the patient's body. Pressing hard, he spread the fingers of his right hand, and a large ball – apparently from inside the patient – began to grow between the first and second fingers. When, in a matter of seconds, it had reached the size of a tennis ball, an assistant reached over with a pair of forceps and lifted the lump clear of the patient's abdomen. He then snipped away at the thread of tissue still connecting the cyst to the patient's body until it came clear, and dropped it into Watson's hand. Watson commented: 'It is warm and when I press it, only a little blood oozes out. It seems to be hard inside.'

After the healer had finished his work and the remainder of the blood had been wiped off the patient's stomach, there was, astonishingly, no visible wound. 'I rub my hand over her skin,' says Watson. 'It is hot, but there is nothing on it, not a mark of any kind.' The woman got up slowly and walked away.

Many others were to make the trip to the Philippines to observe, speculate and wonder. Thousands also travelled to receive treatment from the psychic surgeons, often as a last resort when orthodox medicine had failed to help. Conflicting accounts are given by both patients and investigative groups. Some have said that they experienced or witnessed events that could not be explained away as fraud. Others wrote off psychic surgery as a hoax. By the early 1970s, a great deal of interest was being generated in Europe and the USA, but it seemed that the more the phenomenon was studied, the more polarised investigators' views became.

SLEIGHT OF HAND?

Tom Valentine, a Chicago journalist, published his version of the facts in his book *Psychic Surgery*. Describing one particular episode, he wrote:

'I was convinced that the operations in that house on that morning were not wrought by sleight of hand. We were not hypnotized, and I certainly wasn't allowing myself to be suggestible... Psychic surgery is not impossible, not fakery, not hypnotic suggestion, not a hoax, not a miracle, and is not limited to the Philippines.'

A fact-finding mission comprising experts in medicine, psychiatry, biology, physics, chemistry, parapsychology and conjuring from seven different countries went to the Philippines in March 1973 and April 1975 under the leadership of George Meek. Their party included patients as well as monitoring equipment.

They found that there were indeed fraudulent practitioners among those who claimed to be genuine healers. But the team stated that: 'the factual existence and daily practice of several types of psycho-energetic phenomena by several native healers was clearly established. The practice of materializing and dematerializing human blood, tissue and organs as well as non-human objects was found.'

Yet other investigators have not come to this conclusion. Quite to the contrary, they condemn outright the practice of psychic surgery as fraudulent. They too have taken out their own experts and followed up the experiences of patients treated but not entirely cured. Does this mean that one group has reached a totally erroneous conclusion? Or could the picture be more complex than these black-and-white judgements suggest?

In London, in November 1990, questions about the nature of psychic surgery were again raised when two Filipino psychic surgeons – Sister Flor Cometa and Emilio Laporga – gave a demonstration of their powers before an audience of several hundred people, which included clinical doctors. Among the patients were a man with subcutaneous cysts on the arm, and a woman with a large facial lump, both of whom were treated with relatively little pain. All the operations were recorded on film, and discussed by eminent doctors, bishops, parapsychologists and magicians. No one appears to have reached any definite conclusions, however.

AGENTS OF THE DARK

RARELY – IF EVER –
DO THE THREATS OF THE
MYSTERIOUS MEN IN BLACK,
FOLLOWING A CLOSE
ENCOUNTER, COME TO
ANYTHING. SO WHAT COULD
BE THE PURPOSE BEHIND
THEIR VISITS?

In September 1976, Dr Herbert Hopkins, a 58-year-old doctor and hypnotist, was acting as consultant on an alleged UFO teleportation case in Maine, USA. One evening, when his wife and children had gone out leaving him alone, the telephone rang and a man identifying himself as vice-president of the New Jersey UFO Research Organisation asked if he might visit Dr Hopkins that evening to discuss certain details of the case. Dr Hopkins agreed: at the time, it seemed the natural thing to do. He went to the back door to switch on the light so that his visitor would be able to find his way from the parking lot, but while he was there, he noticed the man already climbing the porch steps. 'I saw no car, and even if he did have a car, he could not have possibly gotten to my house that quickly from any phone,' Hopkins later commented in delayed astonishment.

At the time, Dr Hopkins felt no particular surprise as he admitted his visitor. The man was dressed in a black suit, with black hat, tie and shoes, and a white shirt. 'I thought, he looks like an undertaker,' Hopkins later said. His clothes were immaculate – suit unwrinkled, trousers sharply creased. When he took off his hat, he revealed himself as completely hairless, not only bald but without eyebrows or eyelashes. His skin was dead white, his lips bright red. In the course of their conversation, he happened to brush his lips with his grey suede gloves, and the doctor was astonished to see that his lips were smeared and that the gloves were stained with lipstick!

An MIB visited Dr Herbert Hopkins and warned him to discontinue his investigations into an alleged UFO teleportation case on which he was working at the time. Taking a coin from Dr Hopkins, as illustrated above, the MIB promptly made it disappear, remarking that neither Hopkins nor anyone else on this plane would ever see that coin again.

It was only afterwards, however, that Dr Hopkins reflected further on the strangeness of his visitor's appearance and behaviour. Particularly odd was the fact that his visitor stated that his host had two coins in his pocket. It was indeed the case. He then asked the doctor to put one of the coins in his hand and to watch the coin, not himself. As Hopkins watched, the coin seemed to go out of focus, and then gradually vanished. 'Neither you nor anyone else on this plane will ever see that coin again,' the visitor told him. After talking a little while longer on general UFO topics, Dr Hopkins suddenly noticed that the visitor's speech was slowing down. The man then rose unsteadily to his feet and said, very slowly: 'My energy is running low – must go now – goodbye.' He walked falteringly to the door and descended the outside steps uncertainly, one at a time. Dr Hopkins saw a bright light shining in the driveway, bluish-white and distinctly brighter than a normal car lamp. At the time, however, he assumed it must be the stranger's car, although he neither saw nor heard it.

MYSTERIOUS MARKS

Later, when Dr Hopkins' family had returned, they examined the driveway and found marks that could not have been made by a car because they were in the centre of the driveway, where the wheels could not have been. But the next day, although the driveway had not been used in the meantime, the marks had vanished.

Dr Hopkins was very much shaken by the visit, particularly when he reflected on the extraordinary character of the stranger's conduct. Not surprisingly, he was so scared that he willingly complied with his visitor's instruction, which was to erase the tapes of the hypnotic sessions he was conducting with regard to his current case, and to have nothing further to do with the investigation.

Subsequently, curious incidents continued to occur both in Dr Hopkins' household and in that of his eldest son. He presumed that there was some link with the extraordinary visit, but he never heard from his visitor again. As for the New Jersey UFO Research Organisation, no such institution exists.

Dr Hopkins' account is probably the most detailed we have of an MIB (Man in Black) visit, and confronts us with the problem at its most bizarre. First we must ask ourselves if a trained and respected doctor would invent so strange a tale, and if so, with what conceivable motive? Alternatively, could the entire episode have been a delusion, despite the tracks seen by other members of his family? Could the truth lie somewhere between reality and imagination? Could a real visitor, albeit an impostor making a false identity claim, have visited the doctor for some unknown reason of his own, somehow acting as a trigger for the doctor to invent a whole set of weird features?

In fact, what seems the *least* likely explanation is that the whole incident took place in the doctor's

CASEBOOK

THE ODD COUPLE

On 24 September 1976 – only a few days after Dr Herbert Hopkins' terrifying visit from an MIB – his daughter-in-law Maureen received a telephone call from a man who claimed to know her husband John, and who asked if he and a companion could come and visit them.

John met the man at a local fast-food restaurant, and brought him home with his companion, a woman. Both appeared to be in their mid-thirties, and wore curiously old-fashioned clothes. The woman looked particularly odd: when she stood up, it seemed that there was something wrong with the way that her legs joined her hips. Both strangers walked with very short steps, leaning forward as though frightened of falling.

They sat awkwardly together on a sofa while the man asked a number of detailed personal questions. Did John and Maureen watch television much? What did they read? And what did they talk about? All the while, the man was pawing and fondling his female companion, asking John if this was all right and whether he was doing it correctly.

John left the room for a moment, and the man tried to persuade Maureen to sit next to him. He also asked her 'how she was made', and whether she had any nude photographs.

Shortly afterwards, the woman stood up and announced that she wanted to leave. The man also stood, but made no move to go. He was between the woman and the door, and it seemed that the only way she could get to the door was by walking in a straight line, directly through him. Finally the woman turned to John and asked: 'Please move him; I can't move him myself.' Then, suddenly, the man left, followed by the woman, both walking in straight lines. They did not even say goodbye.

Towards the end of Dr Hopkins' MIB visit, he noticed that the man's speech and movements seemed to be slowing down. Then the MIB got up unsteadily and left, walking very shakily. Dr Hopkins watched him walk down the front steps of his house and into the driveway, where there was a bright bluish-white light – as shown **left** *– but he failed to see or hear anything else as the stranger departed.*

imagination. When his wife and children came home, they found him severely shaken, with the house lights blazing, and seated at a table on which lay a gun. They confirmed the marks on the driveway and a series of disturbances to the telephone that seemed to commence immediately after the visit. So it would seem that some real event occurred, although its nature remains mystifying.

The concrete nature of the phenomenon was accepted by the United States Air Force, who were concerned that persons passing themselves off as USAF personnel should be visiting UFO witnesses. In February 1967, Colonel George P. Freeman, Pentagon spokesman for the USAF's Project Blue Book, told UFO investigator John Keel in the course of an interview:

'Mysterious men dressed in Air Force uniforms or bearing impressive credentials from government agencies have been silencing UFO witnesses. We have checked a number of these cases, and these men are not connected with the Air Force in any way. We haven't been able to find out anything about these men. By posing as Air Force officers and government agents, they are committing a federal offence. We would sure like to catch one. Unfortunately the trail is always too cold by the time we hear about these cases. But we are still trying.'

But were the impostors referred to by Colonel Freeman and Dr Hopkins' strange visitor similar in kind? UFO sightings, like sensational crimes, attract a number of mentally unstable persons, who are quite capable of posing as authorised officials in order to gain access to witnesses; and it could be that some supposed MIBs are simply pseudo-investigators of this sort.

One particularly curious recurrent feature of MIB reports is the ineptitude of the visitors. Time and again, they are described as incompetent: and if they are impersonating human beings, they certainly do not do it very well, arousing their victims' suspicions by improbable behaviour, by the way they

look or talk, and by their ignorance as much as their knowledge. But, of course, it could be that the only ones who are spotted as impostors are those who are no good at their job, and so there may be many more MIB cases that we never learn about simply because the visitors successfully convince their victims that there is nothing to be suspicious about, or that they should keep quiet about the visit.

UNFULFILLED THREATS

A common feature of a great many MIB visits is indeed the instruction to a witness not to say anything about the visit, and to cease all activity concerning the case. (Clearly, we know of these cases only because such instructions have been disobeyed.) One Canadian UFO witness was told by a mysterious visitor in 1976 to stop repeating his story and not to go further into his case, or he would be visited by three men in black. 'I said, "What's that supposed to mean?" "Well," he said, "I could make it hot for you . . . It might cost you certain injury." A year earlier, Mexican witness Carlos de los Santos had been stopped on his way to a television interview by two large black limousines. One of the occupants – dressed in a black suit and 'Scandinavian' in appearance – told him: 'Look, boy, if you value your life and your family's, too, don't talk any more about this sighting of yours.'

However, there is no reliable instance of such threats ever having been carried out, though a good many witnesses have gone ahead and defied their warnings. Indeed, sinister though the MIBs may be, they are notable for their lack of actual violence. The worst that can be said of them is that they frequently harass witnesses with untimely visits and telephone calls, or simply disturb them with their very presence.

While, for the victim, it is just as well that the threats of violence are not followed through, this is

UFO theorist David Tansley, **below, *has suggested that MIBs are some kind of demonic psychic entity.***

> ❚❚ THREE MEN IN BLACK SUITS WITH THREATENING EXPRESSIONS ON THEIR FACES... THREE MEN WHO WALK IN ON YOU AND MAKE CERTAIN DEMANDS... AFTER THEY GOT THROUGH WITH YOU, YOU WISHED YOU'D NEVER HEARD OF THE WORD SAUCER. YOU TURNED PALE AND GOT AWFULLY SICK. YOU COULDN'T GET ANYTHING TO STAY ON YOUR STOMACH FOR THREE LONG DAYS. ❚❚
>
> **GRAY BARKER, THEY KNEW TOO MUCH ABOUT FLYING SAUCERS**

for the investigator one more disconcerting aspect of the phenomenon – for violence, if it resulted in physical action, would at least help in establishing the reality of the phenomenon. Instead, it remains a fact that most of the evidence is purely hearsay in character and often not of the highest quality: cases as well-attested as that of Dr Herbert Hopkins are unfortunately in the minority.

Another problem area is the dismaying lack of precision about many of the reports. Popular American writer Brad Steiger alleged that hundreds of ufologists, contactees and chance percipients of UFOs claim to have been visited by ominous strangers – usually three, and usually dressed in black; but he cites only a few actual instances. Similarly, John Keel, an expert on unexplained phenomena, claimed that, on a number of occasions, he actually saw phantom Cadillacs, complete with rather sinister Oriental-looking passengers in black suits; but for a trained reporter, he showed a curious reluctance to pursue these sightings or to give chapter and verse in such an important matter. Such loose assertions are valueless as evidence: all they do is contribute to the myth.

And so we come back once again to the possibility that there is nothing more to the phenomenon than myth. Should we perhaps write off the whole

business as delusion, the creation of imaginative folk whose personal obsessions take on this particular shape because it reflects one or other of the prevalent cultural preoccupations of our time? At one end of the scale, we find contactee Woodrow Derenberger insisting that the 'two men dressed entirely in black' who tried to silence him were emissaries of the Mafia: while at the other, there is theorist David Tansley, who suggested that they are psychic entities, representatives of the dark forces, seeking to prevent the spread of true knowledge. More matter-of-factly, Dominick Lucchesi claimed that they emanated from some unknown

A Mexican witness, Carlos de los Santos, was stopped by MIBs travelling in two large black limousines on his way to a television interview about his UFO sighting. The MIBs warned him to keep silent – as illustrated above – and he cancelled the interview. Two weeks later, however, he changed his mind and made the broadcast. Not a word was heard from the MIBs, despite their threats.

civilisation, possibly underground, in a remote area of Earth – the Amazon, the Gobi Desert or the Himalayas.

But there is one feature that is common to virtually all MIB reports, and that perhaps contains the key to the problem. This is the possession, by the MIBs, of information that they should not have been able to come by – information that was restricted, not released to the press, known perhaps to a few investigators and officials but not to the public, and sometimes not even to them. The one person who does possess that knowledge is always the person visited. In other words, the MIBs and their victims share knowledge that perhaps nobody else possesses. Add to this the fact that, in almost every case, the MIBs appear to the witness when he or she is alone – in Dr Hopkins' case, for example, the visitor took care to call when his wife and children were away from home, and established this fact by telephone beforehand – and the implication has to be that some kind of paranormal link connects the MIBs and the persons they visit.

TRUTH – OR PARANOIA?

To this must be added other features of the phenomenon that are not easily reconciled with everyday reality. Where are the notorious black cars, for instance, when they are not visiting witnesses? Where are they garaged or serviced? Do they never get involved in breakdowns or accidents? Can it be that they materialise from some other plane of existence when they are needed?

These are only a few of the questions raised by the MIB phenomenon. What complicates the matter is that MIB cases lie along a continuous spectrum ranging from the easily believable to the totally incredible. At one extreme are visits during which nothing really bizarre occurs, the only anomalous feature being, perhaps, that the visitor makes a false identity claim, or has unaccountable access to private information. At the other extreme are cases in which the only explanation would seem to be that the witness has succumbed to paranoia. In *The Truth About the Men in Black*, UFO investigator Ramona Clark tells of an unnamed investigator who was confronted by three MIBs on 3 July 1969. 'On the window of the car in which they were riding was the symbol connected with them and their visitations. This symbol had a profound psychological impact upon this man. I have never encountered such absolute fear in a human being.'

That first meeting was followed by continual harassment. There were mysterious telephone calls, and the man's house was searched. He began to hear voices and to see strange shapes. 'Black Cadillacs roamed the street in front of his home, and followed him everywhere he went. Once he and his family were almost forced into an accident by an oncoming Cadillac. Nightmares concerning MIBs plagued his sleep. It became impossible for him to rest, his work suffered and he was scared of losing his job.'

Was it all in his mind? One is tempted to think so. But a friend confirmed that, while they talked, there was a strange-looking man walking back and forth in front of the house. The man was tall, seemed about 55 years old – and was dressed entirely in black.

with a study of haunted castles, and had reached the conclusion that the thick damp walls of ancient buildings served as 'Faraday cages', shutting out radio and other electromagnetic waves, and creating anomalous electrical phenomena.

A BBC television programme broadcast in 1966, showing Herbert and his team investigating the allegedly haunted Sandford Orcas Manor in Dorset, resulted in a good deal of publicity for the Paralab's activities, and an invitation for Herbert and his research officer Manfred Cassirer to attend a symposium on psychotronics in Prague in September 1970 followed. The contacts made there with Russian, Czech and other Eastern bloc scientists led to invitations to visit such places as Moscow and Leningrad. Through these meetings, Herbert and his Paralab soon became part of the international network of paraphysical research, and he went on to develop particularly strong links with Soviet parapsychologists.

SOVIET INFLUENCE

Soviet parapsychology had attracted a good deal of interest among psychical researchers in the early 1960s. In Britain, this was sparked off by the publication of a translation of *Experiments in Mental Suggestion* by Professor Leonid Vasiliev of Leningrad University, who had been working on telepathic hypnosis, using subjects in chambers shielded from electromagnetic waves. Then, in 1968, Benson Herbert's newly established *Journal of Paraphysics* reported on the international conference on *psi* held in Moscow in June of that year.

EVIDENCE FROM THE PARALAB

BENSON HERBERT UPSET THE PSYCHIC ESTABLISHMENT WHEN, IN THE 1960S, HE SET OUT TO INVESTIGATE THE PARANORMAL THROUGH THE LAWS OF PHYSICS

I n 1966, a scientist who had for several years been researching into psychokinesis (PK) set up a research laboratory in a remote farmhouse at Downton, Wiltshire – an area of Britain free from traffic vibration and widespread electrical interference, both of which had, in London, previously upset his delicate research instruments.

The newly established Paraphysical Laboratory (or 'Paralab', as it is familiarly called) soon became a controversial centre for paranormal research in Britain. Its director, Benson Herbert, had started his career as a physicist, with an interest in archaeology and mythology. In the years before the Second World War, he had carried out a survey of archaeological sites in Britain and Ireland, combining this

Benson Herbert is seen in his Paraphysical Laboratory (Paralab), which he set up in Wiltshire in 1966, above. Here, he is recording the level of electrical energy given off by his subject's right hand.

In FOCUS

WITHOUT FEAR OR FAVOUR

After the Second World War, Benson Herbert took part in experimental seances organised by R.G. Medhurst, a member of the Society for Psychical Research (SPR). After six months, the sitters began to experience some vigorous table phenomena, which appeared to be communications from a family of 'controls'. In order to investigate, Herbert agreed to be put in an experimental trance. While 'under', he acquired a Chinese 'guide' who claimed to have lived 1,000 years ago. However, he assumed that this guide was no more than a projection from his own subconscious. This practical approach to reality was to make his work particularly acceptable to the East Europeans, whose interpretation of phenomena was essentially materialist at the time.

But the fact that Herbert had participated in a seance and experienced physical phenomena did not make him popular with the main body of parapsychologists, who had not had such experience and were sceptical of psychokinesis (PK). At a time when research into altered states of

The new journal was viewed balefully by the psychic establishment, however, primarily because Benson Herbert was breaking all the rules (as understood in the 1960s) for exploring paranormal phenomena. In the first place, he styled himself a paraphysicist. As he said in 1964:

'We are trying to carry out precise and systematic research into the physics of the paranormal... No one knows just how far subconscious dramatisation is involved in purely mental phenomena such as trance.'

Statements like this did nothing to endear him to psychologists, who at that time dominated psychical research.

A NEW REALITY

But for Herbert, it had been the work of physicists that had first made him aware of the strange and exciting possibilities in the Universe. At university, he had eagerly absorbed Albert Einstein's theory of relativity, Arthur Eddington's theory of the expanding Universe, Karl Heisenberg's principle of indeterminacy, as well as the ideas of quantum mechanics and polydimensional geometry. It was clear to him that the world was certainly not at all what it seemed, and that 'our senses were crude and inefficient instruments which created an artificial barrier of illusion between our brains and the mysterious reality outside.'

His first introduction to *psi* came through the pages of science fiction. While still at school, he even wrote science fiction stories for an American magazine; and it was in the science fiction writing

Benson Herbert attempts, right, to tap a group's subconscious mind through use of a device known as an octo-tron. Each participant places his fingers lightly on the square board at the end of one of the eight arms which usually move quite soon afterwards, pointing to letters of the alphabet spread beneath. It is virtually impossible for any member of the group to dominate the proceedings.

consciousness had scarcely begun, the fact that he had ignored the boundary between scientist and subject, and had allowed himself to be put into a trance, was thought quite shocking.

His editorial line in the *Journal of Paraphysics* exacerbated the scandal. 'Are witches psychic?' he asked in an early issue. Answering the question in the affirmative, he said that many witches had a high degree of dissociation, and were therefore suitable

Sybil Leek, a witch who cooperated with Herbert during his investigations, is seen here with sceptic Dr R. Hope and his wife.

subjects for research. He also reported on his experiments with a group of witches, who had claimed that, by incantation, they could make a candle flame flicker at predetermined intervals. He then went on to observe the effects when witches danced outdoors around a fire, and concluded that ESP might be stimulated by absorption of negative ions through the skin.

'It would appear', he wrote in the journal, 'that witchcraft provided a rich field of research in paraphysics, and we trust that our many witch friends will continue to give their valuable cooperation to facilitate eventual control of the powers which some of them certainly seem to possess.' In 1963, he joined a witch, Sybil Leek, in a seance at an allegedly haunted building in Southampton and was filmed by the BBC.

Herbert's fascination with witches was totally abhorrent to most parapsychologists, who were at pains to distance themselves from what they saw as primitive links with the occult. Another group with whom he fraternised were ufologists, equally unpopular in the mid 1960s. In an article on ufology and paraphysics, Herbert suggested: 'There is a continuous gradation from the poltergeist-type activity to the UFO-type activity.' By the 1980s, this link had become accepted by many more students of the paranormal; but in 1967, it was still a heresy.

time as a kind of "heat", but which now, after much reflection, I believe to be more akin to a mild electric shock.'

A year later, when he visited Kulagina again, Herbert submitted to a repeat experiment in which she held his arm lightly above the wrist: after several minutes, he collapsed, concluding, on this occasion, that it was indeed heat that was being transmitted. Indeed, his arm was so badly burnt that the marks remained there for the following eight days.

In the *Proceedings* of the Society for Psychical Research, Herbert reported on his experiences with Nina Kulagina and firmly rejected the accusations of fraud that had been made against her by James Randi and others.

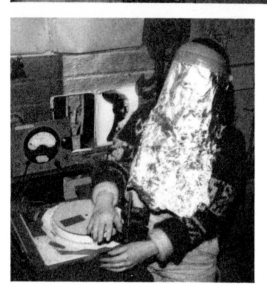

of H. G. Wells that he was first to meet the suggestion that the phenomena of ghosts and poltergeists could perhaps be explained by postulating the existence of extraspatial dimensions.

Herbert eventually became convinced that a new breakthrough in physics lay in the study of the paranormal, and this was to be the starting point for his life-long attempt to demonstrate that there is a physical basis to such things as clairvoyance, PK, psychic healing and the curious phenomenon of 'dermo-optics' – the alleged ability to see through one's skin.

In fact, throughout the early 1970s, the *International Journal of Paraphysics* concentrated on the Eastern bloc's research along these lines. In 1972, Herbert actually met the remarkable Nina Kulagina when visiting Leningrad. She was credited with extraordinary abilities in skin vision and PK, and was reportedly able to move substantial objects either by some kind of gesture or simply by fixing them with her eyes.

On hearing that Herbert was interested in the possible link between PK and healing, Kulagina gripped his left arm. For two minutes, he felt nothing. Then, quite abruptly, as he put it, he 'experienced a new sensation which I described at the

Benson Herbert and the psychic healer Josephine Blatch are shown **top**, *using infra-red equipment at the Paralab.*

Sarah Dodd, one of Herbert's subjects, uses a device known as 'Rodeo' (rotational dermo-optics), **above left**. *She wears an aluminium foil blindfold and rests her left hand on a switch that, as long as it is depressed, keeps the turntable running. When the red card is beneath her outstretched right hand, she has to release the switch, stopping the turntable.*

A tube of haemoglobin is concealed in a box that has 64 compartments, **above**. *The aim is for the subject to determine which one it is in.*

Another remarkable psychic investigated by Herbert was Suzanne Padfield, the clairvoyant whose ability in psychometry enabled her to identify the killer of a little girl in Moscow, 1,700 miles (2,736 kilometres) away, when the child's possessions and a photograph of the girl were put in her hands. In Herbert's Paralab, an experiment was later carried out to determine her ability to deflect a beam of light. This involved apparatus that generated a polarised beam of light that could be registered on a metering device. Suzanne Padfield placed her hands near the tube through which the beam passed, and attempted to affect it. She found she was able to lower the meter reading a significant number of times.

Subsequent projects at the Paralab included an investigation into psychic healing, experiments with bacteria and viruses, and the study of dermo-optics (skin vision), including the ability to sense colours and writing through the fingers – an ability which could be of enormous benefit to the blind, and to those with deficient colour vision.

Benson Herbert's death in April 1991 is widely regarded as a great loss to psychical research – all the more because, as is not generally known, he himself seemed to have impressive psychic abilities.

THE PUZZLE OF THE PYRAMIDS

FOR MORE THAN 40 CENTURIES, THE PYRAMIDS OF ANCIENT EGYPT HAVE BEEN A SOURCE OF WONDER. HOW WERE THESE ENIGMATIC MONUMENTS BUILT, AND WHY?

Pyramids are the very symbol of Egypt – an ancient civilisation infinitely complex and splendid in its powers. There they stand, each one a massive, brooding presence set against the empty desert, its simple shape apparently easy to comprehend and yet somehow ambivalent, confusing, mysterious.

The scene, below, shows workers hauling building blocks up a ramp that wound round the basic structure – one of the most likely means of raising a pyramid.

Egyptian pyramids are huge. That makes a difference. Seen in a mere diagram or as a model, a pyramid looks straightforward: it has four faces, a topmost point and passageways leading to a chamber within the structure. But stand close beside an Egyptian pyramid, now raise your eyes towards the summit, and thoughts of faces and points are bound to become irrelevant. Suddenly, half the world seems to be of stone; the other half is sky. Climb inside a pyramid, and the cramped and humid passageways will quickly disorient you.

Pyramids also keep their secrets. We can only guess at why the Egyptians raised them, while we also have to speculate about the building techniques used. We have no definitive solutions to these problems because no account survives from ancient Egypt. The only real record lies in the pyramids themselves.

The first pyramid, the Step Pyramid of King Zoser, was constructed during the Third Dynasty, in about 2650 BC, and today still dominates the Saqqâra skyline, 10 miles (15 kilometres) south of present-day Cairo. Imagine the impact when it was first built! The citizens of Memphis, then the capital of Egypt, no doubt lifted up their eyes to the hills that marked the beginning of the western desert to see the six levels of this memorial to their dead king rising up some further 200 feet (60 metres). This first pyramid is also a remarkable record of experiment in stone – previous tombs had always been made of mud brick.

Zoser's pyramid began with a single-storey tomb of solid stone, with a burial chamber driven about 100 feet (30 metres) into the rock beneath. The builders then set about extending it; but, before completing this stage, they apparently had an idea that sparked off the pyramid age – they added three more layers to make a four-step pyramid. Even so, they were still not done. They then extended the base still further and added the final two steps. It is possible that this stepped pyramid represents the dead king's stairway to the stars.

Structures around the pyramid pose problems of interpretation, too. Were the buildings and courtyards the scene of some royal or religious ceremony while Zoser was alive, or the haunt of priests and pilgrims who maintained his cult after his death, or even an arena where the dead king's spirit could work its magic? Later pyramids featured a fairly standard complex, which included the pyramid itself, a mortuary temple, or offering place, built against its eastern face, and a causeway that connected it with a valley temple on the edge of the cultivated plain bordering the Nile.

Zoser's successors left the beginnings of two or three more aborted step pyramids before turning to the first attempt at a true pyramid with smoothed-off faces, at Maidûm, situated about 40 miles (65 kilometres) south of Cairo. Maidûm, today, is a ruin,

The first true pyramid, above, was raised over the tomb of King Zoser at Saqqâra in about 2650 BC. Its original height was probably over 200 feet (60 metres).

Some 40 important pyramids can be found at various sites along the Nile, some of which are indicated on the map, left; but the positioning of the Great Pyramid is remarkable. It stands exactly halfway between the eastern and western boundaries of ancient Egypt, while a quarter circle drawn with the pyramid at its centre closely circumscribes the Nile delta.

The view of the Great Pyramid, below, shows clearly how its stones were fitted together.

its central core rising 250 feet (75 metres) or so from a mound of rubble that was once part of the pyramid itself. But it started as a step pyramid, the sides of which were then faced to form one continuous slope. Unfortunately, however, the extended base rested on sand instead of bedrock, and as a result the pyramid collapsed, possibly before having been completed.

GREAT HEIGHTS

The builders learned from this experiment. The next king, Sneferu, the first king of the Fourth Dynasty (which lasted roughly from 2500 BC to 2400 BC), built two substantial pyramids at Dashûr, just south of Saqqâra. Then came the three pyramids at Gîza: the Great Pyramid of Cheops, with the Egyptian name of Khufu; its immense companion built by Chephren or Khafre; and the smaller pyramid of Mycerinus or Menkaure. The Great Pyramid is unique in having passageways and chambers high in its structure: virtually all other pyramids have a single passage leading down to a small chamber at ground level or in the rock below. It is also the high point of pyramid construction, both literally and figuratively. Originally, it stood just over 480 feet (146 metres) high, on a base extending to just under 760 feet (231 metres) along each side, although the smooth facing stones have long since been taken off to be incorporated in the medieval buildings of Cairo, and so its height today is about 450 feet (137 metres). No one was to build a pyramid that high again, nor one that was executed to such a high standard.

After Gîza, Fifth and Sixth Dynasty kings built pyramids at Saqqâra and at nearby Abu-Sîr. In even the best of these, the interior stones were roughly worked, and in the later ones the core consisted of small stones bonded with Nile mud. Once the limestone facing had been stripped away by later generations, the core fell apart. By the end of the Sixth Dynasty, about 2180 BC, Egypt had split into a confusion of provinces, and vast monuments went out of favour. The Eleventh and Twelfth Dynasties then saw Egypt united once again; and during a period lasting from 2000 BC to 1750 BC, kings once more raised pyramids. These were less than half the height of the Great Pyramid and often roughly built.

MEDITERRANEAN SEA

29°50'E   32°38'E

Port Said

Alexandria

Abu Rauwâsh
Gîza
Zawiyet el-Aryân
Saqqâra
Lake Qârûn
Seila
Hawara
Illahun

Cairo
Abu Sîr
Dashûr
Mazghûna
Lisht
Maidûm

Suez

Gulf of Suez

River Nile

E G Y P T

Zawiyet el-Mayitin

Tel-el-Amarna

N

official western boundary

official eastern boundary

0   25   50   75 miles
0   50   100 kilometres

Deir el-Bahri
Luxor

El Kûla

In some cases, the inner core consisted mainly of mud bricks, held in place with reinforcing walls. These were the last pyramids to be constructed. Later kings opted instead to build extensive temples, which would demonstrate their might while still alive, and hidden tombs, which would keep them safe when dead.

Gîza and the Great Pyramid of Cheops seem to encapsulate all the mysteries associated with the building of the pyramids, and pose many questions. But what was the purpose of the Great Pyramid? A fairly obvious suggestion is that it may have been a tomb, and there is indeed a sarcophagus in what is now called the King's Chamber. However, there is no indication that any actual funeral took place. The last passageway before the King's Chamber is the magnificent Grand Gallery – at its base, 156 feet long, 28 feet high, 7 feet wide (47.5 by 8.5 by 2 metres), but stepping in towards the ceiling and sloping steeply up at an angle of 26 degrees. It may be that Cheops' ritualists planned a final great procession up the incline, but this still leaves a problem unsolved: the corridor that runs up to the start of the Grand Gallery is so low that anyone climbing it has to bend double.

Why, too, was the Great Pyramid built on that site? The ancient Egyptians are thought to have built their pyramids on the scarp of the Nile valley, where all the royal tombs were built, because that

The cross-section of the Great Pyramid, below, was prepared by Charles Piazzi Smyth, the Astronomer Royal for Scotland and Professor of Practical Astronomy at Edinburgh University, in 1864. Smyth believed that the entrance passage was aligned with the position of the star alpha Draconis in the year 2170 BC.

The majestic complex of pyramids at Giza is shown bottom.

Professor Stecchini also considers that the Egyptians laid out their entire country to demonstrate this knowledge, positioning borders, cities and major temples at points significant in terms of latitude and longitude and at distances measured in round numbers. The length of Egypt as a whole thus became exactly 1,500,000 royal cubits (a cubit was approximately equal to the length of a man's forearm). So powerful was this notion that other peoples, too, Stecchini claims, located their own important centres at sites chosen for their distances from, and their angles to, the main Egyptian meridians.

GOLDEN SECTION

This is not all; the Great Pyramid seems to incorporate other messages, too. Stecchini and others have claimed that the relation between its height and its base gives the value of *pi*, the ratio of the circumference of a circle to its diameter. Likewise, the Pyramid is said to embody *phi*, the golden section that divides a line so that the ratio of the shorter to the longer equals the ratio of the longer part to the whole. Centuries later, the golden section played an important role in Classical Greek architecture, as it was thought to provide particularly harmonious proportions for a building. In the case of the Great Pyramid, however, calculations based on the principle of the golden section would make the area of each face of the Pyramid equal to the area of a square drawn on its height. Modern estimates of the original height of the Great Pyramid are not exact enough to solve the conundrum once and for all.

The most accurate measurements of the Great Pyramid were taken in 1925 by James Humphrey Cole, who was able to identify the original position of the corners, although the blocks themselves are missing, and to measure the sides with an error of less than 12 inches (3.8 centimetres). He published these dimensions for the sides of the Pyramid: north, 755.414 feet (230.253 metres); south, 756.073 feet (230.454 metres); east,

was the western horizon. From Memphis, the shapes could be seen silhouetted against the setting sun, with which the destinies of the dead kings' spirits were held to be linked.

Lately, however, some researchers have speculated that there may perhaps have been more to the choice of site than that. According to these theorists, whose views are explained in detail by Professor Livio Catullo Stecchini in Peter Tompkins' book *The Secrets of the Great Pyramid,* the ancient Egyptians probably had a much more advanced awareness of geography and cosmology than is generally acknowledged. Stecchini claims that the Egyptians knew, for example, that the Earth was round and were able to calculate distances for degrees of latitude and longitude, an operation equivalent to measuring the circumference of the Earth.

755.866 feet (230.391 metres); west, 755.755 feet (230.357 metres). This made the difference between the longest and the shortest sides a matter of only 7.9 inches (20.1 centimetres), and he found that the 'worst' oriented side was less than one tenth of a degree off true north.

Cole made no attempt to estimate the original height of the Great Pyramid, but he accepted that the faces sloped at approximately 50°51' and this gives a figure of 481.12 feet (146.65 metres). An earlier survey by the archaeologist Sir Flinders Petrie, published in 1883, made the height 481.30 feet (146.70 metres).

Most estimates suggest that the Great Pyramid took between 20 and 30 years to build; that between 4000 and 10,000 men worked on it continuously, with hundreds more in the quarries; and that during the three or four months of late summer, when the Nile flooded, levies of up to 100,000 men hauled the next year's supply of stone to the site and raised finished blocks to the construction level. Much of the poorer-quality stone for the core came from nearby quarries – the Sphinx is carved from an outcrop of harder rock left in one of them – but granite to line the internal chambers came from far up the Nile, and the finer limestone for the facing stones came from the Tura quarries, burrowed into the Muqattam hills, which lie across the river to the east of Cairo.

HARD LABOUR

Petrie spelt out how he thought 100,000 men organised their work. A party capable of handling a block of average size – 40 cubic feet (11.32 cubic metres) or 2.5 tonnes – would consist of eight or so men. Each of these, he thought, would transport 10 blocks during three months' labour, taking a fortnight to bring them down the causeway at the quarries, a day or two of good wind to take them across the river, and six weeks to carry them up the pyramid causeway. They would then have four weeks in

The step pyramid of Zoser is shown above, to the left, besides another, crumbling, at Saqqâra.

An unfinished obelisk, left, lies as it was left in the quarry at Aswan. It is clear that the masons were confident that they would be able to move this as a single massive piece of stone: but how?

which to raise finished blocks into place on the pyramid. At every stage, they almost certainly dragged the blocks along on wooden sledges, a slurry of mud and water being poured in front of the sledges to lubricate the runners.

---

*In*FOCUS

POWER FROM

THE PYRAMID

No other structure has been the subject of so many theories as the Great Pyramid at Giza. It has been described as a tomb, and even a storage place for the history of Atlantis, the 'lost continent'. And because the pyramid's alignment and construction to specific proportions almost defy understanding, it has been suggested that its builders must have received help from an outside force, perhaps from another planet.

Other theories, however, focus on the strange powers that pyramids appear to exert on objects placed within them. This idea stems in part from discovery in the Great Pyramid of the remains of creatures that had become mummified rather than decayed. This convinced many that the pyramid's shape has a preservative power. Today, claims that the pyramid shape gives off an inexplicable energy abound.

One of the most famous claims was made by a Czech radio engineer, Karl Drbal, who in 1949 filed a patent for a small cardboard model of the Great Pyramid of Cheops which

he dubbed a 'Pharaoh's shaving device'. Its cavity, he said, could actually keep the steel edge of a razor blade sharp for more than 100 daily shaves. (The patent was granted in 1959 after he had convinced the examiners – by detailed technical evaluation – of its genuineness.)

Experiments with pyramids and humans have also produced interesting results. Volunteers, placed inside pyramids six and eight feet high, have felt contrasting feelings: in the lower area of the pyramid, they experienced a soothing warmth; but on raising their hands into the apex, they felt needle-like pricking sensations. Many people who use pyramid tents at home in which to meditate claim to lose tension and worries, gain greater psychic energy and see their past incarnations. Some claim that it can even slow the aging process, while others say that coffee stored in a pyramid-shaped container tastes less bitter. Conclusive proof as to the secret power of the pyramids remains to be found, however.

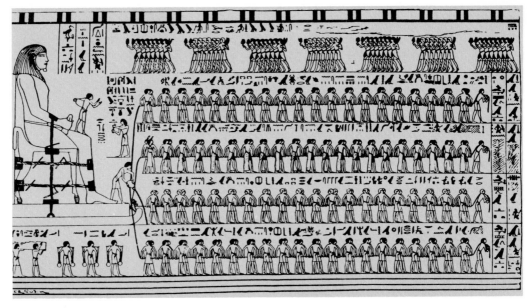

Documentary evidence to support the theory that the building stones for the pyramids were transported on wooden sledges is reproduced right. Here, a team of about 150 men moves a giant statue of a seated figure. Notice in particular the timekeeper standing on the figure's knee and the man pouring some sort of lubricant from a jar in front of the sledge runners.

Over the years, engineers with an interest in Egyptology have ruminated on the construction methods that the Egyptians might have used to build the pyramids. One, for example, has suggested that the builders installed rudimentary cranes at various levels of the pyramid, with long lifting ropes running down through a series of pulleys to a giant capstan at ground level. (Others, however, claim that the Egyptians did not have pulleys.) A French architect, August Choisy, thought that the Egyptians might have used twin levers to lift the blocks straight up before sliding them sideways on to higher levels. Others have returned again and again to the idea of the balance arm – a stout beam supported on a pillar about 6 feet (2 metres) high. By slinging a block from the shorter arm of such a beam, which might be about 3 feet (1 metre) long, and hanging counterweight rocks from the other arm, which could be up to 15 feet (4.5 metres) long, workers could raise the block into the air and position it on a sledge or some other support. One of the engineers to plump for the balance arm in recent years, Olaf Tellefsen, a Norwegian-born naval architect, also came up with a theory of 'direct assault', suggesting that gangs of 25 or 30 men might have pulled the laden sledges up greased slipways set directly against the sloping faces of the pyramids.

As an alternative to the theory of a spiral ramp winding round a pyramid under construction, it has been suggested that the stones may have been brought up a single ramp that was widened and strengthened as it was gradually raised to a greater height, as illustrated below.

Many people have also suggested that the Egyptians may have hauled the blocks of stone up mud-brick ramps. One tomb painting does indeed show a ramp in use for the setting up of temple columns, and remains of ramps can be found at a couple of pyramid-building sites. A papyrus has also survived in which are noted calculations to determine the number of bricks needed for a ramp 1,200 feet (366 metres) long and 90 feet (27.5 metres) wide, leading up to a height of 100 feet (30.5 metres). Unfortunately, there is a daunting difference between a modest ramp of this size and one many times longer that would have been needed for the Great Pyramid. Some people, meanwhile, think the Egyptians may have relied on ramps that wound around the Pyramid, in spite of the objection that these would provide too insecure a base for levering large blocks into position.

Certain Arab historians, however, blandly assured their readers that the ancient Egyptians laid magic talismans atop the blocks, which could then be shifted easily from place to place. But Sir Flinders Petrie also proposed that the Egyptians might have used sledge-like rockers with curved runners. They would place a block on a rocker, he suggested, and then start swinging it backwards and forwards. They would then slip thin planks beneath each end alternately, as they pushed on the block to keep it rocking. In this way, it would gradually 'climb' upwards. John Fitchen, Emeritus Professor of the Fine Arts at Colgate University, New York, extended this idea by suggesting that the builders purposely made part of the face of the unfinished pyramid into a giant stone staircase. Gangs of workers could then jack the blocks up, step by step.

Sadly, as no ancient Egyptian description of how the pyramids were built has been found, the method of their construction may well be a secret they are fated to retain. According to Kurt Mendelssohn, author of *The Riddle of the Pyramids*, what was important for the Egyptians was the actual building of the pyramids as a spectacular and unifying common task for the enormous work force they wanted to band together. Once formation of a centralized state had been achieved, such large-scale building then discontinued.

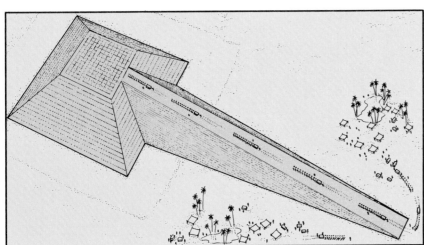

TURNING IN THEIR GRAVES

THE MYSTERIOUS MOVEMENT OF LEAD-CASED COFFINS IN A SEALED TOMB IN BARBADOS DURING THE 19TH CENTURY WAS BELIEVED BY MANY TO BE THE WORK OF SUPERNATURAL FORCES

They say that the dead tell no tales. And since the corpses interred in a Barbadian graveyard vault early last century were, apparently, the only agencies present when the coffins they were laid in moved, there naturally exists no immediate first-hand account of this eeriest of mysteries.

The so-called 'creeping coffins of Barbados' passed, with some alacrity, into West Indian folk-lore some time between 1812 and 1820. But this was no isolated, strange incident: rather, it was a phenomenon that repeated itself with chilling regularity until the nerve both of the vault's owners and of local dignitaries finally ran out. At the time, the tomb in question, situated near the entrance to the graveyard of Christ Church, overlooking the bay at Oistins on the south coast of the island, belonged to the Chase family. It was a solid affair, built of large, cemented blocks of coral, 12 feet long by 6 feet wide (4 metres by 2 metres), that were sunk halfway into the ground and sealed off by a great marble slab. Anyone trying secretly to get in (or out) of the vault would have found it something of an arduous if not impossible task.

Two burials took place before anything happened. On 31 July 1807, Mrs Thomasina Goddard's funeral was held; and on 22 February 1808, that of the infant Mary Anna Maria Chase. Then, on 6 July 1812, pallbearers and mourners arrived to lay to rest Dorcas Chase, the elder sister of Mary Anna Maria. Several of the men heaved the door open – struggling with its great weight – and the coffin was lifted down to the portals of the tomb. Peering into the darkness from the few first steps, the leading pallbearers were greeted by a truly astonishing sight.

Mary Anna Maria's coffin had moved to the corner opposite the one in which it had been placed, and Mrs Goddard's had been flung aside against a wall. Something more than a draught had moved them, for both coffins were cased in lead. Without pausing to ask questions, the labourers lifted the coffins back into position, placed Dorcas' coffin among them and sealed up the vault again. But who or what had tampered with the dead – and why? Amazed and frightened, the mourners chose to put the blame on black slaves who had assisted at the funeral of the first Chase sister.

So were the slaves to blame? Certainly, there was reputedly little love lost between the patriarch Thomas Chase and the blacks he employed. Chase was by all accounts a cruel man whose tyrannical behaviour had driven his daughter Dorcas to kill herself. It seems improbable, though, that anyone bearing a grudge against him would have gone to such lengths to inflict such trivial damage.

MALIGN SPIRITS?

As it was, Chase himself died within the month; and on 9 August 1812, his coffin was placed with the other three, which this time remained undisturbed. A few years then slipped by, during which there was no reason for anyone to believe that anything untoward was taking place in the Oistins churchyard.

But, on 25 September 1816, the vault was reopened for the burial of a little boy, Samuel Brewster Ames; once more the coffins lay in disarray and the accusing eye was again turned on the black labourers, who promptly denied all charges and shrank in fear from what they considered the work of malign spirits. They regarded the dead with great superstition and were, in reality, the most unlikely of suspects. There was little the mourners could do, however, but return the coffins to their rightful places, leave Master Ames among them

and block up the doorway with the great slab—which they did, hastily.

The tomb was then opened again on 17 November for the interment of another Samuel Brewster, whose coffin was being transferred to the Chase vault from its original home in a St Philip graveyard. The mystery surrounding the vault was now so well-known that a crowd gathered in anticipation of fresh disturbances.

They were not to be disappointed, for it was found that all of the coffins had shifted ground and that of Mrs Goddard, who had been lying in 'rest' now for nearly a decade, had finally given up under the strain and fallen apart. An exhaustive search of the vault proved futile – the walls, floor and roof were as solid and unyielding as ever. And yet, for the third time, there were unmistakable signs of violent activity within. One wonders with what sense of dreadful, resigned foreboding the mourners repositioned the coffins (tying and bundling the remnants of Mrs Goddard's against the wall) and cemented the great door back into place.

Nearly three years were now to pass before the vault was opened again – during which time it received thousands of curious visitors. On 17 July 1819, the funeral of Thomasina Clarke took place. It seems that the mystery was now a major national issue, for Viscount Combermere, the Governor of Barbados, and two of his officials attended the funeral. In front of hundreds of hushed spectators, the marble slab was cut free by masons and dragged aside by a team of slaves.

Inside, all was chaos: every coffin had moved, save only the shattered fragments of Mrs Goddard's, which had remained in their little pile. The vault was searched again but there was nothing, not one clue. Undeterred, the labourers lugged the coffins back. Sand was sent for and sprinkled

The bay at Oistins on the south coast of Barbados received thousands of visitors in the years between 1812 and 1820. Tourists flocked to Christ Church graveyard to see at first hand the vault of the Chase family where, it was rumoured, someone – or something – was tampering with the dead.

over the floor of the tomb so that it formed a smooth, thick carpet that would surely show the footprints of the mysterious coffin mover. Then, once the door was replaced, Combermere left the impression of his seal in the cement and others did the same.

Public speculation and excitement about the strange goings-on finally mounted to such a degree that no one had the patience to wait for someone to pass on before the mystery could be finally solved or abandoned. After prolonged debate that could lead to only one conclusion, Viscount Combermere, the Honourable Nathan Lucas, Major J. Finch (secretary to the Governor), Mr R. Bowcher Clarke and Mr Rowland Cotton journeyed to Christ Church, collected the Reverend Thomas Orderson and repaired to the graveyard on 18 April 1870 with a band of quaking black labourers.

The seals on the cement were intact: no one had therefore since removed the door and entered that way. From the outside, the vault was also as solid as ever. Combermere ordered the cement to be chipped away, and the huge slab was dragged aside, causing a strange, grating noise. This was the result of one of the larger lead coffins having been thrown up against the door, where it now lay. Mary Anna Maria's tinier coffin, meanwhile, clearly had been sent flying to the far end of the vault with such violence that it had damaged the coral wall. The other coffins were scattered about, but there were no telltale marks in the sand to suggest

what it was that might have moved them. The Honourable Nathan Lucas, reporting the incident, had this to say:

'I examined the walls, the arch, and every part of the vault, and found every part old and similar; and a mason in my presence struck every part of the bottom with his hammer, and all was solid. I confess myself at a loss to account for the movements of these leaden coffins. Thieves certainly had no hand in it; and as for any practical wit or hoax, too many were requisite to be trusted with the secret for it to remain unknown; and as for negroes having anything to do with it, their superstitious fear of the dead and everything belonging to them precludes any idea of the kind. All I know is that it happened and that I was an eye-witness of the fact!'

Whatever, or whoever, it was that caused the coffins in the Chase vault to wander between those four walls was given no further opportunity to do so, for all of the coffins were lugged out and given more peaceful resting places elsewhere in the same churchyard.

WEREWOLVES AND VAMPIRES

There have been other cases, too, of coffins refusing to stay put. Discussing the Barbados mystery in his book *West Indian Tales of Old,* Sir Algernon E. Aspinall makes reference to the *European Magazine* of September 1815, for instance, which cites a vault at Stanton in Suffolk, England, where on at least three separate occasions – and, as at Oistins – behind a sealed door, coffins had moved off their raised biers. During one of these 'manoeuvres', the heaviest coffin – another eight-pallbearer affair – had climbed on to the fourth step of the vault. 'Whence arose this operation, in which it was certain that no-one had a hand?' asked the *European Magazine*. Needless to say, the people of Stanton were as shocked as the Barbadians. In 1867, F. C. Paley, son of the rector of Gretford, near Stamford in Lincolnshire, England, also wrote to *Notes and Queries* concerning the repeated movement of heavy lead coffins (also cased in wood) in a local vault, his letter corroborated by a witness who commented that some of the coffins had moved to a leaning position against the wall.

The superstitious people of Arensburg on the Baltic island of Oesel immediately blamed vampires and werewolves when similar trouble occurred in the town cemetery in 1844. The crisis started in June that year with the 'spooking' of horses belonging to visitors to the graveyard. Some of these horses bolted, others fainted or dropped dead; and many, so the story goes, went mad. The fault was laid at the door of the Buxhoewden family vault. When a funeral service in the family chapel was interrupted by eerie sounds from the adjacent burial chamber, the bravest of the Buxhoewdens entered the tomb to find that the coffins of their late relatives had been thrown around. Rumours of devilry spread, and there was great fear and consternation in Arensburg. The president of the local ecclesiastical court, the Baron de Guldenstabbe, headed an official enquiry and personally visited the vault, which had been put back in order and locked. But the coffins had moved again.

Determined to get to the bottom of the mystery, the Baron set up a committee to investigate it. They

The Chase vault at Oistins, **above, has stood open and empty since 1820, when all the coffins it contained were removed and buried in another, more peaceful place on the island.**

Viscount Combermere, the Governor of Barbados, **below, supervised the sealing of the Chase vault after the funeral of Thomasina Clarke on 17 July 1819. When he returned nine months later to check on the state of the tomb, Combermere found the coffins in total disarray, yet the seals on the door had remained intact.**

went further than their Barbadian cousins and had the floor of the vault ripped up – hoping, in vain, to find a secret passage. They suspected ghouls, though none of the coffins had in fact been robbed. Forced to give up their fruitless search, the committee laid not sand but ash throughout the vault and chapel and, as at Oistins, left secret seals that would break if the door were opened by any means. For three days and nights, the place was also guarded by soldiers. Then the committee returned: the seals were unbroken, the ashes were untouched and yet the coffins were everywhere they should not have been – some standing on their heads, and one so badly cracked that a bony arm protruded

> **THE CONSISTENT FEATURE OF ALL THESE CASES IS THAT METAL OBJECTS CAN BE CAUSED TO MOVE BY SOME UNKNOWN FORCE, POSSIBLY WITH THE PROVISIONS THAT THE METAL MUST BE LEAD, OF A CERTAIN WEIGHT, SHAPE AND BULK, RESTING IN CERTAIN PLACES AT PARTICULAR TIMES. SIMILAR CONDITIONS SWITCH FROM THE STRANGE TO THE FAMILIAR WHEN THE METAL OBJECT HAPPENS TO BE A NEEDLE OF MAGNETISED IRON.**
>
> **ERIC FRANK RUSSELL, GREAT WORLD MYSTERIES**

from it. Lacking the patience of the Barbadians who had put up with this sort of thing for eight years, the Arensburg committee and the Buxhoewdens immediately had the coffins moved elsewhere and thereby put an end to the vault's activities.

But what is it that causes coffins to move about, whether they are in vaults in Barbados, in England or on an island in the Baltic Sea? There seems to be no ready explanation. The 'traps' set up by various investigators – the unbroken seals and untouched sand- or ash-covered floors – strongly indicate that no human villains are involved.

Among those who have considered the supernatural and paranormal possibilities was Sir Arthur Conan Doyle, who believed that the Oistins coffins moved because of the strange physical powers that are supposed to reside in the bodies of the prematurely dead – the young Chase girls and Samuel Brewster Ames. But perhaps more credence should be given to the theory proffered by George Hunte, author of *Barbados*, who suggests that 'gas from decomposing bodies and not malevolent spirits was

Drawings were made by eyewitness Nathan Lucas to show how the coffins were originally placed in the vault at Oistins, below left, and how they were found in April 1820, below right. However, there are discrepancies between the account given by Lucas and those of other witnesses, and a second set of drawings, bottom, said to have been made on the spot and at the time the tomb was opened, is generally accepted to be a more accurate portrayal of the arrangement of the coffins.

gations carried out by the Barbadians themselves. At the time of the last burial there in 1819, someone saw fit to make a drawing of the vault with the coffins laid out in a state of orderliness, and another of its supposedly chaotic appearance when it was opened for the final time in April 1820. Eric Frank Russell compared the two sets of drawings in his chapter on the coffin phenomenon in *Great World Mysteries*:

'As first placed, three large coffins were put in a neat row with the middle one set slightly further away from the vault's door. Three smaller coffins sat tidily on top of the big ones. All had their feet towards the door, their heads towards the back of the vault, their longitudinal axes parallel to the side walls.

'When found out of place, all coffins were in varying but fairly regular stages of reversal, their heads now being more or less towards the door, their feet more or less towards the back wall. They look exactly as if caught when rotating at snail's pace around their own centres of gravity, some having twisted farther than others, their axes now cutting through an arc of about 120 degrees. The picture they present is that of a swirl, or a spiral effect, like so many metal shapes, heavier at one end than the other, spun around by some force gravitational, gyroscopic, electromagnetic or goodness knows what.'

However inconclusive, Russell's suggestion seems to be the most plausible. Superstition and fear, though – slamming the door shut on the case of the creeping coffins of Barbados and then abandoning the vaults – have precluded further scientific research into the whole weird business, which still remains wreathed in mystery. All that is known for sure is that for eight macabre years in the Chase vault at Oistins, on the island of Barbados, there were, to adapt the words of Emily Brönte, 'unquiet slumbers for the sleepers in that quiet earth'.

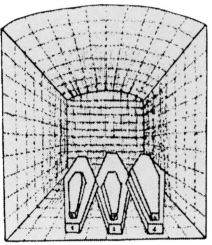

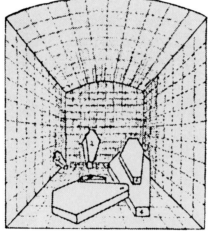

responsible for the violent separations and disarray of the sober arrangements which were made by undertakers'.

What about water in the vaults? Could the coffins possibly have floated? The Chase vault was not only watertight but high and dry, too; so underground currents can certainly be ruled out. And since the events at Arensburg all took place within a few weeks, any sign of flooding would surely have been noticed by investigators – none was. Lead coffins can certainly float – they need something to float on, however.

The movements of the Oistins coffins could perhaps be ascribed to the effect of violent earth tremors. Barbados lies on a seismic belt and is framed by fracture zones; moreover, there is a volcano on the nearby island of St Vincent. Even the slightest underground tremor could have displaced the coffins to a degree – but why should this have affected only those in the Chase vault? The theory is dubious. Stanton, Gretford and Arensburg are not known for seismic activity.

Most of the coffins in the vault at Barbados were made of lead, so we can infer that ordinary magnetic forces did not cause the mischief. And yet some such force may still provide the answer to the mystery. One vital clue has emerged from investi-

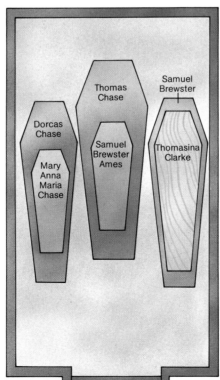

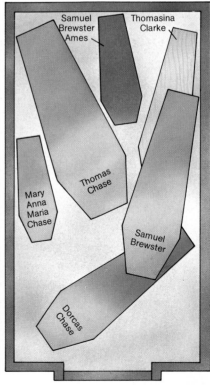

CONTROLLED BY THE SUN

INCESSANT TURMOIL ON THE SUN'S SURFACE IS SAID BY SOME TO INFLUENCE CHEMICAL, BIOLOGICAL AND SOCIAL ACTIVITY ON EARTH

Dark blotches on the face of the Sun have been observed and recorded for 2,000 years, but have been studied in detail only since telescopes were first used in astronomy in the early 17th century. We now know that these 'sunspots' come and go in cycles of just over 11 years and that they are closely associated with solar flares, intense outbursts of radiation on the Sun's surface. But why sunspots appear when and where they do, how they are formed, and what effects they have upon life on Earth are matters still not fully understood.

Sunspots first become visible as 'holes' in the swirling, granular surface of the Sun. Some cluster together to form groups. These can reach enormous dimensions: an average group, for instance, may be several times the diameter of the Earth. Groups can also merge into larger formations, with areas of up to 7,000 million square miles (18,000 million square kilometres).

Sunspots appear dark, we now know, because they are about 2,000°C (3,632°F) cooler than the surrounding area; and their number is estimated by a somewhat arbitrary formula, with the result expressed as a Wolf number, after the Swiss astronomer – Rudolf Wolf – who devised the method in 1852. It can vary from 0 to 300, and may increase very rapidly. From 8 to 18 February 1956, for example, it shot up from 26 to 270; and then, in the next 10 days, fell back to 125. This fluctuation formed a small peak within the overall cycle.

The main sunspot cycle averages 11.1 years in length, although individual cycles have ranged from 7 to 17 years. There is also a longer cycle of 179 years, apparently related to the movement of the Sun around the centre of mass of the solar system. In addition, there is a 25-month sunspot cycle, apparently linked to changes in the rate of emission of subatomic particles, known as neutrinos, from the Sun's deep interior.

DISTURBING THE EARTH

Orthodox scientists now recognise that sunspots influence the Earth in certain fairly well-understood ways. Solar flares, for instance – sudden outbursts of energy that always occur near sunspots – and the electrically charged particles that issue from them, may cause auroral displays in the Earth's

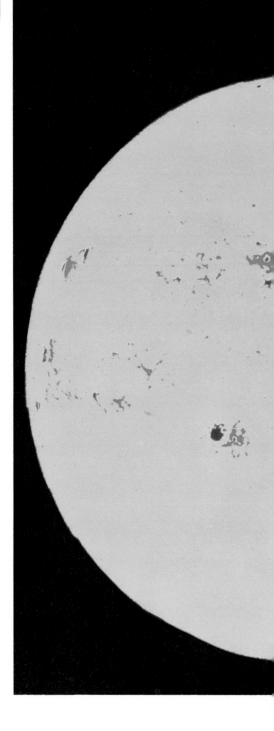

The vast globe of the Sun, capable of swallowing up a million Earths is blotched by huge sunspot groups, as shown right. Each group is like a great magnet, and the two poles of the magnet are represented in different colours in this computerised picture. Magnetic fluctuations on the Sun certainly seem to influence the Earth's magnetic field, and this in turn may affect living things.

The graph below shows sunspot cycles over a period of 280 years. The number and extent of sunspots vary in a cyclic way, reaching a peak roughly every 11 years. At the least active part of the cycle, there may be no spots for several days.

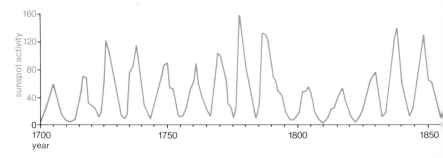

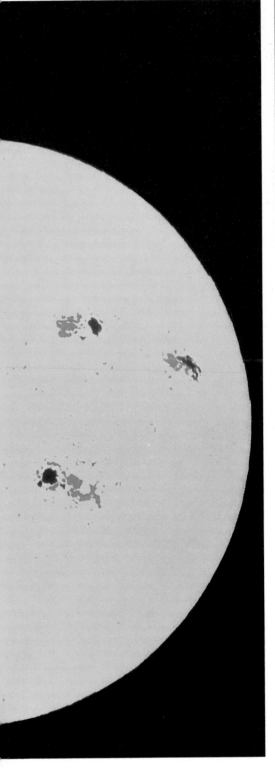

Soviet scientists have emphasised Sun-Earth links in books such as **The Geomagnetic Field and Life,** *top,* **by A.P. Dubrov and Complete Harmony in Nature,** *centre,* **by L.V. Golovanov. They have expressed the view that the Sun's influence is due to magnetic fields that burst through the surface at sunspot sites, as above.**

1900   1950

atmosphere. They can also cause sharp fluctuations in the Earth's magnetic field. A major solar flare may even bring about minute changes in the Earth's rotation by its effect on the terrestrial magnetic field.

Ironically, a costly attempt to study the Sun was actually brought to a premature end by sunspot activity. The 80-tonne American Skylab space-station, empty after having been occupied by a number of crews on scientific missions, was circling the Earth in 1979. Solar activity affected the Earth's atmosphere, causing it to expand and increase the drag experienced by Skylab. As a result, the craft broke up and fell to Earth over Western Australia in July 1979.

What else, we might well ask, is the Sun doing to us, apart from knocking a space-station out of orbit and putting an occasional brake on the Earth's rotation? The close correlation that has now been established between the solar cycle and variations in the Earth's magnetic field may also imply a corresponding influence on life on the Earth. Indeed, there is now generally accepted evidence that the Earth's magnetic field influences a wide variety of processes in all manner of living things – everything from micro-organisms to human beings – and electromagnetic ecology is now considered to be a scientific discipline in its own right.

According to Soviet scientist Dr A.P. Dubrov, the nervous system, the skin's electrical resistance, blood count, blood clotting rate, heart and eye function, onset and duration of a woman's menstrual period, and even the incidence in the population of neurosis, epilepsy and schizophrenia – all can be influenced by variations that may occur in the Earth's magnetic field.

A LIVING SUNDIAL

In experiments that lasted more than 20 years, Dr Maki Takata of Japan showed, for instance, that blood clotting rates respond precisely and immediately to both short- and long-term cycles in solar activity. 'Man is a living sundial,' he concluded. His findings supported those of Professor Giorgio Piccardi of Florence, in Italy, concerning ordinary water. Piccardi claimed, after conducting thousands of tests throughout an entire solar cycle, that the rate of certain chemical processes in water exactly matches day-to-day sunspot counts, the occurrence of magnetic storms and that of solar flares. The process in question was the precipitation from water of a dissolved compound – that is, the substance involved, bismuth oxychloride, came out of solution and formed a solid deposit.

Piccardi then turned his attention to blood, and found that its coagulation time could be increased by up to 50 per cent, simply by shielding it from the Earth's magnetic field. 'All living beings,' he concluded, 'are bound more intimately to the external world than one would think.'

The claims of Takata and Piccardi have been supported by numerous reports from the former Soviet Union (now the CIS), where heliobiology – the study of the Sun's influence on life – is an accepted discipline. Scientists there are particularly interested in the so-called Kursk anomaly. In the region around the Russian city of Kursk, the Earth's magnetic field reaches three times its average

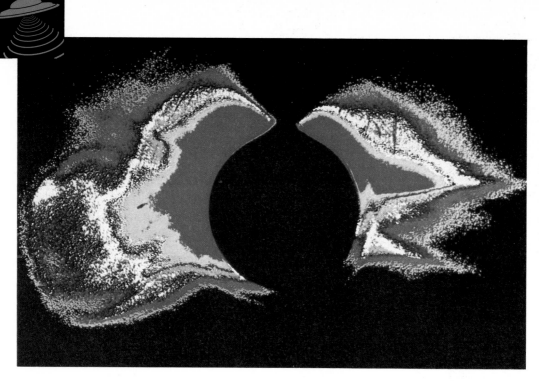

strength. The incidence of certain diseases is 160 per cent higher than the average, and yields of a wide range of crops are consistently lower.

There have been all too few attempts in the West to follow up Soviet research in heliobiology. However, there have been some surprises. One report published in the prestigious scientific journal *Nature*, for instance, described a significant correlation between fluctuations in the terrestrial magnetic field and emergency cardiac admissions to two Indian hospitals over a six-year period. This lends some support to Dubrov's claim, based on at least 14 Soviet studies, that magnetic storms are 'one of the direct causes of cardiovascular accidents [heart attacks]'.

But some of the boldest claims of all in this field were made by the late Russian scientist A. L. Chizhevsky. He studied sunspots for 10 years and correlated their appearance with his own state of health, declaring:

'We must assume that there exists a powerful factor outside our globe which governs the development of events in human societies, and synchronises them with the Sun's activity . . . we must assume that the electrical energy of the Sun is the superterrestrial factor which influences historical processes.'

He supported this startling claim with a mass of evidence covering 2,400 years. It revealed, he said, the existence of a 'universal cycle of historical

The huge extent of the solar corona, the Sun's 'atmosphere', is revealed in the Skylab computerised picture, above left. The corona is shaped by the Sun's magnetic field.

RCA technician John H. Nelson above, is seen projecting an image of the Sun on to a circular screen at his observatory in New York. Nelson predicted radio 'weather' from sunspots and planetary positions in this way.

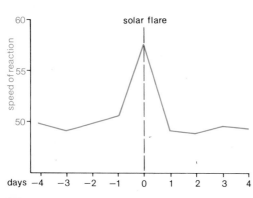

Same of the suggested influences of solar activity are shown in the four graphs reproduced here. Admissions of heart cases (blue) at an Indian hospital seem to keep step through the year with disturbances in the Earth's magnetic field, left. A chemical reaction in the open took place more quickly on the day of a solar eruption, below left. The number of warm days in the year (blue) measured at a Scottish site kept in step with sunspot numbers over a 50-year period, above right. Even Soviet government purchases of white hares (blue), valuable for their fur, seem to depend on sunspot numbers, though there is an interval of five years between a sunspot peak and a peak in hare purchases, as shown right.

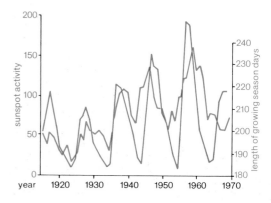

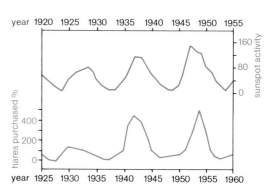

events' locked to that of the Sun. Each cycle came in four phases of roughly equal duration, he said. In the first, people were peaceful but apathetic; in the second, new ideas and leaders emerged; in the third (coinciding with a maximum of solar activity), nations reached 'maximum excitability', realising their greatest achievements, good or bad; while in the fourth, everybody became exhausted and slipped into the first phase of the next cycle.

Chizhevsky believed he had found cycles everywhere: in the emigrations of Jews, the outbreaks of diphtheria and influenza epidemics, strikes, terrorism, all major wars and even the voting patterns in Britain. Absurd as some of these claimed correlations may seem, Chizhevsky might not have been surprised by the coincidence of maximum solar sunspot activity and, for instance, the Soviet invasions of Hungary, Czechoslovakia and Afghanistan, the agitation by Polish workers in 1980 and the still officially unexplained influenza pandemics of 1957 and 1968.

MAVERICK SUNSPOTS

One man who put the study of sunspots to practical use was J. H. Nelson, chief analyst of shortwave radio propagation for RCA Communications in New York. He studied them carefully for more than 20 years, until his retirement. Before the days of satellite communication, radio companies were at the mercy of the Sun, for the state of the ionosphere influenced the range and quality of shortwave radio communication. After careful study of individual sunspots and solar flares, Nelson made an important discovery: some sunspots heralded radio blackouts, while others did not.

Looking more closely at the disruptive 'maverick' sunspots, as he called them, Nelson made an even more important discovery: they were invariably associated with certain positions of the planets. Nelson was not a professional astronomer, and certainly not an astrologer, but a technician with a practical job to do. Eventually, he was able to announce that there was a direct relationship between bad radio 'weather', severe magnetic storms, and planetary angles. Moreover, the 'maverick' angles of 0°, 90° and 180° coincided with the traditionally unfavourable angles of astrology, while the 'favourable' angles of 60° and 120° were also favourable in astrology.

By taking into account the positions of all the planets – even distant Pluto – Nelson eventually achieved, he believed, an accuracy of 85 per cent in his forecasts of radio 'weather'. His chief also acknowledged his work to have been of enormous importance to his company, the world's largest in this field.

Nelson never discovered the nature of the influence that could cause this relationship, however. The planets raise 'tides' on the surface of the Sun by their gravitational attractions, but these are minute. Furthermore, the gravitational fields of the planets differ considerably from each other: that of Jupiter is over 30 times stronger than that of Mercury, which is much closer to the Sun. Yet Nelson found that his forecasting system worked only when all the planets were taken into account. Gravity could not give them all an equal 'vote' in this manner. So Nelson was led to conclude, some-

what lamely, that 'unknown forces' were involved in the process.

Whether or not the radiation from solar flares reaches us according to a timetable drawn up by the planets, it certainly has a direct effect on our magnetic environment; and this in turn is known to affect many biological processes. Such radiation is certainly not the only influence on worldwide events, but it is a cyclic influence, and may well determine the timing of a wide variety of occurrences: heart attacks, influenza epidemics, the very moment of birth – or even the rise of political and religious movements. Today, after three centuries of research and speculation, we still cannot give a definite answer to the question: 'Are we all slaves of the Sun?'

According to the radio engineer J. H. Nelson, when Sun-planet directions make angles of 90° or 180° with each other, as illustrated below, sunspots that happen to occur at the same time will cause magnetic 'storms' on Earth. Any planets can be involved, including the three outer planets not shown here. Angles of 60° and 120°, on the other hand, are associated with an absence of magnetic disturbances.

// RESEARCH CARRIED OUT OVER A NUMBER OF YEARS AT THE TOMSK MEDICAL COLLEGE HAD FOUND A RELATION BETWEEN ROAD ACCIDENTS AND SOLAR ACTIVITY... AFTER THE ERUPTION OF A SOLAR FLARE, ROAD ACCIDENTS INCREASED, SOMETIMES BY AS MUCH AS FOUR TIMES ABOVE THE AVERAGE. //

NEW SCIENTIST

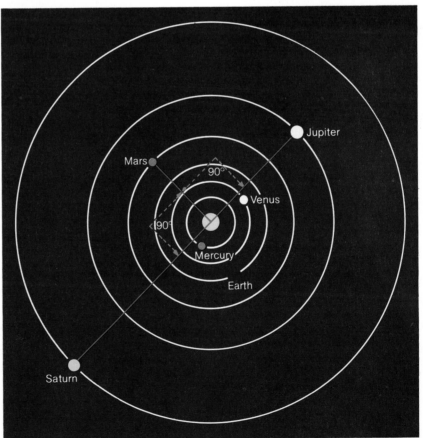

FURTHER EXPERIMENTS IN ASTRAL TRAVEL

WHAT HAPPENS WHEN SOMEONE'S 'ASTRAL BODY' VISITS A PLACE DURING AN OUT-OF-THE-BODY EXPERIENCE? PROFESSOR A. J. ELLISON DESCRIBES FURTHER EXPERIMENTS

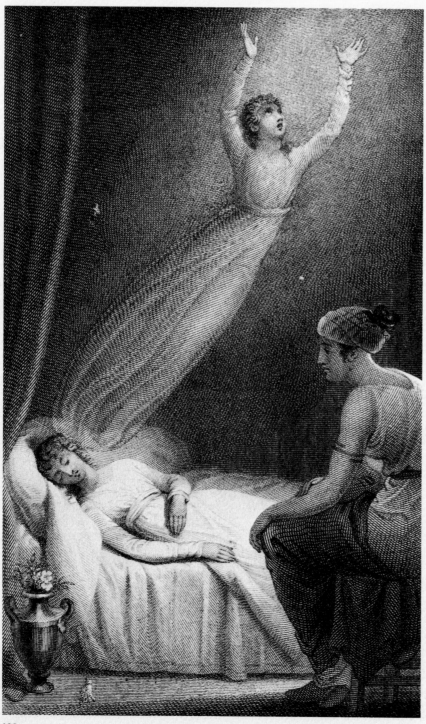

One of the major difficulties in psychical research is how to eliminate the possible intervention of telepathy. The problem is especially acute in the investigation of out-of-the-body experiences (OOBEs). The obvious way to test an OOBE is to ask the person undergoing the experience to 'visit' a place that he or she has never seen when awake, and then to ask for a detailed description of the surroundings, which can later be checked. But it seems that there is no way of knowing whether a real OOBE is involved, or whether the subject could be using clairvoyance to gain such information. Another interesting suggestion has been made: that having an OOBE may act as a trigger, bringing to the surface information that is lying passive in the subject's subconscious. Indeed, it could be that even everyday experiences such as seeing, hearing, touching, smelling and tasting are all mere illusions, and that we in fact sense the physical world by clairvoyance.

To combat this problem, I had built several years ago a box containing some fairly sophisticated electronic circuitry. With the subject of the experiment in an OOBE state, I could – by pressing a button at the front of the machine – make a three-digit random number appear at the back – out of my sight. I would then ask the subject to tell me the number at the back of the machine, and enter the number he or she gave me on another dial at the front of the machine. The machine would tally the numbers on the two dials and note whether or not the subject had been successful in stating the original number correctly. This procedure could be repeated any number of times to give a run of experiments. At the end of a run, the dials could then be set to display the number of successes. (The machine could also indicate how many of the separate digits corresponded on each occasion, if it should be that this information was required.)

The important point about this method is that, since at no time – before, during or after the experiment – are the random numbers in the mind of the experimenter, the influence of telepathy of any kind is thereby ruled out. The next step was to use the box to test a number of subjects who, as previous experiments had shown, were able to have OOBEs when this suggestion was made to them under hypnosis. (It is an ability fairly common among good hypnotic subjects.)

I started with two or three trial runs in which, for speed, I looked at the numbers at the back of the box while the first subject was attempting to tell me what they were. These runs were remarkably successful. So we started a run of 25 tries in which I did not look at the numbers in the window at the back, but used the method described above. Almost at once, the subject seemed to be in difficulty, and said that she was finding it impossible to 'read' the numbers clearly, as they were 'too small'.

The astral body is said to leave the physical body at death, as shown in the illustration by the French artist Corbould, far left. People who experience OOBEs often describe them in terms of a journey undertaken by the 'astral body'; but what actually happens during an OOBE is still the subject of debate.

Professor Arthur Ellison, left, devised a method for investigating the nature of OOBEs. A figure produced by a random number generator appears; the subject of the experiment is then asked to go in his 'astral body' and read the number. The number he sees is recorded on the dial at the front of the machine, and the machine checks whether or not the reading is correct. At no time is the original random number seen in the ordinary sense by anyone. Thus, a successful reading by the subject indicates that his OOBE is not dramatised telepathy.

❚❚ MY MEMORY OF THE DETAILS SEEN WHEN STILL UNCONSCIOUS IS STILL VIVID AND THERE IS NO DOUBT IN MY OWN MIND THAT MY VANTAGE POINT AT THAT MOMENT WAS DETACHED FROM MY BODY. **❚❚**

LYALL WATSON, THE ROMEO ERROR

I suggested that she practise with small numbers set up by a friend at home (and looked at afterwards, for the recording of 'right' or 'wrong'), and asked her to return in a month or two to continue more rigorous experiments using the box. It was no surprise to me, however, when she did not reappear as arranged.

A second hypnosis subject proved even less successful, was unable to read the figures at the back of the box under any conditions, and did not continue the experiments.

BEATING THE ODDS

My third subject was a famous American psychic who came to our laboratory during a visit to Britain and was told about the machine I had developed. He volunteered to try a run immediately – unfortunately, not giving us time to check that the box was in fact functioning properly. He indicated confidently that the numbers would 'just appear' in his mind, and an OOBE experience was not necessary in his particular case. This, of course, raises some interesting questions about the nature of OOBEs. There is certainly plenty of evidence that information can appear in the mind without any particular procedure, such as inducing an OOBE, being necessary. The psychic ran through a series of around 20 'guesses'. At the end, I turned the dial to see how many he had got right, expecting to find a zero score – and, to my astonishment, the window indicated eight.

But the following morning, I decided to investigate further, and did a run myself, and also scored eight. Clearly, there was something wrong. Careful examination indicated a non-visible fault in a microcircuit, resulting in all seven bars of the units digit being illuminated, forming the figure eight. The psychic's score had therefore been due to a misreading. Careful cleaning of the component in question reduced my score on a subsequent run to its usual zero.

The fourth subject to use the box was a famous British psychic. This time, the experiment was

PERSPECTIVES

TESTING A VIEWPOINT

Investigators into astral projection have been presented with many different accounts of out-of-the-body experiences by way of evidence that the phenomenon exists, and have also embarked upon scientific experimentation; but the possibility that clairvoyance or telepathy of some kind are involved still remains.

In his book *To Kiss Earth Goodbye,* American artist Ingo Swann tells how, as a small child, he once left his body while on the operating table as the surgeon removed his tonsils, and even saw the scalpel accidentally cut the back of his tongue. He also heard the surgeon swear at his mistake. This ability to leave his body at will continued and was later tested at Stanford University with quite spectacular results. Swann seemed able, for instance, to project himself way beyond this planet and described with considerable accuracy the features of Mercury, right down to the shape of its magnetic field – all this some time before Mariner 10 was able to confirm his descriptions. Researchers found, however, that his description

of Jupiter was nowhere near as detailed and even misinformed in some respects.

Accurate descriptions were also given by Bob Morrell who, when subjected to torture while in the Arizona State Penitentiary, claimed often to have left his body as a direct reaction to such treatment and to have wandered freely outside the jail. Thus he was able to outline to researchers events that occurred in the streets of San Francisco that he could not otherwise possibly have known about. Strangely, once he was no longer subjected to torture, the facility for astral travel promptly disappeared.

In his book *Mysteries,* Colin Wilson, meanwhile, points out potential uses for out-of-the-body experiences. Criminals, for instance, could conceivably use astral travel to help them plan burglaries. He also reminds us of the rather startling claim that occultist Aleister Crowley is said to have used astral travel to commit psychic rape on those women he wanted to possess.

planned and the box carefully checked for correct operation. I did a run or two, and my research assistant did the same. We obtained typically low scores. After allowing plenty of time for the circuitry to warm up and stability to be established, as well as a final check, the visiting psychic made the first run of 20 tries. A score of eight ensued. A check by myself gave another score of eight. Again, there had to be something wrong with the equipment – and, sure enough, careful cleaning of the microcircuit proved necessary. I now did a run, and my research assistant did a run – both resulting in the usual low scores. Everything was working correctly. The psychic did another run – and obtained another score of eight. But when we recleaned the equipment and tried again, we obtained our average low scores. Had the equipment again been at fault? It was impossible to tell.

A sceptical observer might well say that it was mere chance that a fault appeared in the equipment we were using on two occasions when well-known psychics were the subjects of experiment. An experienced psychical researcher, on the other hand, might observe that this kind of thing often happens. It is as though the unconscious mind of the psychic, knowing that a high score was required, achieved

this by the easiest available method – by using PK on the microcircuit rather than by means of clairvoyance. But no one is currently able to prove this contention: it merely remains a possibility.

Dr Karlis Osis, the Research Officer of the American Society for Psychical Research, conducted some interesting experiments with Alex Tanous to try to determine whether observations during OOBEs are performed with something similar to the human eye. Osis required Tanous, in his OOBE state, to 'look' through the window of a box in which was an optical system superimposing images that gave a certain appearance to normal sight when viewed from a certain point in space. This appearance was, in effect, an illusion – something that did not physically exist – and the experiment

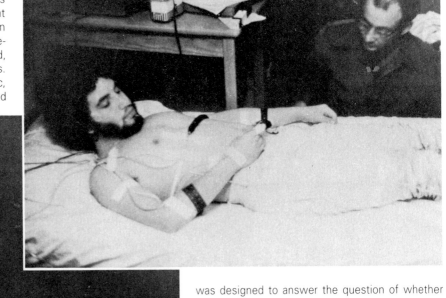

was designed to answer the question of whether OOBEs can be regarded as a kind of dramatised clairvoyance, or whether something (perhaps the 'astral body') actually travels from place to place during an OOBE. Osis claimed that his results indicated some support for the idea of a presence in the physical space in front of the box. There are, however, problems in the interpretation of his results: the limits of clairvoyance are, after all, unknown; and, even though it was possible to choose the target patterns randomly so that no one knew what their appearance to the human eye would be, it may have been possible for the unconscious mind of the subject to deduce the appearance from clairvoyant knowledge of the relative positions of the components in the box, and to dramatise the experience to produce the correct result. Osis claimed that later experiments, in which he placed physical sensors (strain gauges) in front of the window of the optical box, seemed to indicate that some kind of physical object might be there during OOBE observations. There seemed to be a tendency for more 'hits' on the optical targets when the gauges indicated activity.

Further interesting experiments involving psychic Stuart Blue Harary were conducted at America's Psychical Research Foundation in Durham, North Carolina. The aim was to observe

InFocus

MISS Z AND THE HIDDEN NUMBER

The first fully controlled laboratory experiment set up in order to investigate the nature of OOBEs was conducted by Dr Charles Tart, *left*, of the University of California. Dr Tart's subject was a Miss Z, who reported having experienced OOBEs since childhood.

After wiring her up to an electroencephalograph (EEG), Dr Tart then asked Miss Z to put herself into an OOBE state. On a shelf above her head was a slip of paper on which was written a number that had been selected by Dr Tart from mathematical random number tables before the beginning of the experiment. The wires that led from Miss Z's head to the electroencephalograph were designed to be of such a length that she could not physically get up at any point and look at the number on the shelf without causing an obvious interruption in the pattern that appeared on the electroencephalograph print-out.

Nothing significant happened on the first night of the experiment. On the second night, however, Miss Z was successful in experiencing an OOBE, in the course of which she said that she saw a clock on the wall above the shelf – she could not have seen this while lying down – and had 'read' the time as being 3.15 a.m. A check on the electroencephalograph print-out revealed unusual brainwave patterns at that time. On the third night, she had a similar experience.

It was not until the fourth night that she attempted to read the figure on the slip of paper – and, remarkably, did so with complete success. She reported the time of her experience – by the laboratory clock – as somewhere between 5.50 and 6.00 a.m. At 5.57 a.m. on the electroencephalograph tape, it was noted that her brainwave patterns showed a disturbed output. Dr Tart's experiment seemed to show that something paranormal was indeed going on during Miss Z's OOBEs.

" GOING OUT [ASTRAL PROJECTION] IS A DRAMATIC EXPERIENCE... THERE IS A VERY POWERFUL AND VERY RAPID SPIRAL THRUST OF ENERGY... "

JOHN HERON,

CONFESSIONS OF A JANUS-BRAIN

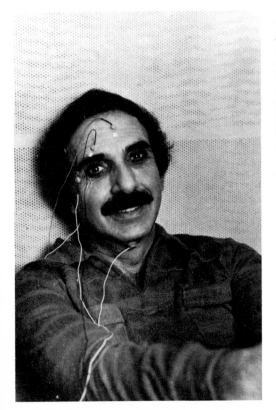

Does anything actually leave the physical body during an OOBE? Dr Karlis Osis, above, of the American Society for Psychical Research, conducted experiments in which he placed strain gauges in front of the site that the subject, psychic Alex Tanous, left – shown wired up to an electroencephalograph as he was during the experiments – is asked to visit.

closely the behaviour of small rodents, snakes and kittens in the presence of an 'astral projection'. The kittens were put in a large, open test box that had been marked into squares. The normal random activity of the kittens could be expressed in terms of the number of squares occupied by a kitten in a given period of time. In normal experimental conditions, the kittens tended to be frightened, cry and move about a great deal. Harary 'went', in an OOBE state, to the kittens' box and tried to calm them. One of the kittens did indeed change in behaviour, its movement and activity both decreasing during the times when Harary was having an OOBE. The other kitten took no notice, however. Later experiments were not very significant, but it appears from the work done by Harary and other researchers that it might be worthwhile to investigate whether animals are actually better than machines as detectors of subjects having OOBEs.

One can reasonably conclude from all this that it may not be meaningful to take subjects' descriptions of their own experiences of OOBEs too literally. Indeed, an OOBE may well be a mental construction, consisting of memories of the physical world, with some information obtained through telepathy or clairvoyance superimposed on it. Eastern scriptures suggest that the 'astral world' to which many people believe we go after death (and which we visit in the 'astral body' during an OOBE) is a 'world of illusion', based perhaps on a combination of our memories of this world and our desires, both conscious and unconscious. As Professor H.H. Price has pointed out, such a world of mental images would be just like the world that is frequently described by mediums and psychics, with all the individual differences one would expect. However, as Professor Price also pointed out, such a 'next world' would not be at all dissimilar from what some philosophers say this world is really like. Perhaps a study of the OOBE would in fact help us towards a better understanding of ourselves, our perceptions and mental processes.

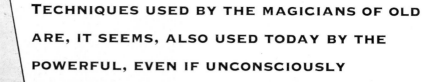

RITUAL MAGIC

The art of creating changes in consciousness in accordance with will is today practised in every great city of the Western world. For a body of theory and practice that the confident mid-Victorian materialist regarded as a sad relic of the irrational past, doomed to be swept into the dustbin of history, has in fact survived and flourished. It is impossible to be sure just how many men and women regularly engage in ritual magic, but there is a fair number certainly, for several thriving businesses exist to supply their needs. In England, for example, there are mail order firms issuing catalogues that contain a large selection of magical paraphernalia: swords, daggers, ceremonial candles and incenses appropriate to every type of magical rite are included.

Many modern magicians appear to live ordinary enough lives. They have jobs and families, they mow their lawns, go on holiday, and pay their taxes just like their neighbours. But there is no denying that their private beliefs are sometimes odd to the point of what some would describe as eccentricity. They see the Universe as a living being, its visible appearance veiling its real nature; and they regard symbol and allegory, dream and vision as more truly conveying ultimate reality than all the equations of the mathematician and the astrophysicist.

The various physical and psychological techniques employed today by magicians are quite as strange as the beliefs that inspire them. The modern magician, for instance, will hold his body in painful and unlikely postures for long periods of time. He will spend weeks in the visualisation of, and meditation upon, some simple coloured symbol – perhaps a red triangle or a yellow square. He will half-choke himself with the smoke of exotic incenses; he will whirl like a spinning top until he falls senseless to the ground; he may clad himself in strange robes and stand, amid circles and symbols, chanting the words of evocation that, so he believes, will bring the gods down to earth and help him, in turn, become supremely powerful.

It has been suggested, however, that many others besides an occult minority have practised ritual magic this century. Politicians and clergymen,

Few political or military movements in modern times have used special effects, such as lights, music and stirring speech, in order to manipulate the minds of the masses as successfully as the Nazis, top left. No detail was overlooked; and the blood banner that had been carried by Hitler in the putsch of 1923 was used in every ceremony consecrating new swastika banners, as shown above. Yet total concentration on blood and death was to backfire – their vision of martial glory ending in the snows of Stalingrad, above left, and the ruins of Berlin.

speakers at protest meetings and strike leaders – all, so it is argued, *unconsciously* employ magical techniques. They have learned from others, or have themselves developed on the basis of experience, the same methods of altering consciousness employed by modern magicians: but while the magician is usually concerned only with altering the state of consciousness of himself and perhaps a few close associates, the politician or priest is intent on altering the feelings and actions of hundreds, thousands, or, in the case of such revolutionaries as Adolf Hitler and Eva Peron, maybe many millions of people.

MAGICAL PERFORMANCES

Ritual magicians employ light, colour, sound and highly theatrical spectacle to achieve what some have called 'one-pointedness' – in other words, the directing of the mind towards one particular idea, or universal factor. If, for example, a contemporary magician wants to concentrate his consciousness upon, and flood his mind and spirit with, the ideal of benevolent power, he will 'invoke Jupiter' – that is, he will either play the chief part or be the only actor in a 'mystery play' in which he identifies himself with this god and surrounds himself with theatrical 'props' that are traditionally associated with the deity and his attributes.

Inside his magic circle, he will outline a square or a four-pointed star – four is the number sacred to Jupiter – with chalks or paints of Jupiter's colours – violet, purple and shades of blue. He will decorate his 'temple', the room in which he carries out his ceremonial workings, with sprays of oak and poplar leaves, associated with the god since classical times. In his censer, or incense burner, cedar wood and saffron, recognised as perfumes of Jupiter, will smoulder on a bed of glowing charcoal. And if he is one of that small minority of ritualists who employ mind-altering drugs, some opium may also have been placed in the censer or he will have smoked opium before the ceremony.

Once this setting for the Jupiterian mystery play has been prepared, the magician will begin to act out his role, identifying himself with the god in exactly the same way that a 'method' actor identifies himself with the character he is portraying. Every word the magician will say during his performance, every act he will carry out, every 'Name of Power' he chants, will be associated with the Jupiterian principle of benevolent power. And by the end of the rite, the magician's mind will – if he has been successful – be filled with that principle to the exclusion of all else.

// NOBODY IN CREATION IS CLEVERER

THAN THE HUMAN BEING. POSSESSED

OF THE MOST ACCESSIBLE

TECHNIQUES, HE CAN MAKE ALL

CREATION HIS SERVANT... **//**

KO HUNG, REJOINDER

TO POPULAR CONCEPTIONS

Today, too, the ritual magician, above, invokes the gods by flooding his mind with the concept of supreme power and surrounding himself with traditional symbols.

Exactly the same system – that of using ceremony to alter emotions and consciousness – is also employed in many respects by politicians and statesmen. Take, for example, the May Day processions that would take place in any Communist country. The fluttering red flags, the pictures of revolutionary heroes and martyrs borne aloft, the thousands of clenched fists and stamping feet, and the dais upon which stand the party leaders beneath vast romanticised portraits of Marx, Engels and Lenin – all are the political equivalents of the furnishings and decorations of the magician's temple, and there is no doubt that the consciousness of the onlookers and participants in the revolutionary ceremony becomes changed. Drab working lives, inadequate housing and food, fears for the future are all forgotten. Instead, the people feel themselves to be part of a great marching army, a rushing tide of progress destined, by the laws of history, to smash down all that stands in its way, in the attempt to create a new and better world.

Perhaps the greatest masters of such 'political ritual magic' were the leaders of the Nazi Party. Indeed, some occultists have gone so far as to suggest that Adolf Hitler and his closest associates had studied the techniques of occult ceremony, deliberately applying them to political purposes. This theory has long been debated, with no firm conclusions forthcoming. At one period of his early

come up with anything more effective than the ceremonies employed at Nuremberg.

Some occultists claim that those who raise the old gods from the depths of the unconscious run the risk of being destroyed by them. Certainly, many of the young men who invoked Mars at Nuremberg eventually fell as sacrifices – at Stalingrad, at Kursk, and in the fire and smoke of besieged Berlin.

At the present day, no statesman or politician conducts, consciously or otherwise, 'magical' ceremonies either as impressive or as sinister as those performed at Nuremberg. But similar use of light, colour and sound to alter the thought and feelings of an audience can be discerned in other aspects of contemporary life, in religious celebrations, and even in rock concerts. It has even been said that anyone who saw the late Janis Joplin in action in many ways witnessed a ritual evocation of the spirit of Venus quite as effective as any carried out by magicians, past or present.

Giant idealised portraits of the former USSR's officially approved heroes, above, served at May Day celebrations to direct the minds of the participants towards a single goal – furtherance of the Communist state.

life, the future Führer undoubtedly read a great deal of occult literature; and what does seem certain is that the Nazi's Nuremberg Rallies were extremely formalised, elaborately staged ceremonies, designed to exert a particular effect upon the minds both of the participants and of those who later saw films of them.

Fanfares from assembled trumpeters in traditional costume or the theatrical black and silver uniforms of the SS, the stirring marches played to the gathering crowds, and the concerts of Wagner's music that usually preceded each rally – all caused mental associations with the ideas of Germanic myth and tradition, military glory and National Socialism (Nazism). At each rally, the massed swastika banners – black, white and red, traditionally a colour combination associated with war, terror and death – brought into the consciousness of the participants the entire Nazi ideology. The high point and prime ritual of the rallies, meanwhile – Hitler ceremonially consecrating new swastika banners by clasping them to the 'blood banner' that had been carried by him and others in the unsuccessful Munich *putsch* of 1923 – was the most potent element in the Nazis' loathsome 'mystery play'. Indeed, the emotions conveyed by it were such that the minds of living Nazis were, in a sense, linked with the thoughts and actions of National Socialist martyrs. One might say it was almost a sacrament.

The magical and quasi-religious aspects of these rallies were emphasised by the fact that their climax always came after darkness and took place in what Albert Speer, the Nazi technocrat, described as 'a cathedral of light' – an open space surrounded by upright beams, reminiscent of the pillars of Gothic architecture, emanating from anti-aircraft searchlights pointed directly up towards the sky.

The Nuremberg Rallies undoubtedly achieved their intended effects. The overwhelming majority of those who either witnessed or participated in them found their minds overflowing with ideas of glory, military struggle and self-sacrifice for the good of the Aryan race. Even if an occultist of great expertise had spent years in devising a ritual to invoke Mars, he would have been unlikely to have

" MAGIC IS IN EXISTENCE IN EVERY

CULTURE IN THE WORLD – AND

IS, IN ADDITION, STRIKINGLY

UNIFIED DESPITE THE DIVERSITY

OF CULTURES – BECAUSE IT IS

A REFLECTION OF ETERNAL

PRINCIPLES AND AS SUCH

MUST EXIST SO LONG AS THERE

ARE CULTURES. "

ARTHUR VERSLUIS,

THE PHILOSOPHY OF MAGIC

The late Janis Joplin, right, gave electric stage performances that embodied – unknowingly, it is thought – all the elements of an invocation of Venus.

SACRED GEOMETRY

SACRED BUILDINGS HAVE ALWAYS BEEN DESIGNED TO BE TANGIBLE EXPRESSIONS OF MAN'S BELIEFS. HOW HAVE THEY SYMBOLISED HARMONY WITH CERTAIN COSMIC LAWS?

More than 2,000 years ago, during the lifetime of the Greek philosopher Plato (c. 427-347 BC), the people of Delos were struck down by a terrible pestilence. In despair, they consulted the oracle, and asked what steps they should take. The oracle set them a problem: they were to double the volume of a cubic altar, while preserving its shape. The governors of Delos sent to the geometers of the Academy, imploring them to find the answer and thereby save their city. In fact, to solve the problem, it is necessary to find the cube root of two; but with the mathematics that the ancient Greeks had at their disposal, this was impossible. So it seems that the problem set by the oracle was – to say the least – mischievous; but the story does show how highly geometry (which has the literal meaning 'measuring the Earth') was regarded in ancient Greece.

On the Greek island of Delos, below, 2,400 years ago, the people consulted the oracle to discover what steps they should take to escape from a plague that was ravaging their community. The oracle then set them a geometrical problem that they found impossible to solve.

Ancient Greek geometers inherited the knowledge of the ancient Egyptians who, in the third millennium BC, first developed this science as a practical method of surveying land. Every year, the flooding of the river Nile destroyed all boundary markers within its alluvial plain, and these had to be reestablished by central government in order to prevent disputes among landowners. The method of surveying had to be simple and accurate, and it had to facilitate the measurement of both length and area. This required an easy method of producing a right angle.

The solution adopted by the ancient Egyptians involved two men and a length of rope with 13 knots in it, marking 12 equal divisions. Laid out straight, the rope could be used for measuring distance; and by arranging it in the shape of a triangle, with one side three units long, another four, and another five, a right angle was formed. Using this simple method, it was also easy to lay out rectangles and other more complex geometrical figures, and the method was used, in particular, for laying out the foundations of sacred buildings.

In ancient Egypt, organised religion pervaded life to such an extent that almost every action was a ritual act of worship. Indeed, the very laying out of

tombs and temples involved the most complex ceremonies. There has been much speculation about the significance of the dimensions of ancient Egyptian buildings, in particular the pyramids; but there is no doubt that every aspect of Egyptian sacred building was in fact infused with religious symbolism. The actual practice of 'cording the temple' – laying out its foundations – is described as follows in a wall carving at Dandara, north of Luxor:

'The living god, the magnificent son of Asti, nourished by the sublime goddess in the temple, the sovereign of the country, stretches out the rope in joy; with his glance towards the *ak* of the Bull's Foreleg constellation, he establishes the temple-house of the mistress at Dandara, as took place there before.'

In other words, the priest fixed the orientation of the temple upon the constellation of the Bull's Foreleg – the constellation we now know as Ursa Major, the Great Bear. Surveyors then fixed a line at right angles to this one, using the knotted rope to form a right-angled triangle – thus imbuing the building from the very beginning with rich symbolic meaning.

For measuring and surveying, the ancient Egyptians used a rope, as shown above, divided by knots into 12 sections, with which they could form a right angle. The wall painting, right, from the tomb of Menena at Thebes, shows such a knotted rope being used to measure the harvest.

Other cultures have chosen different ways to enrich their buildings with symbolic meaning, however. The Tower of Babel, the Babylonian Etemenanki, for example, was designed as a miniature representation of the Universe, with seven stages, each representing one of the seven heavens of Babylonian cosmology. Each level was identified with a planet, and painted in a corresponding colour. The bottom layer was painted black to represent Saturn; the next one, orange, for Jupiter; the third, red, for Mars; the fourth, yellow, for the Sun; the fifth and sixth, green and blue, for Venus and Mercury; and the top, white, probably for the Moon.

SYMBOLIC ARK

The *Old Testament*, in fact, contains many detailed descriptions of buildings obviously designed as physical expressions of the ancient Jewish art of *gematria*, or number symbolism. The dimensions are believed to have been received by direct revelation from God, and clearly had a transcendent significance. For instance, the instructions for the construction of the ark began in this way, according to *Genesis 6: 14—16*:

'And this is the fashion which thou shalt make it of: the length of the ark shall be three hundred cubits, the breadth of it fifty cubits, and the height of it thirty cubits. A window shalt thou make to the ark, and in a cubit shalt thou finish it above; and the door of the ark shalt thou set in the side thereof; with lower, second and third storeys shalt thou make it.'

Noah's ark was thus divided into three storeys, each with 11 sections, which gives a total of what is considered a sacred number, 33. The ark had two openings: the main entrance in the lowest storey, through which the animals passed into the plane of physical life, and the small one-cubit window at the top through which the spirit, in the shape of the dove that Noah sent out to look for land at the height of the Flood, was released. In his book *The Canon*, William Stirling goes so far as to connect

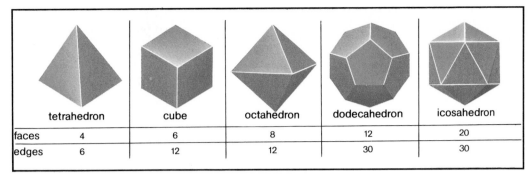

	tetrahedron	cube	octahedron	dodecahedron	icosahedron
faces	4	6	8	12	20
edges	6	12	12	30	30

The five shapes known as Platonic solids, in which all edges and interior angles are equal, shown left, were regarded by Plato as essential forms that acted as links between the spiritual and physical worlds. However, it seems probable that these five regular solids were in fact known long before the time of Plato. Indeed, the spherical stones, left, carved in the shape of the five solids and dating from Neolithic times, were found in Britain, and can be seen at the Ashmolean Museum, Oxford.

In the drawing, far left, from an Ethiopian manuscript, Noah's ark is shown with three storeys. According to Kabbalistic tradition, each storey was divided into 11 sections, making a total of 33, a sacred number.

the dimensions of the ark with the size of the planet Earth. As he puts it:

'If this is correct, we must conceive, by the proportions of the ark, the vast figure of a man, in the likeness and the image of God, whose body contains the measure of the sun's path in the ecliptic, the circuit of the Earth, and the orbits of the seven planets.'

HARMONIOUS MAN

Fanciful as they may seem, such cosmological schemata can be found throughout ancient architecture, particularly in Egypt and Babylonia. Indeed, the ark is in many ways the image of the righteous man who is taken away from an old and evil world and fitted into a new and God-given plan. Some would even say that those who fit the cosmic scheme survive; those who do not, perish.

For the ancient Greeks, and Plato in particular, it was in geometry that the harmony of the cosmos could be expressed. For them, the world was governed by the proportions given by the two geomet-

ric progressions of Pythagoras: 1, 2, 4, 8 and 1, 3, 9, 27; and in his work *Timaeus,* Plato went on to assert that the forms that best reflected this harmony were cubes and squares with sides in these specific proportions.

For later Platonists, geometry even accounted for all known states of matter. Especially important were the series of Platonic solids, four of which represented the four elements. The tetrahedron,

// AN ELABORATE RITUAL DICTATED

THE LOCATION AND DIRECTION OF

THE APARTMENTS WHICH THE

EMPEROR WOULD OCCUPY AT

DIFFERENT TIMES OF THE YEAR,

SO THAT HIS ACTIONS WOULD

BE IN ACCORDANCE WITH

HEAVEN'S PRINCIPLES. //

DEREK WALTERS,

FENG SHUI

In the Hindu tradition, purusha, or cosmic Man, represents the Universe. The plan of a Hindu temple, below, can be seen to accommodate the cosmic human form.

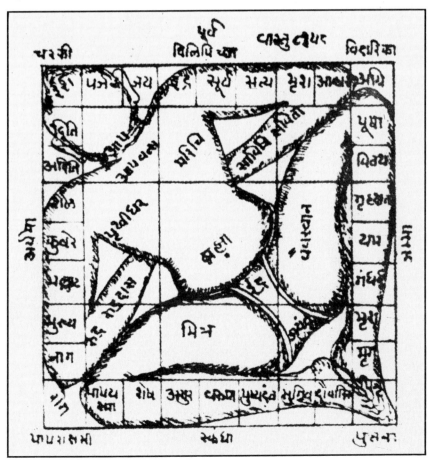

being the simplest regular geometrical solid, represented fire, the lightest of the elements; the octahedron, bounded by eight equilateral triangles and considered next in lightness to the tetrahedron, was assigned to air. Then came the cube, a solid and immovable figure that stood for the element earth; while the icosahedron, the 'heaviest' of the regular solids bounded by triangles, represented water. An extraordinary footnote to the symbolism of the Platonic solids is the find, in Britain, of a series of spherical stones, at least a thousand years old, carved to represent the same solids. Indeed, megalithic monuments seem to indicate sophisticated astronomical and geometrical knowledge on the part of their builders.

For other civilisations, the reflection of divine harmony in the proportions of buildings was a less abstract matter. If God made Man, then the proportions of the human body must echo the harmony of the divine plan. A Hindu architectural *sutra* says: 'The Universe is present in the temple by means of proportion'; and the Hindu temple plan is seen superimposed on the body of the *purusha,* or cosmic Man.

In western tradition, the same idea is found in the work of the architectural theoretician Marcus Vitruvius Pollio. More commonly known simply as Vitruvius, this Roman, who worked in the first century BC, codified his rules for good building in his ten books, *De Architectura* ('Of Architecture'). After the fall of the Roman Empire, his books were lost for a millennium until rediscovered by the architects of the Renaissance through whom, in their effort to recreate classical architecture, *De Architectura* gained a stature far greater than any importance it had enjoyed in classical times.

According to Vitruvius, architecture depends on order, arrangement, eurhythmy – beauty and fitness in the relationship of the parts of the building to the whole – symmetry, propriety and economy.

" To the ancient mind, propitious building was not merely a matter of analysing the physical characteristics of the surrounding countryside. Buildings were also designed to reflect the harmony between Man and the universe. *"*

The idea that cosmic harmony could be expressed through the human form was taken up with enthusiasm by Renaissance designers. Leonardo da Vinci's Vitruvian Man, *left, for instance, is shown fitted into the cosmic circle. Michelangelo's painting* The Creation of Adam, *below, on the ceiling of the Sistine Chapel in the Vatican, also celebrates the beauty of the human body and the essential harmony between God and Man.*

In an influential 10-volume book on architecture, the Roman architect Vitruvius laid down rules for good design – including the correct use of Corinthian, Doric and Ionic columns, illustrated left to right, above.

The Hongkong and Shanghai Bank in Hongkong, right, is shown under construction in 1983. The bank was sited – by its English architect, Norman Foster – in accordance with ancient Chinese geomantic principles.

Eurhythmy is achieved, said Vitruvius, through an elaborate system of proportion. In temples, this proportion is to be derived from the proportions of the human body which, he said, had been 'formed with such propriety that the several members are commensurate with the whole'. No building, he asserted, 'can possess the attributes of composition in which symmetry and proportion are disregarded [and] unless there exists the perfect conformation of parts which may be observed in a well-formed human being . . .'

This foundation of the proportions of architecture on those of the human body was also taken up with enthusiasm by the architects of the Renaissance. Proportions were worked out explicitly and in detail, and employed in church facades, in foundations and in paintings. In particular, dimensions were related via geometric and harmonic proportions. In 1525, a Franciscan monk named Francesco di Giorgio published a treatise entitled *De Harmonia Mundi Totius* ('Concerning the Harmony of the Whole World') that effectively blended the Platonic geometrical tradition, aspects of the Jewish Kabbalistic tradition, and Vitruvius' system based, as it was, on the proportions of the human body.

The quality which Vitruvius called propriety was defined by him as the perfection of style that results from the correct construction of a building, and he was to record the correct rules for building in the classical tradition – among them, explicit guidelines for the use of the various types of classical column – Corinthian, Ionic and Doric – in temples dedicated to the various gods. Doric was to be used for temples in honour of Jupiter, lightning, the heavens, the Sun or Moon, Minerva, Mars or Hercules; Corinthian for Venus, Proserpine, spring water and nymphs; and Ionic for Juno, Diana and Bacchus, and others.

Propriety was also to be achieved by the correct siting of the building. Temples were to be built in healthy neighbourhoods where suitable springs of fresh water existed, and were to be oriented in such a way that the light could be used to the maximum effect. The ancient Chinese art of geomancy, *Feng Shui,* was – and still is – concerned precisely with such questions. It is essentially a method of ensuring the propitious siting of buildings in the

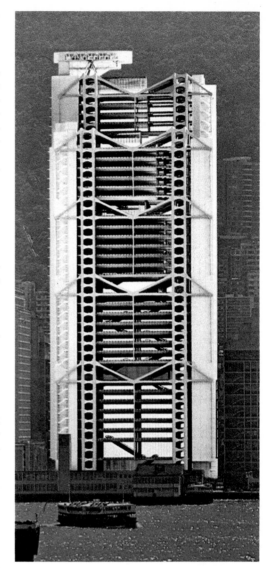

surrounding physical terrain. To the ancient mind, however, such propitious building was not merely a matter of analysing the physical characteristics of the surrounding countryside. Buildings were also designed to reflect the harmony between Man and the Universe.

PERSPECTIVES
MAGICAL MEASUREMENTS

According to the principles of *Feng Shui* – an ancient Chinese form of geomancy – particular dimensions and proportions are likely to bring good fortune. The Chinese geomancer, even today, therefore uses a special ruler – known as *ting lan* – on which significant measurements are marked. These are vital in planning a building.

The *Feng Shui* foot is equivalent to approximately 43 cms (17 ins) and is divided into eight principal sections, each corresponding to a named portent. The first, measuring up to 5.4 cms (2⅛ ins) and termed *Ts'ai,* corresponds to wealth; the second,

measuring from 5.5–10.7 cms (4¼ ins), *Ping,* points to sickness; while the third, measuring from 10.8–16.1 cms (6⁵⁄₁₆ ins), *Li,* indicates separation. The fourth, *I,* measuring from 16.2–21.4 cms (8³⁄₁₆ ins), promises righteousness; and the fifth section, *Kuan,* from 21.5–26.8 cms (10½ ins), is said to mean promotion. The sixth, *Chieh,* from 26.9–32.1 cms (12⅝ ins) signifies likely robbery; the seventh, *Hai,* from 32.2–37.5 cms (14¾ ins) is equally inauspicious and indicates accidents; while the eighth section, *Pen,* measuring from 37.6–42.9 cms (16¹⁵⁄₁₆ ins), signifies a new start.

THE OZ FACTOR

TIMELESSNESS AND A FEELING OF DISLOCATION ARE OFTEN REPORTED AFTER CLOSE ENCOUNTERS WITH UNIDENTIFIED FLYING OBJECTS. WHAT IS IT THAT CAUSES THIS SENSE OF ALIENATION?

There is indeed, a marked social dimension to the UFO enigma. The phenomenon is not a fixed thing: it changes with the times and, perhaps, has done so for centuries. The airship waves of the 1890s in the USA, and those in 1909 and 1913 in Britain, for instance, showed UFOs keeping one step ahead of current technology; and the apparent similarities between the ancient fairy lore of many cultures and modern UFO entity sightings is equally striking. Note also the way that aliens, according to contemporary witnesses, no longer come from the solar system but from other stars or even other galaxies, now that our space probes have shown no sign of advanced life on any of our sister worlds.

The influence of science-fiction movies is relevant, too. *The Day the Earth Stood Still*, for instance, used the motif of electromagnetic interference with vehicles, some time before claims of this effect had even arisen in UFO accounts.

It has also been realised that identified flying objects (IFOs) are of great significance. Since more

The nature of UFO sightings seems to change with the times. In the 1890s, airships, like the one above, were widely seen in California. Later, after films such as The Day the Earth Stood Still, *above right, made in 1951, aliens and other forms of spacecraft were more frequently reported.*

There has been serious study of the UFO phenomenon ever since 1947; but one of the most frequent criticisms made of ufology is that no progress whatsoever has been made during this time. We are no nearer a solution, it is sometimes said, than on the day when Kenneth Arnold first encountered a formation of discs over Mount Rainier in Washington State, USA, all those years ago. Such an attitude dismisses out of hand, however, many important discoveries.

We now realise, for instance, that there is not just one type of UFO phenomenon but two – at least. On the one hand, there are physical occurrences, involving energy behaving in poorly understood ways. These are called unidentified atmospheric phenomena, or UAPs: on the other, there is interaction with UFOs involving human beings.

than 90 per cent of reported UFOs are in fact identified, it was always foolish just to dismiss them. Indeed, now there has been closer study of intriguing IFO cases, in which witnesses were fooled, by such commonplace sights as the Moon, into believing they had witnessed a UFO.

Ufology is now diversifying into a variety of subdivisions; and the scientific study of UAPs may even become a field of research on its own. UAPs, however caused, seem to be amorphous balls of energy that emit broad–band radiation. They could perhaps be related to ball lightning, whatever atmospheric physicists eventually prove that to be. Indeed, ball lightning may be a sub–category of

UAPs, rather than the reverse. Another important kind of UAP may be a piezoelectrical impulse squeezed from the ground into the atmosphere. These lightforms may or may not be proven to exist, but such theories are at least providing ufologists with testable hypotheses.

But whereas UAPs may be seen by a number of independent observers, UFOs are very often totally subjective, or else perceived only by a small number of witnesses who are associated with each other in some way and who occupy a small area. But there has been speculation – by, for example, researcher Dr Michael Persinger – that UAP events may account for the more mysterious UFO close encounters as well.

PSEUDO-MEMORIES

According to Persinger, radiation emitted by the UAP may interfere with the brain functioning of any percipient who is close enough to it – that is, within the phenomenon's 'sphere of influence'. This proximity triggers hallucinatory experiences, which also feature unconsciousness, trauma, time-loss and pseudo-memories of an alien encounter, which are personally relevant but individually variable. They are said to be stimulated by the interpretation of the event (and made in the seconds before the UAP/brain interaction takes place) in terms of a culturally conceived 'alien device'. Many years ago, the same phenomenon would have been culturally conceived as demonic, or as from the fairy realm, during the same moments of interaction.

Dr Alvin Lawson and William McCall have attempted to prove an origin for subjective interpretations in terms of repressed memories of the birth process. Some factor such as this, present in all cases, is certainly necessary to explain the otherwise puzzling threads that interlink stories of alien contact from so many different countries – for the UFO enigma is world-wide in extent and also highly consistent.

Such research may be all that is necessary to establish a basic understanding of the UFO enigma. However, many problems remain. Why is there frequently gross distortion of normal stimuli, precipitating extraordinary close encounters? Why does there appear to be a connection between close encounter witnesses and psychic phenomena? Why do close encounter witnesses often become 'repeaters', having frequent UFO contacts, often from childhood?

Such difficulties, among others, give one cause to speculate as to whether a better, all–embracing or even additional theory to encompass the remaining cases may still be necessary. One important clue regarding this may be the existence of the 'Oz factor'.

The Oz factor comprises a set of features that stand out among UFO close encounter reports. Individually, they have been recognised for several years, but nobody had sought to tie them together into a collective experience. The following typical quotations from close encounter witnesses sketch in the outline of the Oz factor. 'All sounds around me suddenly ceased . . . it was like being at the bottom of a very deep well.' 'I felt isolated and alone, suddenly not a part of the environment.' 'It was as if I were half in this world and half out of it.' 'Time

In the film The Wizard of Oz, Dorothy and her dog Toto, seen bottom in a scene with the scarecrow, were transported out of their everyday life by a whirlwind. Those who have encounters with UFOs likewise often feel sucked into a void – hence the term 'Oz factor'.

▌▌ I HAVE SPOKEN TO NUMEROUS WITNESSES... WHO TOLD ME THEY HAD BEEN CAUGHT IN A WHIRLWIND, HAD SEEN STRANGE CREATURES, AND HAD BEEN LEFT WONDERING AND CONFUSED... ALL I COULD OFFER THEM WAS THE ASSURANCE THAT THEY WERE NOT ALONE, THAT MANY OTHERS SHARED THE SAME EXPERIENCE, AND THAT I BELIEVED FUTURE SCIENCE WOULD EVENTUALLY ACCEPT AND UNDERSTAND IT AS AN IMPORTANT SOURCE OF NEW KNOWLEDGE. ▌▌

JACQUES VALLEE, DIMENSIONS

seemed to slow down and then stand still. As this thing passed over, it literally took ages to do so.'

Essentially the Oz factor is a sense of timelessness and sensory isolation: the witness feels as if the UFO has temporarily sucked him out of the real world and into a kind of void where only he and the phenomenon co-exist. The name was given by analogy with the experience of Dorothy and Toto who, in *The Wizard of Oz*, were taken by a whirlwind to the land of Oz. The extent of this experience in the UFO records makes its importance obvious, for it is not something that investigators generally seek out. Rather, as a rule, it is reported spontaneously.

Often, a witness will come out of an encounter suffering considerable confusion about the length of time it has lasted. Indeed, it seems perfectly reasonable to suggest that cases of time-loss or time-lapse in contacts and abductions are the result of the Oz factor. This might very well suggest that many close encounters (possibly all) involve some degree of the Oz factor. After all, a time-loss of three or four minutes during a typical UFO experience could easily go unnoticed.

Memories retrieved hypnotically from time-loss cases seem to imply that some kind of 'message transfer' takes place during the 'lost' time. There is a disturbing consequence to be drawn from all this. A message transfer might indeed be present in all UFO close encounters, with the encounter itself being a mere side-effect. But in the majority of instances, this transfer, if it does take place, is never even suspected by the witness: it takes place beyond his normal conscious awareness.

SHARED EXPERIENCES

The existence of the Oz factor certainly points towards the consciousness of the witness as the focal point of the UFO encounter, for it is clearly here that the effects take place, whatever their cause may be. That this is so receives further vindication from an unexpected source, for the Oz factor, it seems, is not confined to UFO cases. Consider this description: 'I got this cold feeling . . . and I raised myself on my elbow. I could not hear the clock ticking and it was only a foot away from me. Everything was – how should I explain it? – like everything had stood still.'

This account comes from a witness about to see a ghost and evidently involves something akin to the Oz factor. Similar features have also been detected in out-of-the-body experiences, timeslips and precognitive visions. As the only obvious common denominator between all of these things is the mind of the percipient, suspicion must be directed

---

The spectrum of reality

objective reality

normal waking consciousness

QC experience

– – – halfway

lucid dreams

hypnagogic/ hypnopompic hallucinations

dreams/ creative fiction

subjective reality

On the reality spectrum, above, QC (quasi-conscious) experiences lie on the upper half of the scale between objective and subjective reality. Close encounters, out-of-the-body experiences, timeslips and precognitive visions all appear to be quasi-conscious experiences.

American airline pilot Captain E. J. Smith, right, uses a dinner plate to illustrate the flying saucers he saw on 6 July 1947 over Oregon, USA.

" UFONAUTS MAY EXISTS LARGELY IN THE EYE OF THE BEHOLDER. AFTER ALL, THE UFOS THEMSELVES MAY BE PLASMIC GLOBULES OF PURE INTELLIGENCE, AND THE UFONAUTS MAY BE NOTHING MORE THAN EXTERNALISED MENTAL PROJECTIONS RATHER THAN THE INDEPENDENT PILOTS THEY APPEAR TO BE. "

BRAD STEIGER,

MYSTERIES OF TIME AND SPACE

A cartoon from a Sheffield newspaper of 1913, left, shows the genesis of an airship sighting in the north of England.

The disc-like object emitting a vapour trail, below, was photographed over Namur, Belgium, on 5 June 1955. According to the theory of quasi-conscious experience, subjective data may manipulate objective reality to such an extent that an image such as this can be projected by the human mind and subsequently photographed.

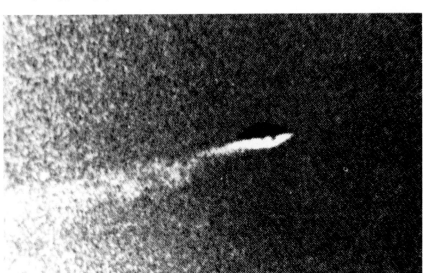

at consciousness once again. This is the stage on which the events are acted out.

Close encounters and many paranormal phenomena do indeed seem to have correspondences, if not necessarily exactly the same origin, so a general name is required for them. The term 'quasi-conscious experience' (or QC experience) has been adopted, as these events certainly come in the guise of normal reality and yet, in some ways, are very clearly not this.

A number of researchers, such as Patrick Austin and Hilary Evans, have suggested that we need a 'spectrum' to describe various facets of reality, and a development of this idea has proved invaluable in this connection. What we might call the 'spectrum of reality' would stretch from totally subjective experiences, such as dreams, to totally objective experiences, such as everyday waking consciousness. Both these extremes are, in fact, subject to

'interference' from other parts of the spectrum. For example, objective environmental factors, such as a cold breeze or loud noise, may affect a sleeper and make an appearance in another form in the subjective world of his dreams. The gulf between the two ends of the spectrum is far from empty. Lucid dreams, in which the dreamer is aware that he is dreaming and maintains some degree of control over dream imagery, seem to locate themselves towards the subjective end of the spectrum, but closer to the middle than the ordinary dream. Other phenomena, such as hypnagogic and hypnopompic hallucinations (the vivid images seen on the brink of sleeping and waking), also require to be placed towards the subjective end of the spectrum.

The QC experience fills what is otherwise a somewhat disconcerting gap on the spectrum between the middle and the objective end. Had we not known of it, we might have been tempted to invent it to prevent a lack of balance. The QC experience may even occupy quite a broad band of the spectrum not just a narrow one – but it is best appreciated as a kind of mirror image of the lucid dream. Whereas, in a lucid dream, objective information coming in from outside manipulates subjective dream reality, in the QC experience the reverse occurs: the subjective information manipulates what is experienced as objective reality.

This need not be seen as mind literally altering matter (although it remains an interesting possibility in view of quantum physics and brain/mind psychology, both of which may in some circumstances permit reality to be what our consciousness decides it to be). Possibly, in very rare instances, reality is manipulated sufficiently strongly to allow a photograph to be taken revealing the fact – and this may account for the few seemingly unimpeachable shots of UFOs. Usually, the manipulation of reality is not external, in the sense that it is visible to others or could be photographed, but takes place within the sensory systems of the percipient. What we perceive of the outside world is largely what our brain interprets from incoming signals. That is why optical illusions occur, and continue to occur, even when we know we are being fooled. And so, under the influence of a QC experience, our eyes might 'see' the Moon but our mind might 'experience' a UFO close encounter. Subjective information from some source has over-ridden the perception of objective reality to create the distortion – hence the very puzzling IFO cases. The overwhelming majority of close encounters might, on this basis, be reducible to ordinary stimuli seen 'under the influence', as it were.

Obviously, much work needs to be done to make progress with such hypotheses. But if they are in any way correct, we need to explore the origin of the subjective data that over-rides objective reality. It could be internal (from a deeper level of ourselves) or external (for example, from some other intelligence). It may even be both.

COSMIC CHAT SHOWS

If alien intelligence does exist, it is most unlikely to use primitive technology – radio telescopes, for instance. The intelligence may not have eyes or ears, for example. But consciousness itself may be the true radio telescope of the cosmos. On this basis, mind-to-mind chat shows may be going on around us all the time, while we search forlornly with our multi-million-dollar radio telescope toys. Only a few people (the psychic repeater witnesses, perhaps) may have sufficient receptiveness to 'tune in' to such cosmic conversations. If we did pick up such messages, our minds might be forced to replay them in terms of ideograms from our memory store (based on cliché interpretations of science fiction films and little green men). Each individual may produce a different picture, based on his personal image store, but there would be an essential similarity, since our views of images fitting the concept 'alien' are likely to be similar. Since this kind of 'similar but different' pattern is just what we find within UFO data, the theory may have some merit, despite its admittedly speculative nature.

Ever since that classic sighting by Kenneth Arnold, ufologists' own findings have been gradually eroding the 'extra-terrestrial hypothesis' in its usual form – the theory that UFOs are spaceships. The odd thing is that, now that we have found a number of mechanisms that seem to explain at least some aspects of the enigma in rational terms, we may be heading back full circle to a new but very different alien hypothesis: that UFOs are associated with alien consciousness making contact by way of the human mind.

SEX, SORCERY AND SEANCES

MANY VICTORIANS REGARDED SEANCES – USUALLY HELD IN DARKENED ROOMS – AS A CLOAK FOR SCANDALOUS IMPROPRIETY. FOR SOME OCCULTISTS, HOWEVER, THERE SEEMS TO HAVE BEEN A LINK BETWEEN SEX AND PSI

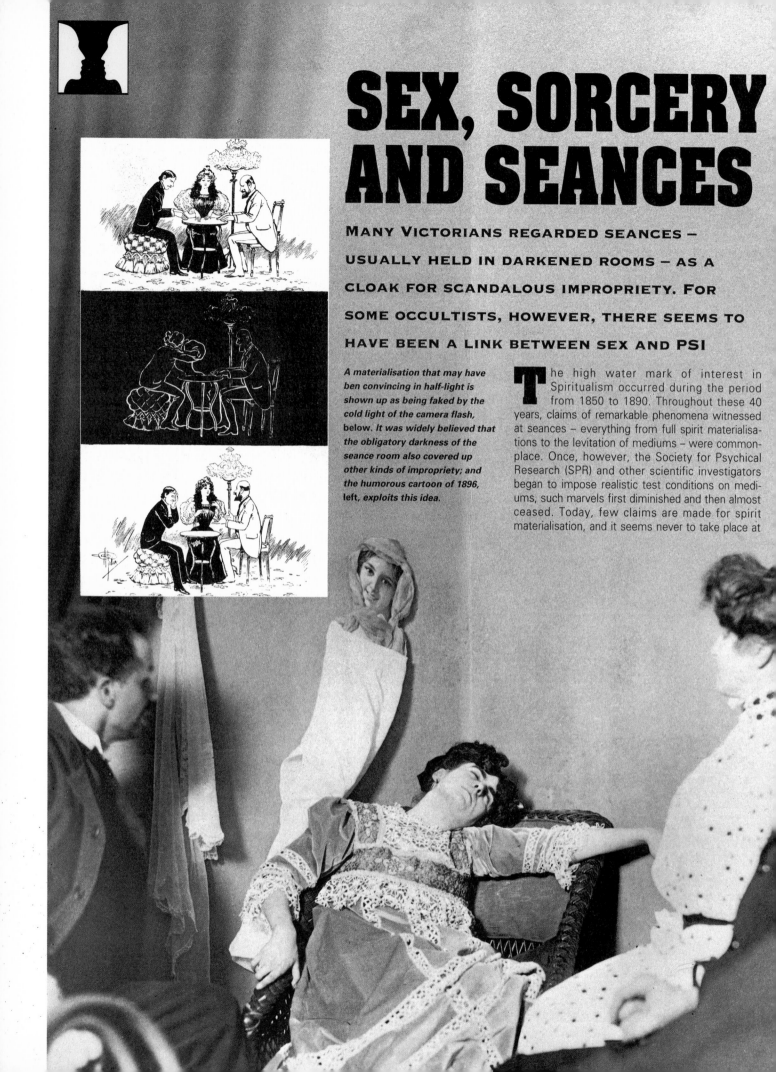

A materialisation that may have ben convincing in half-light is shown up as being faked by the cold light of the camera flash, below. It was widely believed that the obligatory darkness of the seance room also covered up other kinds of impropriety; and the humorous cartoon of 1896, left, exploits this idea.

The high water mark of interest in Spiritualism occurred during the period from 1850 to 1890. Throughout these 40 years, claims of remarkable phenomena witnessed at seances – everything from full spirit materialisations to the levitation of mediums – were commonplace. Once, however, the Society for Psychical Research (SPR) and other scientific investigators began to impose realistic test conditions on mediums, such marvels first diminished and then almost ceased. Today, few claims are made for spirit materialisation, and it seems never to take place at

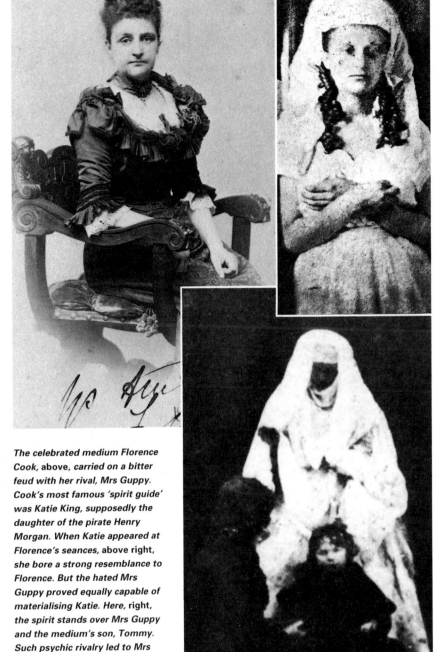

The celebrated medium Florence Cook, above, carried on a bitter feud with her rival, Mrs Guppy. Cook's most famous 'spirit guide' was Katie King, supposedly the daughter of the pirate Henry Morgan. When Katie appeared at Florence's seances, above right, she bore a strong resemblance to Florence. But the hated Mrs Guppy proved equally capable of materialising Katie. Here, right, the spirit stands over Mrs Guppy and the medium's son, Tommy. Such psychic rivalry led to Mrs Guppy's underhand attempts to sabotage Florence Cook's seances. In return, she was accused of running a house of assignation.

" MRS GUPPY USED HER PRETENDED MEDIUMSHIP FOR BASE PURPOSES, AND GAVE SEANCES SOLELY... TO ENABLE CERTAIN DISREPUTABLE PARTIES TO FURTHER CARRY OUT THEIR LEWD PROPENSITIES. "

all in the presence of non-believers and under rigid test conditions.

There is, in fact, strong reason to believe that every professional Victorian medium, with the possible exception of D.D. Home, practised fraud at one time or another. Even those who may have possessed genuine paranormal powers were not averse to practising deception when 'the power was weak' or 'the guide could not be reached'. So it is perhaps not surprising that men and women who were prepared to produce fake spirit phenomena in order to extract money from the pockets of the bereaved were also prepared discreetly to defy Victorian morality. Some female mediums became notorious for this, and even Spiritualist newspapers made veiled references to 'moral degeneration' as an occupational disease of mediumship, usually attributing it to possession by evil spirits. A more likely explanation, however, is that some mediums simply did not care about Victorian society's attitude towards sex.

Allowance must also be made for the normally sternly repressed sexual emotions, fantasies and memories, which were likely to erupt when any respectable Victorian entered a trance. In 1888, for example, one anonymous member of the SPR reported that he or she had seen: 'a medium, at others times calm and respectable, suddenly under some mysterious influence or control, break out into a tirade of the most horrible blasphemous and obscene language.'

Curiously enough, the writer of the above report fell victim to the same kind of phenomenon when experimenting with automatic writing: 'At last... the pencil settled down to steady writing, and there came the most filthy, vile language such as the mind could never have imagined.'

A CLOAK FOR PROSTITUTION?

Spiritualism seems even to have served as a cloak for prostitution and similar activities. Indeed, a feud between two mediums, Florence Cook and Mrs Guppy, involved some curious allegations concerning the latter. Mrs Guppy was a powerful physical medium whose accomplishments had included the materialisation at seances of such diverse objects as fresh flowers and a large block of ice. But in January 1873, she found that her clients were being drawn away by what she referred to as the 'doll face' of Florence Cook, who was young and attractive. It is of interest that Mrs Guppy should consider Florence's appearance, rather than her psychic abilities, to be the reason for increasing popularity.

Mrs Guppy, therefore, decided to take drastic measures. In the guise of enquirers, a certain James Clark and two other friends of Mrs Guppy were to attend one of Florence Cook's seances. When a 'spirit' – whom they suspected to be Florence Cook in disguise – manifested itself, they were to throw oil of vitriol (concentrated sulphuric acid) in its face.

Mrs Guppy also tried to enlist the help of two American mediums, Mr and Mrs Holmes, in her scheme, but they indignantly refused and sent a warning to the intended victim. In revenge, Mrs Guppy regularly sent roughs to break up the Holmes' seances. Such activity ceased only when, in a letter to the London Dialectical Society, Holmes

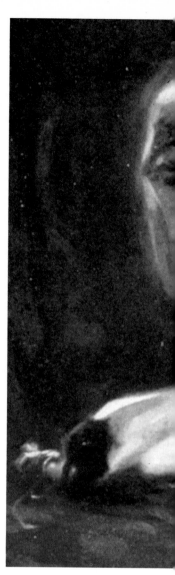

threatened to expose her: 'If necessary, I can give you the details of the infamous transactions of Mrs Guppy with Miss Emily Berry, 1 Hyde Park Place, also why Mrs Guppy used her pretended mediumship for base purposes, and gave seances solely for assignation to better enable certain disreputable parties to further carry out their lewd propensities.'

In the 19th century, so-called 'black' magicians were usually those occultists who employed sex in the attempt to unlock those gates that lead to the paranormal. There were a surprising number of such practitioners. Of course, they took care to avoid adverse publicity and tended to speak and write of their activities in coyly symbolic language. One was P.B. Randolph, an American who called himself a Rosicrucian. He believed that, in the course of human copulation, both men and women produce 'psychic secretions', as well as the more familiar male semen and female lubricants. These positive and negative psychic secretions, said Randolph, are 'thesis and antithesis', and combine into a 'new and higher unity' that sets in flow a current of psychic force. If certain secret techniques are used for directing this current into the proper channels, both participants in the sexual act will receive physical, mental and spiritual benefits.

In typically vague and flowery language, Randolph described how he had acquired this knowledge: 'I made love to, and was loved by, a dusky maiden . . . I . . . learned the fundamental principle of the White Magic of Love; subsequently I became acquainted with some dervishes . . . and of these devout practices of a simple but sublime and holy magic . . . I obtained . . . the ELIXIR OF LIFE . . . the water of beauty and perpetual youth, and the philosopher's stone.'

Another 19th-century practitioner of sexual occultism was Thomas Lake Harris – English by birth but American by naturalisation. His method involved something he called 'archnatural respiration' – probably nothing more than deliberate hyperventilation of the lungs. But he also dabbled in an occult sexual technique – *sympneumata* – that involved a couple breathing in unison while they made love.

ASTRAL EROTICISM

An adaptation of *sympneumata* has also been employed by black magicians of the present century for purposes of sexual seduction. The would-be lover sits as near as possible to his intended victim, who is totally unaware of his intentions at first. He gauges her breathing by the rise and fall of her breasts and, once he has established the exact rhythm, begins to breathe in precise unison with her. The sorcerer continues this for a period of between three and five minutes, and then contracts the muscles of his anus for five to ten seconds. This, supposedly, establishes an 'astral link' between the two people involved, by bringing into action the man's *muladhara chakra*, a centre of psychic activity that, according to some occultists, controls the libido. It is situated, they claim, in a part of the 'subtle body' corresponding to the area between the anus and the genitals.

▐▐ THE POWER OF THE ORGASM AND THE MAGIC STUFF THAT COMES WITH IT WILL SUFFUSE THE ROOM OR TEMPLE AND THE WORSHIPPER IS INFLAMED WITH BLISS. ▐▐

PETER REDGROVE, THE BLACK GODDESS AND THE SIXTH SENSE

THE FAMOUS FLYING GUPPY

During the late Victorian era, Mrs Samuel Guppy was one of London's most prominent mediums. Born Agnes Nichols, her mediumistic powers were first discovered in 1866 – the year before she married Samuel Guppy – by the great British naturalist Alfred Russel Wallace during investigations into Spiritualism. He found young Agnes at his sister's house where she was conducting seances that included raps, table movements, levitation and apports. So renowned did Mrs Guppy become that her seances were even attended by minor European royalty, such as Princess Marguerite of Naples (who asked for, and received, cacti, which dropped from the air on to the seance table). Other apports included stinging nettles, lobsters, live eels and butterflies.

In spite of her success, however, Mrs Guppy was known to be highly jealous of another London medium, Florence Cook. Some said this was because Miss Cook was more attractive. Whatever the case, rumour also implicated Mrs Guppy in a potential scandal when an American medium claimed that Mrs Guppy's seances were, in fact, a hotbed of sexual intrigue.

The most famous incident in Mrs Guppy's career occurred on 3 June 1871 when she was, apparently, transported – within three minutes – from her home in Highbury, North London, to the house of another medium, Charles Williams, at 61 Lamb's Conduit Street, some three miles away. Williams was holding a seance, when a sitter jokingly asked the spirit control, Katie King, to bring Mrs Guppy. She arrived at the seance – out of nowhere, crash-landing on the table – in a loose dressing gown and wearing a pair of bedroom slippers. She seemed to be in a trance, and had one arm over her eyes. Before long, her boots, hat and clothes also miraculously travelled from her home.

The magician then gradually increases his rate of breathing until it reaches the rate characteristic of the height of sexual activity. The 'astral link' ensures that the emotions normally associated with this rapid breathing are communicated to the woman, and she immediately experiences arousal.

Some of those who practise *sympneumata* attempt to establish 'astral links' with their victims for more than mere sexual satisfaction. Indeed, once the established link has been sufficiently strengthened, the bedmate can be transformed into a disciple. Thus, it is claimed, one more black magician comes into existence.

All this is very reminiscent of an ancient idea about vampirism – that victims themselves in turn become vampires, seeking out the living for nourishment. Many occultists have been well aware of such similarities and have theorised elaborately on the subject of 'psychic vampirism', by means of which psychosexual energy is drained from the victim. This can be done in several ways: some vampires are supposed to be sufficiently powerful to absorb energy simply by sitting in the same room as the objects of attack, while others have to engage in 'astral projection' and, in ghostly form, visit their victims as they sleep. Still others can extract energy from a partner only via sexual activity. Really expert vampires, one group asserts, can sexually exhaust their victims to the point of death. In this way, the vampire not only obtains the physical strength of the victim but acquires his or her soul as a familiar spirit.

THE MASTER SATURNUS

An offshoot of the group that produced this occult teaching was 'Saturn-Gnosis', active in Germany from the 1920s until its suppression by the Nazis. It was later revived, around 1950, by a man who called himself the 'Master Saturnus'.

The leaders of Saturn-Gnosis taught an extraordinarily complex system of sex magic, either based on their own imagination and fancy or on some secret tradition. Indeed, the system is so involved that it seems hardly worth the trouble of following it, however beneficial the supposed results. For example, before engaging in sexual activity, initiates of the group were instructed to consult ephemerides (tables giving the daily positions of the Sun, Moon and planets in relation to the zodiac). If Venus and Mars were square – at an angle of 90° to one another, as seen from the Earth – copulation should be carried out in a sitting position. The exact nature of the sitting position would also have to be decided in accordance with astrological conditions: thus if Venus were in a 'stronger' zodiacal position than Mars, the woman would sit on the man's lap. When the couple eventually decided on their appropriate posture, they were not to start their activities before burning incense and placing defensive occult symbols around themselves.

The type of sex magic associated with Saturn-Gnosis and similar European groups spread across the Atlantic in the 1920s and has continued to flourish ever since. For example, the Great Brotherhood of God was led by a one-time resident of the Abbey of Thelema. It was extremely active in the 1930s and attracted a surprisingly large membership. Louis Culling even published a detailed account of

his progress in this society. He had to pass numerous tests, during one of which he was required to engage in continuous sexual intercourse, without ejaculation, for a period of three hours. Culling not only passed all his tests, rising to high office in the brotherhood, but carried out much research in the field of occult sexuality. His major triumph was his discovery that *damiana*, a Mexican herb traditionally reputed to possess stimulant qualities, was a 'psychic aphrodisiac'. Those taking it, he claimed, benefited not only physically, by becoming more potent, but also astrally: apparently, they became so filled with psychosexual energy that they were irresistible to members of the opposite sex.

If Culling's published account is to be believed, a series of experiments he carried out in 1962 proved the paranormal effects of *damiana* beyond all reasonable doubt. The 69-year-old researcher began to drink a daily cupful of an infusion of the wondrous herb. After only 10 days, women over 30 years younger than himself began to take an interest in him. Four days later, his libido bursting with the energy of a man half-a-century younger, he left his Los Angeles home for a short holiday in the Mexican border town of Tijuana.

With no trouble at all, he got into conversation with a young waitress, who agreed to visit him at his hotel. Fortified by *damiana,* the couple engaged in extended and ecstatic copulation. The waitress is said to have been delighted by her experience.

Such, then, are the claims of the sexual occultists. They range from the absurd to the plausible, and suggest a two-way traffic between the psychosexual energy of the libido and the outer world: the libido, it is said, can move matter, as in poltergeist phenomena; and it can itself be revitalised and manipulated by drugs, by rituals, or by feats of psychic exertion. Diverse as these beliefs are, they are alike in the stress placed on a 20th-century obsession – the central importance of sex.

The erotic element in the conventional vampire tale is made explicit in the painting, above, which comes from a Viennese postcard of 1900. Some forms of sex magic are said to be akin to vampirism, the victim becoming a disciple of the magician.

Louis Culling, right, gained high office in a brotherhood of sex magicians.

179

DREAM WINNERS

FEW PRECOGNITIVE DREAMS ARE POTENTIALLY AS PROFITABLE AS THOSE THAT GIVE ACCURATE DESCRIPTIONS OF FUTURE WINNERS AT HORSE RACES. YET SOMETIMES, IT SEEMS, EVEN NON-GAMBLERS RECEIVE SUCH PSYCHIC TIPS

It is a common belief that no one can, or should, make money out of his or her paranormal abilities. Indeed, many sensitives believe that, since their talents are gifts from God, it would be immoral in the extreme to use them to further their own fortunes. If they did so, they say, the gift would be removed or, worse still, the fortune acquired would bring with it tragedy and disaster.

H. E. Saltmarsh, the British psychical researcher, made a number of studies of precognition cases published in the *Proceedings* and *Journal* of the Society for Psychical Research (SPR), and found it necessary to accept the reality of premonitions. In his book *Foreknowledge,* he cites two particular cases involving the winners of horse races.

A certain Mr John H. Williams, a Quaker, was about 80 years of age, and a staunch opponent of gambling, in fact. On 31 May 1933, at 8.35 a.m.,

According to Dr Samuel Johnson (1709-1784), above: 'By pretension to second sight, no profit was ever sought or gained.' But this is not always the case. Indeed, considerable sums have been won at the races as a direct result of precognitive dreams.

Williams woke from a dream that had concerned the Derby. In the dream, he had been listening to a running commentary on the race on the radio. The commentator gave the names of the first four horses. Williams remembered two of them – *Hyperion* and *King Salmon.*

The Derby was to be run at 2 p.m. that day. Williams told a neighbour whom he met on a bus that morning about his dream. He also recounted it to a business acquaintance.

That afternoon, although so strongly antagonistic towards gambling, Williams listened to the radio commentary on the race and heard his very dream over again, the commentator using identical expressions and giving the same names. Saltmarsh states that he corresponded with Williams, as well as the two men to whom he had recounted his dream that morning and who confirmed Williams' story.

Dame Edith Lyttleton, a member of the SPR and herself a gifted sensitive, also collected a number of such cases for her book *Some Cases of Prediction,* all but one of them sent to her by people who had heard a radio broadcast she made on precognition. From the large number of letters she received, she selected the most promising for investigation. Every case in her collection was corroborated by at least one person, sometimes by two or three, who had heard of the prediction before fulfilment. Dame Edith stated: 'That some predictions are cases of definite precognition, I personally have no doubt at all.' Among these cases, there are no less than eight where the result of a horse race or a football match was predicted.

One subject had dreamed that he visited Lincoln and remained so long in the Cathedral that, on arriving at the racecourse, he found he had missed the

Hyperion, above, *won the 1933 Derby. The night before the race, John H. Williams, a Quaker and a staunch opponent of betting, woke from a dream about the Derby in which he had heard a radio commentator give the names of the first four horses. One of these was Hyperion.*

number of dreams and impressions occurring, there must be a few chance 'hits' that are remembered, while the rest are forgotten. This is why, he claimed, we get sets of cases that we falsely imagine to be precognitive, but which are really only due to natural chance.

This of course is a strong argument, and one often put forward. But even Tyrrell – among other investigators – has pointed out that additional factors must be taken into account. For example, precognitive dreams are usually exceptionally vivid and the feelings within them, strong. These features often compel the percipient to tell his circle of friends to take some action.

A RUN FOR HIS MONEY

The following case is one for which the corroborative evidence is quite remarkable. It concerns John Godley, later Lord Kilbracken, and began on 8 March 1946 when he was an undergraduate at Balliol College, Oxford. This strange chapter in his life ended 12 years later.

Godley found that he could often dream precognitively. Moreover, the subjects of his precognitive dreams were the winners of horse races. The punters' dream – or the bookies' nightmare – seemed to have homed in on Godley.

On the night of 8 March, he dreamed that, in Saturday's evening paper, he read the racing results and noticed that two horses, *Bindal* and *Juladin*, had both won at starting prices of 7-1. When Godley woke up, he went to a café in town where he met a friend, Richard Freeman. He told him of his dream, they looked at *The Times* and found that *Bindal* was indeed running at Plumpton

first race, the Lincoln Handicap, but was told that it had been won by *Outram*. On waking, he related his dream to a friend. This was in November, and the list of entrants in the race was not published until January of the following year. In March, the race was indeed won by *Outram*, with rather long odds laid against it.

It is, of course, possible that such cases could be attributed to chance. Psychical researcher G. N. M. Tyrrell (1879-1952) argued that, given the

CASEBOOK

WIN SOME, LOSE SOME

J. H. Jung-Stilling (1740-1817), German writer, physician and psychical researcher, *right,* told the story of Dr Christopher Knape who, in 1768, dreamed that he received the winning numbers of the State lottery. He duly bought some tickets and, amazingly, won some money. About eight years later, the dream recurred. Again, he was presented with winning numbers, but unfortunately a noise woke him up and, as a result, he was able to remember only the first two digits. Nevertheless, he bought a few tickets and made a small sum.

A year later, his dream returned yet again. Encouraged by his earlier successes, Knape felt he must be on to a certainty. However, he was to win nothing: a short time before the draw, his ticket money was returned to him as all the tickets had been sold.

that afternoon. Later that morning, he found, in the *Daily Express*, that *Juladin* was running at Wetherby.

The undergraduate was now, understandably, very excited. He told some of his friends, who placed bets, while Godley himself backed both horses. *Bindal* won at 5-4. Godley then put his winnings on *Juladin*, which duly won its race.

Not unnaturally, the news spread through the undergraduate community; and for a fortnight after the event, many were the morning enquiries made of Godley as to whether he had had any racing dreams. Godley was worried. He suspected, probably with good reason, that if he did dream any more horse names but failed to win, he would never be forgiven by those friends and acquaintances who had put their shirts on them.

But it did happen again – on Thursday, 4 April 1946 – when Godley was at home in Ireland. Again in a dream, he found himself looking at a list of winners. On waking, the only horse he remembered was *Tubermore*, and he told his family at breakfast. At that time, the family lived in such isolation that they would not get Tuesday's edition of *The Times* and Wednesday's *Irish Times* until Thursday. Godley therefore telephoned the local postmistress, who checked the daily papers and found that a horse called *Tuberose* was indeed running in the Grand National. The name seemed close enough and he and members of his family backed it. The BBC news at 6 p.m. that day told them that *Tuberose* had won.

By now, Godley was taking the matter seriously. He kept records of his dreams when he returned to Oxford, but it was only on 2 July 1946 that he experienced this sort of dream again. In it, he telephoned his bookmaker from a telephone box in the Randolph Hotel, Oxford, to ask for the result of the last race. The dream was so vivid that Godley even

Lord Kilbracken, seen above with film actress Jayne Mansfield, had an astonishing run of dream predictions. As an undergraduate, for instance, he dreamed that two horses, Bindal and Juladin, had both won their respective races. The next day, he discovered that these horses were indeed running and backed them successfully.

felt how stuffy the box was. He was told that *Monumentor* had won at 5-4. Next morning, he checked the runners. There was a horse called *Mentores*. He backed it. It won at odds of 6-4.

The fourth time Godley had one of these dreams, a year later, he dreamed he was at a race meeting. He noticed not only that the horse had an easy win but also that it carried the colours of the Gaekwar of Baroda: what is more, he recognised the jockey, the Australian Edgar Britt. The next race found everyone shouting for the favourite – *The Bogie*. In fact, the excited clamour woke Godley.

In a fine state of excitement, he went downstairs and consulted *The Times*. The Gaekwar of Baroda's horse – *Barod Squadron* – was being ridden by Edgar Britt at Lingfield that afternoon. What was more, in the next race, the favourite was *The Brogue* – again, a close-sounding name.

Godley backed both horses. He also told a number of people, including his girlfriend, Angelica Bohm, and his friend, Kenneth Harris. He wrote a statement about his predictions, had it dated and witnessed by three people, and took it to the post office. Here, it was placed in an envelope which, after sealing, was stamped by the postmaster with his official time-stamp and locked up in the post office safe. Both horses won.

Fame then came to Godley as newspapers all over the world got hold of the story and, perhaps as a result, he was given the post of racing correspondent on the *Daily Mirror*. Predictably, he also became inundated with mail from those who hoped he would share his good fortune with them (or at least give them a few winners), those willing to pay him a percentage of their winnings for information, and those seemingly in dire need.

His episodic and unpredictable gift stayed with him. On 29 October 1947, he dreamed of a horse called *Claro*. He backed it, but it was unplaced. However, on 16 January 1949, he dreamed again of the racing results. On waking, he recalled that one of the winners had been a horse called *Timocrat*. Godley backed it – and it won. On 11 February of the same year, he dreamed of two winners, *Monk's Mistake* and *Pretence*. *Pretence* won – but *Monk's Mistake* lost.

Nine years later, Godley dreamed that a horse called *What Man?* won the Grand National. He backed the horse with the most similar name – *Mr What* – and won the largest amount of money in his career.

Lord Kilbracken had no idea why he should have demonstrated such a remarkable gift in this way, except that he was mildly interested in horses and, like all impecunious undergraduates, naturally had a strong motivation to back winners.

But even if we accept that his case, and certain others, show evidence of a precognitive faculty at work, the idea of people predicting and backing winners may still be dismissed by some as 'wrong' or 'frivolous'. However, they are still worthy of study for, in their effects, clues regarding the mysterious nature of time and that of the human psyche ultimately may be discerned.

Mr What, below, *won the 1958* ***Grand National, the most popular*** ***British Classic, bottom. Lord*** ***Kilbracken (then John Godley) had*** ***dreamed that a horse called*** **What** **Man?** *had won the race; he* ***therefore chose the horse with*** ***the nearest name – and won the*** ***largest sum of money since he*** ***had become a dream punter.***

IS THERE A 'MAP' OF
THE WHOLE BODY IN
THE IRIS OF EACH EYE? AND
CAN IT PROVIDE A GUIDE TO
VARIOUS DISORDERS AND
THEIR TREATMENTS?
IRIDOLOGISTS CLAIM SO

From earliest antiquity, the eye has been believed to be one of the very best indicators of personality, temperament, romantic feelings and spiritual condition. It has been regarded, to use the language of the ancients, as the 'mirror of the soul'.

But quite apart from interest in the eye as an indicator of the emotional state, there has been scientific study of the eye as a guide to physical wellbeing. Many people are familiar with the routine ophthalmological investigations carried out by a doctor. He scrutinises the retina, the layer on the inside back of the eyeball, by looking through the pupil, the opening at the front of the eye, using an instrument called an ophthalmoscope. The retina is the only place in the body where nerve endings and blood vessels may be viewed directly, and its state is significant in assessing the general health and condition of the patient, particularly when it comes to anaemia.

Long before the importance of retinal examination was recognised, however, another type of eye diagnosis existed – iridology, the art (or science) of assessing bodily conditions by studying the iris, the coloured part of the eye.

The origins and history of iris diagnosis are disputed by various writers. But the practice of iridology, as we know it today, is a European phenomenon, dating from the middle of the 19th century.

While interest in the diagnostic value of the iris (a word derived from the Latin for 'rainbow') can be credited to several physicians in the 19th century, one man was outstanding in his systematic work in this field. Indeed, Dr Ignatz von Peczely, a Hungarian, justly deserves to be known as the father of iridology. He was a man of remarkable powers of observation and original thought, and demonstrated great bravery. He faced enormous opposition throughout his life, died in comparative obscurity, and is only now beginning to be appreciated.

Iris diagnosis was born in von Peczely's garden in Budapest. At the age of 11, he had caught a wild owl there; and in the ensuing struggle to maintain his hold on the creature, the bird's leg was broken. As the captive glared at its captor, the boy noticed a black line appear in the '6 o'clock' position in the owl's iris. Since the owl has a large iris, the boy was easily able to observe subsequent developments in the bird's eye as the leg healed. Slowly, the black line shrank and was enveloped in white lines. When the leg had fully healed, there was only an indistinct mark left in the iris. Von Peczely was to remember this acute observation throughout his life.

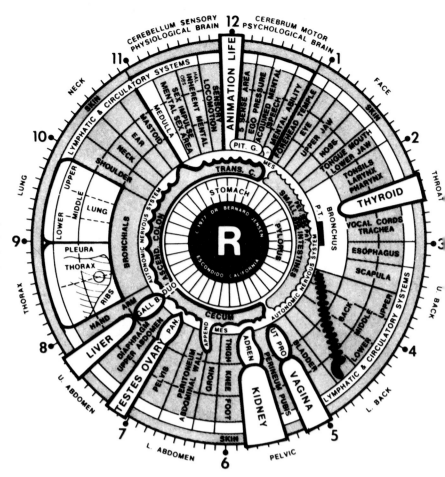

THE EYES HAVE IT

Having an adventurous spirit, the youth took up the highly controversial study of homoeopathy and achieved such success in treating his impoverished neighbours that he attracted the enmity of the medical profession and was forbidden to continue experimenting with the technique. Feeling that he had a vocation in healing, however, he resolved to qualify in orthodox medicine so that afterwards he could continue his work in the respectable guise of a physician.

While a medical student in Vienna, von Peczely became involved with the growing revolutionary movement and was imprisoned for a short while. During this period, he sought outlets for his restless intelligence, and began studying the eyes of his fellow prisoners. Over and over again, he found correlations between known medical problems and markings to be seen on the iris, and resolved to dedicate himself to a serious study of the eye when he was free.

After his release, von Peczely began a systematic examination of the irises of his hospital patients,

The charts, above, were developed by a leading iridologist, Dr Bernard Jensen. Dark or light spots and lines in the iris are believed to indicate the condition of the organs marked in the corresponding areas of the chart.

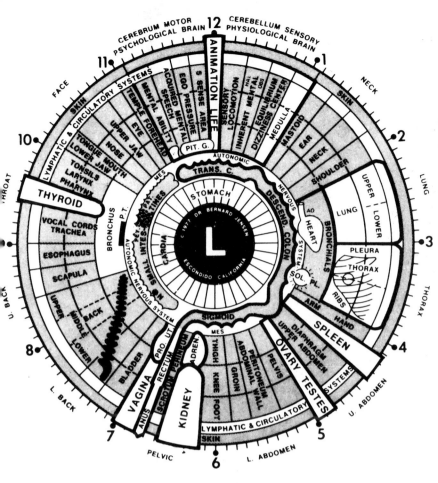

At the same time that von Peczely was working in Hungary, a Lutheran minister, Pastor Nils Liljequist, was making his own iris examinations in Sweden. Pastor Liljequist was treated for fever allopathically (that is, with large concentrations of drugs intended to suppress the disease by creating an opposite condition). In the 19th century, that meant being heavily drugged with quinine. During the course of treatment, Liljequist observed a change in the overall colour of his iris from blue to yellowish-green. This led him to study the relationship between eye colour and the use of medical drugs, especially the heavy metals, commonly used by doctors at the time, and wrote widely circulated monographs on his findings.

Most of the medical world in Europe turned a cold shoulder to this research, however, perhaps snubbing iridology because of von Peczely's homoeopathic interests. Happily, this was not the case everywhere. Naturopathic workers in Germany and the United States of America had 'rediscovered' the findings of von Peczely and amalgamated them with the observations of Liljequist.

The writings of the American, Henry Lindlhar, in the first two decades of the 20th century, make especially interesting reading. Working before iris photography had been perfected, he made elaborate drawings of his own eyes as he experimented on himself with dietary changes, fasting and various medicines, and became the first to use the iris as a means of diagnosis, as iridologists use it today. He catalogued inflammations and organic dysfunctions in himself and in his patients, realising that the iris could reveal the internal functioning of the body without the need for painful and dangerous exploratory operations. He also concluded that homoeopathic preparations bring about beneficial changes in the body without becoming 'trapped' in the body's tissues; and so, unlike conventional drugs, they do not leave colour traces in the iris.

quickly becoming convinced that he could demonstrate a relationship between the limbs and organs of the body and the several parts of the iris. He painstakingly mapped out his findings on an 'iris chart', essentially the same as the one that iridologists use today.

*London iridologist John Morley, below, **is seen photographing a patient's eyes with a specially designed camera.***

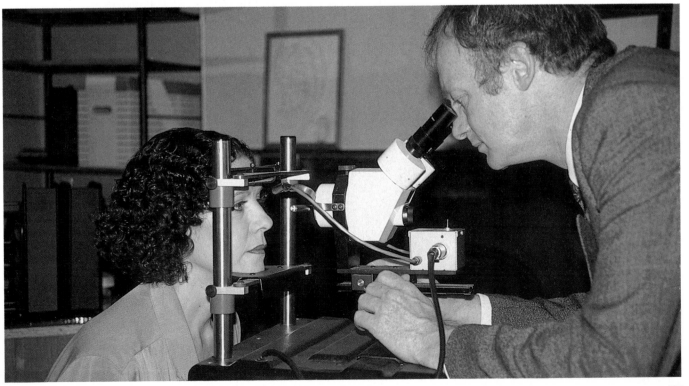

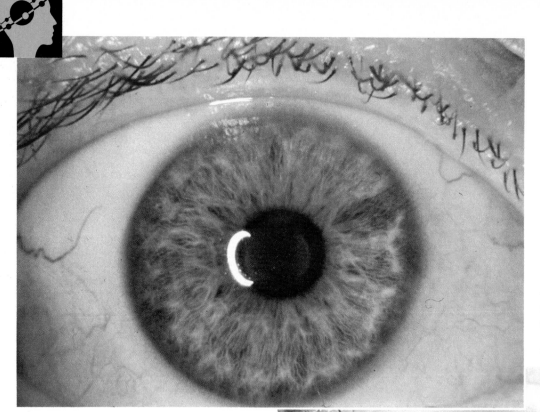

A dark area and a separation of the fibres at the 'two o'clock' position in the iris of the eye, shown left, indicate an underactive thyroid gland.

The eye, below, was once blue. The iridologist's analysis is that toxins accumulated in the area of the digestive tract have caused brown pigmentation. The dark 'spokes' indicate that the poisons have affected the entire body.

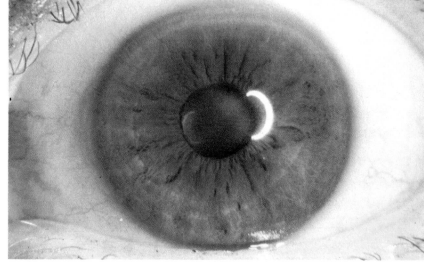

During the Second World War, homoeopathy and naturopathy were eclipsed in the United States, and iridology became all but forgotten. It took the exertions of an American chiropractor, Dr Bernard Jensen, to revive the science. After vast research and the acquisition of much practical experience, he produced, in 1952, the definitive work on the subject, *The Science and Practice of Iridology*. It is a large, well-illustrated work that has been reprinted many times.

Iridological research has emphasised the fact that the human being is a whole, interrelated organism and must be viewed as such when being treated. Thus, the iris diagnostician has the entire medical state of the patient and also a great deal of the patient's medical history displayed before him when he examines the iris: he cannot view the patient simply as having a 'bad heart' or an 'arthritic knee'. This holistic attitude to the patient has especially appealed to practitioners of complementary therapies; and it is perhaps this emphasis that has failed to endear iris diagnosis to the orthodox medical doctor, who may prefer not to be distracted by the totality of body functions.

Iridology is gradually becoming more generally accepted, however, particularly in the United States. Universities on the West Coast offer courses, and one or two hospitals experiment with it. In Europe, iridology is growing in popularity among practitioners of complementary medicine.

Despite such neglect, iris diagnosis is believed by its practitioners to be a scientifically based tool. It has potential for use as an accurate, inexpensive and quick form of diagnosis that could save time, money, pain and perhaps lives, they say. Indeed, if public interest became great enough to draw the attention of the medical establishment to iridology, the right kind of research into its potential and limitations might well draw it out of the realms of 'the unexplained'.

" IRIDOLOGY GIVES YOU THE OPPORTUNITY TO UNDERSTAND YOUR INDIVIDUAL BODY, ITS STRENGTHS AND WEAKNESSES, WHAT YOU HAVE INHERITED AND HOW YOUR BODY HAS BEEN AFFECTED BY HOW YOU HAVE LIVED IN THIS WORLD. "

DR FARIDA SHARAN,

THE BRITISH SCHOOL

OF IRIDOLOGY

SURVIVAL – THE SOLID EVIDENCE?

PERHAPS THE MOST CONTROVERSIAL AREA OF PSYCHICAL RESEARCH IS THAT OF PHYSICAL MEDIUMSHIP. HOW GENUINE MIGHT IT BE?

Author and debunker William Marriott is seen below, surrounded by a fake medium's materialisation props. In normal lighting – and without benefit of the heightened atmosphere of the seance room – such sheeted masks look laughably crude. Yet these very fabrications fooled a great many witnesses.

One of the ironies of the paranormal is that often the best evidence offered for the existence of a spiritual realm is actually produced in a physical form. To some, it may seem absurd that raps, moving tables and levitating trumpets are manifestations produced by spirits; but explaining such phenomena in other ways is, perhaps, no more persuasive.

Such physical phenomena do not occur in isolation: a human catalyst almost always seems to be responsible. The birth of Spiritualism in Hydesville, in the United States, in 1848, actually came about through simple raps that apparently formed the basis of communication between a dead pedlar and the Fox family. Within a few years, the three Fox sisters – Kate, Margaretta and Leah – became world-famous as mediums, and many others discovered that, under the right conditions, they could produce physical phenomena, too.

SPIRIT MACHINE

Elsewhere in the United States, during the early 1850s, farmer Jonathan Koons began conducting his own experiments with physical mediumship. He claimed that the spirits had told him he was 'the most powerful medium on earth'. Following their instructions, he built a small log cabin alongside his farmhouse in Ohio, so that he and his eight children – all of whom were said to be psychic – could hold seances. It was equipped with musical instruments and other items with which the spirits could play. In appearance, it was like a tiny theatre, with seats for up to 30. When the audience was settled, Koons would turn out the lights and play hymns on his fiddle until unseen hands would lift other musical instruments and join in. During such noisy concerts, a tambourine would circle above the heads of the audience, trumpets floated in the air and voices spoke. Spirit hands held phosphor-coated paper to illuminate some of the manifestations. Koons even built a 'spirit machine' – a complex piece of zinc and copper apparatus that the spirits said would help collect and focus the magnetic aura used for their physical demonstrations. According to Koons, when this device was in service, the spirits could triumph over the laws of gravity and cohesion, enabling them to move heavy objects at speed and play instruments.

Just 3 miles (5 kilometres) away, and without the help of a 'spirit machine', John Tipple and his children gave very similar performances in his 'spirit house', which was also said to have been built under instructions from the next world.

Jonathan Koons never charged for the seances he held and there is no evidence of fraud. But, despite Spiritualism's general popularity at that time, he encountered open hostility, particularly from his neighbours. His home was attacked by

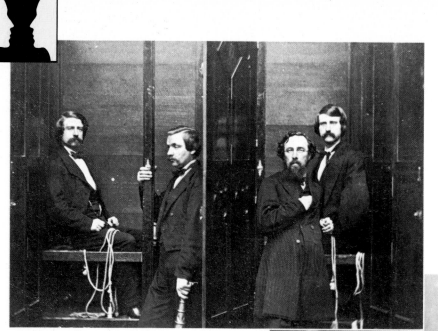

mobs, his children were beaten, and his barns and fields were set alight, forcing him to leave the area. He and his family eventually became Spiritualist missionaries.

Another American family with a similar, eventful seance room were the Davenports. Physical phenomena in the form of raps and strange noises were said to have been heard in their Buffalo, New York, home in 1846, two years before the Hydesville episodes. At that time, Ira Davenport was seven years old and his brother William was five. Four years later, the two boys and their sister Elisabeth began table-turning with impressive results. The table moved, raps were heard and a spirit was said to have controlled Ira's hand and to have written messages. The three children are also reported to have levitated simultaneously at least once. On the

The Davenport brothers were two of the most famous mediums of the late 19th century, exciting both extreme adulation and bitter hostility. Their stage show featured what was, in effect, a portable seance room – a three-doored cabinet, as shown top. When Harry Houdini met Ira Davenport, in the early 1900s, above, he claimed that Davenport confessed to the fact that he and his brother were never anything but conjurers and that they had taught the famous magician Harry Kellar, left, many of his tricks.

fifth night of their experiments, Ira was told by the raps to take a pistol and shoot at a corner of the room. He did so; and at the moment it fired, they saw another phantom figure holding the pistol. It then vanished and the gun fell to the floor.

According to the Davenport children, they were told by the spirits to allow investigators to tie them up in ropes to prove that they were not producing the noises and other manifestations that occurred in their darkened room. This they did to the satisfaction of many visitors, including sceptics.

The Davenports' mediumship was no more remarkable than that of other physical mediums in the mid to late 1800s, but what set them apart was their decision to demonstrate their powers in public. In order to do this, the Davenport brothers constructed a three-door cabinet that was, in effect, a portable seance room. Members of the audience were invited to tie them up securely. But as soon as the doors were closed, strange phenomena occurred. Raps and bangs were heard, hands waved through a small window in the cabinet's centre door, and musical instruments were played. A member of the audience was often invited to sit inside the darkened cabinet while these manifestations were being produced – yet at the end of the demonstrations, the brothers were always still found to be securely tied.

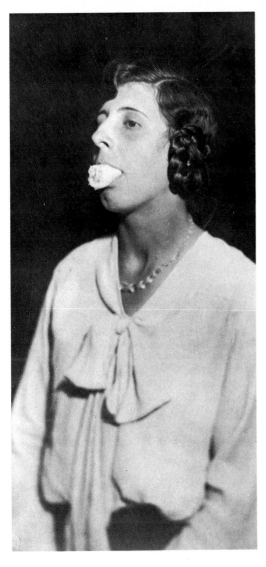

untied and the professor had the rope twisted around his neck. But even so, the newspaper did not award its $500 prize to the Davenports.

The controversy over the boys from Buffalo came to a head when they took their show on the road in Europe where they encountered hostile audiences. Their reception in London and other English cities was particularly sour and things became difficult in Liverpool where two members of the inspection committee, selected by the audience, secured Ira and William with a complicated knot. The brothers claimed that it was restricting their circulation – but a doctor who examined them disagreed. The problem was resolved by a helper who used a knife to cut the knot. A riot broke out on the following night, and the Davenports left Liverpool in haste. Elsewhere in Britain, they received threats that made them decide to end their tour prematurely. As they wrote at the time:

'Were we mere jugglers, we should meet with no violence, or we should find protection. Could we declare that these things done in our presence were deception of the senses, we should no doubt reap a plentiful harvest of money and applause... But we are not jugglers, and truthfully declare that we are not, and we are mobbed from town to town, our property destroyed and our lives imperilled.'

Harry Houdini, the famous escapologist and illusionist, tells a different story. He befriended Ira in the early 1900s, and claimed that Ira admitted that they were no more than conjurers. There is no evidence to support that charge; but it is a fact that Harry Kellar, who was also an internationally famous magician, was employed by the Davenports at one time and, in Houdini's words, 'afterwards learned to do tricks which altogether surpassed their efforts in rope-tying and escape.'

It is impossible to know now, over a century later, if the Davenports were genuine or fraudulent,

It was an impressive and entertaining display, and large audiences flocked to the best theatres in town when the Davenport brothers took their 'public cabinet seance' on tour in America. But it created the same sort of controversy between believers and sceptics as Uri Geller was to bring about in the early 1970s. Certainly, any competent escapologist could get in and out of tied ropes in the way the Davenports did, but that does not necessarily make them frauds. They never claimed to be Spiritualists, but they did maintain that their powers were paranormal – which was why, when the *Boston Courier* offered a $500 prize for the production of genuine physical phenomena, the Davenports applied.

A committee of professors from Harvard University tested them on behalf of the newspaper. Ira and William were tied up, and the ropes passed through holes bored in the cabinet and knotted on the outside. One of the committee members, Professor Benjamin Pierce, then climbed into the cabinet and the doors were closed.

What happened next is a little uncertain. We know that the *Boston Courier* denied one version of the event, which was written by T.L. Nichols, the Davenports' biographer – this was apparently fairly favourable. But Professor Pierce would neither confirm nor deny it. What is certain is that, when the cabinet doors were opened, the brothers were

and the theatricality that surrounded their seances must have made it just as difficult for eyewitnesses to decide. But experiments with physical mediums under carefully controlled conditions have occasionally provided very strong evidence in favour of the genuineness of the manifestations they produce. Sir William Crookes was one of the first physicists to explore the psychic force responsible for producing raps and movements. He tested the most famous of all physical mediums, Daniel Dunglas Home, and became convinced that he possessed strong psychic powers.

Another early investigator of physical forces was Marc Thury, professor of physics and natural history at the University of Geneva, Switzerland, who witnessed the simultaneous levitation of two pianos in the presence of an 11-year-old boy, in the 1850s. Professor Thury suggested that the human body was able to exude a substance that was then manipulated by an unseen force to produce such startling effects. This was the forerunner of the

Kate Goligher, an Irish medium of the 1920s, is seen below, *apparently levitating a table with the aid of ectoplasmic rods. These seem to be obviously fake, especially when seen in close-up,* opposite, centre; *yet Goligher was never proved to be fraudulent.*

ectoplasmic theory, and one that gained ground with many investigators whose observations appeared to provide a degree of confirmation.

LOOK – NO HANDS!

What is puzzling in such cases as the levitating pianos is that, even if the boy had the opportunity to cheat, there is no way in which he could have lifted two such heavy items – or even one of them for that matter. Dr d'Oliveira Feijao, professor of surgery at Lisbon University in Portugal, made a similar observation in the presence of a non-professional medium, Countess Castelwitch, who discovered her powers in 1913. The doctor testified that at her seances: 'Blows were struck, the loudest being on the glass of the bookcase. Articles of furniture sometimes moved. Heavy chairs moved about the room . . . large and heavy books were flung on the floor (our hands being linked all the time).'

At one of the countess' seances, a table, weighing 160 pounds (73 kilograms), was raised on two legs when she touched it lightly. Another smaller table that was strengthened with sheet-iron was torn into 200 pieces by invisible hands, which then piled the pieces into a corner of the room.

A few years earlier, Dr Julien Ochorowicz, an eminent European psychical researcher, had carried out experiments with a young Polish girl, Stanislawa Tomczyk, who was reported to have the ability to move objects without touching them, to stop the hands of a clock and even influence a roulette wheel when she chose the numbers. Dr Ochorowicz not only witnessed the levitation of small objects between Stanislawa Tomczyk's fingers, he also managed to capture the phenomenon on photographs. Sceptics, however, suggested that he had been fooled and that the medium was suspending the items with very thin thread. The researcher replied that, during these demonstrations, he had passed his hand between the object and the medium's fingers and the levitation was maintained. He put forward the theory that she was able to produce 'rigid rays' from her hands to cause these paranormal effects. Stanislawa Tomczyk never gave seances professionally. She confined the displays to scientific experiments and married Everard Feilding, one of the Society for Psychical Research's leading and most sceptical investigators.

Another physical medium who allowed her powers to be studied in the laboratory was Anna Rasmussen, a Danish woman who discovered her startling powers at the age of 12. A number of scientists conducted experiments with her in the 1920s, including Professor Christian Winther of the Polytechnic Academy of Copenhagen.

The professor held 116 seances with her in 1928, at each one of which some form of physical phenomenon was produced. The medium remained conscious throughout and usually sat talking, reading or taking refreshments, apparently unconcerned and detached from the manifestations that repeatedly occurred in her presence. These included the production of raps – apparently emanating from her left shoulder – which would answer questions. What impressed the scientists most, however, was the degree of control she could exert over the phenomena. In full daylight, she was able to cause the movement of pendulums suspended in a sealed

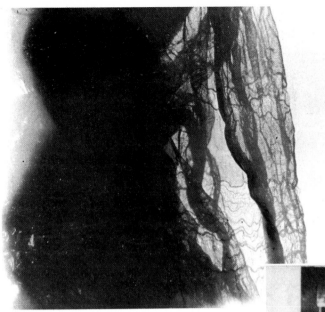

" I AM CONVINCED THAT

BECOMING AWARE OF THE

NEXT STAGE OF EXISTENCE

BEYOND THE EARTH

BIOSPHERE IS VERY LARGELY

A MATTER OF BECOMING

ATTUNED TO ITS VIBRATIONS. **"**

ARTHUR FORD,

THE LIFE BEYOND DEATH

glass case at a distance from her. She was even able to move one pendulum at a time, leaving the others undisturbed, and to make it move in whatever direction was requested.

FRAUD-PROOF EXPERIMENTS?

Nearly 30 years later, the same medium – then Anna Rasmussen Melloni – was asked by psychical researchers if she could repeat the demonstration for them. Several successful experiments were carried out in 1956; but because her own pendulums were used to produce the most impressive results, this detracted from her achievement in the opinion of some experimenters.

While the early tests with Anna Rasmussen were being conducted in Denmark, a British medium was giving the last seances of her brief but spectacular (and strictly nonprofessional) career. Stella Cranshaw, a young nurse, had been discovered by the colourful and controversial psychical researcher Harry Price in the early 1920s. She agreed to be tested at his National Laboratory of Psychical Research in London and he devised elaborate, ingenious equipment, including a supposedly fraud-proof seance table, to test her powers, as well as imposing stringent controls.

This table was really two – one inside another. The top of the inner table was fitted with a hinged trap door that could be opened only from the underside. Musical instruments, such as a harmonica or bell, were placed on a shelf between the legs of the inner table, and a length of gauze was wrapped around the legs. The sides of each table were also enclosed in wooden trellises. These precautions made it impossible for anyone to be able to touch the objects on the inner shelf.

Stella Cranshaw sat at this table with other sitters, two of whom held her hands and feet throughout the proceedings. Soon after she had gone into a trance, sounds – such as the ringing of a bell or the playing of a harmonica – were heard coming from within the table. The trap door in the table top was pushed up from inside and, when a handkerchief was placed over it, sitters felt finger-like forms moving beneath it.

The dark, lace-like ectoplasm, above left, was produced at one of the Goligher seances in Belfast in the 1920s. Almost all such samples are said to have dematerialised, and only one specimen remains in the possession of the Society for Psychical Research – but it is indisputably cheesecloth.

Stella Cranshaw, below left, a young British nurse, was discovered to be a powerful medium in the 1920s. Despite her undoubted gifts, she was never really interested in mediumship and never gave public seances.

The greatest achievement of Stella Cranshaw's mediumship, in Harry Price's eyes, was the successful manipulation of a telekinetiscope – a sensitive piece of apparatus that he had designed himself. It consisted of a small red light bulb, a battery and a telegraph key. When the key was pressed, the light would come on. To prevent this happening by normal means, Price designed the apparatus so that a soap bubble covered the key. During the course of a seance in the presence of Stella Cranshaw, the device would be placed inside a glass shade to prevent the soap bubble from drying out. The light would then be turned on, apparently by psychokinesis; and when the device was inspected later, the soap bubble was always found to be still intact.

Stella Cranshaw was tested over five years, but in spite of the remarkable phenomena witnessed during such demonstrations, she had little interest or enthusiasm for psychic work; and when she married in 1928, she stopped giving seances altogether. Other mediums, however, have continued to produce what seems to be tangible evidence of their strange abilities.

THE TERROR OF LONDON

WHO WAS THE FRIGHTENING FIGURE – A MAN KNOWN ONLY AS SPRING-HEELED JACK – WHO TERRORISED THE PEOPLE OF BRITAIN'S CAPITAL FOR DECADES? AN EXTRAORDINARY LEGEND HAS BUILT UP AROUND THIS BIZARRE CHARACTER

On the tombstone, with upraised arms and rage in every feature, towered the terrific form of Spring-Heeled Jack. Freezer and Links stood transfixed; their ghastly burden slipped slowly to the grass, but they remained gaping, terror-struck. Vengeance had fallen!

The lonely lanes and commons of 19th-century suburban London were haunted by the weird and terrifying figure of Spring-heeled Jack, who pounced upon passers-by, sometimes wounded them severely, and bounded away in enormous leaps. Today, the antics of Spring-heeled Jack are almost forgotten, or dismissed as a figment of the imagination – a mere character in Victorian horror literature, or a bogeyman used by mothers as a threat to errant children. Kellow Chesney, in his book *The Victorian Underworld*, says that Jack is 'pure legend' – perhaps the invention of servants reluctant to admit negligence when thieves robbed their master's home.

But Jack was not a character in fiction, folklore or legend. He was real, and his attacks were widely reported in the local and national press. Nobody seems certain when Jack first appeared. Many sources say that reports of a peculiar leaping man were in circulation as early as 1817; but it was not until 1838 that Spring-heeled Jack became a figure of considerable interest and speculation.

On 9 January 1838, the Lord Mayor of London, Alderman Sir John Cowan, revealed, at a public session held in the Mansion House, the contents of a letter he had received several days earlier. He had withheld it, he said, in the hope of obtaining further

SPRING-HEELED JACK... HAD BEEN SEEN DRESSED IN A SUIT OF SHINING BRASS ARMOUR AND, ON ANOTHER OCCASION, IN ONE OF BURNISHED STEEL. ONCE, IN HACKNEY, HE APPEARED AS A LAMPLIGHTER, WHO WALKED UPON HIS HANDS AND CARRIED HIS LADDER BETWEEN HIS FEET. HIS ABILITY TO MAKE PRODIGIOUS LEAPS WAS POPULARLY ASCRIBED TO SPRINGS THAT WERE ATTACHED TO HIS BOOTS.

Tod Slaughter is seen above, as Spring-heeled Jack in the spine-chilling film The Curse of The Wraydons, made in 1946.

Spring-heeled Jack parts lovers, left, in an illustration from a 19th century penny dreadful. Jack was the inspiration for several of these weekly serials. Although usually portrayed as the villain of the piece, often terrorising young women, as shown above left, he occasionally appeared as the hero – an avenger of crime and a punisher of wrongdoers, as on the cover of a Victorian comic, reproduced below left.

information. The correspondent, who signed the letter 'a resident of Peckham', wrote that, as the result of a wager, a person of the highest rank had adopted several frightening guises and set out to scare 30 people to death. He had 'already succeeded in depriving seven ladies of their senses', two of whom 'were not likely to recover, but likely to become burdens to their families.' The resident of Peckham continued: 'The affair has now been going on for some time, and strange to say, the papers are still silent on the subject. The writer has reason to believe that they have the whole history at their finger-ends but, through interested motives, are induced to remain silent.'

Spring-heeled Jack had appeared as a milk-white bull, a white bear, and an enormous baboon; and he had been seen dressed in a suit of shining brass armour and, on another occasion, in one of burnished steel. Once, in Hackney, he appeared as a lamplighter, who walked upon his hands and carried his ladder between his feet. His ability to make prodigious leaps was popularly ascribed to springs that were attached to his boots.

On Wednesday, 18 February 1838, 18-year-old Lucy Scales and her sister Margaret were returning home after visiting their brother, a butcher who lived in a respectable part of the district of Limehouse. Lucy, slightly ahead of her sister, was passing the entrance to Green Dragon Alley when a figure leapt upon her from the shadows. The apparition breathed fire into Lucy's face and then bounded away as the girl fell to the ground, seized by violent fits.

Two days later, 18 year-old Jane Alsop replied to a violent ringing of the bell at the front gate of her parents' home in east London. Outside was an extremely agitated man who identified himself as a policeman. 'For God's sake bring me a light,' he cried, 'for we have caught Spring-heeled Jack in the lane!'

Jane fetched a candle, but when she handed it to the 'policeman', the man discarded his all-enveloping cloak. On his head was a large helmet, he wore a skin-tight suit of what looked like white oilskin and, in the light of the candle, his protuberant eyes burned like coals.

Without uttering a word, he vomited blue and white flames into Jane's face and grabbed the temporarily blinded and frightened girl with talon-like fingers, which tore her dress and raked her skin. Attracted by her screams, Jane's sisters, Mary and Sarah, came to the girl's assistance. Somehow Sarah pulled Jane from the fiend's grasp, thrust her indoors and slammed the door in Jack's face.

A week later, Jack tried the same deception, but for some reason his intended victim was suspicious and Jack was forced to flee. A witness claimed that, under his cloak, Jack had been wearing an ornate crest and, in gold filigree, the letter 'w'.

After these attacks, Jack's infamy grew. His exploits were reported in many newspapers and became the subject of no less than four 'penny dreadfuls' (Victorian comics), as well as melodramas performed in the cheap theatres that abounded at that time. But, perhaps as a result of the publicity, Jack's appearances became less frequent and occurred over a larger area.

IMAGE OF THE DEVIL

It was not until 1843 that terror of Spring-heeled Jack again swept the country. Then he appeared in Northamptonshire, in Hampshire – where he was described as 'the very image of the Devil himself, with horns and eyes of flame' – and in East Anglia, where he took particular delight in frightening the drivers of mail coaches.

Then, in 1845, reports came from Ealing and Hanwell, in west London, of a weird figure, leaping over hedges and walls, shrieking and groaning as it went. The perpetrator turned out to be a practical joker, a butcher from Brentford.

Later that year, Jack was seen at Jacob's Island, Bermondsey, a disease-ridden slum of decaying houses linked by wooden galleries across stinking ditches. This area had been immortalised by Charles Dickens seven years earlier as the lair of Fagin and his motley band in *Oliver Twist*. Jack cornered a 13-

year-old prostitute named Maria Davis on a bridge over Folly Ditch. He breathed fire into her face and hurled her into the stinking, muddy ditch below. The girl screamed terribly as the muddy waters claimed her. Witnesses reported the affair to the police, who dragged the ditch and recovered the poor girl's body. The verdict at the subsequent inquest was one of death by misadventure, but the inhabitants of the area branded Jack as a murderer.

There were isolated reports of Spring-heeled Jack over the next 27 years, none of them well-attested. Then, in November 1872, the *News of the World* reported that London was 'in a state of commotion owing to what is known as the Peckham Ghost . . . a mysterious figure, quite as alarming in appearance as Spring-heeled Jack, who terrified a past generation.'

In 1877, Jack gave a virtuoso performance at Aldershot Barracks. The terror began one night in early March. A sentry on duty at the North Camp peered into the darkness, his attention attracted by a peculiar figure bounding across the common towards him. The soldier issued a challenge, which went unheeded or unheard, and the figure disappeared from sight for a few moments. Then it was beside the guard and delivered several slaps to his face with a hand as cold and clammy as a corpse.

There were several more attacks on guards at Aldershot. Once a soldier shot at Jack; and afterwards, a rumour that Jack was invulnerable to bullets spread rapidly. In fact, the soldier had fired blanks at him. Various theories were advanced at the time, but no real clues ever emerged. The identity of the miscreant and the purpose of his attacks remains unknown.

It was 10 years before Jack's activities made further headlines – this time in Cheshire, where he frightened several young ladies. One was playing the piano in the drawing room of her father's house in Oxton, when a black-clad figure rushed into the room, swept every ornament off the mantlepiece and vanished as suddenly as he had appeared. According to an article in the *Liverpool Citizen*, it was widely rumoured that a number of young 'swells... sons of well-known men and bearing

Jacob's Island in east London, left, was the scene of the murder of young Maria Davis. Witnesses stated that Spring-heeled Jack was the culprit, but that he bounded away before he could be apprehended. A verdict of death by misadventure was recorded at the inquest.

Jack is seen outwitting everyone with one enormous leap in a further illustration from a penny dreadful, right.

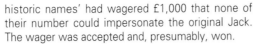

historic names' had wagered £1,000 that none of their number could impersonate the original Jack. The wager was accepted and, presumably, won.

Spring-heeled Jack made his final bow in a sensational appearance in Everton, Liverpool, in 1904. According to the *News of the World* of 25 September, crowds of people gathered to watch Jack scampering up and down William Henry Street, where he executed tremendous leaps, some of which are said to have exceeded 25 feet (7.5 metres). Finally, he leaped clean over the houses and vanished forever.

Although this story of Spring-heeled Jack's final bow has been widely told and might seem to be one of the best-attested examples of his prowess, investigation has proved it to be untrue. Only four days before the report quoted above, the *Liverpool Echo* contained an article about a house in William Henry Street that was said to be haunted by a poltergeist. 'The story,' said the *Echo*, 'as it passed from mouth to mouth, reached sensational dimensions.' At about the same time, further excitement was caused by a man suffering from religious mania who would climb upon the roof of his house and cry out that his wife was a devil or witch. The police or a fire-engine would attempt to bring the man down, but he would escape them by jumping from one roof to the next. From these incidents, the spurious story of Spring-heeled Jack's appearance in Everton was born.

But who or what was the original Spring-heeled Jack? One suggestion is that he was an insane circus fire-eater or acrobat: other theories range from a kangaroo dressed up by a demented animal trainer to, more recently, the inevitable UFO occupant. But Jack was almost certainly a human being – or,

to be more precise, more than one, for it is unlikely that the apparition that appeared at Aldershot in 1877 was the same as the one that had spread terror in suburban London some 40 years earlier. Jack is certainly known to have had his imitators, such as the Brentford butcher and, perhaps, the perpetrators of the Cheshire scare of 1887.

NOTORIOUS PRANKSTER

A very plausible candidate for the title of the Spring-heeled Jack behind the terror that reigned from 1837 to 1838 is Henry de la Poer Beresford, Marquis of Waterford. He had already been an inveterate and notorious prankster during his days at Eton and Oxford, where he was also an outstanding boxer and oarsman. He even once proposed to a railway company that they should arrange for two locomotives to crash, at his expense, simply so that he could witness the spectacle. One night in 1837, having been to the races, he painted the town red, literally – his decorative activities including doors, windows and one of the town watchmen. He and his associates were each fined £100 for this escapade.

Later in that year, *The Herald*, of Fife in Scotland, reported the following: 'The Marquis of Waterford passed through this town the other day, on the top of a coach, with a few of his associates. In the course of the journey they amused themselves with the noble occupation of popping eggs from a basket at any individual who happened to be standing at the wayside.'

The Times commented on this incident: 'This vivacious person is a long time sowing his "wild oats". He is nearly 27 years old.' The activities of the Marquis were not always so entertaining, however. Once he evicted more than 30 tenant families from their homes on his estate at a moment's notice. He also habitually treated people and animals with cruelty.

The young Lord Waterford visited Blackheath Fair in October, 1837; on the same day, Polly Adams, a 17-year-old serving-girl, was brutally attacked as she left the fair. Earlier, it was revealed, she had been accosted by someone with 'pop eyes', whom she believed to be a nobleman. Waterford's eyes had always been noticeably protuberant. His family emblem also fitted the description of a crest that was noticed on the clothes of Jack in one attack, and the whereabouts of the Marquis during this period are entirely consistent with the locations of Jack's appearances.

Waterford's cruel and bullying exploits gradually ceased after this time, and he became a model of respectability after his marriage in 1842. But the idea that Waterford had been Spring-heeled Jack was treated virtually as established fact by newspapers later in the century.

Never caught, and never positively identified, Spring-heeled Jack, together with his numerous escapades, is all but forgotten today. Hardly anyone remembers the penny dreadfuls, the melodramas, or the only film that has been made about Jack – *The Curse of the Wraydons*, shot in 1946 and starring Tod Slaughter. And the names of new bogeymen now come far more readily to the lips of mothers who, a century ago, would have cried: 'Be good or Spring-heeled Jack will get you!'

DISASTER FORETOLD

The R101 is seen as a charred skeleton, below, in the fields near Beauvais, France. Miraculously, its ensign still flies.

Within two days of the disaster, medium Eileen Garrett, right, was 'speaking' to the R101's dead captain.

THE WORLD WAS STUNNED WHEN THE VAUNTED *R101* AIRSHIP CRASHED IN FLAMES IN 1930. WHAT WAS EQUALLY STARTLING WAS A WARNING OF THE CALAMITY FROM BEYOND THE GRAVE AND SUBSEQUENT CONTACT WITH THE DECEASED PILOT

Eugene Rabouille, a 57-year-old poacher, was distracted from his task of setting rabbit snares by the sound of engines overhead. He looked up into the rain-soaked night and saw a confused image of bright lights and an enormous illuminated shape. It was very low in the sky, moving slowly and falling steadily – and it was heading his way. On it came, the drone of the engines getting louder as it approached. And as Rabouille stood rooted to the spot, the gigantic object suddenly pitched forward, corrected itself, and then slid almost gently into the side of a small hill about 100 yards (90 metres) from where he stood. The next moment, he found himself stretched out on the ground, stunned by shock waves, deafened by noise, and blinded by light.

A wall of flames shot hundreds of feet into the air; and as Rabouille picked himself up, he could hear terrible screams through the fire's roar. He saw, too, in the middle of the inferno, human figures rushing about, alive for a moment or two, but irretrievably lost. Rabouille put his hands to his eyes to shield them from the heat, and from the searing

R 101

vision. Then he turned and fled. It was just after 2 a.m. on 5 October 1930.

What Rabouille had witnessed were the final moments of the British airship *R101,* and of the 48 passengers and crew who perished that rainy night near the town of Beauvais, in northern France. He had also seen the event that would crush instantly and irrevocably British faith in the whole idea of rigid airships. It would spark off, too, bitter and lasting recriminations, and provides the backdrop to one of the most curious episodes in the annals of psychic phenomena.

Within two days of the *R101's* sickening destruction, no less a medium than Mrs Eileen Garrett was apparently in touch with the skipper of the enormous craft, Flight-Lieutenant H. Carmichael Irwin. Not only that, it turned out that another airman had actually foretold the end of the *R101* – also from beyond the grave. Three weeks after the calamity, Mrs Garrett found herself in contact again, this time in front of different witnesses, with the airship's dead captain.

PSYCHIC EVIDENCE

Public fascination with these revelations was intense, naturally, as no one knew what had happened during the last few hours on board. The evidence produced by Mrs Garrett was therefore crucial, not only for those who may have wanted to add ammunition to the case for survival after death, but to a question of immediate practical import – the viability of the craft. To gauge how the psychic evidence adds to both debates, it is first necessary to review, in detail, the sad tale of the *R101's* development.

In 1924, the British government had decided that the interests of the Empire could be well served by the construction of a fleet of large passenger airships. Now, the traditional way of going about such an enterprise would have been simply to place an order for a prototype with some suitable

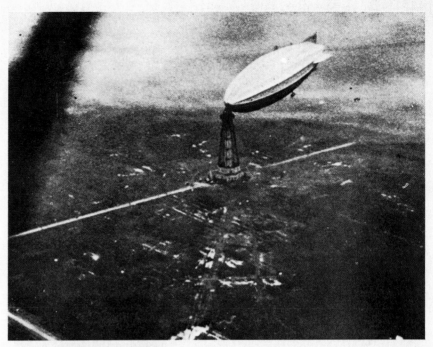

The R100, *is seen,* **top,** *at rest after her successful flight to Montreal in July 1930.*

It was the genius of Barnes Wallis, **above,** *that contributed so much to the success of the* R100.

The R101, *the largest airship ever built at that time,* **left,** *basks in floodlights at her mooring at Cardington. The hangar that housed her there was the biggest building in the British Empire.*

private firm. However, under a Labour government, there was strong pressure from within its ranks to give a practical demonstration of the merits of state enterprise. In the best spirit of British compromise, the decision was therefore reached that two airships should be built simultaneously, one by the Air Ministry itself and the other by a Vickers subsidiary, the Airship Guarantee Company.

The specifications and standards of performance laid down for the two airships were more or less identical, and they were impressive – more sophisticated even than those for the future *Graf Zeppelin.* They were to be, by a huge margin, the largest airships the world had seen – kept aloft by 5 million cubic feet (140,000 cubic metres) of hydrogen. This would give them a gross lift of 150 tonnes; and with a stipulated maximum weight of 90 tonnes for the airships themselves (unloaded), they would provide a 'useful' lift of 60 tonnes – again far in advance of anything to date.

What this amounted to was a specification for a pair of airships that could transport 100 fare-paying passengers in considerable luxury to the four corners of the globe, and at the respectable cruising speed of 63 miles per hour (100 km/h). This altogether grand vision was by no means as fanciful as it may look in retrospect, however.

The Vickers team set up shop in a disused hangar at Howden, Yorkshire, and over the next five years put together an airship of the highest quality, the *R100.* They accomplished their formidable task in relative peace and quiet, away from the glare of publicity and political meddling. Meanwhile, the Air Ministry team resurrected the wartime airship base at Cardington, near Bedford. There, unlike their rivals, they found themselves as goldfish in a bowl. How great a factor this was in the final débâcle is a matter for speculation, but what finally emerged in a blaze of public anticipation was a majestic flying coffin – the much-vaunted *R101.*

The first in the sorry catalogue of mistakes made at Cardington was probably the worst. Because of the competitive element, it was decided

In a desperate attempt to make the R101 *effective, the enormous structure of the doomed craft was split in two to take in an extra gasbag.*

not to pool information with Howden. The design and construction of such advanced airships were bound to throw up problems of both a theoretical and practical nature. Original thinking would be at a premium and there was not a lot of it in the world of British airship design at this time. What the Air Ministry did – deliberately – was to dilute what little there was.

Vickers was in the enviable position of having a truly outstanding designer for the *R100* – Barnes Wallis – who was even then an acknowledged inventive genius and would later become a living legend. During the five years it took to build the two airships, Wallis repeatedly suggested collaboration, but his appeals fell on deaf ears. It was almost as though the Cardington men thought they had nothing to learn from others.

Take the engines, for example. Early on, a newly designed diesel type was adopted because it was marginally safer (from the standpoint of accidental fire) than the conventional petrol type. This should have been weighed against a rather more significant disadvantage of the new diesel engines: they

were far too heavy. The Howden team, too, experimented with diesel, saw quickly that they were too heavy and reverted to proven Rolls-Royce Condor engines. Such pragmatism was out of the question at Cardington. Considerable publicity had been given to the new diesels and they would stay, overweight or not.

The huge gasbags inside the rigid metal frame (16 of them in all) were held in place by an elaborate system of wiring. But the wiring was such that the bags continually rubbed against the girders and rivets of the framework itself. As bad, or worse even, when the airship rolled (a natural enough occurrence), the valves in the gasbags opened slightly, which meant there was an ever-present risk of highly flammable hydrogen wafting around outside the gasbags, but still inside the body of the airship.

CURIOUS SOLUTIONS

The hurried solutions to these fundamental problems were bizarre – some would say comical even, were it not for the dreadful outcome. There were only two ways of getting more lift: either reduce the weight of the airship or increase the volume of hydrogen. The former was difficult to do to any significant degree (without scrapping the diesel engines), but the latter gave scope to fevered imaginations. Why not simply chop the airship in two and stick an extra bay in the middle? And surely there was an easy way of managing to squeeze more hydrogen into the existing gasbags? Simply loosen the wiring to allow them to expand a little more (and chafe a little more as well). If the gasbags showed an annoying tendency to puncture themselves on bits of the framework, track down the offending projections and stick a pad over them. (Some 4,000 pads were finally fitted).

The immediate results (like the final result) of this kind of folly were roughly what one might have expected. The 'new' *R101* was hauled out of the hangar to her mooring mast under perfectly tolerable weather conditions. At once, a gaping hole 140 feet (33 metres) long appeared along the top, where the fabric had merely given way. It was taped up. So was another smaller tear that appeared the next day.

In FOCUS

CAPTAIN HINCHLIFFE'S PREDICTION

Even while the *R101* was stumbling toward completion, there was a psychic portent of catastrophe. On 13 March 1928, a dashing war hero, Captain W. G. R. Hinchliffe, accompanied by heiress Elsie Mackay, took off from Cranwell aerodrome in eastern England in an attempt to fly the Atlantic. They were never to be seen again. It was assumed that their craft had met with an accident, and that they had possibly drowned. Then, on 31 March, Mrs Beatrice Earl was startled by a message that came through on her ouija board: HINCHLIFFE TELL MY WIFE I WANT TO SPEAK TO HER.

Mrs Earl managed to get the message to the aviator's widow, Emilie, who in turn agreed to let Eileen Garrett (whom Mrs Earl knew) try to contact her dead husband. (He, incidentally, had once called Spiritualism 'total nonsense'.) In the sessions that followed, it was found that Hinchliffe's spirit was becoming deeply concerned about the *R101:* 'I want to say something about the new airship... the vessel will not stand the strain.' He pleaded that his old friend Squadron-Leader Johnston, the *R101's* navigator, be told of this doubt about the craft's safety. But the men at Cardington were unmoved. His last message was received as the *R101* headed for France. It ran: STORMS RISING. NOTHING BUT A MIRACLE CAN SAVE THEM.

By then, the medium Eileen Garrett had begun to have dramatic visions of the new airship bursting into flames in a tragic accident . . .

In defence of the beleaguered men at Cardington, it should be said that they were working under intolerable pressure. In July 1930, the unheralded *R100,* having completed her trials successfully, flew to Montreal and back again a fortnight later. It was rumoured that only the more successful of the two airships would serve as a prototype for future development. To the rattled men at Cardington, it was now vital that the *R101* should demonstrate her superiority quickly. The destination for the maiden flight was India, a longer and more glamorous voyage than the *R100's* to Montreal, and guaranteed to put Cardington back in the limelight.

CALENDAR OF WOE

So we come to the final grim chapter, and to the man who must bear most of the blame for the fiasco that cost his and many other lives – the Air Minister himself, Lord Thomson of Cardington. His devotion to the *R101* project bordered on the fanatical (his choice of title when elevated to the peerage provides a pointer to this). He also combined this passion with unslakable ambition. His sights were set on becoming the next Viceroy of India, and by happy coincidence there was an Imperial Conference in London starting in late October. How better to draw attention to his claim than by descending on the conference, fresh from a round trip to the Subcontinent, aboard his beloved *R101?*

A September departure was impossible. Thomson accepted this, but with ill-disguised resentment. Early October was the latest departure date that would get him to India and back in time to fulfil any of his commitments at the conference. The airship must be ready by the fourth of the month because 'I have made my plans accordingly', he said.

Aside from the fact that the airship was unfit for such a voyage, or even for a Sunday excursion for that matter, there was another hitch. It was essential to have a Certificate of Airworthiness, which could only be issued after the successful completion of exhaustive trials. But a temporary certificate was wangled, with the droll proviso that final speed trials be completed during the journey itself.

At 6.36 p.m. on 4 October, the awesomely beautiful silver craft (for she was that) struggled

Lord Thomson of Cardington, above, had a driving ambition to get the R101 into the air. It only served, however, to hasten its end – and his own death.

The press immediately latched on to the strange aftermath of the disaster, as shown in the headline below.

Spectators, bottom, are dwarfed by the burnt-out wreckage of the 777-foot (237-metre) long airship.

away from her mooring mast. And it was a real struggle. Four tonnes of water (half the ballast) had to be jettisoned in those first moments, just to get airborne. Pitching and rolling, the airship that was, in Lord Thomson's immortal words, 'as safe as a house, except for the millionth chance', crossed low over the lights of London an hour-and-a-half later, with one of the five engines already out of commission. At 8.21 p.m., Cardington received the laconic message: 'Over London. All well. Moderate rain.'

THE LAST MESSAGE

At 9.35 p.m., she reached the Channel at Hastings, still flying low and experiencing worse weather – hard rain and a strong southwesterly wind. Two hours later, she crossed the French coast near Dieppe. At midnight, Cardington received its final wireless message. After reporting the *R101's* position as 15 miles (24 kilometres) south of Abbeville, the message ended on a cosy note: 'After an excellent supper, our distinguished passengers smoked a final cigar, and having sighted the French coast have now gone to bed to rest after the excitement of their leavetaking. All essential services are functioning satisfactorily. The crew have settled down to a watch-keeping routine.'

What seemed to pass unnoticed aboard the airship was her low altitude. It did not go unnoticed by some observers on the ground, however, one of whom was alarmed to see the gigantic craft flying overhead at an estimated 300 feet (90 metres), less than half her own length. That was at about 1 a.m., and he judged her to be moving in the direction of Beauvais.

In the next part of this feature, we find out what happened at the seances held by Eileen Garrett and how the dead captain was heard to speak.

> THERE IS ALSO A NEW TYPE OF ENGINE THEY ARE TRYING OUT WHICH INTERESTS ME. IT IS NOT GOING TO BE A SUCCESS... TELL THEM TO BE CAREFUL. IT IS NOT STABILIZED AS IT SHOULD BE.
>
> **CAPTAIN W.G.R. HINCHLIFFE,**
> **POSTHUMOUSLY**

ALIEN VARIATIONS

COULD TODAY'S ALIENS PERHAPS BE THE FAIRIES AND DEMONS OF YESTERYEAR? AND DO SUCH SIGHTINGS MAYBE POINT TO SOME BASIC HUMAN NEED?

On the morning of 4 January 1979, Jean Hingley, a factory worker from near Birmingham in the English Midlands, had what she described as the strangest experience of her whole life. 'At 7 o'clock my husband was going to work by car, and I stood at the back door to wave him off. Hobo, our Alsatian dog, was by my side. When my husband had gone, I saw a light in the garden and thought he had left the light on in the

Many children dream up 'invisible playmates', sometimes resembling fairies, to keep them company – and these 'friends' often become very real. According to one theory, the supernatural creatures seen by adults are more sophisticated 'playmates', called into being for the same kinds of reason that children also need unseen companions.

car port. So I went down, but saw that the light was off. As we turned to go back to the house, I saw an orange light over the garden which gradually turned white. It lit the whole garden. We then went into the back door of the house.

'Suddenly, with a sound like *zee . . . zee . . . zee*, three "beings" floated past me through the open door. They glowed with a brilliant light and seemed to float about a foot [30 centimetres] above the floor. As they floated past me into the lounge, I saw that they had wonderful wings.'

Describing the wings in detail, Mrs Hingley said that they glowed with rainbow colours so breathtakingly beautiful that they made our earthly colours look somehow 'chemical'. Both Jean Hingley and her dog were overwhelmed by the experience. The dog flopped on to the floor and lay stiff, as if drugged. Mrs Hingley also felt paralysed. 'After a while the fear seemed to leave me. I felt as if I were lifted up. I seemed to float into the lounge. The three "creatures" were shaking and tugging at the little Christmas tree – three little, slim "men" in silvery-green tunics and silver waistcoats with silver buttons or press studs. They were about 3 feet 6 inches to 4 feet [1 – 1.2 metres] high, all alike. Their pointed hands and feet were covered in the same silvery-green, and they had pointed caps on their heads of the same colour, and with something like a lamp on top. They were floating round the lounge touching everything – the Christmas cards, the clock, the radio and all the furniture. At last, when I could speak, I said: "Three of you and one of me. What are you going to do? What do you want with me?"'

A somewhat awkward conversation followed, in the course of which the creature revealed that they came from the sky. They said they had visited Australia, New Zealand and America. 'We came down here to try to talk to people, but they don't seem to be interested.'

Although she was very nervous, Jean Hingley talked to them about her life, and they seemed interested in whatever she said. She offered them some mince pies, and when they took them, their hands seemed magnetic. Then she started to show them how to smoke because they seemed curious about her cigarettes, but they were frightened when she lit one, and floated out into the garden.

Jean Hingley herself still seemed to be floating as she followed them. They went towards a glowing, orange-coloured 'space-ship' sitting in her garden. She estimated it to be between 8 and 10 feet (2.4 – 3 metres) long and about 4 feet (1.2 metres) high, with round windows. The creatures still held the mince pies as they entered the object and closed the door. As the craft lifted, they flashed the lights twice – as if, Mrs Hingley thought, saying goodbye. Then the object disappeared. After they had gone, she saw a deep impression in the garden where the 'space-ship' had been; and the packed ice and snow, which had lain for days in the severe winter, had melted away completely.

Jean Hingley said that, after the beings had left, she felt 'warm and happy . . . as though I had been blessed'.

Many commentators have suggested that today's alien visitors are the space age equivalent of fairies, and a case like Jean Hingley's lends support to such an idea. Both her description and a sketch she made of the aliens could apply just as well to fairies as to extra-terrestrial visitors, and the emphasis on the wings is a particularly noteworthy feature. Although many strange winged creatures have been reported in connection with UFOs – notably by John Keel in his investigation of the 'mothman' sightings in West Virginia in late 1966 – few of the aliens with whom witnesses claim to have made direct contact have had wings.

HISTORICAL PARALLELS

In his classic study *Passport to Magonia*, the ufologist Jacques Vallee presented many examples of similarities between fairy and UFO sightings, and inferred that the two phenomena are basically one. Jean Bastide, in *La Mémoire des Ovni*, took the hypothesis further, saying that 'modern contacts established with extra-terrestrials respect precisely the same rules as contacts in the past with beings more or less human in form.' The parallels are certainly striking, and they have helped to encourage the growth of the notion of 'ancient astronauts'. Adherents claim that many of the anomalous phenomena of the past can best be accounted for by the hypothesis that extra-terrestrials either originated the human race or have interacted with it throughout its history. On the basis of existing evidence, however, this hypothesis remains little more than an intriguing speculation.

On the psychological level, however, there is some reason for supposing that yesterday's fairies were indeed the precursors of today's aliens.

Putting aside for a moment the question of the 'reality' of experiences like Jean Hingley's, it is interesting to consider the role played by such entities, their ostensible purpose in manifesting at all, and the effect that their actions have on witnesses.

Right away, we notice that some encounters with entities seem quite accidental and others seem to be clearly directed. Could some manifestations occur in response to a hidden need, a psychological state that calls for outside intervention of some kind? Jean Hingley was certainly in a somewhat troubled state at the time: she had just left her church over a conflict, leaving a gap in her life.

Such considerations have prompted the French ufologist Jean-Francois Boedec, in his book *Fantastiques Rencontres au Bout du Monde*, to suggest that we should conceive of sightings as starting long before the actual experience. Indeed, he points to many cases in which witnesses had premonitions that something was about to happen, or for some reason went home by a different routes or took an unaccustomed walk. Somehow, it would seem, the witnesses were being prepared – or were preparing themselves – for the experience they were about to undergo.

The only way in which this hypothesis could be tested would be by carrying out a psychological examination of every witness, which is hardly possible. We must therefore draw what conclusions we can from what we know of the witnesses' individual circumstances.

It is certainly common for children to dream up 'invisible playmates' to keep them company, and they even sometimes come to believe in the actual existence of these 'friends'. Are fairies, demons and alien visitors perhaps more sophisticated 'playmates', called into being in response to needs, representing our hopes, fears, and expectations?

The sketch, left, depicting a spaceship swooping down and capturing three women in Kentucky in 1976, was made by one of the abductees. Many such encounters with UFOs and alien entities seem to have no apparent cause, but others seem to answer a particular need of the witness.

" ARE THOSE WHO BELIEVE IN THE EXISTENCE OF THESE ENTITIES ALREADY HALFWAY TOWARDS SEEING THEM? "

According to one school of thought, alien sightings – such as that depicted in the artist's impression, below – could be projections from the collective unconscious.

Demons, meanwhile, may meet an intellectual as well as an emotional need. Without demons, theologians would be hard put to account for the existence of evil in the Universe. Consequently, virtually every religion includes not only God, but enemies of God. From this basic assumption, theologians have gone on to picture Earth as the battlefield on which angels and demons fight for people's souls. UFO-related entities have even been identified as agents of Satan.

For an even greater number of people, however, the aliens represent good rather than evil: they are our intellectual and moral superiors who come to Earth to help us sort out our problems – to put an end to wars, social inequality, disease, suffering and all the other evils of the world.

But does it follow that the entities in such cases were conjured up in the witnesses' minds for this purpose?

Some experiences may not be visual at all; or rather, the entity may manifest in a form that seems to rule out altogether any physical identity. Science fiction also contains many variations on the theme of alien invaders 'taking over' humans for sinister purposes. But more people probably still believe that any 'body invaders' are demons from hell rather than aliens from space.

Dr Robert L. Hymers, pastor of the Open Door Community Church in Los Angeles, gives this alarming account of a young man who came to him for help.

'One of our perhaps over-zealous young people had given Don a book to read. The book explained

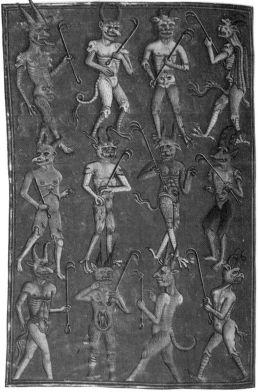

how people can become demon-possessed through the occult. Don clutched the book and leaned forward in his chair. "I've been reading this book all night, I know I'm demon-possessed. I know it."

"How do you know?" I asked, amid the sounds of his crying.

"I tried to drive over to San Francisco. Something kept grabbing the wheel. Voices in my head kept saying 'Drive off the road! Kill yourself!' I didn't know what to do, so I came here to you... Pastor, please pray for me! Please pray for me now! I'm going insane!"

'I closed my eyes and began. "Father, I pray that you'll give peace to Don. I pray that . . ." but I was stopped by a growling sound, like that of a vicious dog. Dr Hymers then continues:

'I opened my eyes just in time. Don was coming towards me, his fingers moving in a menacing way, his eyes wild, froth dribbling from his mouth. A horrible, vicious voice came from deep in his throat. "I'm going to kill you!"

'I leaped from the chair and dashed to the other side of the room. One thought rushed through my mind. "He's dangerous and he's bigger than me,

Some theologians believe that demons – as represented in a 15th-century French manuscript, above left – and angels – depicted on a 19th-century German postcard, above – are in a constant battle for people's souls. Such entities may also answer an intellectual need to explain the existence of evil. The idea has even been mooted that fairies and aliens, too, may answer human needs by representing our hopes, fears and expectations.

and I'm alone!" Then I did the only thing I could think of. I pointed my finger at the advancing figure and said, "Demon, I bind thee in the name of Jesus Christ." His body fell heavily to the floor at my feet.

'In the next few minutes, as I bent in prayer over Don's writhing body, he began to grow calm. Finally, he looked up at me. "I feel better now, Pastor," he said.'

Anyone familiar with the current spate of doom-laden tracts from the fundamentalist churches of the United States will recognise that dramatic story as typical of its genre – that of demon possession. The psychiatrist, on the other hand, would be inclined to explain it in terms of an altered state of consciousness in which a suppressed emotion externalises itself, choosing to do so in this dramatic form. Could a similar process be at work in cases where an actual entity is allegedly seen? In the mid-19th century, the French occultist Eliphas Lévi observed: 'He who affirms the devil, creates the devil.' Could this apply to angels and aliens as well? Are those who believe in the existence of these entities already halfway towards seeing them?

203

CORAL POLGE HAS THE SPECIAL TALENT OF BEING ABLE TO DRAW EXACT LIKENESSES OF PEOPLE SHE HAS NEVER SEEN OR KNOWN – PEOPLE WHOSE FACES COME TO HER FROM BEYOND THE GRAVE THROUGH HER REMARKABLE PSYCHIC POWERS

Many thousands of people believe they have received tangible proof of life after death. It has been given to them in the form of portraits of their loved ones, drawn by a London medium, Coral Polge.

These pencil and pastel sketches, which now adorn walls in homes around the world, often show a striking likeness to dead relatives and friends. Not only are their features recognisable, but sometimes they are dressed in a characteristic style.

Psychic artist Coral Polge does not see the dead, nor is her hand controlled by spirits in the way that automatic writing mediums claim to receive their scripts. 'I just "feel" the people coming through', she told the Spiritualist newspaper

PORTRAITS FROM THE OTHER SIDE

Psychic News in 1972. 'I usually know what to draw without thinking about it too much, rather as one does when doodling.'

In the early stages of her career, Coral Polge gleaned the information for some of her portraits by holding letters written to her by those anxious to discover the fate of people near to them who had died. Nowadays, she concentrates on personal sittings, enabling enquirers to see the sketches as she produces them. She also demonstrates her remarkable talent in public, using an overhead projector or large sheets of paper so that audiences can witness the drawings being made.

It was during one of these public performances that she drew the features of an elderly man with a droopy moustache. Among those in the audience was Phyllis Timms of Salisbury, Wiltshire, who

Coral Polge, above, often gives public demonstrations of her skills as a psychic artist by projecting a drawing on to an overhead screen while working on it.

Coral Polge's drawing, made at a public demonstration, of a man called Herbert Light, above right, is shown above. Light's granddaughter, who was in the audience, recognised his features immediately. But it was only after Coral had given further information – which could not have been acquired by normal means – that she acknowledged the portrait.

Drawings made by Coral Polge are shown left, beside actual photographs of the subjects. She produces her sketches in a matter of minutes, which makes her ability to capture her unseen 'communicators' all the more remarkable. Sometimes, the results are unexpected, as one sitter discovered. She was hoping for a portrait of former UN Secretary-General Dag Hammarskjöld, whose biography she was writing. When Coral drew a 'pretty little girl', above left, the sitter was disappointed until she remembered a family portrait featuring him as a child that showed that Coral's depiction of Hammarskjöld was in fact very accurate.

recognised the man as her grandfather, Herbert Light, who had died of cancer.

But Mrs Timms did not acknowledge the portrait immediately: she wanted 'absolute proof'. In addition to drawing likenesses of the dead, Coral Polge also picks up psychic impressions that help to confirm their identity. In this case, she announced that she felt the elderly man was related to someone in the audience in a green dress. No one responded: indeed, Mrs Timms was not wearing green. The psychic artist was insistent, however, that green was important as a link with the man she had drawn. It then occurred to Mrs Timms that her maiden name was Green – and she raised her hand to accept the portrait. The event is described in Coral Polge's book *Living Images – The Story of a Psychic Artist.*

The introduction to Spiritualism came through her parents, both of whom received spiritual healing in the 1940s. Then, during a visit to Harrow Spiritualist Church, she was told by a medium that she would be a psychic artist. Coral was trained as an artist at Harrow Art School, but she confesses that she was then hopeless at portraits – her particular interest was textile design. Nevertheless, the medium's prediction was not met with scepticism.

Coral took her first psychic circle in 1950. Over four decades later, she has stopped keeping count of the pictures she has drawn, giving up after she passed the 10,000 mark.

To begin with, many of the people she drew were spirit guides – Red Indians, nuns, wise Chinese, smiling monks; but although they pleased the sitters, they did not provide definite proof of survival, for no one could positively identify the subjects as having once lived on earth. She therefore made a special effort to produce more portraits of relatives. The results can sometimes be very impressive. Indeed, it is not unusual for a sitter to burst into tears as he or she sees recognisable features appear on the psychic artist's pad. 'If I never get any more evidence for as long as I live, this is enough to convince me Spiritualism is true,' one woman told her.

Coral Polge cannot produce portraits to order, however. 'It creates barriers when people come expecting or wanting me to draw someone in

Compare a drawing by Coral Polge of the celebrated opera singer Maria Malibran, left, with a portrait from life, right. In this case, the picture was not produced for a relative, but for another singer.

In the early part of her career, Coral Polge often drew spirit guides, as shown below, but this meant little to those who wanted to communicate with someone known to them. She then made a special effort to sense her sitters' relatives.

particular. I draw whoever is able to get through.' Yet people do visit her with high expectations, sometimes raised by messages from dead relatives that they have received through other mediums.

THE PROMISED SKETCH

One such visitor, who went to see Coral Polge anonymously, was expecting a portrait of a 'special person'. What Coral did not know was that the woman was writing a biography of Swedish-born Dag Hammarsjköld, the former United Nations Secretary-General who died in an aeroplane crash in Africa in 1961. The woman had a keen interest in Spiritualism and had apparently received several communications from the statesman through other mediums. In one of these, he promised her a portrait if she visited a psychic artist. It was therefore with some disappointment that she watched as Mrs Polge drew a pretty little girl. At first, she thought the sitting was a failure; but slowly, as the portrait took shape, it began to look strangely familiar. Soon, she was smiling with pleasure: Hammarskjöld had produced his portrait after all.

While researching her book, the woman had seen many family photographs. One, she recalled, showed Hammarskjöld at the age of two, sitting on his mother's knee, with long hair and wearing a dress. In this, he looked just like a pretty little girl.

A portrait produced by Coral Polge also provided corroboration of spirit messages received by singer Grace Brooks. When Grace visited the psychic artist, she received a portrait of a young woman with an unusual hair style. 'This is a Spanish singer named Maria,' Coral told her.

Grace had received messages from Maria through the automatic writing of a young Australian singer, Deidre Dehn, whom she met on the set of the film *Oliver!* At first, Maria had simply given Deidre her Christian name and the surname Garcia; later, however, she supplied the name Malibran. Deidre subsequently discovered that Maria Malibran (née Garcia) had been a celebrated opera singer.

When Deidre Dehn returned to Australia, Grace believed her contact with Maria Malibran to be broken. But the link persisted, it seems; and the drawing produced by Coral Polge is strikingly similar to a portrait Grace found at the British Museum.

The British medium has demonstrated her psychic art in most European countries, as well as Canada, the United States and Australia. But she still finds time to travel around Great Britain to serve some of the little Spiritualist churches where her work began. She has also made numerous television appearances. During a six-week tour of Australia in 1980, she was featured on the nationwide *Don Lane Show*. On this occasion, Coral was asked to draw just one portrait: she produced a picture of a young man, saying that he had three brothers and a father who was in poor health. A member of the studio audience recognised him immediately as the son of a friend: he had been killed in a car crash a year earlier.

Coral Polge also spent three weeks in Canada in 1980, when she gave 80 private sittings and several newspaper interviews. She appeared in public twice, sharing the platform with another medium, David Young – she drew the spirit communicators, while he conveyed messages from them.

Not everyone accepts that Coral's drawings provide evidence of survival beyond the grave. Some regard them as extraordinary examples of extra-sensory perception, while sceptics dismiss them as coincidence. Not all the faces she draws are of the dead: she has occasionally produced portraits of babies before they were even born. And she once did a drawing for a Norwegian television producer who was in Britain with a camera crew: he recognised the portrait immediately – it was of a member of the crew who had been unable to visit Britain right at the last moment.

What does Coral Polge think of her strange gift? 'After producing so many drawings, you don't try to rationalise it,' she says. 'But I still feel a slight amazement that it had anything to do with me.'

WHAT KILLED THE DINOSAURS?

Triceratops, *one of the later dinosaurs, was equipped with three horns and a bony protective frill, as depicted* above.

A Triceratops *skeleton is dwarfed by the colossal form of* Diplodocus, below, *in London's Natural History Museum.*

DINOSAURS ARE USUALLY THOUGHT TO HAVE BEEN CLUMSY, SLOW-WITTED MONSTERS, DOOMED TO FAIL IN THE STRUGGLE FOR LIFE. BUT THEY FLOURISHED FOR 160 MILLION YEARS BEFORE THEY BECAME EXTINCT. WHAT THEORIES HAVE PALAEONTOLOGISTS TO OFFER ABOUT WHY THEY FINALLY DIED OUT?

The age of the dinosaurs, known to science as the Mesozoic era, began about 225 million years ago. Geologists divide it into three principal periods: the Triassic, which lasted about 32 million years; the Jurassic, which lasted about 57 million years; and the Cretaceous, which lasted some 71 million years.

This time span is so vast as to be almost beyond comprehension, but we can gain some idea of its magnitude if we consider that Man's ape-like ancestors appeared only within the last 1.5 million years, and that *Homo sapiens,* modern Man, has existed for only 50,000 years. When dinosaurs ruled, Mankind's ancestors were tiny, rodent-like mammals, and probably formed part of the dinosaur diet.

The term 'dinosaur' was coined by anatomist Sir Richard Owen in 1841. Derived from two Greek words, *deinos* and *sauros,* 'dinosaur' can be said to mean 'fearful reptile', or 'terrible lizard'. But these great animals were not lizards at all. Indeed, in the final stages of their development, they combined features that are characteristic of present-day reptiles, mammals and birds.

Dinosaurs are generally classed into two great orders: the saurischians ('lizard-hipped creatures') and the ornithischians ('bird-hipped creatures'), named after the distinctive structures of their hip bones. One group of dinosaurs looked rather like ostriches, but had stereoscopic vision (both eyes looked forward, giving double views of a scene and providing three-dimensional vision, as our eyes do). They had fine, finger-like claws capable of delicate handling, and they had large brains. In fact, the brains of some of these creatures were seven times as large as those of modern reptiles, according to Dr Dale Russell of the National Museum of Natural Sciences in Ottawa, Canada. 'In other words,' says Dr Russell, belying the popular image of dinosaurs as the slowest-witted creatures ever to exist, 'they were as intelligent as primitive man.'

GIANTS OF THE EARTH

Some of these giants of the past walked upright on their hind legs and were about the same height as human beings. But hundreds of other dinosaur species came in weird and varied shapes and sizes, ranging from the flesh-eating *Cynognathus,* which was about as big as an Alsatian dog, to the 50-tonne herbivorous *Brachiosaurus.* Through millions of years of evolution, dinosaurs dominated every part of the Earth, except the Antarctic regions. They adapted to extremes of heat and cold, ate fish, meat, herbs and foliage; and, in the case of some nimble species, may have had sufficiently swift reflexes to snatch primitive birds in flight.

And yet, suddenly – at least compared with the considerable length of their tenure of the Earth – these conquering creatures, with their great range of abilities, died out, leaving behind only a few distant cousins, such as the crocodiles and turtles. What happened to cause such devastation to the dinosaurs, who had hitherto survived for millions of years? This question has been hotly debated among palaeontologists – scientists who study fossils – for well over a hundred years; but it is only since the early 1970s that satisfactory theories have been put forward.

The chart below shows the lineage of the dinosaurs during prehistoric times. Whatever caused them finally to disappear, scientists agree that Man may never have evolved had they not become extinct.

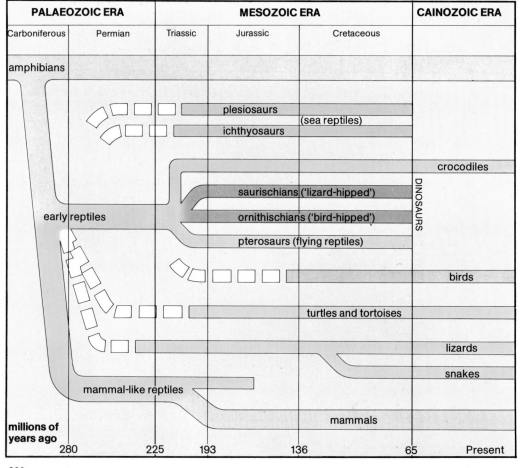

PALAEOZOIC ERA		MESOZOIC ERA			CAINOZOIC ERA
Carboniferous	Permian	Triassic	Jurassic	Cretaceous	
amphibians					
		plesiosaurs			
			(sea reptiles)		
		ichthyosaurs			
					crocodiles
			saurischians ('lizard-hipped')		
early reptiles			ornithischians ('bird-hipped')		DINOSAURS
		pterosaurs (flying reptiles)			
					birds
		turtles and tortoises			
					lizards
					snakes
mammal-like reptiles					
		mammals			

millions of years ago
280   225   193   136   65   Present

The geological strata of the Earth dating from the Mesozoic era are rich in the remains of the dinosaurs and of the plants, insects, fish and animals that they fed on. From this long-buried debris, scientists have been able to build up an accurate picture of the life that flourished during the era.

Like the reptiles, early dinosaurs evolved from amphibians, sea-dwelling creatures that crawled ashore to lay their eggs. These were amniotic, like a hen's egg, with a hard, leathery shell that enclosed the embryo in a sac of liquid. They contained a reservoir of yolk, too, on which the embryo fed until its limbs were formed and it was finally ready to emerge.

A variety of creatures evolved from these amphibians. One of the most important adaptations in the dinosaurs was in the jaw structure. Generally speaking, the jaws and teeth of reptiles are simple affairs: often, the lower jaw consists of two or more loosely articulated bones, enabling them to swallow huge lumps of food that their primitive teeth are incapable of chewing. Fossil remains from the early Triassic period – particularly rich in southern Africa and North America – show that the early dinosaurs had developed a single lower jawbone. The disused extra bones had developed into ossicles – bony plates that make up the structure of the inner ear. The teeth, too, had developed from the simple reptilian spike-like forms, resembling crocodiles' teeth, into front incisors for biting, canines for tearing, and flat-topped molars for chewing.

Otherwise, the many varieties of dinosaur seem to have had surprisingly little in common with each other. This was largely because of the changing nat-

A clutch of eggs laid by **Protoceratops,** *ancestor of the horned dinosaurs, is shown* **above. Many such nests, containing as many as 18 eggs, have been found in the Gobi Desert of Mongolia.**

Apatosaurus, *erroneously known as* Brontosaurus *for a long time, is a heavier version of* **Diplodocus,** *one of the best-known of all the dinosaurs.*

ural conditions of the Mesozoic era and the differing environments in which each variety lived.

At the beginning of the Triassic period, the climate over about three-quarters of the world's surface was warm and even, so that trees and shrubs thrived well inside the areas that now lie in the Arctic Circle. Lush tropical vegetation and swamps covered much of Europe, Asia and the Americas – though the land had not yet broken up into the present-day continents. For most of the Jurassic period, too, dinosaurs were able to wander freely over much of the Earth's surface.

THE EARTH'S CHANGING FACE

Towards the end of the 71-million-year Cretaceous period, however, a mountain-building process, termed the Laramide Revolution, occurred. The oceans retreated from the plains of North America as ranges such as the Rockies were forced into being. Much of Europe and Asia consisted of large islands and finger-like promontories. It was also at this time that many modern forms of plant life appeared, including both conifers, such as fir and pine trees, and deciduous trees, such as elm, oak and beech, as well as many grasses and shrubs that are still familiar today.

An early, tentative theory suggested that changes in the Earth's foliage must have affected the dinosaurs' diet, rendering the huge beasts sluggish and less able to take care of themselves. They may also have become less well-equipped to fend off the little rodent ancestors of Man, who could pillage their eggs, thereby bringing about the giants' slow extinction.

This idea was based on the reptilian characteristics of the dinosaurs. Some modern reptiles, such as the Florida alligator, for example, become inefficient even when the temperature changes by very little; and a greater variation can kill them.

But recent research has shown that the dinosaurs can be equated only superficially with the reptiles that are known today. Some, like the giant plant-eaters *Brachiosaurus* and *Camarasaurus*, were almost certainly warm-blooded, while even a scaly meat-eater, such as *Tyrannosaurus*, may have been more mammal than reptile. The most reptilian of the dinosaurs, such as *Stegosaurus*, had triangular

but the largest and fiercest predators, but the increased ratio of body weight to surface area helps the beast to conserve body heat, thus cutting down its expenditure of energy.

So the problem of the dinosaurs' extinction is not solved by the notion that they were too slow, clumsy and weak-brained to cope with nimbler competitors. This idea will certainly not explain the disappearance of creatures such as *Brachiosaurus*, which flourished for millions of years; still less will it explain the passing of the fierce meat-eating dinosaurs. *Allosaurus* was typical of these: it was about 39 feet (12 metres) long and moved on powerful hind legs, its body counterbalanced by a heavy tail, which could also be used as a club. Its forelimbs were savagely clawed, and its jaws were equipped with ferocious, razor-sharp teeth.

Even more formidable was *Tyrannosaurus rex*: up to 46 feet (14 metres) long, and standing 16 feet (5 metres) high, it weighed about 7 tonnes. All its armament was in its head, which was equipped with double rows of sabre-like teeth, 6 inches (15 centimetres) long. *Tyrannosaurus* may have had impressive brain power, too.

The other order of dinosaurs, the 'bird-hipped' ornithischians, also included some species that

plates on its back, which may have acted as efficient thermostats to control body heat. So, all in all, heat, or the lack of it, was probably not the direct cause of the death of the dinosaurs.

In any case, how could a climatic variation of a few degrees affect such species as the plesiosaurs, marine leviathans that numbered among their species *Kronosaurus*, with a 12-foot (3.7-metre) skull?

A 19th-century theory looked to the sheer bulk of the majority of dinosaurs for an answer to the problem. In essence, it suggested that the hypophysis, the gland controlling growth, went berserk and increased the size of the dinosaurs to an impossible degree. The known characteristics of some of the big vegetarians, such as *Brachiosaurus* of Africa and America and *Apatosaurus* of North America, seem at first to support this view. Between 60 and 80 feet (18 and 24 metres) long, *Brachiosaurus* weighed up to 50 tonnes. Its legs were short and stumpy – powerful enough to enable them to move about on land; but this enormous creature may have preferred to spend most of its time in swamps and lakes – like the modern hippopotamus – where its weight would be buoyed up by the water.

These creatures fed on marine plant life, although their long, slender necks enabled them to supplement their diet with foliage from trees. At the end of the neck sat a ludicrously small head with weak jaws, housing a brain the size of a duck egg. The body was in fact controlled by a secondary 'brain' – a swelling of the spinal cord located in the pelvic region.

Brachiosaurus was, in effect, an eating machine, laboriously consuming around one-third of a tonne of plant life a day. According to the 'giantism' theory, they spent most of their energy eating, and little remained for anything else – even reproduction.

However, 20th-century research has shown that the supposed disadvantages of giantism were often actually advantages, particularly in reptile-like creatures. Giantism not only affords protection from all

The plesiosaur, as shown in the foregound of the illustration above, has been seen as a marine cousin of the dinosaurs. In the distance, a school of air-breathing ichthyosaurs leaps from the water. Pterosaurs, flying reptiles that were also related to the dinosaurs, are seen swooping on fish above the sea.

The break-up of the continents is depicted right. In Triassic times, top, the world's land formed one super-continent (the darker areas are continental shelves, which were not covered by sea at all times), and dinosaurs roamed the world. Towards the end of the Jurassic period, centre, Laurasia and Gondwanaland had started to break apart and the Atlantic Ocean had appeared. By the time that the dinosaurs died out, bottom, the continents had largely assumed their present form.

200 million years ago

140 million years ago

65 million years ago

It has been suggested that the ammonites had formed a major part of the diet of plesiosaurs, and that the disappearance of one led to the extinction of the other. But this argument merely pushed the problem one stage back. What, then, caused the death of the ammonites?

Palaeobotanists came up with another strand to the problem. At the very end of the Mesozoic era, about 50 per cent of all plant life had also vanished. Significantly, plant life of all kinds had been worst hit in a broad band between the Urals of Asia and the Rockies of North America.

It also became apparent that no less than 70 per cent of all life on Earth – plants, insects, fish, birds and reptiles – perished in this great wave of extinctions heralding the so-called Tertiary period. What influence could have had this wide-ranging effect? Could it have been extraterrestrial in origin?

Fundamentalist Christian groups, especially in America, believe they know the reason. The extinction of the dinosaurs was, they claim, an act of God, in order to promote the development of the mammals, and especially Man.

To scientists, such theories seem absurd, explaining nothing. But we now know that, had the dinosaurs not perished, it is extremely unlikely that the mammals would ever have evolved beyond the level of the rodents, and it is therefore unlikely that human beings would ever have established a commanding position on the globe.

Some scientists held that climatic change brought dinosaurs such as the **Tyrannosaurus rex, left,** *to their end; others, that it should be put down to a meteorite or to volcanic activity.*
A sub-tropical landscape of about 120 million years ago is depicted below. The **Iguanodon,** *shown here, was herbivorous, had a beak rather than incisor teeth, and grew up to 33 feet (10 metres) long.*

possessed well-developed defences. They included *Stegosaurus*, the 'plated lizard', which appeared in the Jurassic period. It was a four-footed herbivore, which carried a powerful armament in its tail in the form of a four-pronged spike. Along its spine, it sported a double row of triangular plates, which served, probably, as a thermostat, like the 'sail' of *Pelycosaurus*.

Whether fast-moving predators or slow-moving heavily armoured herbivores, the dinosaurs included some of the most successful and best-adapted animals that the world has seen. Whatever wiped them out, it is unlikely to have been any inherent deficiency in their design.

This fact was emphasized when, with the advance of palaeontology, it was realised that the dinosaurs had not been the only lifeforms to have suffered at the end of the Mesozoic era. Mysteriously, much marine life died out at the same time. For example, the ammonites, an ancient type of mollusc, which sometimes grew to the diameter of a tractor wheel, disappeared, too.

EVIDENCE FROM THE SEANCE ROOM

Reports of the calamity that had befallen the *R101* began trickling into London and Cardington during the small hours of Sunday morning, 5 October 1930. At first, they were guarded: even as late as 5.30 a.m., Reuters in Paris would go no further than to say that 'alarm' had been caused by an 'unconfirmed report that the airship has blown up'. But this was quickly followed by the death knell: *R101* HAS EXPLODED IN FLAMES – ONLY SIX SAVED.

The parallel with the sinking of the *Titanic* was inescapable – a vessel of heroic proportions, the largest and most advanced thing of its kind, safe 'but for the millionth chance', and yet hideously fated on her very first voyage. Public grief was unrestrained on both sides of the Channel.

But even in the midst of that grief, certain starkly insistent questions cried out for answers. How had it happened? Whose fault was it? A special Court of Inquiry was set for 28 October, amid angry

*The *R101* is seen cruising over the outskirts of London, above, during her first test flight on 15 October 1929. Thousands of sightseers had crowded to see her take to the air.*

*The captain of the *R101* was Flight-Lieutenant H. Carmichael Irwin, above right. The testimony of his spirit voice may well have helped the Court of Inquiry that investigated the tragedy.*

rumours that its unspoken function would be to whitewash the Air Ministry in general, and the dead Lord Thomson in particular.

Getting at the truth about the flight, and particularly what happened during those final minutes, proved exceptionally difficult. Fate had been awkward in its selection of survivors. All the passengers were dead; so were all the officers. The only survivors were six lucky crewmen, none of whom was in the main control car (which was crushed) and none of whom was in a position therefore to know precisely how it was that the mighty *R101* kept her rendezvous with that small hillside outside Beauvais. Put together, their recollections of the final moments added little of importance to what had been seen from the ground

The Court of Inquiry, sitting under the distinguished statesman Sir John Simon, delivered its verdict in April 1931. As the immediate cause of the crash, the Court settled for a sudden loss of gas in one of the forward gasbags. This, if the airship were dangerously low to begin with (as she undoubtedly was), taken in conjunction with a sudden downdraught (which was plausible), would be bound to spell disaster, and was certainly as good a guess as any.

It may well be, however, that what the Court did not consider in evidence held greater significance than what it did. There was considerable testimony that, had it been given credence, would have shed a much clearer light on the disaster and, because of its nature, on issues of vastly greater significance. It was testimony of an extraordinary kind from an extraordinary source – the dead captain of that very airship.

On the afternoon of the Tuesday following the crash, four oddly assorted characters assembled at the National Laboratory of Psychical Research in West London. Harry Price, who had set up the laboratory a few years earlier, was a singular man – wealthy, mercurial, an amateur magician, and a passionate investigator of all sorts of psychic phenomena. And, what was of great importance in the light of what was to follow, he was a savage foe of what he saw as Spiritualist hokum, whether of the deliberately fraudulent variety (which as a magician, he was perfectly equipped to expose) or of the innocent type (in which genuine paranormal experiences, such as telepathy, were wrongly ascribed to 'voices from beyond').

One of Price's guests that day was the celebrated medium Eileen Garrett, a woman of unimpeachable integrity, whose paranormal faculties continually astonished her as much as they did those who witnessed them. Despite the fact that, in trances, she frequently delivered weirdly plausible messages seemingly from beyond the grave, she refused to classify herself as a Spiritualist. And she backed up her strange powers with a disarming eagerness to expose them to the most searching examinations that could be devised by the Harry Prices of this world.

The other principal guest was an Australian journalist, Ian Coster, whom Price had persuaded to sit in on what promised to be a potentially fascinating seance. Sir Arthur Conan Doyle had died a few months earlier. He and Price had wrangled for years

Harry Price, above, arranged the seance at which Flight-Lieutenant Irwin's spirit was first heard.

The bodies of those killed in the disaster lie in state in flag-draped coffins, in Westminster Hall, London, below. Public reaction to the crash was intense; and the French provided full military honours before the bodies were brought across the Channel by two Royal Navy destroyers. An estimated half-million Londoners watched the funeral procession; and world leaders from Hitler to the Pope sent condolences.

– Conan Doyle huffy about Price's acerbic views on Spiritualism, Price discerning a credulity verging on dottiness in the celebrated author.

Conan Doyle had vowed to prove his point in the only way possible – from the afterlife; and Price had arranged the seance with Mrs Garrett to give him his chance. Coster, a sceptic, was there as a witness. Eileen Garrett, as always, did not know the purpose of the seance, nor did she know who Coster was. As far as she knew, it was a straightforward, clinically controlled investigation into her strange psychic talents.

The three of them, along with a skilled shorthand writer, settled down in the darkened room, and Mrs Garrett quickly slipped into a trance. Soon she began to speak, not in her own voice but that of her regular 'control', known as Uvani. He had first manifested himself years before and claimed to be an ancient Oriental whose purpose in establishing himself as a link between Mrs Garrett and departed spirits was to prove the existence of life after death. Sometimes he would relay messages in his own voice, using deep, measured cadences; at other times he would stand aside, as it were, and allow the spirit to communicate directly.

THE UNINVITED SPIRIT

Today, after announcing his presence, Uvani gave Price a few snippets of information from a dead German friend (of whom, incidentally, Price was certain Eileen Garrett was perfectly ignorant), but nothing that excited him. Then, suddenly, Eileen Garrett snapped to attention, became extremely agitated, and tears started rolling down her cheeks. Uvani's voice took on a terrible broken urgency as it spelled out the name I R V I N G or I R W I N. (Flight-Lieutenant H. Carmichael Irwin had captained the *R101*.) Then Uvani's voice was replaced by another, speaking in the first person and doing so in rapid staccato bursts:

'The whole bulk of the dirigible was entirely and absolutely too much for her engine capacity. Engines too heavy. It was this that made me on five occasions have to scuttle back to safety. Useful lift too small.'

The voice kept rising and falling, hysteria barely controlled, and the speed of delivery that of a machine gun. Price and Coster were amazed as a torrent of technical jargon began to tumble from the lips of Eileen Garrett.

'Gross lift computed badly. Inform control panel. And this idea of new elevators totally mad. Elevator jammed. Oil pipe plugged. This exorbitant scheme of carbon and hydrogen is entirely and absolutely wrong.'

There was more, much more, all delivered fiercely at incredible pace. '... Never reached cruising altitude. Same in trials. Too short trials. No one knew the ship properly. Airscrews too small. Fuel injection bad and air pump failed. Cooling system bad. Bore capacity bad . . . Five occasions I have had to scuttle back, three times before starting.

'Not satisfied with feed . . . Weather bad for long flight. Fabric all water-logged and ship's nose down. Impossible to rise. Cannot trim . . . Almost scraped the roofs at Achy. At inquiry to be held later, it will be found that the superstructure of the envelope contained no resilience... The added

middle section was entirely wrong . . . too heavy. . . too much overweighted for the capacity of the engines.'

The monologue petered out at last, and Uvani came back to ring down the curtain on this portion of the astonishing seance.

Three weeks later, on the eve of the Inquiry, there began a sequel to this mystifying occurrence that was every bit as strange. Major Oliver Villiers, a much decorated survivor of aerial scraps over the Western Front, was badly shaken by the *R101* catastrophe. He had lost many friends in the crash, in particular Sir Sefton Brancker, Director of Civil Aviation and Villiers' direct superior at the Air Ministry. Indeed, he had driven Brancker to the airship on the day of departure.

Villiers was entertaining a house-guest who had an interest in Spiritualism, and late one night, when his guest and the rest of the household had gone to bed, he suddenly had an overwhelming impression that Irwin was in the room with him. (The two men had known each other well). Then he heard, mentally, Irwin crying out to him: 'For God's sake, let me talk to you. It's all so ghastly. I must speak to you. I must.' The lament was repeated, then: 'We're all bloody murderers. For God's sake help me to speak with you.' In the morning, Villiers recounted this most disturbing experience to his guest, who promptly arranged a session with the medium Eileen Garrett.

The first of several seances was held on 31 October and, like its successors, it took a significantly different form from the Price-Coster episode.

*In*Focus

THE LAST FEW MINUTES

None of the survivors seemed to know what had caused the *R101* to dive into the ground. One had just dozed off in his bunk when he was jolted awake by the chief coxswain rushing by and shouting: 'We're down lads! We're down!' Another was relaxing over a drink in the specially sealed-off smoking lounge when he felt the airship dip, dip again – and then erupt into flames. Two more, who had been in separate engine cars, were no better informed.

Engine man Joe Binks, however, had glanced out of a window only two minutes before the disaster, and was terrified to see the spire of Beauvais cathedral, 'almost close enough to touch.' He shouted to engineer Bell, another survivor, when the floor seemed to drop away, and then the ship lurched. At the same moment, a message was coming through from the main control car: SLOW. A few moments' silence followed... and then the holocaust.

The Air Ministry clamped down on any news of the crash, yet during the first seance, two days later, 'Irwin' described how he had failed to achieve cruising height: 'Fabric all waterlogged and ship's nose down... '

Three survivors, left, *stand near the wreck.*

Rather than merely listening to Irwin, Villiers was able to converse freely with him through Mrs Garrett. Moreover, while in the first seance Irwin came through alone, in later seances he was joined by several of his colleagues.

Villiers was not served by shorthand, but he claimed the gift of total recall. This, in conjunction with notes hastily scribbled during the 'conversations', convinced him that the transcripts he made were virtually dead accurate. They make absorbing reading, and a short extract from the first one will give their flavour:

Villiers: Now try to tell me all that happened on Saturday and Sunday.

Irwin: She was too heavy by several tons. Too amateurish in construction. Envelope and girders not of sufficiently sound material.

Villiers: Wait a minute, old boy. Let's start at the beginning.

Irwin: Well, during the afternoon before starting, I noticed that the gas indicator was going up and down, which showed there was a leakage or escape which I could not stop or rectify any time around the valves.

Villiers: Try to explain a bit more. I don't quite understand.

Irwin: The goldbeater skins are too porous, and not strong enough. And the constant movement of the gasbags, acting like bellows, is constantly causing internal pressure of the gas, which causes a leakage of the valves. I told the chief engineer of this. I then knew we were almost doomed. Then later on, the meteorological charts came in, and Scottie and Johnnie (fellow officers) and I had a consultation. Owing to the trouble of the gas, we knew that our only chance was to leave on the scheduled time. The weather forecast was no good. But we decided that we might cross the Channel and tie up at Le Bourget before the bad weather came. We three were absolutely scared stiff. And Scottie said to us: 'Look here, we are in for it – but for God's sake, let's smile like damned Cheshire cats as we go on board, and leave England with a clean pair of heels.'

Price and Villiers did not know one another, nor were they aware of each other's seances with Eileen Garrett. They therefore arrived independently at the conclusion that the 'evidence' they had should be placed before Sir John Simon. (Price also informed the Air Ministry). Neither the Court of Inquiry nor the Ministry was prepared to accept that these unusual happenings contributed to an understanding of the *R101* tragedy, however.

// HE [VILLIERS]... WENT UNASHAMEDLY FOR THE PREMISE THAT HE WAS COMMUNICATING WITH DEAD FRIENDS, WITHOUT A DOUBT IN HIS MIND. //

JOHN G. FULLER,

THE AIRMEN WHO WOULD NOT DIE

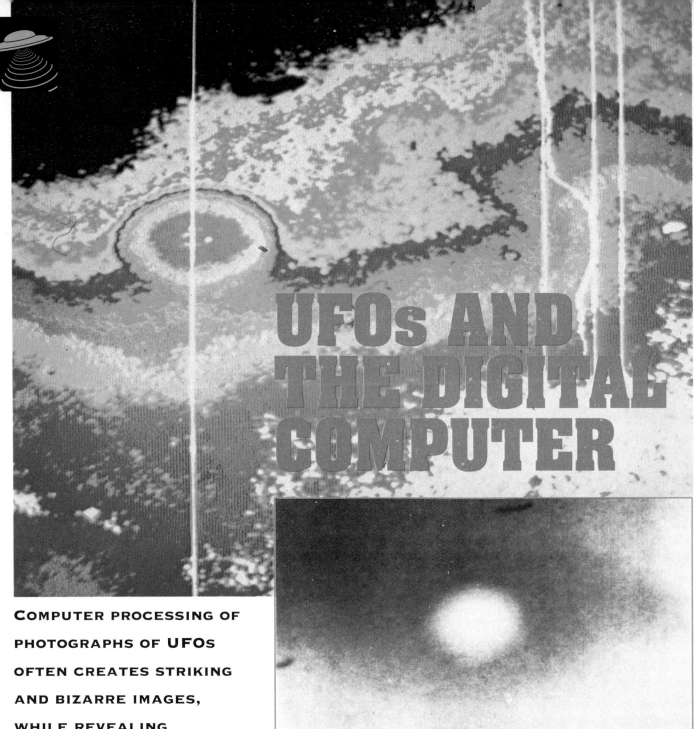

UFOs AND THE DIGITAL COMPUTER

COMPUTER PROCESSING OF PHOTOGRAPHS OF UFOS OFTEN CREATES STRIKING AND BIZARRE IMAGES, WHILE REVEALING SUBTLETIES THAT ARE DIFFICULT TO DISCERN IN THE ORIGINALS

The swirl of vivid hues, top, is a 'computer eye view' of the photograph of a glowing disc seen over Colorado, USA, inset. The colours represent different brightness levels in the original image. The lines on the coloured image are drawn by the computer as it makes a number of measurements.

Most photographs of unidentified flying objects are disappointing. They are blurred, lacking in detail and uninformative at a casual glance. Often, too, they lack the context of landscape that would enable us to judge the size and distance of the UFOs. Usually, too, any that are sharp and clear turn out to be fakes.

It is the task of the UFO photo analyst to sift through such low-grade material, to weed out the frauds and the misidentified aircraft, birds and astronomical objects, and to call attention to any residue of photographs that resist all attempts at being explained away.

Traditionally, UFO photo analysts have been limited to a few techniques of study. By measuring shadows, they may be able to show that a fake picture consists of a landscape shot combined with a picture of a model taken under totally different lighting conditions. By studying the focus on the UFO, they may also be able to show that it was much closer to the camera than the witness claimed, and was therefore much smaller than it appears. By enlarging details, the presence of any tell-tale trade mark can also be revealed. More frequently, we can identify the shot as showing some natural object – even the sceptics' favourite, the planet Venus, seen under unusual atmospheric conditions.

But, all too often, the label 'unidentified' has remained on a photograph because there was apparently too little information to resolve the question: 'What is this mysterious object in the sky?' Yet even in the fuzziest photograph, there are many subtle clues hidden away. Now, a powerful new tool, the computer, promises to disclose them.

One UFO investigation group, Ground Saucer Watch, has applied the computer to the analysis of UFO photographs on a large scale. Ground Saucer Watch was founded in Cleveland, Ohio, USA, in 1957 in order to bring a high level of technical expertise to the study of UFO reports. The group wanted, in the words of a statement made then, to 'see positive scientific action taken to end the elements of foul-up and cover-up in UFO research'. A large network of scientific and engineering consultants assists it in this task.

The computer has proved itself invaluable as an aid. It has enabled Ground Saucer Watch, for instance, in a study of 1,000 photographs that had *prima facie* plausibility, to reject all but 45 as misidentifications or hoaxes. The techniques used to sift such quantities of material are fascinating.

Pictures may be analysed with a so-called Computer Eye that uses a television-type camera to scan a picture and break it down into nearly a quarter of a million tiny 'pixels' (picture cells), in an array that comprises 512 columns and 480 rows.

Although the colours of the photographs provide important information, they do not necessarily come into such computer analyses. The scanner measures the brightness of each pixel and assigns it a rating on a 'grey scale' from 0 (completely dark) to 31 (bright white). So the whole picture is reduced to a quarter of a million numbers, which are stored in the computer's memory. They can be recalled and used to build up a black and white image, a direct copy of the original, on a television screen linked to the computer. But they can also be manipulated in countless different ways to generate new images, which may reveal the presence of unsuspected information in the original picture, or display it in unfamiliar and striking ways.

At the touch of a button, the computer operator can do most of the things that a photo technician can do only at the cost of several hours' work in his

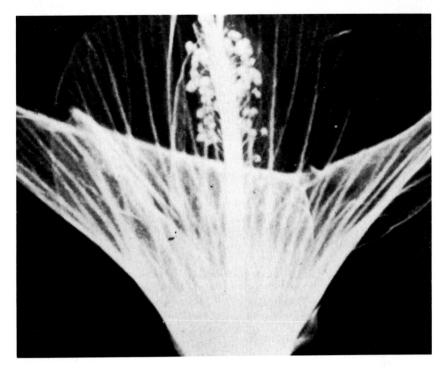

In the X-ray photograph of a flower, above, lighter areas represent thicker tissues which absorb X-rays more strongly than the thinner areas.

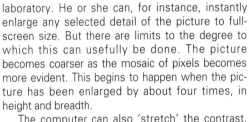

The computer processed version of the picture, below, shows edges separating light and dark areas that have been enhanced. UFO pictures can be similarly clarified.

laboratory. He or she can, for instance, instantly enlarge any selected detail of the picture to full-screen size. But there are limits to the degree to which this can usefully be done. The picture becomes coarser as the mosaic of pixels becomes more evident. This begins to happen when the picture has been enlarged by about four times, in height and breadth.

The computer can also 'stretch' the contrast, brightening the light areas and darkening the shadows, thereby emphasising the detail in a murky original. (This is what you do to you television picture when you turn up the contrast control.)

ENHANCING THE IMAGE

Measurements of distances and angles on the image become extremely easy with the aid of a computer. Crossed lines can be superimposed on the picture and moved at will, in order to identify points of interest The computer can then measure the positions of those points and instantly calculate distance and angles.

All this makes life easier for photo analysts, and enables them to plough through much more material than they could cope with otherwise. But the computer can also easily accomplish a number of feats that are impracticable, or even impossible, for the photo technician to perform.

It can, for example, enhance the edges of the features seen in a photograph. This effect is illustrated on this page with a picture that is a little more conventional than a UFO photo. The X-ray picture is of a flower and is in black and white. Each shade of grey carries information about the flower's thickness, and hence its ability to absorb X-rays at that point. In this negative image, the brighter areas correspond to thicker areas of plant tissue. There is a great deal of delicate structure to be seen in the petals and the central pistil.

But the eye's ability to distinguish shades of grey is limited. The result obtained when the edges are enhanced is also shown on this page.

Areas of uniform shade in the original are represented as a medium grey in the computer-processed picture. Wherever the original increases in lightness (from left to right), the computer draws a bright line; while where there is a transition from light to dark, it draws a dark line. The result is arresting. The flower's structure, which was lost in the subtle, veil-like X-ray image, is now laid bare in a tracery of metallic clarity.

Edge enhancement has little relevance to the indistinct forms visible in many UFO pictures. However, it is revealing when applied to UFO images showing faint detail. These are generally dark objects seen against the daytime sky. But another technique, colour coding, can extract information from the brightness pattern in the original pictures. This exploits the fact that the eye can distinguish colours far more readily than it can distinguish shades of grey.

In order to colour-code a picture, the computer is linked to a colour television set. Each pixel is then assigned a colour according to its brightness. Thus, in the X-ray picture of the flower, the darkest areas are shown as black. The darkest shades of grey (the

Like an artist with a taste for poster paints, the computer has transformed the X-ray flower picture on the opposite page into a bold pattern of colours, below. All the detail is present in the original picture but is now presented in a form more easily 'read' by the human eye and brain.

thinnest parts of the flower) are rendered as shades of violet and red. Increasingly light areas are shown as shades of yellow, green and blue. The lightest areas (the thickest parts of the plant) are rendered as white.

The resulting picture is of a gaudier flower than nature ever created, with all the details of structure leaping out at the eye. Radiographers also use this type of colour coding on X-ray pictures to improve their view of the interior of the human body.

Astronomers and space engineers apply a similar technique to the pictures they take with ground-based telescopes, and to the television images sent back from space satellites and probes. In the original pictures, brightness levels may represent the actual brightness of a planet's surface, or the temperature of a gas cloud in space, or the intensity of radio waves from distant galaxies. The patterns in the computer-generated image will represent this information in terms of colour.

AN AMBIGUOUS MESSAGE

What, then, can the procedure reveal specifically about UFOs? The brightness pattern of light and dark in the image of a UFO is a complex and ambiguous 'message', involving the shape of the object, the amount of light it may be emitting at each point, its intrinsic lightness or darkness, if it is being seen by reflected light, the effects of glare and atmospheric haze, and so on. Emphasising the pattern by means of a colour-coding technique often reveals the true nature of the object immediately. A broken, uneven density may indicate a cloud. A cylindrical shape with protuberances may appear, indicating an aircraft body and wings partly hidden by glare. Alternatively, the contours of a 'daylight disc' (meaning any daytime UFO) may be revealed, and often turn out to be suspiciously like those of a camera lens cap, a pie plate, or a hub cap.

Ground Saucer Watch has employed these techniques on thousands of photographs. Take, as an example, the two famous 'Colorado pictures', shown opposite. They indicate a single UFO, sighted and photographed at precisely 6.20 a.m. local time on 28 August 1969 by Norman Vedaa and his passenger while driving north-east on State Route 80S, approximately 70 miles (110 kilometres) from Denver, Colorado. Vedaa described the object as yellow-gold, tremendously brilliant, oval in shape, and soundless. He said: 'The object was bright, hard to look at – and appeared to hover momentarily. The object's glow... was producing a reflective light on – the clouds below... ' Two colour transparencies were taken and do indeed show a bright yellowish glow with well-defined edges, back-lighting the clouds.

The colour-coding technique was used on the Colorado photographs, and the result is reproduced on the first page of this feature. Again, lighter parts of the original are represented by white, blue and yellow, while darker parts are represented by red, violet and black.

The light vertical lines in that picture, and in the one below, shows different ways of displaying brightness information. The computer has taken a 'slice' down the picture along the left-hand line. At the right, it has plotted a graph of the brightness of the scene along that line, shown by the fluctuating

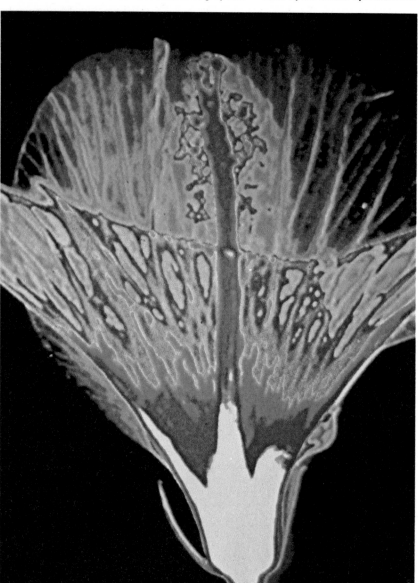

line. Thus, the 'bump' in the wavy line represents the bright centre of the object.

The computer can also speed up detailed study of light and shadow at any selected region of the picture. Ground Saucer Watch has a 'library' of data on the proportion of light that is reflected by each of a large range of materials. In some photographs of UFOS seen by reflected daylight, everyday objects, such as trees or houses, are visible, and the UFO image can be compared with them. This may enable the analyst to make a tentative judgement about the composition of the UFO.

Sometimes, the image of a UFO in the sky is beautifully sharp, while all ground features more than 50 feet (15 metres) away are slightly out of focus. This shows that the object is close to the camera – and so must be a fake (or have been piloted by very little green men).

In its study of the Vedaa pictures, Ground Saucer Watch has been able to rule out more and more explanations that seek to reduce the sightings to causes that are well-known and understood. This was no weather balloon, flock of birds or daylight meteor – the brightness distribution was that of a disc. It was not an aircraft hidden in the glare of reflected sunlight – it was too bright for that, and not a trace of tail or wings could be found. Lens flares, reflections from clouds, mirages and other atmospheric effects are all ruled out: the Sun is in the wrong position for them.

In the near future, photo analysis is likely to be carried out by even more sophisticated computers, working with scanners that can break down the original image into yet finer detail. Soon, it will become virtually impossible to fake a UFO photograph. Then, perhaps, the matter will be solved.

American motorist, Norman Vedaa, saw a brilliant disc and stopped his car to photograph it. It is visible near the upper centre of the picture, top. The second picture, above, was taken within a few seconds and was the original of the processed UFO images on the first page of this article. The disc flew off at high speed.

Measurements of image brightness can be made by computer, as shown right. The measurements are made along the left-hand line. The fluctuating line curves to the right where the photograph is brightest. This curve helped to prove the disc was not a lens flare, weather balloon or aircraft.

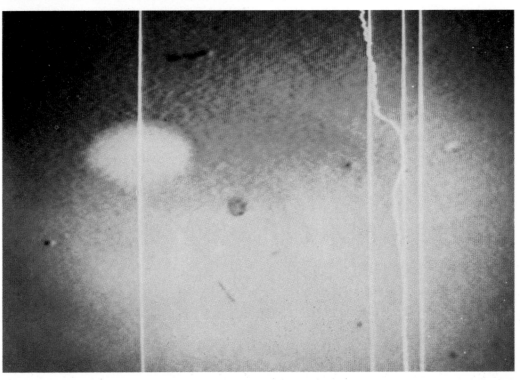

THE MAKING OF A MIRAGE

GIGANTIC SHADOWY FIGURES THAT HAUNT MOUNTAIN RANGES; CITIES AND ARMIES THAT APPEAR IN THE SKIES – SOME ARE AT TIMES PERFECTLY NATURAL PHENOMENA THAT HAVE A SCIENTIFIC EXPLANATION, BUT OTHERS ARE NOT

A giant, wraith-like figure, above, stalks the mountainside, his head surrounded by a multicoloured halo. Known as the Brocken spectre, this terrifying phenomenon is merely the shadow of a man that is cast on to thick cloud.

Desert mirages of water and hills, such as the one in Algeria, below, have often been mistaken for the real objects.

A climber is feeling his way along a precipice high on the Brocken, a 3,747-foot (1,142-metre) peak in the Harz Mountains of Germany, treacherous to all but the most experienced mountaineers. As he moves cautiously from foothold to precarious foothold, he suddenly sees an immense human figure loom out of the mist towards him. In his fright, the climber loses his footing and falls to his death.

It is the classic story of the Brocken spectre. This particular version may be no more than folklore, but it is undoubtedly true that such spectres of the mind exist – and not only on the Brocken. A vivid example of the same phenomenon was reported to *Nature* magazine in 1880. It occurred on Clifton Down, near the Avon gorge, in south-west England. The time was around 10.30 a.m., and the gorge was filled with mist. The witness was standing on the top of nearby Observatory Hill, when he was startled to observe 'a dim gigantic figure apparently standing out through the mist upon one of the lower slopes of Clifton Down'. He soon realised, however, that the figure was not as solid as it seemed. 'A moment's glance sufficed to show me that it was my own shadow on the mist; and as I waved my arms about, the gaunt spectre followed every movement.'

The physical explanation of the Brocken spectre given by the anonymous observer is correct. Such spectres can be seen anywhere that shadows are cast on dense mist and water droplets. While this may be understandable, the suddenness with which these natural phenomena occur can make them startling and even frightening.

The observer on Clifton Down also happened to note a curious feature of the phenomenon. 'A gentleman who stood beside me likewise saw his spectre, but not mine, as we ascertained by the movements executed; nor could I see his, unless we stood so close together that the spectres seemed combined into one.'

But it is not only human figures that cast these strange and dramatic shadows. Adam's Peak, a 7,360-foot (2,243-metre) mountain in Sri Lanka, regularly produces its own spectre. The mountain stands isolated, rising around 1,000 feet (305 metres) above the ridge of which it is a part. The phenomenon, for which the mountain is famous, occurs just after sunrise. To an observer standing on the mountain, the shadow of the peak appears to rise in front of the observer, while the summit is surrounded by a rainbow-hued halo and two dark

streamers leading off into the sky. Suddenly, the shadow either disappears or falls down to the ground.

This sunrise spectre mystified scientists for many years. It was assumed that it must be some kind of mirage, but these are caused by layers of hot and cold air, superimposed on each other, and scientists could not measure any atmospheric temperature differences in this phenomenon. Then, in 1886, a scientist named Ralph Abercromby made the brave decision to spend the night on Adam's Peak in order to see what transpired at sunrise. He and his companions were evidently in low spirits by the time dawn came. According to his journal:

'The morning broke in a very unpromising manner. Heavy clouds lay all about, lightning flickered over a dark bank to the right of the rising Sun, and at frequent intervals masses of light vapour blew up from the valley and enveloped the summit in their mist.'

Then, at around 6.30 a.m., the Sun appeared briefly from behind clouds, and the observers saw the weird shadow of the mountain. It disappeared and then appeared again – and 'seemed to rise up and stand in front of us in the air, with rainbow and spectral arms, and then to fall down suddenly to the earth'. This was the feature of the phenomenon

that had mystified scientists for so long. From his vantage point, however, Abercromby could see what had eluded observers on the ground. 'As a mass of vapour drove across the shadow, the condensed particles caught the shadow... As the vapour blew past, the shadow fell to its natural level – the surface of the Earth.' Abercromby added that, as a good scientist, he had conducted a number of temperature measurements, and the results were enough to confirm his belief that the phenomenon could not have been due to a mirage.

A mirage, however, *is* the explanation for another extraordinary natural oddity – the *Fata Morgana* (Italian for 'Fairy Morgan'). This often impressive phenomenon takes its name from Morgan le Fay, King Arthur's enchantress sister, who could make cities or ports appear anywhere on the open seas – a talent that she apparently found useful when luring sailors to a watery death. Strictly speaking, the *Fata Morgana* is the name of one particular manifestation of this phenomenon – a magnificent city that appears over the Strait of Messina, between Italy and the island of Sicily. As a Dominican friar, Antonio Minasi, described it, in 1773:

It was at the Strait of Messina – the stretch of water that runs between Sicily and mainland Italy, below – that a strange phenomenon was first recorded. On certain calm and sunny days, the image of a magnificent city, complete with palaces and castles, men and animals, appears in the sky above the Strait. The phenomenon is named Fata Morgana *after Morgan le Fay,* left, *the enchantress sister of King Arthur of Britain. Local legend has it that the image is a reflection of her underwater city off the coast at Messina.*

'When the rising sun shines from that point whence its incident ray forms an angle of about 45 degrees on the sea of Reggio [the Strait of Messina], and the bright surface of the water is not disturbed either by the wind or the current, the spectator . . . with his back to the sun and his face to the sea – on a sudden he sees appear in the water . . . various multiplied objects, such as numberless series of pilasters, arches, castles well delineated, regular columns, lofty towers, superb palaces with balconies and windows, extended alleys of trees, delightful plains with herds and

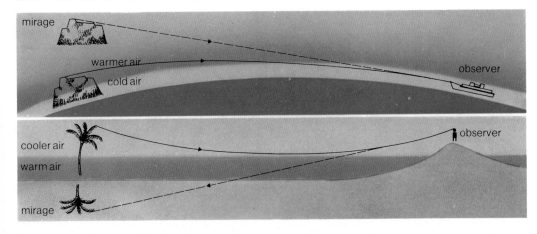

The diagrams, left, *show how mirages are formed. Differences in temperature between layers of air cause differences in density, and these in turn cause light rays to travel in curved paths. The light rays reach the eye as if they have travelled in straight lines – and so the mirage appears above or below the true image.*

flocks, armies of men on foot and horseback, and many other strange figures, all in their natural colours and proper action . . . if the air be slightly hazy and opaque . . . then the objects will appear . . . vividly coloured or fringed with red, green, blue and the other prismatic colours.'

REFRACTED LIGHT

Antonio Minasi believed that the image was a direct reflection of the mainland coast in the water of the Strait of Messina. It appeared where it did, he explained, because the strong currents that exist in the Strait caused the surface of the water to tilt slightly. Today, however, the phenomenon of the mirage is much better understood: differences in temperature can cause patches of air to act in much the same way as lenses, refracting light rays in unpredictable directions. This causes magnified images to appear with great clarity, even at a con- siderable distance from the original object. The commonest example is the mirage of the sky seen in the hot air above a hot road, which gives the impression of shimmering water. At sea, mirages of ships or land, seen while either is still over the hori- zon, are familiar to sailors the world over.

The inverted mirage, above, was allegedly seen over Paris towards the end of the 19th century. Mirages of such extent and accuracy are rare.

In a French engraving from the 16th century, left, an army advances through the sky. Such scenes have been reported as occurring long after the events they depict. Perhaps, therefore, they are mirages in time.

The photograph below, taken in 1887, allegedly shows a mirage of the city of Bristol, England, that appeared in the sky over Alaska, at a distance of 6,000 miles (9,500 kilometres).

" WITH UNCANNY VOLITION, THE SHIP SAILED STEADILY ON... BENT ON SELF-DESTRUCTION SOMEWHERE ON THE SANDS OF STRANDFONTEIN. JUST AS THE EXCITEMENT REACHED ITS CLIMAX, HOWEVER, THE MYSTERY SHIP VANISHED INTO THIN AIR AS STRANGELY AS IT HAD COME. "

THE BRITISH SOUTH AFRICA ANNUAL, 1939

PERSPECTIVES

COASTING UPHILL

Gravity – that is, the force that pulls objects towards Earth – is still only imperfectly understood. Scientists explain it as a force of attraction between masses, but one that varies according to the size of the masses and the distance between them. Mathematically formulated, this law has become the basis of a complex gravitational theory that allows the effects of gravity to be calculated with minute accuracy. The nature of the force, however – the way in which it is transmitted – is still a mystery.

It is agreed among scientists that the force of gravity is not constant on the Earth's surface; indeed, it varies according to the alignments of the heavenly bodies. Alignments of the Sun and Moon, for example, are responsible for spring and neap tides. There also appear to be certain purely local variations that are not connected with the movements of the planets: the lines of prehistoric stones at Carnac in Brittany, France, for instance, mark subtle changes in the magnitude of the gravitational force.

These subtle changes in gravity are discernible only by sensitive instruments . But, occasionally, gravitational anomalies can cause dramatic effects.

The Electric Brae, or Croy Brae, *left,* is a gentle slope overlooking the south side of Culzean Bay near Ayr in the Strathclyde region of Scotland. Motorists driving down it find that, if they park in a layby, and release the handbrake, the car appears to run backwards, uphill, even though this would seem to be an impossibility.

Another example occurs in Belo Horizonte in Brazil. Peanuts Street is a narrow and unpretentious suburban street that runs slightly uphill for around a quarter of a mile (350 metres). But switch off your engine and release your handbrake, and your car will move, slowly but steadily, uphill.

In both cases, the reason for this strange phenomenon is thought to have something to do with magnetic forces induced by surrounding rocks that are rich in iron. But nobody really knows.

In some parts of the world, such mirages are commonplace. For example, the mirage of Tallinn in Estonia, a former Soviet republic, is regularly seen in Helsinki in Finland, 50 miles (80 kilometres) to the north, across the Gulf of Finland. It is said to be so distinct that individual buildings can be recognised. The sky above Alaska in North America is also said to be strangely receptive to impressions of the city of Bristol, 6,000 miles (9,500 kilometres) away in England.

VISION OF BRISTOL

In his book *New Lands*, published in the 1920, Charles Fort mentions the tradition that Bristol is visible over Alaska between 21 June and 10 July every year. He notes that, remarkably, the image is said to have been seen regularly by the Alaskan Indians long before Europeans settled there and identified the city of the mirage. In 1887, a certain Mr Willoughby took a photograph of the mirage, in which several of the buildings of Bristol could be clearly recognised. But many people even protested that the likeness was so good that the photograph had to be of Bristol itself.

But what of cases involving action and movement? The following extraordinary example was reported in the German newspaper *Allgemeine Zeitung* of 13 February 1854. Three weeks earlier, on 22 January 1854, an extraordinary phenomenon had been witnessed by the inhabitants of the village of Büderich, in north-west Germany.

'Shortly before sunset, an army, of boundless extent, and consisting of infantry-cavalry, and an enormous number of wagons, was observed to proceed across the country in marching order. So distinctly seen were all these appearances that even the flashing of the firelocks, and the colour of the cavalry uniform, which was white, could be distinguished. This whole array advanced in the direction of the wood of Schafhauser, and as the infantry neared the thicket, and the cavalry drew near, they were hid all at once, with the trees, in a thick smoke. Two houses, also, in flames, were seen with the same distinctness. At sunset, the whole phenomenon vanished.'

Such armies in the sky have been reported with reasonable regularity, and are often believed to be re-enactments of battles that have taken place in the past. The repeat performances, on four successive Saturday and Sunday nights in 1642, of the English Civil War battle of Edgehill is a particularly well-known example. It seems likely, however, that the Büderich case was a mirage of military manoeuvres that were taking place elsewhere.

In cases such as these, the normal and the paranormal come very close. Science can certainly explain some – but not all – of these bizarre phenomena, and then only partially.

CLAIRVOYANT DISCOVERIES

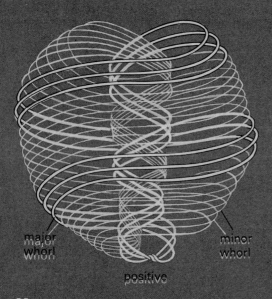

major
whorl

minor
whorl

positive

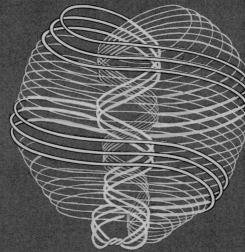

negative

The two kinds of ultimate physical atoms, seen clairvoyantly by Annie Besant and C.W. Leadbeater, are shown left. The atoms, which spun incessantly, consisted of currents of energy forming spiral whorls. Colours constantly flashed out, changing according to which spiral was most active.

MODERN PHYSICISTS ARE PROBING EVER DEEPER INTO THE STRUCTURE OF MATTER, USING COSTLY AS WELL AS HIGHLY SOPHISTICATED TECHNOLOGY. HOWEVER, SOME OF THEIR DISCOVERIES MAY HAVE BEEN MADE BEFORE — BY MEANS OF EXTRA-SENSORY PERCEPTION

Annie Besant and Charles Leadbeater, below, are seen working together. Their observations, when viewing matter on the small scale, were in conflict with the science of their time.

and Leadbeater saw, by occult means, the 'quarks' that physicists now postulate as the building blocks of matter.

The power of viewing the very small is one of the *siddhis*, (or psychic faculties) that, according to Eastern tradition, can be cultivated by yoga meditation. In the ancient yoga *sutras*, the semi-legendary sage Patanjali lists these: one is the power to gain 'knowledge of the small, the hidden, or the distant by directing the light of a superphysical faculty'.

T wo figures who dominated the Theosophical Society at the end of the 19th century – Annie Besant and Charles W. Leadbeater – began, in 1895, a series of researches that was to last nearly 40 years. They were studying the ultimate structure of matter, using methods that orthodox science did not countenance – attempting to view atoms by means of extra-sensory perception. However, the vast amounts of information they produced seemed to bear no relation to the findings of chemists and physicists during those four decades. Only a century later were resemblances noticed between their descriptions and the modern theory of the structure of fundamental particles. Indeed, it now seems possible that Besant

WINDOWS ON THE WHORLS

The diagrams of *micro-psi* atoms drawn from the descriptions provided by the two Theosophists – Annie Besant and Charles Leadbeater – give only a faint impression of the fantastic spectacles they witnessed. But what they saw was also confirmed by later clairvoyants using *micro-psi* (the faculty of viewing the very small) in the late 1950s. Initially, a mist or haze of light would appear when they observed matter on the microscopic scale. With greater magnification, the mist would then become resolved into myriad points of light, they said. These were viewed by them as scintillating and moving chaotically. Some atoms moved in regular orbits, forming the seven minor and three major whorls of the atoms. Some cascaded, rather like showers of meteors. But the motion of the atoms was said to be confined to well-defined volumes of space, in any one of seven different geometric forms. Each 'ultimate physical atom' was enclosed in a 'bubble', as if some sort of transparent membrane was surrounding it. The Theosophists even spoke of space itself being pushed back by the dynamic activity of the matter in the atom. This accorded with the complex theories of Theosophy, which hold that what we normally regard as a vacuum is only one of the seven states of matter.

This ability to acquire knowledge of the small or microscopic is sometimes termed *micro-psi*; and Besant and Leadbeater claimed to have gained their *micro-psi* abilities under the tutelage of their Indian gurus.

To acquire knowledge paranormally that is confirmed by conventional science only years later is perhaps the most convincing type of ESP. In such cases, there is no possibility that the psychic has access to established sources of information. And whether or not the ESP was exercised under controlled laboratory conditions, it is impossible, in principle, to have gained such information either by fraud or by means of the five senses.

The atom of hydrogen, **below left,** *according to Besant and Leadbeater, was a transparent egg-shaped body containing smaller globes arranged in two interlinked triangles. Each one of the globes contained three of the 'ultimate physical atoms'.*

The shapes, **below right,** *are the seven fundamental forms of the* **micro-psi** *atoms, discovered by the Theosophists.*

In 1895, Annie Besant and Charles Leadbeater went so far as to publish pictures of what they claimed were hydrogen, nitrogen and oxygen atoms present in the air. According to a description, given in their book *Occult Chemistry*, a hydrogen atom was:

'Seen to consist of six small bodies, contained in an egg-like form... It rotated with great rapidity on its own axis, vibrating at the same time, the internal bodies performing similar gyrations. The whole atom spins and quivers and has to be steadied before exact observation is possible. The six little bodies are arranged in two sets of three, forming two triangles that are not interchangeable.'

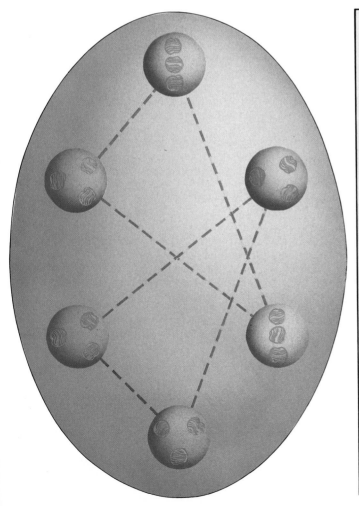

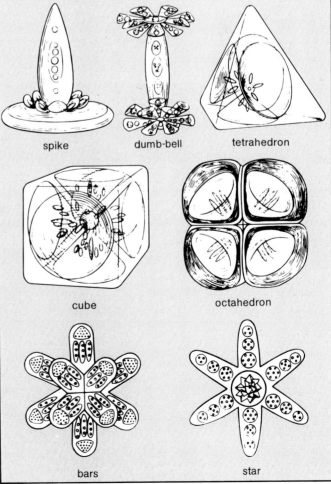

spike

dumb-bell

tetrahedron

cube

octahedron

bars

star

But these 'six little bodies' were not the most basic units of matter. The psychics could magnify the images of them and found that each was composed of a globe enclosing three 'points of light'. When these, in turn, were highly magnified, they appeared as particles of definite size. Besant and Leadbeater called them 'ultimate physical atoms'.

Each of these 'ultimate' particles was seen to be made up of 10 convoluted spiral curves, or whorls, three of which (known as the 'major' whorls) appeared thicker or brighter than the other seven ('minor') whorls. The overall form of the whorls was that of a heart, with one end slightly concave and the other end pointed.

ATOMIC STRUCTURE

The Theosophists' description of matter differed greatly from the contemporary scientific notions of the atom. Two centuries earlier, Sir Isaac Newton (1642-1726), the great English physicist, had conjectured that atoms were 'solid, massy, impenetrable'. By 1895, however, it was suspected that atoms did have a structure and that they were composed of smaller electrically charged particles. One of these, it was believed, was an electron, a negatively charged particle much lighter than an atom. Electric currents were thought to consist of electrons in motion. Then, in 1897, the electron's existence was demonstrated by the English physicist J. J. Thomson. Various models of the structure of the atom were then proposed. But the theory that finally won acceptance, as the result of the experimental and theoretical analyses of the physicists H. Geiger, E. Marsden and Lord Rutherford, was that of the 'nuclear' atom. It showed that the electrons in an atom orbit a tiny nucleus in which all the atom's positive charge and most of its mass are concentrated. When this was first demonstrated, from 1909 onwards, the electrons were supposed to move in well-defined orbits, rather like those of the planets. They were thought to whirl around the nucleus millions of times per second, in a volume with a ten-millionth of the breadth of a pinhead. Then, in the 1920s, with the advent of quantum mechanics (the theory of atomic structure), the electrons and their orbits came to be regarded as 'fuzzy' and ill-defined.

As each scientific picture of the atom was discarded and replaced by the next, Besant and Leadbeater continued to produce remarkably consistent descriptions of their *micro-psi* atoms, which at no time bore any resemblance to the atoms of the orthodox scientists.

Nevertheless, the two Theosophists observed, in 1908, that in certain elements – for example, the inert gases neon, argon, krypton and xenon and the metal platinum – the atoms were not all identical. Neon, for example, had a variant they called *meta-neon*, which had a different atomic weight. This anticipated, by almost six years, the scientific realisation that chemically indistinguishable variants of an element could exist, having atoms of different weights. These variants in turn came to be called 'isotopes'.

One of the most important tools of orthodox chemistry is the periodic table. This is a classification of the elements in terms of their chemical

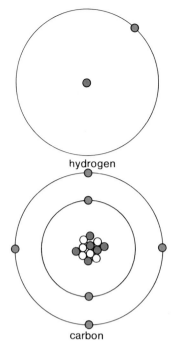

hydrogen

carbon

In conventional science, the nucleus of the hydrogen atom, top, comprises a single positively charged proton. The nuclei of heavier atoms, such as carbon, above, consist of protons and neutral particles called neutrons. Negatively charged electrons orbit the nucleus.

Isotopes of an element such as neon, below, have equal numbers of protons but different numbers of neutrons.

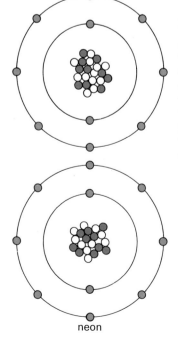

neon

properties and their atomic weights. The atomic weights of the elements increase as you read across the table from left to right, and down it, from top to bottom. Chemical properties change systematically along each row of the table and down each column. Besant and Leadbeater found that the complex shape of the *micro-psi* atom corresponded to the column of the periodic table in which that element lay.

When the psychics began their research, between 60 and 70 elements were known (of the 90 or so that occur in nature) and there were many gaps in the periodic table. Besant and Leadbeater described a number of types of *micro-psi* atom that corresponded, they believed, to gaps in the table. The existence of these elements, and many of their properties, could have been predicted by science, but had not yet been observed.

The atoms that the two psychics described were sometimes seen to be combined into larger units, just as the corresponding chemical atoms combined into larger groupings, called molecules. The *micro-psi* atoms were combined in the same number as the atoms known to science. But, in total violation of all that was known to chemistry, *micro-psi* atoms were observed to be broken up and their constituent particles mixed with those of other atoms. Sceptics felt that this discredited Besant and Leadbeater's claims, since chemical atoms do not split up and mix with each other wholesale when they combine, though they share or transfer some outer electrons.

Other problems emerged. For example, Leadbeater described the *micro-psi* molecule of the compound benzene as being octahedral – that is, as having the overall shape of an eight-faced solid. But chemists already knew that the chemical molecule of benzene was flat and hexagonal. And the psychics described *micro-psi* atoms of several supposed elements for which there was no room whatever in the periodic table

Such problems as these add up to overwhelming evidence against the two Theosophists' interpretation of the *micro-psi* atoms as being the atoms studied by the chemist. Neither could they have been the nuclei of atoms, which do not split up in chemical reactions. What, then, were they? If they were merely hallucinations, why should the forms described by Besant and Leadbeater have correlated with the position of the element in the periodic table? How could the two psychics have 'guessed' that some atoms exist in different forms five years before scientists suspected the existence of isotopes? These aspects of their work remain mysterious even today.

 TO ACQUIRE KNOWLEDGE PARANORMALLY THAT IS CONFIRMED BY CONVENTIONAL SCIENCE ONLY YEARS LATER IS PERHAPS THE MOST CONVINCING TYPE OF ESP. **//**

IF SPECTRAL FIGURES APPEAR ON A PHOTOGRAPH WHEN NOTHING OF THE KIND WAS VISIBLE AT THE TIME THEY WERE TAKEN, PSYCHIC INVESTIGATION IS CLEARLY CALLED FOR. WHO ARE THESE GHOSTLY 'EXTRAS'?

The ease with which 'extras' may be imposed upon photographs has led most people to believe that many, if not all spirit photographs are in some way fraudulent. However, while the greater number of so-called psychic pictures are indeed intended to amuse or defraud, a few have been made in circumstances that place them on a level beyond ordinary understanding.

The most extraordinary spirit photographs of all have been made during seances, often under rigid test conditions; but a few interesting ones have also been made unexpectedly, and by amateurs. Someone takes a snapshot of a friend, of an interior, or of a pet, and afterwards finds, to his astonishment, the image of a face or figure – sometimes recognisably that of a deceased relative or friend. This occurs rarely, but it does happen; and many examples with written accounts have been preserved by archivists and librarians interested in

In the spirit photograph, below, taken by a certain Mrs Wickstead in 1928, an embracing couple – not seen by the photographer at the time – appear in the churchyard. The 'spirits' were not identified; and the Society for Psychical Research, who investigated the matter, could not explain them.

psychic phenomena. The earliest preserved examples of spirit photographs were of this order: they were taken by amateur photographers who had no specialist interest in psychic effects and who were disappointed at their portraits and landscapes being spoiled by the mysterious 'extras'.

It is generally accepted that spirit photography as such began in Boston, Massachusetts, USA, on 5 October 1861, when William Mumler accidentally produced his first spirit picture. But this date may not be entirely accurate. For, according to an early pioneer of Spiritualism in Boston, Dr H.F. Gardner, a few portraits exhibiting a second figure that could not be accounted for had been made previously at nearby Roxbury. The Roxbury photographer was an orthodox Christian who, after hearing about Mumler's pictures, refused to print any negatives containing 'spirits' on the grounds that, if these pictures had anything to do with Spiritualism, they were the work of the Devil.

The fact is that, well over a century later, we still do not know what causes 'spirits' to appear on prints. The majority of psychical researchers involved with spirit photography claim it occurs by the direct intervention of the spirits themselves. If one accepts such a theory, the phenomena may be viewed not so much as 'spirit photography', as 'photography by spirits'.

UNEXPECTED DEVELOPMENTS

The famous English journalist W.T. Stead was an early champion of spirit photography, and many portraits of him show images of recognised 'extras' alongside. After he died in the *Titanic* disaster in April 1912, he continued to converse from the spirit world with his daughter, Estelle, as she reported. And then the matter went further, for his image began to appear as an 'extra' alongside her in pictures. When Estelle asked him to say something about the actual production of such images, Stead insisted that the spirits were themselves involved with them – in order to convince us of the reality of life after death.

The spirit photographs made by professionals and participants in seances are fascinating enough. But it is the innocence and the element of the unexpected that permeate the accidental spirit photographs of amateurs that intrigue the investigator of the genre most.

One such example is a photograph taken in 1964 inside the English church of St Mary the Virgin, in Woodford, Northamptonshire. It was taken by 16-year-old Gordon Carroll who, with a friend, had been on a cycling tour. They had decided to visit the church because of its historic value – it is mentioned in the *Domesday Book*. After checking that the church was empty, Gordon took two pictures of the interior – one looking towards the altar, and another photograph of the rear of the interior.

The spirit of William T. Stead, who had died in the Titanic *disaster, appears, above, in a photograph of his living daughter Estelle. When she asked him how psychic photography came about, he replied that the spirits themselves were involved in producing the unexpected images.*

Arrows, above right, point to the ghostly heads of two drowned sailors, photographed by a passenger on the vessel, Watertown. *The spectres had been seen in the waves for several days after the drowning, and the photographer deliberately took the picture to record this psychic phenomenon.*

*In*Focus

NEGATIVE FINDINGS

The faking of spirit photographs seems to have begun almost as soon as the genuine product appeared in the mid-19th century. One of the most common faking techniques was the double exposure – not a problem with the large plates then in use. But a more cunning method involved the painting of a background screen with a special chemical, invisible to ordinary sight, which would show up on photographic film. This screen was pre-painted and placed behind the sitter. Other complex techniques were also devised by unscrupulous photographers.

The case now known as the 'Moss photographic fiasco' is among the most interesting of the proven frauds. During the early 1920s, G.H. Moss was employed as a chauffeur by a man who was interested in the paranormal. Moss was an amateur photographer, and one day brought a print with a ghostly 'extra' to his employer. The employer showed interest and, after some experiments on his own, introduced Moss to the British College of Psychic Science. Around 1924, Moss was given a year's contract to work under test conditions at the college, on a fixed salary. His work there was impressive and well-received – until, that is, he was exposed as a fraud.

Moss produced a number of spirit images that were recognised as the likenesses of dead relatives and friends by sitters. In one of these, shown *below,* the sitter was a trance medium. She recognised the 'extra' as her dead sister. A cut-out photograph of that sister was mounted alongside the 'extra' to illustrate the resemblance. In another, *right,* the image was recognised by a person observing the photographic session, though it was not clear whether the recognised individual was dead or alive.

A third example of Moss's work, *far right,* was made in a seance with the well-known medium Mrs Osborne Leonard on 5 January 1925. The sitter was informed by 'a voice from beyond' that he would be sitting for a photograph in eight days. The invisible speaker promised that she would reveal herself then.

After the pictures had been processed, the young photographer filed them away and only took them out a year later in preparation for a Christmas slide show. On examining the pictures, he and his friend saw that one of them featured a ghostly figure, apparently kneeling in front of the altar: its head was not visible since it was bowed down as if in prayer. The figure appeared to be wearing a monk's robes. Both Gordon and his friend at the time were convinced there had been no one at the altar when the photograph was taken, nor – according to a film processing expert – had any fraud been involved.

SPECTRAL PORTRAITS

Only rarely do amateur photographers take pictures in the knowledge that they are recording psychic phenomena. One of the few exceptions is the case of the *Watertown* pictures, which contain images of drowned seamen. These were deliberately taken by one of the passengers on board a vessel, the *Watertown*, from which two seamen had been swept overboard and drowned during the course of the journey. For several days afterwards, passengers and crew alike insisted that the seamen's spectral heads could be seen in the waves and spray.

Much more typical is the account of the curious extras on a snapshot taken by a certain Mrs Wickstead in 1928. The snapshot – now quite faded but never of first-rate quality – was one of two taken at the church in the village of Hollybush, not far from Hereford. Mrs Wickstead was on a car tour with friends and had stopped to see the church. She decided to take a photograph of her friend, Mrs Laurie, who in the event can barely be seen in the photograph. After the picture had been taken, Mrs Laurie drew Mrs Wickstead's attention to the grave of a soldier who had died on active service. Alongside this grave was another of a girl who had died shortly afterwards.

'I wonder if they were lovers?' Mrs Laurie had remarked to her companion.

In a letter to Sir Oliver Lodge, later President of the Society for Psychical Research (SPR), Mrs Wickstead wrote that Mrs Laurie had seemed impressed by the two graves and had made a point of showing them to her husband. 'We thought no more about it until about six weeks later when the film was developed and came out as you see, with these two figures on the path in the shadow of the yew tree,' Mrs Wickstead wrote. The two figures were in an embrace. The picture was investigated by the SPR, but the mystery of the 'extras' was never solved.

There have also been cases of sensitives both seeing and photographing spirits that have remained invisible to others present – but these are

That sitting, which had already been arranged without Mrs Leonard's knowledge, did indeed produce an 'extra' – and some of the sitter's friends insisted that the image bore a strong likeness to his recently deceased wife. A portrait of her was then pasted alongside so that a comparison could be made.

Moss was finally unmasked by the astute F. Barlow, at that time the Honorary Secretary for the now defunct Society for the Study of Supernormal Pictures. While Barlow was examining a group of Moss's negatives containing 'extras', he noticed a peculiar roughness on the edges of certain plates.

Closer examination showed that each negative bearing a spirit image had one edge that was filed. Detailed examination of the plate wrappings revealed that they had been skilfully opened by steaming and subsequently resealed.

Moss vehemently denied fraud and even signed a statement declaring his innocence. However, when faced with the filed plates, he made a confession. He had secretly opened certain plates and superimposed an image on them, marking them for later use by filing the edges.

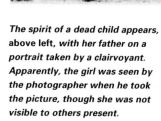

rare. One of the most famous examples has become known as the 'Weston' photograph.

The Reverend Charles Tweedale and his family lived in Weston vicarage, a much haunted house in the town of Otley in West Yorkshire. While having lunch on 20 December 1915, Mrs Margaret Tweedale saw the apparition of a bearded man to the left of her son. The others around the table could see nothing. However, Margaret's husband immediately fetched the camera and took a picture of the area indicated by his wife. When the negative was developed, a portrait of the apparition appeared on the print.

SPIRITUAL INSTRUCTION

An extraordinary picture session that took place in Belgium seems to support the belief that the spirits intervene directly in psychic photography. In this instance, a spirit actually instructed an amateur photographer in the most precise manner as to how and when to take a picture in which the spirit would manifest itself. The picture was taken by Emile le Roux in 1909 and is one of the very few stereoscopic spirit photographs.

The instructions apparently came from a spirit who claimed to be the uncle of le Roux's wife. The spirit made contact through her while she was practising automatic writing in le Roux's presence. Through the automatic script, the 'uncle' said that he could be photographed at a later point in the day and gave instructions as to the time and necessary exposure. Le Roux, a keen amateur photographer, considered the exposure to be far too long; but he followed instructions and took the picture with his stereoscopic camera at the time indicated. The image of the deceased uncle not only appeared, but was quite recognisable. In its day, the plate became very famous – but time after time, le Roux had to defend himself against the usual charges of fraud.

The spirit of a dead child appears, above left, with her father on a portrait taken by a clairvoyant. Apparently, the girl was seen by the photographer when he took the picture, though she was not visible to others present.

The stereoscopic picture, above, shows Madame le Roux practising automatic writing, while the spirit image of her uncle appears beside her face, to the left. Through the writing, the spirit gave the photographer instructions on how the picture shoud be taken.

The unidentified 'extra' on the print, left, was photographed in Gloucester Cathedral around 1910.

The picture of a bottle, above right, was allegedly made by the direct transfer of a thought on to a photographic plate in France in 1896, by a certain Commandant Darget.

The ghost of a woman, dead a week, is seen, right, in a picture taken by her daughter. She is apparently sitting in the back seat. Experts said the photograph had not been tampered with.

His own simple words echo the recurrent story of the amateur caught up in a mysterious process:

'In reality, this photograph was made under the most simple circumstances, and I would say that except for the strangeness of the spirit head, there were so few difficulties both before and after its execution that, in spite of the scepticism which arose within me and which has not yet quite vanished, I am forced to admit that in order to explain this negative, it is necessary to look in another direction than fraud or the double exposure of the plate.'

The subject of spirit photography greatly excited psychical investigators in the 1870s and 1880s, but no organised and sustained study seems to have been made. There are many references to the phenomenon in the *British Journal of Photography*, and a number of articles in the *Journal* of the SPR. But the issue was clouded by the controversy over Spiritualism, and no undistorted and full treatment of psychic photography itself has come down to us.

In any event, psychic photography did not end with the unexplained appearance of spirit forms on prints. One new form that has emerged in recent times is the manifestation of UFOs. What is more, since the main question is whether images on film can be produced without optical processes, thoughtography is of relevance too.

▮▮ MOST PSYCHICAL RESEARCHERS INVOLVED WITH SPIRIT PHOTOGRAPHY CLAIM IT OCCURS THROUGH DIRECT SPIRIT INTERVENTION. ▮▮

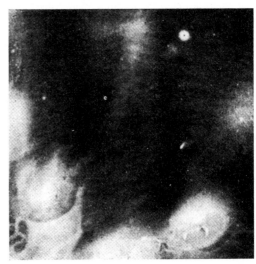

The term 'thoughtography' first came into use in Japan in 1910, following a series of tests by Tomokichi Fukurai of a clairvoyant who accidentally imprinted a calligraphic character on a photographic plate by psychic means. Later, the sensitive found he was able to do this by concentrated effort. Fukurai's work was published in English 20 years later, and experiments similar to his were then undertaken in Europe and the United States. But it was not until 1962 that interest in thoughtography was activated by Pauline Oehler, of the Illinois Society for Psychic Research, through her work with the American psychic Ted Serios.

Serios was much investigated under strictly controlled conditions, particularly by Dr Jule Eisenbud, a psychical researcher working mainly in Denver, Colorado, USA. In many experiments planned by Eisenbud over a period of two years, Serios could produce, at will, pictures of what he was thinking about – an old hotel, cars, a corner of a room, and many other mental images. He could also produce an image of a target set by himself or others. For example, one day he glanced casually at a travel magazine in Eisenbud's waiting room. The next day, he decided to produce a picture of London's Westminster Abbey, which he had noticed in the publication – and succeeded in doing so.

Thoughtography has continued to be subjected to psychical research; and although Ted Serios' ability to transfer his thoughts on to film has never been fully explained, neither has it ever been proved to be fraudulent.

Among the professional spirit photographers of the late 19th century, however, there were undoubtedly frauds – and a number of them were eventually exposed. But that, of course, does not negate the important fact that many 'spirit' images may well have been produced by paranormal means: indeed, it could still be the case today.

TIMESLIPS INTO THE FUTURE ARE IN MANY WAYS EVEN MORE DISTURBING THAN TIMESLIPS INTO THE PAST – IF ONLY BECAUSE THEY SOMEHOW SUGGEST THAT THE COURSE OF OUR LIVES MAY WELL HAVE BEEN FIXED IN ADVANCE. HOW IS IT THAT SOME PEOPLE EXPERIENCE ACCURATE VISIONS OF WHAT IS TO COME?

In 1966, a new incumbent arrived in the parish of Saxmundham in the East Anglian county of Suffolk. He recognised the church, below, as the one that he had seen in the first of a series of dreams the previous year.

Precognition must surely be the strangest kind of disruption of our time experience. Sometimes it is short-term, with only a few minutes, days or weeks elapsing between the experience and the events that bear it out. But sometimes 20 years or more can pass between foresight and fulfilment. On occasions, the precognition is even forgotten until those events foreseen actually occur.

Following a series of television programmes on the subject of timeslips, an English clergyman wrote to the BBC, describing three precognitive dreams that he had experienced during one period of his life. They had occurred in the space of two months in about 1965, when he was vicar of a parish in Nottinghamshire.

Each dream had begun in the same way, in a vicarage that he recognised as being his childhood home. Yet, in each dream, the house seemed to belong to a different church. In the first, he visited a beautiful medieval one. In the second, the church was a large, dark Victorian building. The third included a variation, for the dreamer did not walk from the vicarage to the church, but strolled to the bottom of the garden before seeing what he took to be the ruins of Hadleigh Castle, near Benfleet in Essex.

FUTURE SHOCK

The clergyman then forgot the series of dreams until he was appointed to his next parish, at Saxmundham in Suffolk. Its medieval church precisely matched the church that had appeared in his first dream, the previous year.

Five years now passed before the clergyman's next change of residence. He had dismissed the possibility that the second dream would be fulfilled, for he did not care at all for Victorian churches and thought it therefore highly unlikely that he would ever accept an appointment to one. Yet when, in 1971, he was offered a living in Beckenham, Kent, he accepted it at once, only later recognising its large Victorian church as the very one he had seen in that second dream.

By now, both he and his wife were deeply impressed by the accuracy of the dreams. But they had to wait until 1977 to test the truth of the third. It was then that the clergyman was appointed vicar of St Mary's, Bury St Edmunds, in Suffolk. Here, he discovered that, at the bottom of the very large churchyard, were the ruins of an old abbey. There, he found two sections of wall – resembling closely the two towers of Hadleigh Castle, as witnessed in his dream.

LANDSCAPE OF FEAR

There was a lapse of 12 years between the clergyman's third dream and its fulfilment; but an even greater length of time was spanned by a recurrent precognitive dream that first occurred in 1955. The setting of the dream, experienced by a married English woman, was always the same: a flat landscape of fields with a windmill in the distance, the whole scene enclosed by leafless trees and a hedge. The action of the dream was also basically the same in each repetition: she was always running through grass and mud towards the windmill, with the sound of feet pounding behind her in rapid pursuit. The mill seemed to be her goal and to represent safety – but she never succeeded in reaching it.

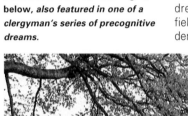

The abbey ruins at Bury St Edmunds in Suffolk, East Anglia, below, *also featured in one of a clergyman's series of precognitive dreams.*

As often happens in recurring dreams, the action developed with time. Soon, no longer did the woman merely hear the sounds of pursuit, she actually came to see the pursuer's shadow on the grass and knew that whoever or whatever was chasing her was gaining ground. The dream was frightening and verged on a nightmare, for although she was never caught by her pursuer, neither did she escape nor find help.

In 1970, the woman and her husband moved to East Anglia. Although the landscape around their home at Sutton, in Norfolk, was flat and agricultural, the woman did not at first connect it in any way with her dream.

Shortly after their move, the husband died. Only then did the wife discover the landscape of her dream. She had often seen the Sutton windmill but not from an angle where she could have identified it with the windmill in the dream – not, that is, until the usual road to the mill was being repaired, and the woman found herself obliged to approach it from its far side. At once, she found herself in the dream landscape – the waving grass, ploughed field, bare trees and the windmill itself were suddenly all too familiar.

It was 12 years after the last of his series of timeslip dreams that the clergyman took up the living at St Mary's, Bury St Edmunds, left – *and thereby fulfilled his third precognitive dream.*

Subsequently, this woman came to feel that the pursuer in her dream was death – or, at least, the disaster represented by the loss of her husband – particularly as her dream had always featured a winter setting, and her husband had indeed died in the month of January, 15 years after the initial dream. After his death, the dream did not recur.

Although the woman had never visited Norfolk when she began to have the dreams, it is possible that, at some time, she had seen a picture of the Sutton mill, the image remaining in her subconscious memory. But it is surely stretching credulity too far to suggest that it was pure coincidence that, years later, she should move to live beside that very mill; and that it was coincidence that she should experience the threat and fear of bereavement in the very place where, in her dream, she had felt just such emotions.

TWO-LEVEL TIMESLIP

This is just one of many examples of such strange, chilling and almost inexplicable long-term precognitions. In another, a small boy in late 19th-century Hanley, Staffordshire, in the English Midlands, was given a severe beating by a sadistic schoolmaster for some minor misdemeanour. The child was very young – seven years old – and sensitive.

'Instead of going to school in the afternoon, I played truant. I remember even now running along the street, scraping my iron-shod boots on the pavement so as to strike sparks; also stopping to listen to organ music coming from a little church, although it was empty and locked up. Across the road at the end of the street, there was (and still is) an archway to a street running at right-angles. It led to the backs of the houses and shops. To the left, it was very short as there were only two (I think) houses, and it was terminated by a blank wall. At the other side of the wall, there was a vast area of waste land.

'On this particular day there was a doorway in the wall; and when I went through, I found myself in a different world – a small town with houses nothing like any I had ever seen before. I went along one street and all the houses were empty. I entered several but came out again without attempting any exploration. Eventually, I stayed in one of the houses and, going upstairs, I came to a large room looking on to a landscape that I had never seen before. The land sloped away to a valley, although I could not see what was at the bottom, and beyond there were low tree-covered hills. Even at that age, I was fascinated by the sun and the stars, and I realised that I was facing east.'

These recollections were described many decades later, when the subject of the experiences had retired from his career as a professor of electrical engineering. Intriguingly, the events that the 'vision' anticipated actually occurred during the First World War:

'Early in 1917, the Germans broke off the Somme battles and made a retirement of about 40 miles [65 kilometres]. Besides taking the High Command completely by surprise, they left a desert 40 miles [65 kilometres] wide.

'I was sent to 4th Army Headquarters which was established a little way east of a deserted village called Villers Carbonnel. It was close to the River

The windmill, above, at Sutton in Norfolk, East Anglia, was all too familiar to a woman who had seen it in a terrifying recurrent dream that plagued her for 15 years.

Somme where it runs northwards before taking an abrupt turn to the west at St Quentin.

'One evening, I had some hours free and I decided to explore some of the neighbouring villages and make a few sketches (which I still have). I came to a village called Misery (most appropriately); and when I entered it, I had that feeling which is described as hair-raising. I was in the street of my earlier vision. All the people were gone, apart from dead Germans I found in several houses I entered and hurriedly left. Then I found a house free of those unpleasant occupants and, going upstairs, I found myself in the large room facing east. The landscape was exactly as I had found it before. The valley was the Somme valley but, as Misery is some way back, the river is not visible.'

There was another curious factor. In his childhood 'hallucination', the subject happened to notice that the village street in which he seemed to find himself was named Windmill Street. When the professor revisited Hanley in about 1960, he found that an estate of houses had now been built on the waste ground, beyond the archway he had used that day in 1896. One of its streets was called Windmill Street.

This is one of the most complex and convincing cases of long-distance precognition. Not only did the 'vision' present in great detail the scene that the professor was to visit 20 years after his childhood experience, it also presented the very street name that would be associated with the site of the experience decades later. In this instance, precognition seems to have worked on two levels: one concerned the personal history of the small boy, 20 years ahead; the other concerned the history of the site of the experience, some 65 years ahead.

In her book *The Mask of Time*, Joan Forman cites several other remarkable examples of timeslips. One concerns a woman who regularly travelled by underground from Stockwell to Chancery Lane, London, in order to get to work. During a light early-morning sleep, she dreamt that she was ascending the steps at Chancery Lane station when a crippled woman passed by her in the opposite direction. At first, on waking, the dreamer was puzzled as to the possible significance of such imagery, but then dismissed the dream as meaningless. She was utterly taken aback, however, when later that morning she met the very same crippled lady on the steps at Chancery Lane. In some strange way, it seemed that her mind had learned about what was to happen prior to the actual event, trivial though it was. Or could it have been sheer coincidence? Perhaps the dreamer had even seen the handicapped

" CAN WE BE THUS PURSUED BY THE FUTURE? OR IS A DREAM OF THIS KIND ONLY A NATURAL EXPRESSION OF HUMAN DREAD OF THE UNKNOWN, OF DEATH, BEREAVEMENT AND PAIN? "

JOAN FORMAN, THE MASK OF TIME

In 1896, in Hanley, part of the industrial city of Stoke-on-Trent in the English Midlands, in an area that was then waste ground, a small boy, playing truant, suddenly found himself in a certain Windmill Street, in a village unlike any he had ever seen. Years later, he was to recognise the village in war-stricken France: decades later still, he found that a Windmill Street, below, now stood on the former waste ground in Stoke-on-Trent.

a previous occasion, but not consciously remembered her.

The extraordinary and arresting phenomenon of precognition, of seeing the future anything from minutes to years ahead of the observer's 'now', can hardly be disputed in the face of evidence that has accumulated throughout the ages. In the cases described here, direct comparisons can be made between the 'visions' and the events that matched them. Doubtless, too, many precognitions occur that are not sufficiently striking to be remembered in this way and so their validity cannot be subsequently confirmed. But perhaps there are also 'visions' that refer to times so far ahead that their date cannot even be guessed at. Indeed, some appear to transport the subject into eras and environments that are barely recognisable.

The village of Misery in the valley of the Somme in western France – seen left, as it looked after the German retreat of 1917 – appears to have been the village seen by the child in Hanley 21 years previously and recognised by him when he was an officer with the British Army in 1917. In his timeslip experience, the village was uninhabited; and when the officer eventually saw it in person, its only occupants were the corpses of German soldiers.

THIS THREE-PART SERIES ABOUT
THE *R101* AIRSHIP DISASTER
CONCLUDES WITH A NEW PERSPECTIVE
ON EVIDENCE FROM BEYOND THE GRAVE

The *R101* affair is a classic of its kind for two reasons. Firstly, the messages purporting to come from Captain Irwin contained information about a matter of widespread general interest, and were couched in technical language. Everyone wanted to know what had happened to cause the catastrophe, and many were in a position to have informed opinions. Moreover, the official verdict was not particularly convincing – composed as it was of a fair bit of speculation wrapped up in careful qualification (necessarily, since there was not much hard evidence to go on). Someone really well informed about airships in general, and the *R101* project in particular, just might come to the conclusion that Irwin's post-mortem account, although conflicting with the official verdict, has more than a ring of truth. This, by itself, would not have been conclusive, but it may have provided undeniably strong circumstantial evidence for spiritual survival.

Secondly, there is little to raise the question of Spiritualism's chronic bugbear – the suspicion of deliberate fraud. There can be no field of investigation where the personal integrity of those 'on trial' looms larger, and therefore comes under closer scrutiny. Yet medium Eileen Garrett went to her grave with an unblemished reputation. Further, the seances were held in circumstances controlled by a world-famous detective of fraudulent mediumship. To arrange a hoax, even had he wanted to, Harry Price would have needed to enlist as fellow-conspirators both Mrs Garrett and Major Villiers, a

The credibility of Eileen Garrett, above, is central to the R101 mystery. She had been in touch with the spirit of the aviator Hinchliffe, who uttered warnings about the airship; had visions of an airship in flames; and received messages from the spirits of those on board the R101 – seen, top, on its initial test flight in October 1929, cruising over St Paul's Cathedral, London.

distinguished and honourable man – and, indeed, several others.

With fraud out of the way, then, the question turns on whether the information said to have come from the dead Captain Irwin is of such a nature that it could have come only from him. Put another way, is there any possible means by which the information that came via Mrs Garrett could have got to her other than by her being in contact – through her guide Uvani – with Captain Irwin's spirit? If not, the case for the survival of the spirit is made – a simple conclusion, but one with profound implications.

Everything hangs on the details of the messages, therefore; and so it is to them that we now turn. The case for accepting the voice as being that of the true Irwin has been presented in considerable detail by John G. Fuller in his book *The Airmen Who Would Not Die*.

None of those present, he explains, knew anything at all about the complexities of airship design or the business of flying one, and so it is impossible that such startlingly specific statements as those made by 'Irwin' – at wild speed and in what was, to those present, a language as foreign as it is to the lay reader today – could have been dredged from the conscious or unconscious mind of any of them. That rules out straightforward telepathy.

One of 'Irwin's' statements was not only highly technical, it referred to something that would not be known outside the inner sanctum of those intimately involved with the airship – the new hydrogen-carbon fuel mix. Another, the reference to Achy

DID THE SPIRITS REALLY SPEAK?

('almost scraped the roofs at Achy'), is just as bewildering. Price tried to find Achy in conventional atlases without success. But when he tracked down a large-scale railway map of the Beauvais area (a map as detailed as the charts Irwin would have carried in the control car), he found it – a tiny hamlet on the railway lines, a few miles north of Beauvais. Where could such a snippet of information have come from, if not from Irwin himself?

Finally, Price had the transcript examined, clause by clause, by an expert from Cardington (who volunteered for the job). Will Charlton – as did other old Cardington hands – professed himself astonished at the technical grasp displayed therein, and by the likelihood of Irwin's account in its essentials. Indeed, Charlton reckoned that no one but Irwin could have been the source of this information – information that explained clearly what had happened during the fateful voyage as against the speculative account in the official report.

SHAKY GROUND

As far as it goes, this sounds pretty convincing. But such evidence begins to fray at the edges somewhat when it is realised that, in Charlton, Price had not found an expert at all – rather, a convinced Spiritualist whose claim to airship expertise rested on the shaky ground of having been in charge of stores and supplies at Cardington. In a review of Fuller's book for *Alpha* magazine in 1980, Archie Jarman, credited by Fuller with knowing more about the subject than any living person, draws attention to some glaring examples of Charlton's ignorance: they are certainly of such a nature as to discredit him as an expert. For example, during one sitting, 'Irwin' made a reference to 'SL8'. Price had no idea what this meant, and it remained for Charlton to come up with the answer: 'The SL8 has been verified as the number of a German airship – SL standing for Shuttle Lanz.' In order to track down this morsel of information, Charlton had to comb through the entire record of German airships.

Now, far from being impressive, such a statement is utterly damning from an expert. 'The SL stands for *Schütte Lanz* (*Schütte*, not 'Shuttle' or 'Shutte' as Fuller variously had it), the German rival airship development before the First World War, one of which was shot down in flames in a celebrated action during a raid on England in 1916 (a mere 14 years previously). Yet Charlton, the expert, had no idea what *SL8* referred to. It is not good enough, and Fuller drives home the point: 'Charlton and his colleagues of Cardington had been strongly impressed with the reference to *SL8*. No one on the staff of Cardington could confirm this designation and number until they had looked it up in the complete records of German airships.'

Furthermore, when Jarman was compiling a report on the affair in the early 1960s, he solicited the opinions of two real experts: Wing-Commander Booth, who had captained the *R100* on the Montreal flight, and Wing-Commander Cave-Brown-Cave, who had been intimately involved in the *R101's* construction.

Wing-Commander Booth spoke for both when he replied: 'I have read the description of the Price-Irwin seance with great care and am of the opinion that the messages received do not assist in any

The official inquiry into the disaster seemed to add little to the account of the great airship's final moments as provided by the poacher, Eugene Rabouille, above, *who saw it plough into the ground.*

way in determining why the airship *R101* crashed...' Cave-Brown-Cave ended with the crushing comment: 'The observations of Mr Charlton should be totally disregarded.'

Booth's verdict on the Villiers material was to prove even harsher in content: 'I am in complete disagreement with almost every paragraph . . . the conversations are completely out of character, the atmosphere at Cardington is completely wrong, and the technical and handling explanation could not possibly have been messages from anyone with airship experience.' The latter remark is surely true. Just to take one example, at one point, 'Irwin' complained about the gas indicator going up and down. Booth's trenchant reply was: 'No such instruments were fitted.'

That technical inaccuracy is bad enough, but it is mild in comparison with what the officers are said to have had in mind from the moment they set off from Cardington. They supposedly knew that the airship was most probably a dud and that they had no chance of reaching their destination. But they thought they might just manage to creep across the Channel and tie up at Le Bourget. There were only four places on Earth with the facilities to cope with such an immense airship, and Le Bourget assuredly was not one of them.

WHEN ALL WAS LOST

After they had crossed the Channel, according to 'Irwin', they 'knew all was lost'. So what did they do? They opted to press on into a brutal headwind, hoping to make Le Bourget (knowing all was lost), 'and try at all costs some kind of landing'. Surely no sane person would attempt any such thing, especially when there was an obvious alternative?

If the Captain and his close colleagues really were terrified about the way things were going, all they had to do was turn around and, with the wind at their backs, limp home to the safety of Cardington. Sane men do not accept certain death (and commit dozens of their fellows to the same fate) rather than admit that they have been defeated by an impossible task.

Jarman's view is that nothing whatever occurred during the seance that cannot be put down to Eileen Garrett's own subconscious and her telepathic powers. Take the reference to Achy, for instance – at first sight so inexplicable. According to Jarman, who knew Mrs Garrett well, she frequently motored from Calais to Paris and Achy is on that road, clearly signposted. Could not Mrs Garrett have retained the name subconsciously? Since it is more than likely that the *R101* did *not* pass directly over Achy, what else are we to believe?

And while Eileen Garrett certainly knew nothing to speak of about the technicalities of airships, the *R101* was much on her mind even before the crash. She had already had visions of an airship disaster, and had discussed her fears at length with none other than Sir Sefton Brancker – Director of Civil Aviation – just 10 days before the accident.

The supposed secret nature of some of the technical information provided by 'Irwin' can also be explained. The fact is that the design and construction of the *R101* (fuel mix and all) was conducted with about as much secrecy as the building of Concorde. Anyone who cared to do so could have amassed immense technical detail about the airship simply by reading the newspapers. And, of course, the press was full of it during the interval between the crash and the seances. As for the savage indictments that form the burden of all the seances, the Cardington follies had been notorious all along, brought finally to the fore, naturally, by the disaster.

Those attending the seances were probably very well up on all this; and so if we accept that Eileen Garrett had telepathic gifts, we need look no further, suggests Archie Jarman in *The R101 Rises Again*. That is a perfectly reasonable explanation.

But perhaps the final word should be left to Harry Price. In his letter to Sir John Simon, which is, incidentally, couched in the language of a disinterested research scientist, he states that he does not believe that it was the 'spirit' of Irwin present at the seance. Then he continues: 'I must also state that I am convinced that the psychic was not consciously cheating. It is likewise improbable that one woman in a thousand would be capable of delivering, as she did, an account of the flight of an airship... Where such information comes from is a problem that has baffled the world for 2,000 years.'

> **❝ I LIVE IN A WORLD FILLED WITH PHENOMENA OF A TRANSCENDENTAL NATURE... I HAVE LEFT THESE PHENOMENA OPEN TO SPECULATION, BUT I SUSPECT THAT THIS FIELD, WHICH IS SURELY DISCREDITED BY THOSE WHO DO NOT EXPERIENCE ITS NATURE, BELONGS TO THE INNER WORKINGS OF WHAT WE CALL MIND, AS YET TO BE EXPLORED. ❞**
>
> **EILEEN GARRETT**

Sir Sefton Brancker, above, discussed the problem of the R101 with Eileen Garrett just before the crash.

The giant airship, left, is manoeuvred by ground crew prior to its last flight.

The stark, burnt-out remains of the R101, below, offered few clues to the precise cause of the appalling disaster.

THE MYSTERIOUS DISAPPEARANCE OF SHIPS AND AIRCRAFT IN AN AREA OF THE NORTH ATLANTIC HAS LED TO A BELIEF THAT THE REGION IS HOST TO STRANGE AND POWERFUL FORCES. HERE, WE TAKE A FURTHER LOOK AT THE BASIS FOR THIS LEGEND

The American author Charles Berlitz, above, has done most to foster the idea that disappearances in the Bermuda Triangle are the result of extraordinary happenings.

Is the island of Bermuda, below, in the Atlantic Ocean, at the centre of a whole series of sinister events, as many have suggested?

Mere mention of the Bermuda Triangle is likely to enliven any flagging conversation and set people's spines tingling almost anywhere in the world. It has been the subject of books, novels, films, television dramas and documentaries, newspaper and magazine articles – even a board game. The Bermuda Triangle – formed by an imaginary line connecting Bermuda with Puerto Rico and the coast of Florida – is the place where scores of ships and aircraft are said to have vanished without trace. Dozens of researchers and writers are convinced that the losses are caused by some kind of force or phenomenon unknown to science.

Charles Berlitz, author of two best-sellers about the region, *The Bermuda Triangle* and *Without a Trace,* has written:

'Large and small boats have disappeared without leaving wreckage, as if they and their crews had been snatched into another dimension . . . in no other area have the unexplained disappearances been so numerous, so well researched, so sudden, and attended by such unusual circumstances, some of which push the element of coincidence to the borders of impossibility.'

In his book *Invisible Residents,* John T. Sanderson states that the number of disappearances in the Bermuda Triangle is seemingly out of all proportion to the number of losses elsewhere. And John Wallace Spencer claims in *The Limbo of the Lost:* 'Tragedies connected with this region continually occur without explanation, without pattern, without warning, and without reason.'

Bermuda has had an evil reputation for generations. Its 300 or so tiny islands were discovered in 1515 by Juan de Bermúdez. Yet, despite an equable climate, plentiful supplies of fresh food and water, and an ideal location for a mid-ocean refuge and provisioning base, the islands were shunned for almost a century after their discovery. They were feared by the tough Elizabethan sailors – Shakespeare called them 'the still-vex'd Bermoothes' – and they gained a reputation as a place of devils. Nobody knows why: perhaps the

TALES FROM THE BERMUDA TRIANGLE

only reasonable explanation is that then, as now, the region was known as the home of inexplicable forces that caused men and ships to disappear.

According to writers on the subject, the modern catalogue of losses in the region begins in 1800 with the disappearance of the *USS Pickering*. In 1854, the British ship *Bella* disappeared en route from Rio de Janeiro to Jamaica, although she was known to have been dangerously overloaded and may simply have capsized. In 1866, the Triangle claimed the Swedish barque *Lotta* and two years later, the Spanish merchantman *Viego* vanished. In 1872, the crew of the *Mary Celeste* disappeared and the vessel was found drifting between the Azores and Gibraltar. Although this is far outside the accepted limits of the Bermuda Triangle, the *Mary Celeste* is often referred to in discussions of the subject. The British training ship *Atalanta* and her 290 cadets and crew also sailed into oblivion in the region in 1880. They were followed, in 1884, by the Italian schooner *Miramon*.

It is said that, in 1902, the German barque *Freya*, sailing from Manzanillo in Cuba to Punta Arenas, Chile, was found in the Triangle. Her crew had disappeared. The vessel itself was listing badly, was partly dismasted and showed every sign of having been caught in a particularly violent storm – except that there had not been any storms: weather records revealed that only light airs had prevailed.

In 1938, the blue skies were cloudless and the sea was still when the steamship *Anglo-Australian* radioed an 'all's well' message before sailing into the Bermuda Triangle. She never emerged.

Although the Bermuda Triangle has been claiming ships such as these since the days when Christopher Columbus sailed its waters, it did not begin to attract attention in a big way until 1945. That year, five US Navy bombers – Flight 19 – vanished after sending a series of baffling and bizarre

The late Ivan T. Sanderson, above, suggested that the Bermuda Triangle is one of 12 'vile vortices' on Earth – regions where the rate of disappearance of ships and aircraft is unusually high.

The Bermuda Triangle, charted below, is usually represented as a region touching Florida and the islands of Puerto Rico and Bermuda. But some writers extend it much further and refer to it as the 'Devil's Triangle' or the 'Limbo of the Lost'.

radio messages. A few years later the writer Vincent Gaddis called the region the Bermuda Triangle. There is little agreement among writers on its size and shape, and each region is given a different name such as 'Devil's Triangle' and 'Limbo of the Lost'. At its smallest, however, the Bermuda Triangle is the size of the United Kingdom and Eire; at its largest, it takes in about half the North Atlantic Ocean.

Charles Berlitz and other writers such as Richard Winer, John Wallace Spencer, Vincent Gaddis, John Godwin, Ivan T. Sanderson, Adi-Kent Thomas Jeffrey and Alan Landsberg have maintained that the mystery of the Triangle cannot be explained away by storms and other natural causes. They believe that the disappearances were caused by a phenomenon unrecognised by orthodox science.

VANISHING AIRCRAFT

In January 1948, the British airliner *Star Tiger* was nearing the end of a routine flight from the Azores to Bermuda when she is said to have radioed: 'Weather and performance excellent. Expect to arrive on schedule.' But the aircraft did not arrive at all. While a search was being made for survivors and wreckage, radio stations picked up a couple of faint messages purporting to be from the aircraft. It was 'as if a final message was being sent or relayed from a far greater distance, in space or time,' wrote Charles Berlitz.

Another airliner, a *Douglas DC-3,* vanished on a flight from Puerto Rico to Florida in December 1948. The pilot allegedly radioed: 'We are approaching the field . . . only fifty miles [80 kilometres] to the south. . . . We can see the lights of Miami now . . . all's well. Will stand by for landing instructions.' But when Miami replied a few minutes later, she received no response: not another word was ever heard from the aircraft. The *DC-3* had vanished over an area where the water was only 20 feet (6

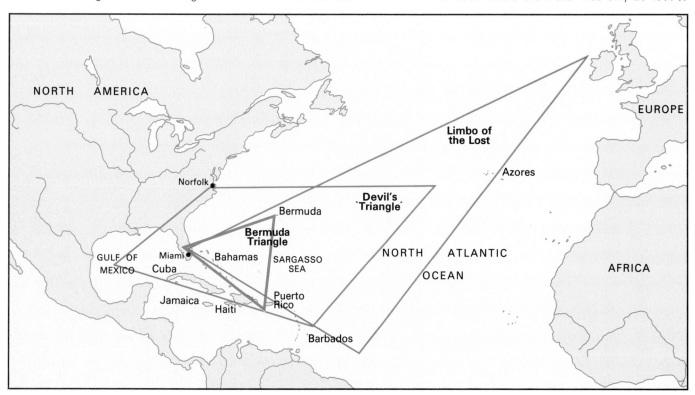

Part of the coast of Florida is shown, left, on a 16th-century map by Lazaro Luis. Christopher Columbus travelled through the area now known as the Bermuda Triangle in the late 15th century and noted that his ship's compass acted erratically. He also recorded that he had witnessed a 'great flame of fire' that fell into the sea.

The Avenger *torpedo bomber, below, is of the type that vanished in December 1945 after leaving Fort Lauderdale naval air base for a brief training flight off the Florida coast. No trace of the five aircraft and 14 crew was ever found, despite an extensive search. This case, one of the most celebrated mysteries of aviation history, has been called 'the Mary Celeste of the sky'.*

" HAVE YOU EVER FELT TWO PEOPLE PULLING ON YOUR ARMS IN OPPOSITE DIRECTIONS? IT FELT THAT WE WERE ON A PLACE OR POINT THAT SOMEBODY OR SOMETHING WANTED, AND SOMEBODY OR SOMETHING WANTED US TO BE IN ANOTHER PLACE FROM WHERE WE WERE GOING. *"*

CAPTAIN DON HENRY, BERMUDA TRIANGLE INCIDENT SURVIVOR

1954, no less than nine large coastal freighters went missing. The authorities were so alarmed that, in 1955, they dispatched a team of scientists aboard the survey ship *Kaiyo Maru No. 5* to investigate the region. To everybody's horror, the *Kaiyo Maru No. 5* and her scientists and crew also inexplicably vanished. As a consequence, the Japanese declared the region an official danger zone.

Unlike their Japanese counterparts, the United States authorities have not declared the Bermuda Triangle to be a danger zone. Indeed, they deny that anything at all unusual is happening there. This official view, however, does not accord with private opinions sometimes expressed in unguarded moments. One Navy spokesman let slip: 'We know there's something strange going on out there, we've always known it, but there doesn't seem to be any reason for it at all.' And a senior intelligence officer of the Third Naval District is on record as

metres) deep, yet search craft failed to locate any wreckage or survivors.

The extent of the Triangle's range of influence startled researchers when Professor Wayne Meshejian announced in 1975 that a sophisticated weather satellite, operated by the National Oceanographic Administration, consistently malfunctioned when over the Bermuda Triangle. It seemed that something prevented the satellite transmitting information to receiving stations. 'We are talking about a force we know nothing about', Meshejian was quoted as saying.

Even more alarming is the claim that the Bermuda Triangle is not unique. The late Ivan T. Sanderson plotted the location of dozens of air and sea losses and concluded that at least 12 similar regions – he called them 'vile vortices' – encircle our globe. 'Planes, ships, and subs have, as we have stressed, been disappearing all over the world,' he wrote in his book *Invisible Residents*, 'but it has to be admitted that many more are reported to have done so in these . . . areas than in any others.'

One such 'vile vortex' has long been known to lie off the coast of Japan. Called the Devil's Sea, it has been claiming small fishing craft of doubtful stability for hundreds of years. Between 1950 and

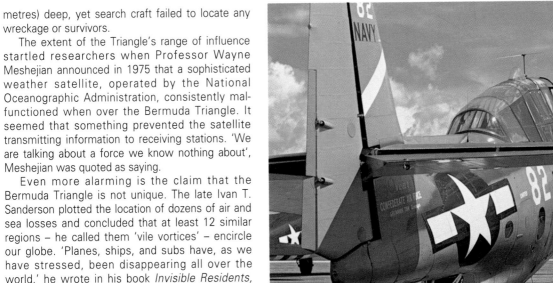

saying: 'Nobody in the Navy sneers at this thing.' The authorities, it seems, could be engaged in a cover-up to conceal their ignorance from the public.

There is little agreement about what 'this thing' in the Bermuda Triangle is. John Wallace Spencer became convinced that UFOs provide the only acceptable solution. Ships and aircraft are actually being taken away from our planet, he said. Looking down instead of up, Ivan T. Sanderson suggested that a highly intelligent civilisation may even have evolved on or below the sea bed and that the disappearances are connected with their periodic examination of mankind.

Other suggestions have ranged from mini black holes to openings to other dimensions where time runs quickly, slowly or not at all.

That this latter theory may not be as absurd as it sounds is indicated by the experience of a young pilot named Bruce Gernon. In 1970, he was piloting a small aircraft when he flew through a strange

> **THERE ARE GOOD REASONS TO CONNECT THESE INCIDENTS TO THE MAGNETIC FIELD OF THE EARTH... PERHAPS... A CHANGE IN THE MAGNETIC SITUATION IS DEVELOPING.**
>
> **H. AUCHINCLOSS BROWN,**
> **CATACLYSMS OF THE EARTH**

The 125-foot (38-metre) schooner Gloria Colita, below, was found wrecked and abandoned in the Gulf of Mexico in early February 1940. She had left Mobile, Alabama, on 21 January, laden with lumber for Cuba.

cloud. On landing at Miami, he discovered that his flight had taken half-an-hour less than it was possible for it to have done. Did Gernon fly into another dimension and out again? Unfortunately, his flight plan is missing and there is no way of checking and corroborating his story.

A similar happening is said to have been experienced by the passengers and crew of a National Airlines aircraft that vanished from the radar at Miami for a full 10 minutes. Emergency operations were launched, but then the airliner reappeared and landed safely. Nobody on board had experienced anything odd, but they had no explanation for the fact that every clock and watch on board was found to be 10 minutes slow.

According to Charles Berlitz, the remains of the fabled lost continent of Atlantis have been found off Bimini in the Bahamas. Many people believe that it was the home of a technological super race and that one of their machines or weapons is possibly still functioning, disintegrating our ships and aircraft.

'Could magnetism or some form of magnetic phenomenon be related to the strange disappearances?' asks Richard Winer, author of *The Devil's Triangle*. Few writers have failed to mention how the compass needle usually points to magnetic North rather than to the actual North Pole – except, however, within the Bermuda Triangle.

It is clearly a strange place and odd things happen there. Hundreds of ships and aircraft have inexplicably vanished without trace. They hardly ever send a distress call and wreckage is rarely found. Furthermore, as John Godwin has written in *This Baffling World*, 'we find that almost monotonously fine weather conditions prevailed at the crucial times.' He goes on to ask: 'Did the lost airplanes and lost ships encounter phenomena unknown to today's science? Do the laws of nature still contain a few paragraphs not covered in our textbooks?'

Gibbs Hill lighthouse, above, has acted as a navigational aid on Bermuda since the 1840s. Has it also been a silent witness of strange disappearances in the surrounding seas?

The Bermuda Triangle mystery provided the storyline for a 1978 film, directed by Richard Friedenburg, as advertised left.

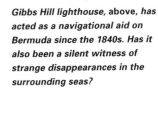

THE SECRET LIFE OF THE MOON

STRANGE BRIGHT LIGHTS

HAVE SOMETIMES BEEN

SEEN DARTING ACROSS THE

MOON'S LIFELESS SURFACE.

WHAT SECRETS ARE

PERHAPS HELD BY THIS

EXTRAORDINARY WORLD?

Apollo XVI astronaut Charles Duke conducts an experiment on the Moon, above.

Manned and unmanned missions to the Moon have enabled astronomers to piece together considerable detail about its present structure and past history – yet mystery still surrounds many aspects of the Moon. Significant results have come from seismometers (moonquake recorders) left behind by astronauts: as well as detecting moonquakes and the impact of meteorites, these readings can be interpreted to give some idea of the internal structure of the Moon. The astronauts also left instruments to record heat emanating from the interior, and their readings can detect the amount of radioactivity within the Moon.

But the most important evidence of all are the rocks returned to Earth by the Apollo missions, and smaller samples brought back by automatic Russian probes from further sites. Detailed analysis has revealed the chemical composition of these rocks, while studies of their radioactive elements has allowed scientists to measure their ages. Both provide vital clues to the history of the Moon.

It is thought to have formed at about the same time as the Earth and the other planets, some 4,600 million years ago. For the first 700 million years, it was continually bombarded by huge rocks from space, pieces of rubble left over from the formation of the solar system.

At first, they fell so thick and fast that their impact melted the outer part of the Moon. As bombardment diminished, the molten rock then solidified at the top, where it was exposed to the cold of space. The rocks that solidified into this crust were the lightest types and contained unusually large amounts of aluminium, calcium and sodium atoms, with proportionally less iron and magnesium. This formed the crust that we still see on the Moon, battered by later meteorites into the crater-scarred terrain of the light-coloured lunar 'highlands'. The largest impacts blew out enormous basins hundreds of miles across; and after two particularly huge impacts 3,900 million years ago, the downfall largely ceased.

The crust had also accumulated a large share of radioactive elements – such as uranium – and the heat from trapped atoms now began to melt isolated small regions within the solid crust. From these pockets of liquid rock, molten lava flowed up to flood the low lying parts of the surface, and particularly the floors of the huge basins. These solidified lava flows form the dark lava plains, or *maria*, that we see on the Moon today. The two last great impact basins became the *Mare Imbrium* and the *Mare Orientale*, vast flat plains over 500 miles (800 kilometres) across

The final lava flows spread over the *Oceanus Procellarum* region some 2,600 million years ago. By then, most of the radioactive elements had decomposed, and the remainder could not supply enough energy to melt rocks. Apart from some smaller impacts – like those that created the craters

Tycho and *Copernicus* – the Moon has been dead ever since.

Or has it? For centuries, astronomers have reported seeing occasional strange lights and glows on the Moon, as well as clouds of dust that obscure crater floors. The total number of transient lunar phenomena (TLP) reports now runs to well over 1,500. One of the first was seen in 1787 by William Herschel, Britain's leading astronomer of the time and discoverer of the planet Uranus. He described the TLP that he saw as a red sparkling glow on the dark side of the Moon. Most of the recent TLP sightings are brilliant reddish markings seen on the Moon's bright side, however, and they concentrate around the edges of the *maria*, especially in particular craters, like *Aristarchus*. Other TLP reports tell of clouds of dust covering the floors of large craters, such as *Alphonsus* and *Plato*.

Some of these reports are undoubtedly due to misinterpretations by inexperienced observers, or to problems with telescopes. The American space agency NASA coordinated a TLP network for a number of years: during this time, none of the TLP sightings reported to it was confirmed by another observatory. But many experienced astronomers have seen TLPs, and their testimony is backed up by a few instrumental observations.

It is very difficult to explain TLP sightings. The glows could be due to electrically charged particles from the Sun hitting the surface and causing certain minerals to shine by the process of fluorescence. But laboratory experiments on lunar rocks and soil show that any such fluorescent glow would be far too faint to account for TLPs.

The only reasonable explanation is a cloud of dust ejected from the lunar surface, presumably carried upwards by gas escaping from a pocket deep within the Moon's crust. Thinly spread clouds could cause obscuration; and denser ones could reflect sunlight and appear bright. The British astronomer Allan Mills also suggested that lightning discharge within a dust cloud could make it glow

Lightning in an electrical storm is seen generated within an erupting volcano, above. Could it be that the strange lights or TLPs – transient lunar phenomena – that astronomers have seen on the Moon are the result of volcanic moonquakes?

One theory about the origin of the Moon is that the Earth and Moon once formed a single, rapidly spinning planet as shown right, top – that later broke in two. Another, the 'accretion' theory, illustrated right, bottom – suggests that both bodies are products of a large cloud of loosely bonded matter that once orbited the Sun, approximately where the Earth is now.

brightly enough to account for even the brightest TLP sightings.

But it takes a lot of energy to raise a tonne or so of dust – the minimum needed to cause a TLP. Gas bursting from a deep pocket would produce severe moonquakes, and the Apollo seismometers show no signs of the frequent, powerful quakes that should accompany TLPs.

Nor does the evidence produced following the Apollo missions provide conclusive proof. The rocks mostly fall into two types – the crust and the later lava plains. These are found together over the plains because rocks from neighbouring crustal high lands have been blasted out over the *maria* by meteorites. But a few rocks from the Apollo XII landing site were of a third type, which turned out to be common at the Apollo XIV site in the highlands of *Fra Mauro*. These rock fragments contain unusual amounts of potassium (symbol K), rare earth elements (REE), and phosphorus (P): they have therefore been named KREEP rocks. No one is sure when or why these rocks appeared on the lunar surface – though they are certainly not more recent than the *maria* – nor why they are concentrated in just a few regions like *Fra Mauro*.

However, the origin of the Moon is still in doubt, even though astronomers had confidently expected the Apollo missions to provide an answer to rival theories.

The first is that the Earth and Moon were once a single, rapidly spinning planet that broke in two. Most astronomers now think this unlikely. One problem is that the Earth-Moon system has too little 'spin': add the Moon's present motion to the Earth's spin, and the combined planet would not rotate fast enough to break up under the effect of its own centrifugal force. Another problem is that the Earth and Moon differ slightly in their chemical composition.

Alternatively, the Moon could have formed from a ring of debris left around the early Earth. Strong support for this theory comes from a study of the isotopes of oxygen on the Earth and Moon. These indicate that the two worlds formed at about the same distance from the Sun. But if they formed together, the Moon and Earth should have similar proportions of all the elements – which, as mentioned above, they do not. And if the Moon formed naturally from a ring of debris around the Earth, why do the other Earth-like planets – Venus and Mars – not have large moons, too?

Many scientists consider that the most likely theory concerning the origin of the Moon is that it was once an independent planet that came within the Earth's gravitational field and was captured by it, as depicted right.

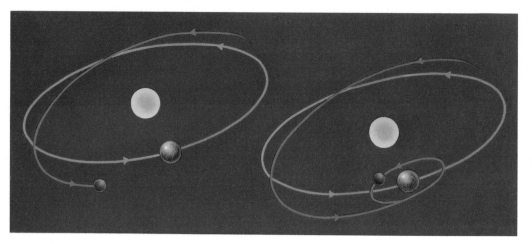

The Apollo missions have also made a surprising discovery. Although the Moon today has no magnetic field, its rocks bear the imprint of a past magnetic field almost as strong as the Earth's. Geologists think that the Earth's field is generated by electric currents flowing in its liquid iron core. The Moon, however, has only a small iron core – if it has one at all. And its internal heat should never have been high enough to melt its central regions, even though the surface melted under bombardment by meteorites.

Astronomers are faced with two alternatives, neither of them very attractive. The Moon may originally have contained some short-lived radioactive elements, which liberated intense heat for the first million years or so. This heat may have melted the Moon throughout, and allowed iron to sink to the centre as a small molten core, which generated a magnetic field. As the radioactive atoms all decayed, the heat source dried up, and the core solidified and lost its ability to generate magnetism. An alternative explanation is that the Moon may have been exposed to a strong magnetic field from outside – a field existing in that part of the solar system where the Moon was born.

A third possibility is that the Moon was originally a separate planet, orbiting the Sun, and was later 'captured' by the Earth. A planet formed closer to the Sun should have more titanium and magnesium than Earth, and less lead, gold and sodium – corresponding very closely to the elemental composition of the Moon. This theory, however, disagrees with the oxygen isotope interpretation, which puts the original Moon at the same distance from the Sun as the Earth.

The actual chance of Earth 'capturing' a passing world is very small – some would say impossibly small. But this low probability could explain why Earth alone has a large moon; and the 'capture' theory is the only one in which the Moon could end up with its orbit tilted, as it is, relative to the equator of the Earth.

Even dismissing the weird ideas of alien beings on, or in, the Moon, our companion world is undoubtedly a strange place. After several visits by manned spacecraft, and numerous unmanned orbits and landings, the Moon still guards its secrets. When men do return to the Moon, it seems quite likely they will discover not just more answers, but also more questions.